POEMS AND TRANSLATIONS
by
DANTE GABRIEL ROSSETTI

Oxford University Press, Amen House, London E.C.4

GLASGOW NEW YORK TORONTO MELBOURNE WELLINGTON
BOMBAY CALCUTTA MADRAS CAPE TOWN

Geoffrey Cumberlege, Publisher to the University

DANTE GABRIEL ROSSETTI

POEMS & TRANSLATIONS
1850–1870
Together with the Prose Story
'HAND AND SOUL'

GEOFFREY CUMBERLEGE
OXFORD UNIVERSITY PRESS
LONDON NEW YORK TORONTO

This edition was first published in 1913, *and reprinted in* 1919, 1926, 1936, *and* 1949

PRINTED IN GREAT BRITAIN

O.S.A.

CONTENTS

POEMS

	PAGE
THE BLESSED DAMOZEL	1
LOVE'S NOCTURN	5
TROY TOWN	9
THE BURDEN OF NINEVEH	12
EDEN BOWER	18
AVE	23
THE STAFF AND SCRIP	26
A LAST CONFESSION	32
DANTE AT VERONA	48
JENNY	62
THE PORTRAIT	73
SISTER HELEN	76
STRATTON WATER	83
THE STREAM'S SECRET	88
THE CARD-DEALER	95
MY SISTER'S SLEEP	97
A NEW YEAR'S BURDEN	99
EVEN SO	99
AN OLD SONG ENDED	100
ASPECTA MEDUSA	101
THREE TRANSLATIONS FROM FRANÇOIS VILLON:	
THE BALLAD OF DEAD LADIES	101
TO DEATH, OF HIS LADY	102
HIS MOTHER'S SERVICE TO OUR LADY	102
JOHN OF TOURS	104
MY FATHER'S CLOSE	105
ONE GIRL	106

CONTENTS

Sonnets and Songs, towards a Work to be called
'THE HOUSE OF LIFE'

SONNETS: PAGE
I. BRIDAL BIRTH 107
II. LOVE'S REDEMPTION 108
III. LOVESIGHT 108
IV. THE KISS 109
V. NUPTIAL SLEEP 109
VI. SUPREME SURRENDER 110
VII. LOVE'S LOVERS 110
VIII. PASSION AND WORSHIP 111
IX. THE PORTRAIT 111
X. THE LOVE-LETTER 112
XI. THE BIRTH-BOND 112
XII. A DAY OF LOVE 113
XIII. LOVE-SWEETNESS 113
XIV. LOVE'S BAUBLES 114
XV. WINGED HOURS 114
XVI. LIFE-IN-LOVE 115
XVII. THE LOVE-MOON 115
XVIII. THE MORROW'S MESSAGE . . . 116
XIX. SLEEPLESS DREAMS 116
XX. SECRET PARTING 117
XXI. PARTED LOVE 117
XXII. BROKEN MUSIC 118
XXIII. DEATH-IN-LOVE 118
XXIV-VII. WILLOWWOOD 119-20
XXVIII. STILLBORN LOVE 121
XXIX. INCLUSIVENESS 121
XXX. KNOWN IN VAIN 122
XXXI. THE LANDMARK 122
XXXII. A DARK DAY 123
XXXIII. THE HILL SUMMIT 123
XXXIV. BARREN SPRING 124
XXXV-VII. THE CHOICE 124-5
XXXVIII. HOARDED JOY 126
XXXIX. VAIN VIRTUES 126
XL. LOST DAYS 127
XLI. DEATH'S SONGSTERS 127
XLII. 'RETRO ME, SATHANA!' . . . 128
XLIII. LOST ON BOTH SIDES 128

CONTENTS

SONNETS (*continued*):   PAGE
- XLIV. THE SUN'S SHAME 129
- XLV. THE VASE OF LIFE 129
- XLVI. A SUPERSCRIPTION 130
- XLVII. HE AND I 130
- XLVIII–IX. NEWBORN DEATH 131
- L. THE ONE HOPE 132

SONGS:
- I. LOVE-LILY 132
- II. FIRST LOVE REMEMBERED 133
- III. PLIGHTED PROMISE 133
- IV. SUDDEN LIGHT 134
- V. A LITTLE WHILE 135
- VI. THE SONG OF THE BOWER 135
- VII. PENUMBRA 137
- VIII. THE WOODSPURGE 138
- IX. THE HONEYSUCKLE 138
- X. A YOUNG FIR-WOOD 139
- XI. THE SEA-LIMITS 139

SONNETS FOR PICTURES, AND OTHER SONNETS:
- FOR 'OUR LADY OF THE ROCKS', BY LEONARDO DA VINCI . 141
- FOR A VENETIAN PASTORAL, BY GIORGIONE . . . 142
- FOR AN ALLEGORICAL DANCE OF WOMEN, BY ANDREA MANTEGNA 142
- FOR 'RUGGIERO AND ANGELICA', BY INGRES . . 143
- FOR 'THE WINE OF CIRCE', BY EDWARD BURNE JONES . 144
- MARY'S GIRLHOOD 145
- THE PASSOVER IN THE HOLY FAMILY 145
- MARY MAGDALENE AT THE DOOR OF SIMON THE PHARISEE . 145
- SAINT LUKE THE PAINTER 146
- LILITH 146
- SIBYLLA PALMIFERA 147
- VENUS 147
- CASSANDRA 148
- PANDORA 149
- ON REFUSAL OF AID BETWEEN NATIONS . . . 149
- ON THE 'VITA NUOVA' OF DANTE 150
- DANTIS TENEBRÆ 150
- BEAUTY AND THE BIRD 151

CONTENTS

	PAGE
A MATCH WITH THE MOON	151
AUTUMN IDLENESS	152
FAREWELL TO THE GLEN	152
THE MONOCHORD	153

POEMS AND A PROSE STORY FROM *The Germ*, 1850:

SONNETS FOR PICTURES	154
THE CARILLON	155
PAX VOBIS	156
HAND AND SOUL	157

THE EARLY ITALIAN POETS

PART I

POETS CHIEFLY BEFORE DANTE

PREFACE	175
TABLE OF POETS IN PART I	180
CIULLO D' ALCAMO	
DIALOGUE. Lover and Lady	189
FOLCACHIERO DE' FOLCACHIERI	
CANZONE. He speaks of his Condition through Love	196
LODOVICO DELLA VERNACCIA	
SONNET. He exhorts the State to vigilance	197
SAINT FRANCIS OF ASSISI	
CANTICA. Our Lord Christ: of order	198
FREDERICK II, EMPEROR	
CANZONE. Of his Lady in bondage	199
ENZO, KING OF SARDINIA	
SONNET. On the Fitness of Seasons	201
GUIDO GUINICELLI	
SONNET. Concerning Lucy	201
CANZONE. Of the gentle Heart	202
SONNET. He will praise his Lady	204
CANZONE. He perceives his Rashness in Love, but has no choice	204
SONNET. Of Moderation and Tolerance	206
SONNET. Of Human Presumption	206

CONTENTS

GUERZO DI MONTECANTI
    SONNET. He is out of Heart with his Time . . . 207

INGHILFREDI, SICILIANO
    CANZONE. He rebukes the Evil of that Time . . 207

RINALDO D'AQUINO
    CANZONE. He is resolved to be joyful in Love . . 209
    CANZONE. A Lady, in Spring, repents of her Coldness . 211

JACOPO DA LENTINO
    SONNET. Of his Lady in Heaven 213
    CANZONETTA. Of his Lady, and of her Portrait . . 213
    SONNET. No Jewel is worth his Lady 215
    CANZONETTA. He will neither boast nor lament to his Lady 215
    CANZONETTA. Of his Lady, and of his making her Likeness 217
    SONNET. Of his Lady's Face 218
    CANZONE. At the End of his Hope 219

MAZZEO DI RICCO DA MESSINA
    CANZONE. He solicits his Lady's Pity 221
    CANZONE. After six years' Service he renounces his Lady 222
    SONNET. Of Self-seeing 224

PANNUCCIO DAL BAGNO PISANO
    CANZONE. Of his Change through Love . . . 224

GIACOMINO PUGLIESI
    CANZONETTA. Of his Lady in absence 226
    CANZONETTA. To his Lady, in Spring 227
    CANZONE. Of his Dead Lady 228

FRA GUITTONE D'AREZZO
    SONNET. To the Blessed Virgin Mary 230

BARTOLOMEO DI SANT' ANGELO
    SONNET. He jests concerning his Poverty . . . 231

SALADINO DA PAVIA
    DIALOGUE. Lover and Lady 231

BONAGGIUNTA URBICIANI, DA LUCCA
    CANZONE. Of the True End of Love; with a Prayer to his Lady 233
    CANZONETTA. How he dreams of his Lady . . . 234
    SONNET. Of Wisdom and Foresight 236
    SONNET. Of Continence in Speech 236

CONTENTS

MEO ABBRACCIAVACCA, DA PISTOIA
    CANZONE. He will be silent and watchful in his Love . 237
    BALLATA. His Life is by Contraries 239

UBALDO DI MARCO
    SONNET. Of a Lady's Love for him 240

SIMBUONO GIUDICE
    CANZONE. He finds that Love has beguiled him, but will trust in his Lady 240

MASOLINO DA TODI
    SONNET. Of Work and Wealth 242

ONESTO DI BONCIMA, BOLOGNESE
    SONNET. Of the Last Judgement 243
    SONNET. He wishes that he could meet his Lady alone . 243

TERINO DA CASTEL FIORENTINO
    SONNET. To Onesto di Boncima, in answer to the Foregoing 244

MAESTRO MIGLIORE, DA FIORENZA
    SONNET. He declares all Love to be Grief . . . 244

DELLO DA SIGNA
    BALLATA. His Creed of Ideal Love . . . 245

FOLGORE DA SAN GEMINIANO
    SONNET. To the Guelf Faction 246
    SONNET. To the Same 246
    SONNET. Of Virtue 247
    TWELVE SONNETS. Of the Months 247
    SEVEN SONNETS. Of the Week 255

GUIDO DELLE COLONNE
    CANZONE. To Love and to his Lady 259

PIER MORONELLI, DI FIORENZA
    CANZONETTA. A Bitter Song to his Lady . . . 261

CIUNCIO FIORENTINO
    CANZONE. Of his Love; with the Figures of a Stag, of Water, and of an Eagle 263

RUGGIERI DI AMICI, SICILIANO
    CANZONETTA. For a Renewal of Favours . . 264

CARNINO GHIBERTI, DA FIORENZA
    CANZONE. Being absent from his Lady, he fears Death . 265

CONTENTS   xi

Prinzivalle Doria   PAGE
    Canzone. Of his Love, with the Figure of a sudden
        Storm 267

Rustico di Filippo
    Sonnet. Of the Making of Master Messerin . . . 268
    Sonnet. Of the Safety of Messer Fazio 269
    Sonnet. Of Messer Ugolino 269

Pucciarello di Fiorenza
    Sonnet. Of Expediency 270

Albertuccio della Viola
    Canzone. Of his Lady dancing 270

Tommaso Buzzuola, da Faenza
    Sonnet. He is in awe of his Lady 271

Noffo Bonaguida
    Sonnet. He is enjoined to pure Love 272

Lippo Paschi de' Bardi
    Sonnet. He solicits a Lady's Favours 272

Ser Pace, Notaio da Fiorenza
    Sonnet. A Return to Love 273

Niccolò degli Albizzi
    Prolonged Sonnet. When the Troops were returning
        from Milan 273

Francesco da Barberino
    Blank Verse. A Virgin declares her Beauties . . 274
    Sentenze. Of Sloth against Sin 275
    Sentenze. Of Sins in Speech 275
    Sentenze. Of Importunities and Troublesome Persons . 276
    Sentenze. Of Caution 279

Fazio degli Uberti
    Canzone. His Portrait of his Lady, Angiola of Verona . 279
    Extract from the 'Dittamondo'. Of England, and of
        its Marvels 282
    Extract from the 'Dittamondo'. Of the Dukes of
        Normandy, and thence of the Kings of England, from
        William the First to Edward the Third . . . 285

Franco Sacchetti
    Ballata. His Talk with certain Peasant Girls . . 288
    Catch. On a Fine Day 289
    Catch. On a Wet Day 290

CONTENTS

ANONYMOUS POEMS   PAGE
   SONNET.   A Lady laments for her lost Lover, by similitude
      of a Falcon 291
   BALLATA.   One speaks of the Beginning of his Love . 292
   BALLATA.   One speaks of his false Lady . . . 292
   BALLATA.   One speaks of his feigned and real Love . 292
   BALLATA.   Of True and False Singing 293

PART II

DANTE AND HIS CIRCLE

INTRODUCTION TO PART II 297

DANTE ALIGHIERI
   THE NEW LIFE (*La Vita Nuova*) 325
   SONNET (TO BRUNETTO LATINI). Sent with the *Vita Nuova* 386
   SONNET. Of Beatrice de' Portinari, on All Saints' Day . 386
   SONNET. To certain Ladies; when Beatrice was lamenting her Father's Death 387
   SONNET. To the same Ladies; with their Answer . 387
   BALLATA. He will gaze upon Beatrice 388
   CANZONE. He beseeches Death for the Life of Beatrice . 388
   SONNET. On the 9th of June, 1290 390
   SONNET (TO CINO DA PISTOIA). He rebukes Cino for Fickleness 391
   SONNET (TO CINO DA PISTOIA). Written in Exile . . 392
   SONNET. Of Beauty and Duty 393
   SESTINA. Of the Lady Pietra degli Scrovigni . . 393
   SONNET. To the Lady Pietra degli Scrovigni . . 395
   SONNET (TO GUIDO CAVALCANTI). He imagines a pleasant Voyage for Guido, Lapo Gianni, and himself, with their three Ladies 402
   SONNET (TO GIOVANNI QUIRINO). He answers the foregoing Sonnet (by Quirino); saying what he feels at the approach of Death 456

GUIDO CAVALCANTI
   SONNET (TO DANTE ALIGHIERI). He interprets Dante's Dream, related in the first Sonnet of the *Vita Nuova* . 396

CONTENTS

GUIDO CAVALCANTI (*continued*)—

	PAGE
SONNET. To his Lady Joan, of Florence	396
SONNET. He compares all Things with his Lady, and finds them wanting	397
SONNET. A Rapture concerning his Lady	397
BALLATA. Of his Lady among other Ladies	398
SONNET (TO GUIDO ORLANDI). Of a Consecrated Image resembling his Lady	398
SONNET. Of the Eyes of a certain Mandetta, of Thoulouse, which resemble those of his Lady Joan of Florence	400
BALLATA. He reveals, in a Dialogue, his increasing love for Mandetta	400
SONNET (TO DANTE ALIGHIERI). He answers the foregoing Sonnet (by Dante), speaking with shame of his changed Love	403
SONNET (TO DANTE ALIGHIERI). He reports, in a feigned Vision, the successful Issue of Lapo Gianni's Love	403
SONNET (TO DANTE ALIGHIERI). He mistrusts the Love of Lapo Gianni	404
SONNET. On the Detection of a false Friend	404
SONNET. He speaks of a third Love of his	405
BALLATA. Of a continual Death in Love	405
SONNET. To a Friend who does not pity his Love	406
BALLATA. He perceives that his highest Love is gone from him	406
SONNET. Of his Pain from a new Love	407
SONNET (TO BERNARDO DA BOLOGNA). He answers Bernardo, commending Pinella, and saying that the Love he can offer her is already shared by many noble Ladies	409
SONNET (TO GUIDO ORLANDI). In Praise of Guido Orlandi's Lady	410
SONNET (TO DANTE ALIGHIERI). He rebukes Dante for his way of Life, after the Death of Beatrice	411
BALLATA. Concerning a Shepherd-maid	412
SONNET. Of an ill-favoured Lady	413
SONNET. To a newly enriched Man; reminding him of the wants of the Poor	413
SONNET (TO POPE BONIFACE VIII). After the Pope's Interdict, when the great Houses were leaving Florence	414
BALLATA. In Exile at Sarzana	414

CONTENTS

GUIDO CAVALCANTI (*continued*)— PAGE
    CANZONE. A Song of Fortune 416
    CANZONE. A Song against Poverty 418
    CANZONE. He laments the Presumption and Incontinence of his Youth 420
    CANZONE. A Dispute with Death 422

CINO DA PISTOIA

    SONNET (TO DANTE ALIGHIERI). He answers Dante, confessing his unsteadfast Heart 391
    SONNET (TO DANTE ALIGHIERI). He answers the foregoing Sonnet (by Dante), and prays him, in the name of Beatrice, to continue his great Poem . . . 392
    SONNET (TO DANTE ALIGHIERI). He interprets Dante's Dream related in the first Sonnet of the *Vita Nuova* . 425
    CANZONE (TO DANTE ALIGHIERI). On the Death of Beatrice Portinari 426
    SONNET (TO DANTE ALIGHIERI). He conceives of some Compensation in Death 428
    MADRIGAL. To his Lady Selvaggia Vergiolesi; likening his Love to a search for Gold 429
    SONNET. To Love, in great Bitterness 429
    SONNET. Death is not without but within him . . 430
    SONNET. A Trance of Love 430
    SONNET. Of the Grave of Selvaggia, on the Monte della Sambuca 431
    CANZONE. His Lament for Selvaggia . . . 431
    SONNET (TO GUIDO CAVALCANTI). He owes nothing to Guido as a Poet 433
    SONNET. He impugns the verdicts of Dante's *Commedia* . 433
    SONNET. He condemns Dante for not naming, in the *Commedia*, his friend Onesto di Boncima, and his Lady Selvaggia 434

DANTE DA MAIANO

    SONNET (TO DANTE ALIGHIERI). He interprets Dante Alighieri's Dream, related in the first Sonnet of the *Vita Nuova* 435
    SONNET. He craves interpreting of a Dream of his . 435
    SONNET. To his Lady Nina, of Sicily 436
    SONNET. He thanks his Lady for the Joy he has had from her 437

CONTENTS

CECCO ANGIOLIERI, DA SIENA

SONNET (TO DANTE ALIGHIERI). On the last Sonnet of the
Vita Nuova 438
SONNET. He will not be too deeply in Love . . . 438
SONNET. Of Love in Men and Devils 439
SONNET. Of Love, in honour of his Mistress Becchina . 439
SONNET. Of Becchina the Shoemaker's Daughter . . 440
SONNET. To Messer Angiolieri, his Father . . . 440
SONNET. Of the 20th June, 1291 441
SONNET. In absence from Becchina 441
SONNET. Of Becchina in a Rage 442
SONNET. He rails against Dante, who had censured his
homage to Becchina 442
SONNET. Of his four Tormentors 443
SONNET. Concerning his Father 443
SONNET. Of all he would do 444
SONNET. He is past all Help 444
SONNET. Of why he is unhanged 445
SONNET. Of why he would be a Scullion . . . 445
SONNET. He argues his case with Death . . . 446
SONNET. Of Becchina, and of her Husband . . . 446
SONNET. On the Death of his Father 447
SONNET. He would slay all who hate their Fathers . . 447
SONNET (TO DANTE ALIGHIERI). He writes to Dante,
then in exile at Verona, defying him as no better
than himself. 448

GUIDO ORLANDI

MADRIGAL (TO GUIDO CAVALCANTI). In answer to the foregoing Sonnet (by Cavalcanti) 399
PROLONGED SONNET (TO GUIDO CAVALCANTI). He finds
fault with the Conceits of the foregoing Sonnet (by
Cavalcanti) 408
SONNET (TO GUIDO CAVALCANTI). He answers the foregoing Sonnet (by Cavalcanti), declaring himself his
Lady's Champion 411
SONNET (TO DANTE DA MAIANO). He interprets the
Dream related in the foregoing Sonnet (by Dante da
Maiano) 436
SONNET. Against the 'White' Ghibellines . . . 449

GIANNI ALFANI

SONNET (TO GUIDO CAVALCANTI). On the part of a Lady
of Pisa 408

CONTENTS

BERNARDO DA BOLOGNA

    SONNET (TO GUIDO CAVALCANTI). He writes to Guido, telling him of the Love which a certain Pinella showed on seeing him 409

DINO COMPAGNI

    SONNET (TO GUIDO CAVALCANTI). He reproves Guido for his arrogance in Love 410

LAPO GIANNI

    MADRIGAL. What Love shall provide for him . 449
    BALLATA. A Message in charge for his Lady Lagia . . 450

DINO FRESCOBALDI

    SONNET. Of what his Lady is 452
    SONNET. Of the Star of his Love 452

GIOTTO DI BONDONE

    CANZONE. Of the Doctrine of Voluntary Poverty . . 453

SIMONE DALL' ANTELLA

    PROLONGED SONNET. In the last Days of the Emperor Henry VII 455

GIOVANNI QUIRINO

    SONNET (TO DANTE ALIGHIERI). He commends the work of Dante's Life, then drawing to its close; and deplores his own deficiencies 456

APPENDIX TO PART II

I. FORESE DONATI.—CECCO D'ASCOLI 457

    SONNET (DANTE TO FORESE). He taunts Forese by the nickname of Bicci 458
    SONNET (FORESE TO DANTE). He taunts Dante ironically for not avenging Geri Alighieri . . . 459
    SONNET (DANTE TO FORESE). He taunts him concerning his Wife 459
    SONNET (FORESE TO DANTE). He taunts him concerning the unavenged Spirit of Geri Alighieri . . . 460

II. GIOVANNI BOCCACCIO

SONNET.	To one who had censured his public Exposition of Dante	463
SONNET.	Inscription for a Portrait of Dante	464
SONNET.	To Dante in Paradise, after Fiammetta's death	464
SONNET.	Of Fiammetta singing	465
SONNET.	Of his last sight of Fiammetta	465
SONNET.	Of three Girls and of their Talk	466

INDEX OF FIRST LINES OF POEMS 467

INDEX OF FIRST LINES OF TRANSLATIONS . . 471

POEMS

[*Author's Note*, 1870]

[Many poems in this volume were written between 1847 and 1853. Others are of recent date, and a few belong to the intervening period. It has been thought unnecessary to specify the earlier work, as nothing is included which the author believes to be immature.]

POEMS

THE BLESSED DAMOZEL

The blessed damozel leaned out
   From the gold bar of Heaven;
Her eyes were deeper than the depth
   Of waters stilled at even;
She had three lilies in her hand,
   And the stars in her hair were seven.

Her robe, ungirt from clasp to hem,
   No wrought flowers did adorn,
But a white rose of Mary's gift,
   For service meetly worn;   10
Her hair that lay along her back
   Was yellow like ripe corn.

Herseemed she scarce had been a day
   One of God's choristers;
The wonder was not yet quite gone
   From that still look of hers;
Albeit, to them she left, her day
   Had counted as ten years.

(To one, it is ten years of years.
   . . . Yet now, and in this place,   20
Surely she leaned o'er me—her hair
   Fell all about my face. . . .
Nothing: the autumn fall of leaves.
   The whole year sets apace.)

It was the rampart of God's house
   That she was standing on;
By God built over the sheer depth
   The which is Space begun;
So high, that looking downward thence
   She scarce could see the sun.   30

THE BLESSED DAMOZEL

It lies in Heaven, across the flood
   Of ether, as a bridge.
Beneath, the tides of day and night
   With flame and darkness ridge
The void, as low as where this earth
   Spins like a fretful midge.

Heard hardly, some of her new friends
   Amid their loving games
Spake evermore among themselves
   Their virginal chaste names ;   40
And the souls mounting up to God
   Went by her like thin flames.

And still she bowed herself and stooped
   Out of the circling charm ;
Until her bosom must have made
   The bar she leaned on warm,
And the lilies lay as if asleep
   Along her bended arm.

From the fixed place of Heaven she saw
   Time like a pulse shake fierce   50
Through all the worlds. Her gaze still strove
   Within the gulf to pierce
Its path : and now she spoke as when
   The stars sang in their spheres.

The sun was gone now ; the curled moon
   Was like a little feather
Fluttering far down the gulf ; and now
   She spoke through the still weather.
Her voice was like the voice the stars
   Had when they sang together.   60

(Ah sweet ! Even now, in that bird's song,
   Strove not her accents there,
Fain to be hearkened ? When those bells
   Possessed the mid-day air,
Strove not her steps to reach my side
   Down all the echoing stair ?)

THE BLESSED DAMOZEL 3

'I wish that he were come to me,
  For he will come,' she said.
'Have I not prayed in Heaven?—on earth,
  Lord, Lord, has he not pray'd?
Are not two prayers a perfect strength?
  And shall I feel afraid?

'When round his head the aureole clings,
  And he is clothed in white,
I'll take his hand and go with him
  To the deep wells of light;
We will step down as to a stream,
  And bathe there in God's sight.

'We two will stand beside that shrine,
  Occult, withheld, untrod,
Whose lamps are stirred continually
  With prayer sent up to God;
And see our old prayers, granted, melt
  Each like a little cloud.

'We two will lie i' the shadow of
  That living mystic tree
Within whose secret growth the Dove
  Is sometimes felt to be,
While every leaf that His plumes touch
  Saith His Name audibly.

'And I myself will teach to him,
  I myself, lying so,
The songs I sing here; which his voice
  Shall pause in, hushed and slow,
And find some knowledge at each pause,
  Or some new thing to know.'

(Alas! We two, we two, thou say'st!
  Yea, one wast thou with me
That once of old. But shall God lift
  To endless unity
The soul whose likeness with thy soul
  Was but its love for thee?)

'We two,' she said, ' will seek the groves
   Where the lady Mary is,
With her five handmaidens, whose names
   Are five sweet symphonies,
Cecily, Gertrude, Magdalen,
   Margaret and Rosalys.

'Circlewise sit they, with bound locks
   And foreheads garlanded ;
Into the fine cloth white like flame
   Weaving the golden thread,
To fashion the birth-robes for them
   Who are just born, being dead.

'He shall fear, haply, and be dumb :
   Then will I lay my cheek
To his, and tell about our love,
   Not once abashed or weak :
And the dear Mother will approve
   My pride, and let me speak.

'Herself shall bring us, hand in hand,
   To Him round whom all souls
Kneel, the clear-ranged unnumbered heads
   Bowed with their aureoles :
And angels meeting us shall sing
   To their citherns and citoles.

'There will I ask of Christ the Lord
   Thus much for him and me :—
Only to live as once on earth
   With Love,—only to be,
As then awhile, for ever now
   Together, I and he.'

She gazed and listened and then said,
   Less sad of speech than mild,—
'All this is when he comes.' She ceased.
   The light thrilled towards her, fill'd
With angels in strong level flight.
   Her eyes prayed, and she smil'd.

(I saw her smile.)   But soon their path
  Was vague in distant spheres :   140
And then she cast her arms along
  The golden barriers,
And laid her face between her hands,
  And wept.   (I heard her tears.)

LOVE'S NOCTURN

MASTER of the murmuring courts
  Where the shapes of sleep convene !—
Lo ! my spirit here exhorts
  All the powers of thy demesne
  For their aid to woo my queen.
        What reports
  Yield thy jealous courts unseen ?

Vaporous, unaccountable,
  Dreamland lies forlorn of light,
Hollow like a breathing shell.   10
  Ah ! that from all dreams I might
  Choose one dream and guide its flight !
        I know well
  What her sleep should tell to-night.

There the dreams are multitudes :
  Some whose buoyance waits not sleep,
Deep within the August woods ;
  Some that hum while rest may steep
  Weary labour laid a-heap ;
        Interludes,   20
  Some, of grievous moods that weep.

Poets' fancies all are there :
  There the elf-girls flood with wings
Valleys full of plaintive air ;
  There breathe perfumes ; there in rings
  Whirl the foam-bewildered springs ;
        Siren there
  Winds her dizzy hair and sings.

Thence the one dream mutually
　　Dreamed in bridal unison,　　　　　　　30
Less than waking ecstasy ;
　　Half-formed visions that make moan
　　In the house of birth alone ;
　　　　And what we
　　At death's wicket see, unknown.

But for mine own sleep, it lies
　　In one gracious form's control,
Fair with honorable eyes,
　　Lamps of an auspicious soul :
　　O their glance is loftiest dole,　　　　　40
　　　　Sweet and wise,
　　Wherein Love descries his goal.

Reft of her, my dreams are all
　　Clammy trance that fears the sky :
Changing footpaths shift and fall ;
　　From polluted coverts nigh,
　　Miserable phantoms sigh ;
　　　　Quakes the pall,
　　And the funeral goes by.

Master, is it soothly said　　　　　　　　50
　　That, as echoes of man's speech
Far in secret clefts are made,
　　So do all men's bodies reach
　　Shadows o'er thy sunken beach,—
　　　　Shape or shade
　　In those halls pourtrayed of each ?

Ah ! might I, by thy good grace
　　Groping in the windy stair,
(Darkness and the breath of space
　　Like loud waters everywhere,)　　　　60
　　Meeting mine own image there
　　　　Face to face,
　　Send it from that place to her !

LOVE'S NOCTURN

Nay, not I ; but oh ! do thou,
　Master, from thy shadowkind
Call my body's phantom now :
　Bid it bear its face declin'd
　Till its flight her slumbers find,
　　　And her brow
　Feel its presence bow like wind.　　　　70

Where in groves the gracile Spring
　Trembles, with mute orison
Confidently strengthening,
　Water's voice and wind's as one
　Shed an echo in the sun.
　　　Soft as Spring,
　Master, bid it sing and moan.

Song shall tell how glad and strong
　Is the night she soothes alway ;
Moan shall grieve with that parched tongue　80
　Of the brazen hours of day :
　Sounds as of the springtide they,
　　　Moan and song,
　While the chill months long for May.

Not the prayers which with all leave
　The world's fluent woes prefer,—
Not the praise the world doth give,
　Dulcet fulsome whisperer ;—
　Let it yield my love to her,
　　　And achieve　　　　　　　　90
Strength that shall not grieve or err.

Wheresoe'er my dreams befall,
　Both at night-watch, (let it say,)
And where round the sundial
　The reluctant hours of day,
　Heartless, hopeless of their way,
　　　Rest and call ;—
　There her glance doth fall and stay.

Suddenly her face is there:
　　So do mounting vapours wreathe
Subtle-scented transports where
　　The black firwood sets its teeth.
　　　Part the boughs and look beneath,—
　　　　　Lilies share
　　Secret waters there, and breathe.

Master, bid my shadow bend
　　Whispering thus till birth of light,
Lest new shapes that sleep may send
　　Scatter all its work to flight;—
　　　Master, master of the night,
　　　　　Bid it spend
　　Speech, song, prayer, and end aright.

Yet, ah me! if at her head
　　There another phantom lean
Murmuring o'er the fragrant bed,—
　　Ah! and if my spirit's queen
　　　Smile those alien words between,—
　　　　　Ah! poor shade!
　　Shall it strive, or fade unseen?

How should love's own messenger
　　Strive with love and be love's foe?
Master, nay! If thus, in her,
　　Sleep a wedded heart should show,—
　　　Silent let mine image go,
　　　　　Its old share
　　Of thy spell-bound air to know.

Like a vapour wan and mute,
　　Like a flame, so let it pass;
One low sigh across her lute,
　　One dull breath against her glass;
　　　And to my sad soul, alas!
　　　　　One salute
　　Cold as when death's foot shall pass.

Then, too, let all hopes of mine,
  All vain hopes by night and day,
Slowly at thy summoning sign
  Rise up pallid and obey.
  Dreams, if this is thus, were they :—
    Be they thine,
  And to dreamland pine away.   140

Yet from old time, life, not death,
  Master, in thy rule is rife :
Lo ! through thee, with mingling breath,
  Adam woke beside his wife.
  O Love bring me so, for strife,
    Force and faith,
  Bring me so not death but life !

Yea, to Love himself is pour'd
  This frail song of hope and fear.
Thou art Love, of one accord   150
  With kind Sleep to bring her near,
  Still-eyed, deep-eyed, ah how dear !
    Master, Lord,
  In her name implor'd, O hear !

TROY TOWN

HEAVENBORN HELEN, Sparta's queen,
      (*O Troy Town !*)
Had two breasts of heavenly sheen,
The sun and moon of the heart's desire :
All Love's lordship lay between.
      (*O Troy's down,
        Tall Troy's on fire !*)

Helen knelt at Venus' shrine,
      (*O Troy Town !*)
Saying, ' A little gift is mine,   10
A little gift for a heart's desire.
Hear me speak and make me a sign !
      (*O Troy's down,
        Tall Troy's on fire !*)

'Look, I bring thee a carven cup;
      (O Troy Town!)
See it here as I hold it up,—
Shaped it is to the heart's desire,
Fit to fill when the gods would sup.
      (O Troy's down,
        Tall Troy's on fire!)

'It was moulded like my breast·
      (O Troy Town!)
He that sees it may not rest,
Rest at all for his heart's desire.
O give ear to my heart's behest!
      (O Troy's down,
        Tall Troy's on fire!)

'See my breast, how like it is;
      (O Troy Town!)
See it bare for the air to kiss!
Is the cup to thy heart's desire?
O for the breast, O make it his!
      (O Troy's down,
        Tall Troy's on fire!)

'Yea, for my bosom here I sue;
      (O Troy Town!)
Thou must give it where 'tis due,
Give it there to the heart's desire.
Whom do I give my bosom to?
      (O Troy's down,
        Tall Troy's on fire!)

'Each twin breast is an apple sweet
      (O Troy Town!)
Once an apple stirred the beat
Of thy heart with the heart's desire :—
Say, who brought it then to thy feet?
      (O Troy's down,
        Tall Troy's on fire!)

TROY TOWN

'They that claimed it then were three :   50
      (O Troy Town !)
For thy sake two hearts did he
Make forlorn of the heart's desire.
Do for him as he did for thee !
      (O Troy's down,
        Tall Troy's on fire !)

'Mine are apples grown to the south,
      (O Troy Town !)
Grown to taste in the days of drouth,
Taste and waste to the heart's desire :   60
Mine are apples meet for his mouth.'
      (O Troy's down,
        Tall Troy's on fire !)

Venus looked on Helen's gift,
      (O Troy Town !)
Looked and smiled with subtle drift,
Saw the work of her heart's desire :—
'There thou kneel'st for Love to lift !'
      (O Troy's down,
        Tall Troy's on fire !)   70

Venus looked in Helen's face,
      (O Troy Town !)
Knew far off an hour and place,
And fire lit from the heart's desire ;
Laughed and said, 'Thy gift hath grace !'
      (O Troy's down,
        Tall Troy's on fire !)

Cupid looked on Helen's breast,
      (O Troy Town !)
Saw the heart within its nest,   80
Saw the flame of the heart's desire,—
Marked his arrow's burning crest.
      (O Troy's down,
        Tall Troy's on fire !)

Cupid took another dart,
    (*O Troy Town!*)
Fledged it for another heart,
Winged the shaft with the heart's desire,
Drew the string and said, 'Depart!'
    (*O Troy's down,
      Tall Troy's on fire!*)

Paris turned upon his bed,
    (*O Troy Town!*)
Turned upon his bed and said,
Dead at heart with the heart's desire,—
'O to clasp her golden head!'
    (*O Troy's down,
      Tall Troy's on fire!*)

THE BURDEN OF NINEVEH

IN our Museum galleries
To-day I lingered o'er the prize
Dead Greece vouchsafes to living eyes,—
Her Art for ever in fresh wise
    From hour to hour rejoicing me.
Sighing I turned at last to win
Once more the London dirt and din;
And as I made the swing-door spin
And issued, they were hoisting in
    A wingèd beast from Nineveh.

A human face the creature wore,
And hoofs behind and hoofs before,
And flanks with dark runes fretted o'er.
'Twas bull, 'twas mitred Minotaur,
    A dead disbowelled mystery;
The mummy of a buried faith
Stark from the charnel without scathe,
Its wings stood for the light to bathe,—
Such fossil cerements as might swathe
    The very corpse of Nineveh.

THE BURDEN OF NINEVEH

The print of its first rush-wrapping,
Wound ere it dried, still ribbed the thing.
What song did the brown maidens sing,
From purple mouths alternating,
  When that was woven languidly ?
What vows, what rites, what prayers preferr'd,
What songs has the strange image heard ?
In what blind vigil stood interr'd
For ages, till an English word
  Broke silence first at Nineveh ?

Oh when upon each sculptured court,
Where even the wind might not resort,—
O'er which Time passed, of like import
With the wild Arab boys at sport,—
  A living face looked in to see :—
Oh seemed it not—the spell once broke—
As though the carven warriors woke,
As though the shaft the string forsook,
The cymbals clashed, the chariots shook,
  And there was life in Nineveh ?

On London stones our sun anew
The beast's recovered shadow threw.
(No shade that plague of darkness knew,
No light, no shade, while older grew
  By ages the old earth and sea.)
Lo thou ! could all thy priests have shown
Such proof to make thy godhead known ?
From their dead Past thou liv'st alone ;
And still thy shadow is thine own
  Even as of yore in Nineveh.

That day whereof we keep record,
When near thy city-gates the Lord
Sheltered his Jonah with a gourd,
This sun, (I said) here present, pour'd
  Even thus this shadow that I see.
This shadow has been shed the same
From sun and moon,—from lamps which came

THE BURDEN OF NINEVEH

For prayer,—from fifteen days of flame,
The last, while smouldered to a name
   Sardanapalus' Nineveh.   60

Within thy shadow, haply, once
Sennacherib has knelt, whose sons
Smote him between the altar-stones:
Or pale Semiramis her zones
  Of gold, her incense brought to thee,
In love for grace, in war for aid: . . .
Ay, and who else? . . . till 'neath thy shade
Within his trenches newly made
Last year the Christian knelt and pray'd—
  Not to thy strength—in Nineveh.[1]   70

Now, thou poor god, within this hall
Where the blank windows blind the wall
From pedestal to pedestal,
The kind of light shall on thee fall
  Which London takes the day to be:
While school-foundations in the act
Of holiday, three files compact,
Shall learn to view thee as a fact
Connected with that zealous tract:
  'Rome,—Babylon and Nineveh.'   80

Deemed they of this, those worshippers,
When, in some mythic chain of verse
Which man shall not again rehearse,
The faces of thy ministers
  Yearned pale with bitter ecstasy?
Greece, Egypt, Rome,—did any god
Before whose feet men knelt unshod
Deem that in this unblest abode
Another scarce more unknown god
  Should house with him, from Nineveh?   90

---

[1] During the excavations, the Tiyari workmen held their services in the shadow of the great bulls. (Layard's *Nineveh*, ch. ix.)

THE BURDEN OF NINEVEH

Ah ! in what quarries lay the stone
From which this pillared pile has grown,
Unto man's need how long unknown,
Since those thy temples, court and cone,
    Rose far in desert history ?
Ah ! what is here that does not lie
All strange to thine awakened eye ?
Ah ! what is here can testify
(Save that dumb presence of the sky)
    Unto thy day and Nineveh ?   100

Why, of those mummies in the room
Above, there might indeed have come
One out of Egypt to thy home,
An alien. Nay, but were not some
    Of these thine own ' antiquity ? '
And now,—they and their gods and thou
All relics here together,—now
Whose profit ? whether bull or cow,
Isis or Ibis, who or how,
    Whether of Thebes or Nineveh ?   110

The consecrated metals found,
And ivory tablets, underground,
Winged teraphim and creatures crown'd,
When air and daylight filled the mound,
    Fell into dust immediately.
And even as these, the images
Of awe and worship,—even as these,—
So, smitten with the sun's increase,
Her glory mouldered and did cease
    From immemorial Nineveh.   120

The day her builders made their halt,
Those cities of the lake of salt
Stood firmly 'stablished without fault,
Made proud with pillars of basalt,
    With sardonyx and porphyry.
The day that Jonah bore abroad
To Nineveh the voice of God,

A brackish lake lay in his road,
Where erst Pride fixed her sure abode
　As then in royal Nineveh.　　　　　　130

The day when he, Pride's lord and Man's,
Showed all the kingdoms at a glance
To Him before whose countenance
The years recede, the years advance,
　And said, Fall down and worship me :—
'Mid all the pomp beneath that look,
Then stirred there, haply, some rebuke,
Where to the wind the Salt Pools shook,
And in those tracts, of life forsook,
　That knew thee not, O Nineveh !　　　140

Delicate harlot ! On thy throne
Thou with a world beneath thee prone
In state for ages sat'st alone ;
And needs were years and lustres flown
　Ere strength of man could vanquish thee :
Whom even thy victor foes must bring,
Still royal, among maids that sing
As with doves' voices, taboring
Upon their breasts, unto the King,—
　A kingly conquest, Nineveh !　　　　150

... Here woke my thought. The wind's slow sway
Had waxed ; and like the human play
Of scorn that smiling spreads away,
The sunshine shivered off the day :
　The callous wind, it seemed to me,
Swept up the shadow from the ground :
And pale as whom the Fates astound,
The god forlorn stood winged and crown'd :
Within I knew the cry lay bound
　Of the dumb soul of Nineveh.　　　　160

And as I turned, my sense half shut
Still saw the crowds of kerb and rut
Go past as marshalled to the strut
Of ranks in gypsum quaintly cut.
　It seemed in one same pageantry

THE BURDEN OF NINEVEH

They followed forms which had been erst;
To pass, till on my sight should burst
That future of the best or worst
When some may question which was first,
   Of London or of Nineveh.

For as that Bull-god once did stand
And watched the burial-clouds of sand,
Till these at last without a hand
Rose o'er his eyes, another land,
   And blinded him with destiny :—
So may he stand again ; till now,
In ships of unknown sail and prow,
Some tribe of the Australian plough
Bear him afar,—a relic now
   Of London, not of Nineveh !

Or it may chance indeed that when
Man's age is hoary among men,—
His centuries threescore and ten,—
His furthest childhood shall seem then
   More clear than later times may be :
Who, finding in this desert place
This form, shall hold us for some race
That walked not in Christ's lowly ways,
But bowed its pride and vowed its praise
   Unto the God of Nineveh.

The smile rose first,—anon drew nigh
The thought : . . . Those heavy wings spread high
So sure of flight, which do not fly ;
That set gaze never on the sky ;
   Those scriptured flanks it cannot see ;
Its crown, a brow-contracting load ;
Its planted feet which trust the sod : . . .
(So grew the image as I trod :)
O Nineveh, was this thy God,—
   Thine also, mighty Nineveh ?

EDEN BOWER

It was Lilith the wife of Adam:
      (Eden bower's in flower.)
Not a drop of her blood was human,
But she was made like a soft sweet woman.

Lilith stood on the skirts of Eden;
      (And O the bower and the hour!)
She was the first that thence was driven;
With her was hell and with Eve was heaven.

In the ear of the Snake said Lilith:—
      (Eden bower's in flower.)   10
'To thee I come when the rest is over;
A snake was I when thou wast my lover.

'I was the fairest snake in Eden:
      (And O the bower and the hour!)
By the earth's will, new form and feature
Made me a wife for the earth's new creature.

'Take me thou as I come from Adam:
      (Eden bower's in flower.)
Once again shall my love subdue thee;
The past is past and I am come to thee.   20

'O but Adam was thrall to Lilith!
      (And O the bower and the hour!)
All the threads of my hair are golden,
And there in a net his heart was holden.

'O and Lilith was queen of Adam!
      (Eden bower's in flower.)
All the day and the night together
My breath could shake his soul like a feather.

'What great joys had Adam and Lilith!—
      (And O the bower and the hour!)   30
Sweet close rings of the serpent's twining,
As heart in heart lay sighing and pining.

EDEN BOWER

'What bright babes had Lilith and Adam!—
    (*Eden bower's in flower.*)
Shapes that coiled in the woods and waters,
Glittering sons and radiant daughters.

'O thou God, the Lord God of Eden!
    (*And O the bower and the hour!*)
Say, was this fair body for no man,
That of Adam's flesh thou mak'st him a woman?

'O thou Snake, the King-snake of Eden!
    (*Eden bower's in flower.*)
God's strong will our necks are under,
But thou and I may cleave it in sunder.

'Help, sweet Snake, sweet lover of Lilith!
    (*And O the bower and the hour!*)
And let God learn how I loved and hated
Man in the image of God created.

'Help me once against Eve and Adam!
    (*Eden bower's in flower.*)
Help me once for this one endeavour,
And then my love shall be thine for ever!

'Strong is God, the fell foe of Lilith:
    (*And O the bower and the hour!*)
Nought in heaven or earth may affright him;
But join thou with me and we will smite him.

'Strong is God, the great God of Eden:
    (*Eden bower's in flower.*)
Over all He made He hath power;
But lend me thou thy shape for an hour!

'Lend thy shape for the love of Lilith!
    (*And O the bower and the hour!*)
Look, my mouth and my cheek are ruddy,
And thou art cold, and fire is my body.

'Lend thy shape for the hate of Adam!
    (*Eden bower's in flower.*)
That he may wail my joy that forsook him,
And curse the day when the bride-sleep took him.

EDEN BOWER

'Lend thy shape for the shame of Eden!
    (*And O the bower and the hour!*)   70
Is not the foe-God weak as the foeman
When love grows hate in the heart of a woman?

'Would'st thou know the heart's hope of Lilith?
    (*Eden bower's in flower.*)
Then bring thou close thine head till it glisten
Along my breast, and lip me and listen.

'Am I sweet, O sweet Snake of Eden?
    (*And O the bower and the hour!*)
Then ope thine ear to my warm mouth's cooing
And learn what deed remains for our doing.   80

'Thou didst hear when God said to Adam:—
    (*Eden bower's in flower.*)
"Of all this wealth I have made thee warden;
Thou'rt free to eat of the trees of the garden:

'"Only of one tree eat not in Eden;
    (*And O the bower and the hour!*)
All save one I give to thy freewill,—
The Tree of the Knowledge of Good and Evil."

'O my love, come nearer to Lilith!
    (*Eden bower's in flower.*)   90
In thy sweet folds bind me and bend me,
And let me feel the shape thou shalt lend me!

'In thy shape I'll go back to Eden;
    (*And O the bower and the hour!*)
In these coils that Tree will I grapple,
And stretch this crowned head forth by the apple.

'Lo, Eve bends to the breath of Lilith!
    (*Eden bower's in flower.*)
O how then shall my heart desire
All her blood as food to its fire!   100

'Lo, Eve bends to the words of Lilith!—
    (*And O the bower and the hour!*)
"Nay, this Tree's fruit,—why should ye hate it,
Or Death be born the day that ye ate it?

' "Nay, but on that great day in Eden.
       (*Eden bower's in flower.*)
By the help that in this wise Tree is,
God knows well ye shall be as He is."

' Then Eve shall eat and give unto Adam;
       (*And O the bower and the hour!*)   110
And then they both shall know they are naked,
And their hearts ache as my heart hath achèd.

' Aye, let them hide in the trees of Eden,
       (*Eden bower's in flower.*)
As in the cool of the day in the garden
God shall walk without pity or pardon.

' Hear, thou Eve, the man's heart in Adam!
       (*And O the bower and the hour!*)
Of his brave words hark to the bravest:—
"This the woman gave that thou gavest."   120

' Hear Eve speak, yea, list to her, Lilith!
       (*Eden bower's in flower.*)
Feast thine heart with words that shall sate it—
"This the serpent gave and I ate it."

' O proud Eve, cling close to thine Adam,
       (*And O the bower and the hour!*)
Driven forth as the beasts of his naming
By the sword that for ever is flaming.

' Know, thy path is known unto Lilith!
       (*Eden bower's in flower.*)   130
While the blithe birds sang at thy wedding,
There her tears grew thorns for thy treading.

' O my love, thou Love-snake of Eden!
       (*And O the bower and the hour!*)
O to-day and the day to come after!
Loose me, love,—give breath to my laughter!

' O bright Snake, the Death-worm of Adam!
       (*Eden bower's in flower.*)
Wreathe thy neck with my hair's bright tether,
And wear my gold and thy gold together!   140

' On that day on the skirts of Eden,
   (*And O the bower and the hour!*)
In thy shape shall I glide back to thee,
And in my shape for an instant view thee.

' But when thou'rt thou and Lilith is Lilith,
   (*Eden bower's in flower.*)
In what bliss past hearing or seeing
Shall each one drink of the other's being !

' With cries of "Eve!" and "Eden!" and "Adam!"
   (*And O the bower and the hour !*) 150
How shall we mingle our love's caresses,
I in thy coils, and thou in my tresses!

' With those names, ye echoes of Eden,
   (*Eden bower's in flower.*)
Fire shall cry from my heart that burneth,—
" Dust he is and to dust returneth ! "

' Yet to-day, thou master of Lilith,—
   (*And O the bower and the hour !*)
Wrap me round in the form I'll borrow
And let me tell thee of sweet to-morrow. 160

' In the planted garden eastward in Eden,
   (*Eden bower's in flower.*)
Where the river goes forth to water the garden,
The springs shall dry and the soil shall harden.

' Yea, where the bride-sleep fell upon Adam,
   (*And O the bower and the hour !*)
None shall hear when the storm-wind whistles
Through roses choked among thorns and thistles.

' Yea, beside the east-gate of Eden,
   (*Eden bower's in flower.*) 170
Where God joined them and none might sever,
The sword turns this way and that for ever.

' What of Adam cast out of Eden ?
   (*And O the bower and the hour !*)
Lo ! with care like a shadow shaken,
He tills the hard earth whence he was taken.

'What of Eve too, cast out of Eden?
  (*Eden bower's in flower.*)
Nay, but she, the bride of God's giving,
Must yet be mother of all men living.   180

'Lo, God's grace, by the grace of Lilith!
  (*And O the bower and the hour!*)
To Eve's womb, from our sweet to-morrow,
God shall greatly multiply sorrow.

'Fold me fast, O God-snake of Eden!
  (*Eden bower's in flower.*)
What more prize than love to impel thee?
Grip and lip my limbs as I tell thee!

'Lo! two babes for Eve and for Adam!
  (*And O the bower and the hour!*)   190
Lo! sweet Snake, the travail and treasure,—
Two men-children born for their pleasure!

'The first is Cain and the second Abel:
  (*Eden bower's in flower.*)
The soul of one shall be made thy brother,
And thy tongue shall lap the blood of the other.'
  (*And O the bower and the hour!*)

AVE

MOTHER of the Fair Delight,
Thou handmaid perfect in God's sight,
Now sitting fourth beside the Three,
Thyself a woman-Trinity,—
Being a daughter borne to God,
Mother of Christ from stall to rood,
And wife unto the Holy Ghost:—
Oh when our need is uttermost,
Think that to such as death may strike
Thou once wert sister sisterlike!   10
Thou headstone of humanity,
Groundstone of the great Mystery,
Fashioned like us, yet more than we!

Mind'st thou not (when June's heavy breath
Warmed the long days in Nazareth,)
That eve thou didst go forth to give
Thy flowers some drink that they might live
One faint night more amid the sands ?
Far off the trees were as pale wands
Against the fervid sky : the sea   20
Sighed further off eternally
As human sorrow sighs in sleep.
Then suddenly the awe grew deep,
As of a day to which all days
Were footsteps in God's secret ways :
Until a folding sense, like prayer,
Which is, as God is, everywhere,
Gathered about thee ; and a voice
Spake to thee without any noise,
Being of the silence :—' Hail,' it said,   30
' Thou that art highly favourèd ;
The Lord is with thee here and now ;
Blessed among all women thou.'

Ah ! knew'st thou of the end, when first
That Babe was on thy bosom nurs'd ?—
Or when He tottered round thy knee
Did thy great sorrow dawn on thee ?—
And through His boyhood, year by year
Eating with Him the Passover,
Didst thou discern confusedly   40
That holier sacrament, when He,
The bitter cup about to quaff,
Should break the bread and eat thereof ?—
Or came not yet the knowledge, even
Till on some day forecast in Heaven
His feet passed through thy door to press
Upon His Father's business ?—
Or still was God's high secret kept ?

Nay, but I think the whisper crept
Like growth through childhood. Work and play,
Things common to the course of day,   51

AVE

Awed thee with meanings unfulfill'd;
And all through girlhood, something still'd
Thy senses like the birth of light,
When thou hast trimmed thy lamp at night
Or washed thy garments in the stream;
To whose white bed had come the dream
That He was thine and thou wast His
Who feeds among the field-lilies.
O solemn shadow of the end   60
In that wise spirit long contain'd!
O awful end! and those unsaid
Long years when It was Finishèd!

Mind'st thou not (when the twilight gone
Left darkness in the house of John,)
Between the naked window-bars
That spacious vigil of the stars?—
For thou, a watcher even as they,
Wouldst rise from where throughout the day
Thou wroughtest raiment for His poor;   70
And, finding the fixed terms endure
Of day and night which never brought
Sounds of His coming chariot,
Wouldst lift through cloud-waste unexplor'd
Those eyes which said, 'How long, O Lord?'
Then that disciple whom He loved,
Well heeding, haply would be moved
To ask thy blessing in His name;
And that one thought in both, the same
Though silent, then would clasp ye round   80
To weep together,—tears long bound,
Sick tears of patience, dumb and slow.
Yet, 'Surely I come quickly,'—so
He said, from life and death gone home.
Amen: even so, Lord Jesus, come!

But oh! what human tongue can speak
That day when death was sent to break
From the tir'd spirit, like a veil,
Its covenant with Gabriel

Endured at length unto the end ? 90
What human thought can apprehend
That mystery of motherhood
When thy Beloved at length renew'd
The sweet communion severèd,—
His left hand underneath thine head
And His right hand embracing thee ?—
Lo ! He was thine, and this is He !

Soul, is it Faith, or Love, or Hope,
That lets me see her standing up
Where the light of the Throne is bright ? 100
Unto the left, unto the right,
The cherubim, arrayed, conjoint,
Float inward to a golden point,
And from between the seraphim
The glory issues for a hymn.
O Mary Mother, be not loth
To listen,—thou whom the stars clothe,
Who seëst and mayst not be seen !
Hear us at last, O Mary Queen !
Into our shadow bend thy face, 110
Bowing thee from the secret place,
O Mary Virgin, full of grace !

THE STAFF AND SCRIP

'Who owns these lands ? ' the Pilgrim said.
  'Stranger, Queen Blanchelys.'
' And who has thus harried them ? ' he said.
  'It was Duke Luke did this :
    God's ban be his ! '

The Pilgrim said : 'Where is your house ?
  I'll rest there, with your will.'
'You've but to climb these blackened boughs
  And you'll see it over the hill,
    For it burns still.' 10

THE STAFF AND SCRIP

'Which road, to seek your Queen?' said he.
  'Nay, nay, but with some wound
You'll fly back hither, it may be,
  And by your blood i' the ground
    My place be found.'

'Friend, stay in peace. God keep your head,
  And mine, where I will go;
For He is here and there,' he said.
  He passed the hill-side, slow,
    And stood below.   20

The Queen sat idle by her loom:
  She heard the arras stir,
And looked up sadly: through the room
  The sweetness sickened her
    Of musk and myrrh.

Her women, standing two and two,
  In silence combed the fleece.
The pilgrim said, 'Peace be with you,
  Lady;' and bent his knees.
    She answered, 'Peace.'   30

Her eyes were like the wave within;
  Like water-reeds the poise
Of her soft body, dainty thin;
  And like the water's noise
    Her plaintive voice.

For him, the stream had never well'd
  In desert tracts malign
So sweet; nor had he ever felt
  So faint in the sunshine
    Of Palestine.   40

Right so, he knew that he saw weep
  Each night through every dream
The Queen's own face, confused in sleep
  With visages supreme
    Not known to him.

'Lady,' he said, 'your lands lie burnt
  And waste : to meet your foe
All fear : this I have seen and learnt.
  Say that it shall be so,
    And I will go.' 50

She gazed at him. 'Your cause is just,
  For I have heard the same :'
He said : 'God's strength shall be my trust.
  Fall it to good or grame,
    'Tis in His name.'

'Sir, you are thanked. My cause is dead.
  Why should you toil to break
A grave, and fall therein ?' she said.
  He did not pause but spake :
    'For my vow's sake.' 60

'Can such vows be, Sir—to God's ear,
  Not to God's will ?' 'My vow
Remains : God heard me there as here,'
  He said with reverent brow,
    'Both then and now.'

They gazed together, he and she,
  The minute while he spoke ;
And when he ceased, she suddenly
  Looked round upon her folk
    As though she woke. 70

'Fight, Sir,' she said : 'my prayers in pain
  Shall be your fellowship.'
He whispered one among her train,—
  'To-morrow bid her keep
    This staff and scrip.'

She sent him a sharp sword, whose belt
  About his body there
As sweet as her own arms he felt.
  He kissed its blade, all bare,
    Instead of her. 80

THE STAFF AND SCRIP

She sent him a green banner wrought
  With one white lily stem,
To bind his lance with when he fought.
  He writ upon the same
    And kissed her name.

She sent him a white shield, whereon
  She bade that he should trace
His will. He blent fair hues that shone,
  And in a golden space
    He kissed her face.

Right so, the sunset skies unseal'd,
  Like lands he never knew,
Beyond to-morrow's battle-field
  Lay open out of view
    To ride into.

Next day till dark the women pray'd:
  Nor any might know there
How the fight went: the Queen has bade
  That there do come to her
    No messenger.

Weak now to them the voice o' the priest
  As any trance affords;
And when each anthem failed and ceas'd,
  It seemed that the last chords
    Still sang the words.

Lo, Father, is thine ear inclin'd,
  And hath thine angel pass'd?
For these thy watchers now are blind
  With vigil, and at last
    Dizzy with fast.

'Oh what is the light that shines so red?
  'Tis long since the sun set;'
Quoth the youngest to the eldest maid:
  ''Twas dim but now, and yet
    The light is great.'

Quoth the other : ' 'Tis our sight is dazed
  That we see flame i' the air.'
But the Queen held her brows and gazed,
  And said, ' It is the glare
    Of torches there.'   120

' Oh what are the sounds that rise and spread ?
  All day it was so still ; '
Quoth the youngest to the eldest maid ;
  ' Unto the furthest hill
    The air they fill.'

Quoth the other ; ' 'Tis our sense is blurr'd
  With all the chants gone by.'
But the Queen held her breath and heard,
  And said, ' It is the cry
    Of Victory.'   130

The first of all the rout was sound,
  The next were dust and flame,
And then the horses shook the ground :
  And in the thick of them
    A still band came.

' Oh what do ye bring out of the fight,
  Thus hid beneath these boughs ? '
' Even him, thy conquering guest to-night,
  Who yet shall not carouse,
    Queen, in thy house.'   140

' Uncover ye his face,' she said.
  ' O changed in little space ! '
She cried, ' O pale that was so red !
  O God, O God of grace !
    Cover his face.'

His sword was broken in his hand
  Where he had kissed the blade.
' O soft steel that could not withstand !
  O my hard heart unstayed,
    That prayed and prayed ! '   150

THE STAFF AND SCRIP

His bloodied banner crossed his mouth
  Where he had kissed her name.
'O east, and west, and north, and south,
  Fair flew my web, for shame,
    To guide Death's aim!'

The tints were shredded from his shield
  Where he had kissed her face.
'Oh, of all gifts that I could yield,
  Death only keeps its place,
    My gift and grace!'

Then stepped a damsel to her side,
  And spoke, and needs must weep:
'For his sake, lady, if he died,
  He prayed of thee to keep
    This staff and scrip.'

That night they hung above her bed,
  Till morning wet with tears.
Year after year above her head
  Her bed his token wears,
    Five years, ten years.

That night the passion of her grief
  Shook them as there they hung.
Each year the wind that shed the leaf
  Shook them and in its tongue
    A message flung.

And once she woke with a clear mind
  That letters writ to calm
Her soul lay in the scrip; to find
  Only a torpid balm
    And dust of palm.

They shook far off with palace sport
  When joust and dance were rife;
And the hunt shook them from the court;
  For hers, in peace or strife,
    Was a Queen's life.

THE STAFF AND SCRIP

A Queen's death now : as now they shake
  To gusts in chapel dim,—
Hung where she sleeps, not seen to wake,
  (Carved lovely white and slim,)
    With them by him.   190

Stand up to-day, still armed, with her,
  Good knight, before His brow
Who then as now was here and there,
  Who had in mind thy vow
    Then even as now.

The lists are set in Heaven to-day,
  The bright pavilions shine ;
Fair hangs thy shield, and none gainsay ;
  The trumpets sound in sign
    That she is thine.   200

Not tithed with days' and years' decease
  He pays thy wage He owed,
But with imperishable peace
  Here in His own abode,
    Thy jealous God.

A LAST CONFESSION

(*Regno Lombardo-Veneto*, 1848)

. . . . . .

Our Lombard country-girls along the coast
Wear daggers in their garters ; for they know
That they might hate another girl to death
Or meet a German lover. Such a knife
I bought her, with a hilt of horn and pearl.

Father, you cannot know of all my thoughts
That day in going to meet her,—that last day
For the last time, she said ;—of all the love
And all the hopeless hope that she might change
And go back with me. Ah! and everywhere,   10
At places we both knew along the road,

A LAST CONFESSION

Some fresh shape of herself as once she was
Grew present at my side ; until it seemed—
So close they gathered round me—they would all
Be with me when I reached the spot at last,
To plead my cause with her against herself
So changed. O Father, if you knew all this
You cannot know, then you would know too, Father,
And only then, if God can pardon me.
What can be told I'll tell, if you will hear.   20

I passed a village-fair upon my road,
And thought, being empty-handed, I would take
Some little present : such might prove, I said,
Either a pledge between us, or (God help me !)
A parting gift. And there it was I bought
The knife I spoke of, such as women wear.

That day, some three hours afterwards, I found
For certain, it must be a parting gift.
And, standing silent now at last, I looked
Into her scornful face ; and heard the sea   30
Still trying hard to din into my ears
Some speech it knew which still might change her heart
If only it could make me understand.
One moment thus. Another, and her face
Seemed further off than the last line of sea,
So that I thought, if now she were to speak
I could not hear her. Then again I knew
All, as we stood together on the sand
At Iglio, in the first thin shade o' the hills.

'Take it,' I said, and held it out to her,   40
While the hilt glanced within my trembling hold ;
'Take it and keep it for my sake,' I said.
Her neck unbent not, neither did her eyes
Move, nor her foot left beating of the sand ;
Only she put it by from her and laughed.

Father, you hear my speech and not her laugh ;
But God heard that. Will God remember all ?

It was another laugh than the sweet sound
Which rose from her sweet childish heart, that day

Eleven years before, when first I found her 50
Alone upon the hill-side ; and her curls
Shook down in the warm grass as she looked up
Out of her curls in my eyes bent to hers.
She might have served a painter to pourtray
That heavenly child which in the latter days
Shall walk between the lion and the lamb.
I had been for nights in hiding, worn and sick
And hardly fed ; and so her words at first
Seemed fitful like the talking of the trees
And voices in the air that knew my name. 60
And I remember that I sat me down
Upon the slope with her, and thought the world
Must be all over or had never been,
We seemed there so alone. And soon she told me
Her parents both were gone away from her.
I thought perhaps she meant that they had died ;
But when I asked her this, she looked again
Into my face, and said that yestereve
They kissed her long, and wept and made her weep,
And gave her all the bread they had with them, 70
And then had gone together up the hill
Where we were sitting now, and had walked on
Into the great red light : 'and so,' she said,
'I have come up here too ; and when this evening
They step out of the light as they stepped in,
I shall be here to kiss them.' And she laughed.

Then I bethought me suddenly of the famine ;
And how the church-steps throughout all the town,
When last I had been there a month ago,
Swarmed with starved folk ; and how the bread was
    weighed 80
By Austrians armed ; and women that I knew
For wives and mothers walked the public street,
Saying aloud that if their husbands feared
To snatch the children's food, themselves would stay
Till they had earned it there. So then this child
Was piteous to me ; for all told me then
Her parents must have left her to God's chance,

A LAST CONFESSION

To man's or to the Church's charity,
Because of the great famine, rather than
To watch her growing thin between their knees. 90
With that, God took my mother's voice and spoke,
And sights and sounds came back and things long since,
And all my childhood found me on the hills ;
And so I took her with me.

                      I was young,
Scarce man then, Father ; but the cause which gave
The wounds I die of now had brought me then
Some wounds already ; and I lived alone,
As any hiding hunted man must live.
It was no easy thing to keep a child
In safety ; for herself it was not safe, 100
And doubled my own danger : but I knew
That God would help me.

                      Yet a little while
Pardon me, Father, if I pause. I think
I have been speaking to you of some matters
There was no need to speak of, have I not ?
You do not know how clearly those things stood
Within my mind, which I have spoken of,
Nor how they strove for utterance. Life all past
Is like the sky when the sun sets in it,
Clearest where furthest off.

                      I told you how 110
She scorned my parting gift and laughed. And yet
A woman's laugh's another thing sometimes :
I think they laugh in Heaven. I know last night
I dreamed I saw into the garden of God,
Where women walked whose painted images
I have seen with candles round them in the church.
They bent this way and that, one to another,
Playing : and over the long golden hair
Of each there floated like a ring of fire
Which when she stooped stooped with her, and when she rose 120
Rose with her. Then a breeze flew in among them,
As if a window had been opened in heaven
For God to give his blessing from, before

This world of ours should set ; (for in my dream
I thought our world was setting, and the sun
Flared, a spent taper ;) and beneath that gust
The rings of light quivered like forest-leaves.
Then all the blessed maidens who were there
Stood up together, as it were a voice
That called them ; and they threw their tresses back,
And smote their palms, and all laughed up at once, 131
For the strong heavenly joy they had in them
To hear God bless the world. Wherewith I woke :
And looking round, I saw as usual
That she was standing there with her long locks
Pressed to her side ; and her laugh ended theirs.

For always when I see her now, she laughs.
And yet her childish laughter haunts me too,
The life of this dead terror ; as in days
When she, a child, dwelt with me. I must tell 140
Something of those days yet before the end.

I brought her from the city—one such day
When she was still a merry loving child,—
The earliest gift I mind my giving her ;
A little image of a flying Love
Made of our coloured glass-ware, in his hands
A dart of gilded metal and a torch.
And him she kissed and me, and fain would know
Why were his poor eyes blindfold, why the wings
And why the arrow. What I knew I told 150
Of Venus and of Cupid,—strange old tales.
And when she heard that he could rule the loves
Of men and women, still she shook her head
And wondered ; and, ' Nay, nay,' she murmured still,
' So strong, and he a younger child than I ! '
And then she'd have me fix him on the wall
Fronting her little bed ; and then again
She needs must fix him there herself, because
I gave him to her and she loved him so,
And he should make her love me better yet, 160
If women loved the more, the more they grew.

A LAST CONFESSION

But the fit place upon the wall was high
For her, and so I held her in my arms:
And each time that the heavy pruning-hook
I gave her for a hammer slipped away
As it would often, still she laughed and laughed
And kissed and kissed me. But amid her mirth,
Just as she hung the image on the nail,
It slipped and all its fragments strewed the ground:
And as it fell she screamed, for in her hand
The dart had entered deeply and drawn blood.
And so her laughter turned to tears: and 'Oh!'
I said, the while I bandaged the small hand,—
'That I should be the first to make you bleed,
Who love and love and love you!'—kissing still
The fingers till I got her safe to bed.
And still she sobbed,—'not for the pain at all,'
She said, 'but for the Love, the poor good Love
You gave me.' So she cried herself to sleep.

Another later thing comes back to me.
'Twas in those hardest foulest days of all,
When still from his shut palace, sitting clean
Above the splash of blood, old Metternich
(May his soul die, and never-dying worms
Feast on its pain for ever!) used to thin
His year's doomed hundreds daintily, each month
Thirties and fifties. This time, as I think,
Was when his thrift forbad the poor to take
That evil brackish salt which the dry rocks
Keep all through winter when the sea draws in.
The first I heard of it was a chance shot
In the street here and there, and on the stones
A stumbling clatter as of horse hemmed round.
Then, when she saw me hurry out of doors,
My gun slung at my shoulder and my knife
Stuck in my girdle, she smoothed down my hair
And laughed to see me look so brave, and leaped
Up to my neck and kissed me. She was still
A child; and yet that kiss was on my lips
So hot all day where the smoke shut us in.

For now, being always with her, the first love
I had—the father's, brother's love—was changed,
I think, in somewise ; like a holy thought
Which is a prayer before one knows of it.
The first time I perceived this, I remember,
Was once when after hunting I came home
Weary, and she brought food and fruit for me,
And sat down at my feet upon the floor
Leaning against my side. But when I felt
Her sweet head reach from that low seat of hers   210
So high as to be laid upon my heart,
I turned and looked upon my darling there
And marked for the first time how tall she was ;
And my heart beat with so much violence
Under her cheek, I thought she could not choose
But wonder at it soon and ask me why ;
And so I bade her rise and eat with me.
And when, remembering all and counting back
The time, I made out fourteen years for her
And told her so, she gazed at me with eyes   220
As of the sky and sea on a grey day,
And drew her long hands through her hair, and asked me
If she was not a woman ; and then laughed :
And as she stooped in laughing, I could see
Beneath the growing throat the breasts half globed
Like folded lilies deepset in the stream.

    Yes, let me think of her as then ; for so
Her image, Father, is not like the sights
Which come when you are gone. She had a mouth
Made to bring death to life,—the underlip   230
Sucked in, as if it strove to kiss itself.
Her face was ever pale, as when one stoops
Over wan water ; and the dark crisped hair
And the hair's shadow made it paler still :—
Deep-serried locks, the darkness of the cloud
Where the moon's gaze is set in eddying gloom.
Her body bore her neck as the tree's stem
Bears the top branch ; and as the branch sustains
The flower of the year's pride, her high neck bore

A LAST CONFESSION

That face made wonderful with night and day. 240
Her voice was swift, yet ever the last words
Fell lingeringly ; and rounded finger-tips
She had, that clung a little where they touched
And then were gone o' the instant. Her great eyes,
That sometimes turned half dizzily beneath
The passionate lids, as faint, when she would speak,
Had also in them hidden springs of mirth,
Which under the dark lashes evermore
Shook to her laugh, as when a bird flies low
Between the water and the willow-leaves, 250
And the shade quivers till he wins the light.

I was a moody comrade to her then,
For all the love I bore her. Italy,
The weeping desolate mother, long has claimed
Her sons' strong arms to lean on, and their hands
To lop the poisonous thicket from her path,
Cleaving her way to light. And from her need
Had grown the fashion of my whole poor life
Which I was proud to yield her, as my father
Had yielded his. And this had come to be 260
A game to play, a love to clasp, a hate
To wreak, all things together that a man
Needs for his blood to ripen : till at times
All else seemed shadows, and I wondered still
To see such life pass muster and be deemed
Time's bodily substance. In those hours, no doubt,
To the young girl my eyes were like my soul,—
Dark wells of death-in-life that yearned for day.
And though she ruled me always, I remember
That once when I was thus and she still kept 270
Leaping about the place and laughing, I
Did almost chide her ; whereupon she knelt
And putting her two hands into my breast
Sang me a song. Are these tears in my eyes ?
'Tis long since I have wept for anything.
I thought that song forgotten out of mind,
And now, just as I spoke of it, it came
All back. It is but a rude thing, ill rhymed,

Such as a blind man chaunts and his dog hears
Holding the platter, when the children run   280
To merrier sport and leave him. Thus it goes :—

    La bella donna [1]
    Piangendo disse :
    ' Come son fisse
    Le stelle in cielo !
    Quel fiato anelo
    Dello stanco sole,
    Quanto m' assonna !
    E la luna, macchiata
    Come uno specchio   290
    Logoro e vecchio,—
    Faccia affannata,
    Che cosa vuole ?

    ' Chè stelle, luna, e sole,
    Ciascun m' annoja
    E m' annojano insieme ;
    Non me ne preme
    Nè ci prendo gioja.
    E veramente,
    Che le spalle sien franche   300
    E le braccia bianche
    E il seno caldo e tondo,
    Non mi fa niente.
    Chè cosa al mondo
    Posso più far di questi
  Se non piacciono a te, come dicesti ? '

[1] She wept, sweet lady,
And said in weeping :
' What spell is keeping
The stars so steady ?
Why does the power
Of the sun's noon-hour
To sleep so move me ?
And the moon in heaven,
Stained where she passes
As a worn-out glass is,—
Wearily driven,
Why walks she above me ?

' Stars, moon, and sun too,
I'm tired of either
And all together !
Whom speak they unto
That I should listen ?
For very surely,
Though my arms and shoulders
Dazzle beholders,
And my eyes glisten,
All's nothing purely !
What are words said for
At all about them,
If he they are made for
Can do without them ? '

La donna rise
E riprese ridendo :—
' Questa mano che prendo
È dunque mia ? 310
Tu m' ami dunque ?
Dimmelo ancora,
Non in modo qualunque,
Ma le parole
Belle e precise
Che dicesti pria.

' *Siccome suole*
La state talora
(Dicesti) *un qualche istante*
Tornare innanzi inverno, 320
Così tu fai ch' io scerno
Le foglie tutte quante,
Ben ch' io certo tenessi
Per passato l' autunno.

' Eccolo il mio alunno !
Io debbo insegnargli
Quei cari detti istessi
Ch' ei mi disse una volta !
Oimè ! Che cosa dargli,'
(Ma ridea piano piano 330
Dei baci in sulla mano,)
' Ch' ei non m' abbia da lungo tempo tolta ? '

She laughed, sweet lady,
And said in laughing :
' His hand clings half in
My own already !
Oh ! do you love me ?
Oh ! speak of passion
In no new fashion,
No loud inveighings,
But the old sayings
You once said of me.

' You said : " As summer,
Through boughs grown brittle,
Comes back a little
Ere frosts benumb her,—
So bring'st thou to me
All leaves and flowers,
Though autumn's gloomy
To-day in the bowers."

' Oh ! does he love me,
When my voice teaches
The very speeches
He then spoke of me ?
Alas ! what flavour
Still with me lingers ? '
(But she laughed as my kisses
Glowed in her fingers
With love's old blisses.)
' Oh ! what one favour
Remains to woo him,
Whose whole poor savour
Belongs not to him ? '

That I should sing upon this bed !—with you
To listen, and such words still left to say !
Yet was it I that sang ? The voice seemed hers,
As on the very day she sang to me ;
When, having done, she took out of my hand
Something that I had played with all the while
And laid it down beyond my reach ; and so
Turning my face round till it fronted hers,—   340
' Weeping or laughing, which was best ? ' she said.

But these are foolish tales. How should I show
The heart that glowed then with love's heat, each day
More and more brightly ?—when for long years now
The very flame that flew about the heart,
And gave it fiery wings, has come to be
The lapping blaze of hell's environment
Whose tongues all bid the molten heart despair.

Yet one more thing comes back on me to-night
Which I may tell you : for it bore my soul   350
Dread firstlings of the brood that rend it now.
It chanced that in our last year's wanderings
We dwelt at Monza, far away from home,
If home we had : and in the Duomo there
I sometimes entered with her when she prayed.
An image of Our Lady stands there, wrought
In marble by some great Italian hand
In the great days when she and Italy
Sat on one throne together : and to her
And to none else my loved one told her heart.   360
She was a woman then ; and as she knelt,—
Her sweet brow in the sweet brow's shadow there,—
They seemed two kindred forms whereby our land
(Whose work still serves the world for miracle)
Made manifest herself in womanhood.
Father, the day I speak of was the first
For weeks that I had borne her company
Into the Duomo ; and those weeks had been
Much troubled, for then first the glimpses came
Of some impenetrable restlessness   370

A LAST CONFESSION

Growing in her to make her changed and cold.
And as we entered there that day, I bent
My eyes on the fair Image, and I said
Within my heart, ' Oh turn her heart to me ! '
And so I left her to her prayers, and went
To gaze upon the pride of Monza's shrine,
Where in the sacristy the light still falls
Upon the Iron Crown of Italy,
On whose crowned heads the day has closed, nor yet
The daybreak gilds another head to crown. 380
But coming back, I wondered when I saw
That the sweet Lady of her prayers now stood
Alone without her ; until further off,
Before some new Madonna gaily decked,
Tinselled and gewgawed, a slight German toy,
I saw her kneel, still praying. At my step
She rose, and side by side we left the church.
I was much moved, and sharply questioned her
Of her transferred devotion ; but she seemed
Stubborn and heedless ; till she lightly laughed 390
And said : ' The old Madonna ? Aye indeed,
She had my old thoughts,—this one has my new.'
Then silent to the soul I held my way :
And from the fountains of the public place
Unto the pigeon-haunted pinnacles,
Bright wings and water winnowed the bright air ;
And stately with her laugh's subsiding smile
She went, with clear-swayed waist and towering neck
And hands held light before her ; and the face
Which long had made a day in my life's night 400
Was night in day to me ; as all men's eyes
Turned on her beauty, and she seemed to tread
Beyond my heart to the world made for her.

Ah there ! my wounds will snatch my sense again :
The pain comes billowing on like a full cloud
Of thunder, and the flash that breaks from it
Leaves my brain burning. That's the wound he gave,
The Austrian whose white coat I still made match
With his white face, only the two were red

As suits his trade. The devil makes them wear 410
White for a livery, that the blood may show
Braver that brings them to him. So he looks
Sheer o'er the field and knows his own at once.

Give me a draught of water in that cup ;
My voice feels thick ; perhaps you do not hear ;
But you *must* hear. If you mistake my words
And so absolve me, I am sure the blessing
Will burn my soul. If you mistake my words
And so absolve me, Father, the great sin
Is yours, not mine : mark this : your soul shall burn
With mine for it. I have seen pictures where 421
Souls burned with Latin shriekings in their mouths :
Shall my end be as theirs ? Nay, but I know
'Tis you shall shriek in Latin. Some bell rings,
Rings through my brain : it strikes the hour in hell.

You see I cannot, Father ; I have tried,
But cannot, as you see. These twenty times
Beginning, I have come to the same point
And stopped. Beyond, there are but broken words
Which will not let you understand my tale. 430
It is that then we have her with us here,
As when she wrung her hair out in my dream
To-night, till all the darkness reeked of it.
Her hair is always wet, for she has kept
Its tresses wrapped about her side for years ;
And when she wrung them round over the floor,
I heard the blood between her fingers hiss ;
So that I sat up in my bed and screamed
Once and again ; and once to once, she laughed.
Look that you turn not now,—she's at your back : 440
Gather your robe up, Father, and keep close,
Or she'll sit down on it and send you mad.

At Iglio in the first thin shade o' the hills
The sand is black and red. The black was black
When what was spilt that day sank into it,
And the red scarcely darkened. There I stood
This night with her, and saw the sand the same.

* * * * * *

A LAST CONFESSION

What would you have me tell you ? Father, father.
How shall I make you know ? You have not known
The dreadful soul of woman, who one day   450
Forgets the old and takes the new to heart,
Forgets what man remembers, and therewith
Forgets the man. Nor can I clearly tell
How the change happened between her and me.
Her eyes looked on me from an emptied heart
When most my heart was full of her ; and still
In every corner of myself I sought
To find what service failed her ; and no less
Than in the good time past, there all was hers.
What do you love ? Your Heaven ? Conceive it spread
For one first year of all eternity   461
All round you with all joys and gifts of God ;
And then when most your soul is blent with it
And all yields song together,—then it stands
O' the sudden like a pool that once gave back
Your image, but now drowns it and is clear
Again,—or like a sun bewitched, that burns
Your shadow from you, and still shines in sight.
How could you bear it ? Would you not cry out,
Among those eyes grown blind to you, those ears   470
That hear no more your voice you hear the same,—
' God ! what is left but hell for company,
But hell, hell, hell ? '—until the name so breathed
Whirled with hot wind and sucked you down in fire ?
Even so I stood the day her empty heart
Left her place empty in our home, while yet
I knew not why she went nor where she went
Nor how to reach her : so I stood the day
When to my prayers at last one sight of her
Was granted, and I looked on heaven made pale   480
With scorn, and heard heaven mock me in that laugh.

O sweet, long sweet ! Was that some ghost of you
Even as your ghost that haunts me now,—twin shapes
Of fear and hatred ? May I find you yet
Mine when death wakes ? Ah ! be it even in flame,
We may have sweetness yet, if you but say

As once in childish sorrow : ' Not my pain,
My pain was nothing : oh your poor poor love,
Your broken love ! '
                     My Father, have I not
Yet told you the last things of that last day   490
On which I went to meet her by the sea ?
O God, O God ! but I must tell you all.

  Midway upon my journey, when I stopped
To buy the dagger at the village fair,
I saw two cursed rats about the place
I knew for spies—blood-sellers both. That day
Was not yet over ; for three hours to come
I prized my life : and so I looked around
For safety. A poor painted mountebank
Was playing tricks and shouting in a crowd.   500
I knew he must have heard my name, so I
Pushed past and whispered to him who I was,
And of my danger. Straight he hustled me
Into his booth, as it were in the trick,
And brought me out next minute with my face
All smeared in patches, and a zany's gown ;
And there I handed him his cups and balls
And swung the sand-bags round to clear the ring
For half an hour. The spies came once and looked ;
And while they stopped, and made all sights and sounds
Sharp to my startled senses, I remember   511
A woman laughed above me. I looked up
And saw where a brown-shouldered harlot leaned
Half through a tavern window thick with vine.
Some man had come behind her in the room
And caught her by her arms, and she had turned
With that coarse empty laugh on him, as now
He munched her neck with kisses, while the vine
Crawled in her back.
                   And three hours afterwards,
When she that I had run all risks to meet   520
Laughed as I told you, my life burned to death
Within me, for I thought it like the laugh
Heard at the fair. She had not left me long ;

A LAST CONFESSION

But all she might have changed to, or might change to,
(I know nought since—she never speaks a word—)
Seemed in that laugh. Have I not told you yet,
Not told you all this time what happened, Father,
When I had offered her the little knife,
And bade her keep it for my sake that loved her,
And she had laughed? Have I not told you yet?   530

'Take it,' I said to her the second time,
'Take it and keep it.' And then came a fire
That burnt my hand; and then the fire was blood,
And sea and sky were blood and fire, and all
The day was one red blindness; till it seemed
Within the whirling brain's entanglement
That she or I or all things bled to death.
And then I found her laid against my feet
And knew that I had stabbed her, and saw still
Her look in falling. For she took the knife   540
Deep in her heart, even as I bade her then,
And fell; and her stiff bodice scooped the sand
Into her bosom.
              And she keeps it, see,
Do you not see she keeps it?—there, beneath
Wet fingers and wet tresses, in her heart.
For look you, when she stirs her hand, it shows
The little hilt of horn and pearl,—even such
A dagger as our women of the coast
Twist in their garters.
              Father, I have done:
And from her side now she unwinds the thick   550
Dark hair; all round her side it is wet through,
But like the sand at Iglio does not change.
Now you may see the dagger clearly. Father,
I have told all: tell me at once what hope
Can reach me still. For now she draws it out
Slowly, and only smiles as yet: look, Father,
She scarcely smiles: but I shall hear her laugh
Soon, when she shows the crimson blade to God.

DANTE AT VERONA

> Yea, thou shalt learn how salt his food who fares
> Upon another's bread,—how steep his path
> Who treadeth up and down another's stairs.
> (*Div. Com. Parad.* xvii.)
>
> Behold, even I, even I am Beatrice.
> (*Div. Com. Purg.* xxx.)

Of Florence and of Beatrice
  Servant and singer from of old,
  O'er Dante's heart in youth had toll'd
The knell that gave his Lady peace;
  And now in manhood flew the dart
  Wherewith his City pierced his heart.

Yet if his Lady's home above
  Was Heaven, on earth she filled his soul;
  And if his City held control
To cast the body forth to rove,
  The soul could soar from earth's vain throng,
  And Heaven and Hell fulfil the song.

Follow his feet's appointed way;—
  But little light we find that clears
  The darkness of the exiled years.
Follow his spirit's journey:—nay,
  What fires are blent, what winds are blown
  On paths his feet may tread alone?

Yet of the twofold life he led
  In chainless thought and fettered will
  Some glimpses reach us,—somewhat still
Of the steep stairs and bitter bread,—
  Of the soul's quest whose stern avow
  For years had made him haggard now.

Alas! the Sacred Song whereto
  Both heaven and earth had set their hand
  Not only at Fame's gate did stand
Knocking to claim the passage through,
  But toiled to ope that heavier door
  Which Florence shut for evermore.

DANTE AT VERONA

Shall not his birth's baptismal Town
  One last high presage yet fulfil,
  And at that font in Florence still
His forehead take the laurel-crown?
  O God! or shall dead souls deny
  The undying soul its prophecy?

Aye, 'tis their hour. Not yet forgot
  The bitter words he spoke that day
  When for some great charge far away
Her rulers his acceptance sought.   40
  'And if I go, who stays?'—so rose
  His scorn:—'and if I stay, who goes?'

'Lo! thou art gone now, and we stay:'
  (The curled lips mutter): 'and no star
  Is from thy mortal path so far
As streets where childhood knew the way.
  To Heaven and Hell thy feet may win,
  But thine own house they come not in.'

Therefore, the loftier rose the song
  To touch the secret things of God,   50
  The deeper pierced the hate that trod
On base men's track who wrought the wrong;
  Till the soul's effluence came to be
  Its own exceeding agony.

Arriving only to depart,
  From court to court, from land to land,
  Like flame within the naked hand
His body bore his burning heart
  That still on Florence strove to bring
  God's fire for a burnt offering.   60

Even such was Dante's mood, when now,
  Mocked for long years with Fortune's sport,
  He dwelt at yet another court,
There where Verona's knee did bow
  And her voice hailed with all acclaim
  Can Grande della Scala's name.

As that lord's kingly guest awhile
  His life we follow ; through the days
  Which walked in exile's barren ways,—
The nights which still beneath one smile   70
  Heard through all spheres one song increase,—
  ' Even I, even I am Beatrice.'

At Can La Scala's court, no doubt,
  Due reverence did his steps attend ;
  The ushers on his path would bend
At ingoing as at going out ;
  The penmen waited on his call
  At council-board, the grooms in hall.

And pages hushed their laughter down,
  And gay squires stilled the merry stir,   80
  When he passed up the dais-chamber
With set brows lordlier than a frown ;
  And tire-maids hidden among these
  Drew close their loosened bodices.

Perhaps the priests, (exact to span
  All God's circumference,) if at whiles
  They found him wandering in their aisles,
Grudged ghostly greeting to the man
  By whom, though not of ghostly guild,   89
  With Heaven and Hell men's hearts were fill'd.

And the court-poets (he, forsooth,
  A whole world's poet strayed to court !)
  Had for his scorn their hate's retort.
He'd meet them flushed with easy youth,
  Hot on their errands.   Like noon-flies
  They vexed him in the ears and eyes.

But at this court, peace still must wrench
  Her chaplet from the teeth of war :
  By day they held high watch afar,
At night they cried across the trench ;   100
  And still, in Dante's path, the fierce
  Gaunt soldiers wrangled o'er their spears.

DANTE AT VERONA

But vain seemed all the strength to him,
   As golden convoys sunk at sea
   Whose wealth might root out penury :
Because it was not, limb with limb,
   Knit like his heart-strings round the wall
   Of Florence, that ill pride might fall.

Yet in the tiltyard, when the dust   109
   Cleared from the sundered press of knights
   Ere yet again it swoops and smites,
He almost deemed his longing must
   Find force to wield that multitude
   And hurl that strength the way he would.

How should he move them,—fame and gain
   On all hands calling them at strife ?
   He still might find but his one life
To give, by Florence counted vain ;
   One heart the false hearts made her doubt ;
   One voice she heard once and cast out.   120

Oh ! if his Florence could but come,
   A lily-sceptred damsel fair,
   As her own Giotto painted her
On many shields and gates at home,—
   A lady crowned, at a soft pace
   Riding the lists round to the dais :

Till where Can Grande rules the lists,
   As young as Truth, as calm as Force,
   She draws her rein now, while her horse
Bows at the turn of the white wrists ;   130
   And when each knight within his stall
   Gives ear, she speaks and tells them all :

All the foul tale,—truth sworn untrue
   And falsehood's triumph. All the tale ?
   Great God ! and must she not prevail
To fire them ere they heard it through,—
   And hand achieve ere heart could rest
   That high adventure of her quest ?

How would his Florence lead them forth,
  Her bridle ringing as she went ;   140
  And at the last within her tent,
'Neath golden lilies worship-worth,
  How queenly would she bend the while
  And thank the victors with her smile !

Also her lips should turn his way
  And murmur : ' O thou tried and true,
  With whom I wept the long years through !
What shall it profit if I say,
  Thee I remember ? Nay, through thee
  All ages shall remember me.'   150

Peace, Dante, peace ! The task is long,
  The time wears short to compass it.
  Within thine heart such hopes may flit
And find a voice in deathless song :
  But lo ! as children of man's earth,
  Those hopes are dead before their birth.

Fame tells us that Verona's court
  Was a fair place. The feet might still
  Wander for ever at their will
In many ways of sweet resort ;   160
  And still in many a heart around
  The Poet's name due honour found.

Watch we his steps. He comes upon
  The women at their palm-playing.
  The conduits round the gardens sing
And meet in scoops of milk-white stone,
  Where wearied damsels rest and hold
  Their hands in the wet spurt of gold.

One of whom, knowing well that he,   169
  By some found stern, was mild with them,
  Would run and pluck his garment's hem,
Saying, ' Messer Dante, pardon me,'—
  Praying that they might hear the song
  Which first of all he made, when young.

DANTE AT VERONA

'Donne che avete'[1] . . . Thereunto
  Thus would he murmur, having first
  Drawn near the fountain, while she nurs'd
His hand against her side : a few
  Sweet words, and scarcely those, half said :
  Then turned, and changed, and bowed his head.

For then the voice said in his heart,   181
  'Even I, even I am Beatrice ; '
  And his whole life would yearn to cease:
Till having reached his room, apart
  Beyond vast lengths of palace-floor,
  He drew the arras round his door.

At such times, Dante, thou hast set
  Thy forehead to the painted pane
  Full oft, I know ; and if the rain
Smote it outside, her fingers met   190
  Thy brow ; and if the sun fell there,
  Her breath was on thy face and hair.

Then, weeping, I think certainly
  Thou hast beheld, past sight of eyne,—
  Within another room of thine
Where now thy body may not be
  But where in thought thou still remain'st,—
  A window often wept against :

The window thou, a youth, hast sought,
  Flushed in the limpid eventime,   200
  Ending with daylight the day's rhyme
Of her ; where oftenwhiles her thought
  Held thee—the lamp untrimmed to write—
  In joy through the blue lapse of night.

At Can La Scala's court, no doubt,
  Guests seldom wept. It was brave sport,
  No doubt, at Can La Scala's court,

[1] 'Donne che avete intelletto d'amore : '—the first canzone of the *Vita Nuova*.

DANTE AT VERONA

Within the palace and without;
  Where music, set to madrigals,   209
  Loitered all day through groves and halls.

Because Can Grande of his life
  Had not had six-and-twenty years
  As yet. And when the chroniclers
Tell you of that Vicenza strife
  And of strifes elsewhere,—you must not
  Conceive for church-sooth he had got

Just nothing in his wits but war:
  Though doubtless 'twas the young man's joy
  (Grown with his growth from a mere boy,)
To mark his 'Viva Cane!' scare   220
  The foe's shut front, till it would reel
  All blind with shaken points of steel.

But there were places—held too sweet
  For eyes that had not the due veil
  Of lashes and clear lids—as well
In favour as his saddle-seat:
  Breath of low speech he scorned not there
  Nor light cool fingers in his hair.

Yet if the child whom the sire's plan
  Made free of a deep treasure-chest   230
  Scoffed it with ill-conditioned jest,—
We may be sure too that the man
  Was not mere thews, nor all content
  With lewdness swathed in sentiment.

So you may read and marvel not
  That such a man as Dante—one
  Who, while Can Grande's deeds were done,
Had drawn his robe round him and thought—
  Now at the same guest-table far'd
  Where keen Uguccio wiped his beard.[1]   240

---

[1] Uguccione della Faggiuola, Dante's former protector, was now his fellow-guest at Verona.

DANTE AT VERONA

Through leaves and trellis-work the sun
  Left the wine cool within the glass,—
  They feasting where no sun could pass:
And when the women, all as one,
  Rose up with brightened cheeks to go,
  It was a comely thing, we know.

But Dante recked not of the wine;
  Whether the women stayed or went,
  His visage held one stern intent:
And when the music had its sign   250
  To breathe upon them for more ease,
  Sometimes he turned and bade it cease.

And as he spared not to rebuke
  The mirth, so oft in council he
  To bitter truth bore testimony:
And when the crafty balance shook
  Well poised to make the wrong prevail,
  Then Dante's hand would turn the scale.

And if some envoy from afar
  Sailed to Verona's sovereign port   260
  For aid or peace, and all the court
Fawned on its lord, 'the Mars of war,
  Sole arbiter of life and death,'—
  Be sure that Dante saved his breath.

And Can La Scala marked askance
  These things, accepting them for shame
  And scorn, till Dante's guestship came
To be a peevish sufferance:
  His host sought ways to make his days
  Hateful; and such have many ways.   270

There was a Jester, a foul lout
  Whom the court loved for graceless arts;
  Sworn scholiast of the bestial parts
Of speech; a ribald mouth to shout
  In Folly's horny tympanum
  Such things as make the wise man dumb.

Much loved, him Dante loathed. And so,
  One day when Dante felt perplex'd
  If any day that could come next
Were worth the waiting for or no,   280
  And mute he sat amid their din,—
  Can Grande called the Jester in.

Rank words, with such, are wit's best wealth.
  Lords mouthed approval ; ladies kept
  Twittering with clustered heads, except
Some few that took their trains by stealth
  And went. Can Grande shook his hair
  And smote his thighs and laughed i' the air.

Then, facing on his guest, he cried,—
  ' Say, Messer Dante, how it is   290
  I get out of a clown like this
More than your wisdom can provide.'
  And Dante : ' 'Tis man's ancient whim
  That still his like seems good to him.'

Also a tale is told, how once,
  At clearing tables after meat,
  Piled for a jest at Dante's feet
Were found the dinner's well-picked bones ;
  So laid, to please the banquet's lord,   299
  By one who crouched beneath the board.

Then smiled Can Grande to the rest :—
  ' Our Dante's tuneful mouth indeed
  Lacks not the gift on flesh to feed ! '
' Fair host of mine,' replied the guest,
  ' So many bones you'd not descry
  If so it chanced the *dog* were I.' [1]

But wherefore should we turn the grout
  In a drained cup, or be at strife
  From the worn garment of a life

---

[1] ' *Messere, voi non vedreste tant 'ossa se cane io fossi.*' The point of the reproach is difficult to render, depending as it does on the literal meaning of the name *Cane*.

To rip the twisted ravel out? 310
  Good needs expounding; but of ill
  Each hath enough to guess his fill.

They named him Justicer-at-Law:
  Each month to bear the tale in mind
  Of hues a wench might wear unfin'd
And of the load an ox might draw;
  To cavil in the weight of bread
  And to see purse-thieves gibbeted.

And when his spirit wove the spell
  (From under even to over-noon 320
  In converse with itself alone,)
As high as Heaven, as low as Hell,—
  He would be summoned and must go:
  For had not Gian stabbed Giacomo?

Therefore the bread he had to eat
  Seemed brackish, less like corn than tares;
  And the rush-strown accustomed stairs
Each day were steeper to his feet;
  And when the night-vigil was done,
  His brows would ache to feel the sun. 330

Nevertheless, when from his kin
  There came the tidings how at last
  In Florence a decree was pass'd
Whereby all banished folk might win
  Free pardon, so a fine were paid
  And act of public penance made,—

This Dante writ in answer thus,
  Words such as these: 'That clearly they
  In Florence must not have to say,—
The man abode aloof from us 340
  Nigh fifteen years, yet lastly skulk'd
  Hither to candleshrift and mulct.

'That he was one the Heavens forbid
  To traffic in God's justice sold
  By market-weight of earthly gold,

Or to bow down over the lid
  Of steaming censers, and so be
  Made clean of manhood's obloquy.

'That since no gate led, by God's will,
  To Florence, but the one whereat   350
  The priests and money-changers sat,
He still would wander; for that still,
  Even through the body's prison-bars,
  His soul possessed the sun and stars.'

Such were his words. It is indeed
  For ever well our singers should
  Utter good words and know them good
Not through song only; with close heed
  Lest, having spent for the work's sake
  Six days, the man be left to make.   360

Months o'er Verona, till the feast
  Was come for Florence the Free Town:
  And at the shrine of Baptist John
The exiles, girt with many a priest
  And carrying candles as they went,
  Were held to mercy of the saint.

On the high seats in sober state,—
  Gold neck-chains range o'er range below
  Gold screen-work where the lilies grow,—
The Heads of the Republic sate,   370
  Marking the humbled face go by
  Each one of his house-enemy.

And as each proscript rose and stood
  From kneeling in the ashen dust
  On the shrine-steps, some magnate thrust
A beard into the velvet hood
  Of his front colleague's gown, to see
  The cinders stuck in the bare knee.

Tosinghi passed, Manelli passed,
  Rinucci passed, each in his place;   380
  But not an Alighieri's face

DANTE AT VERONA

Went by that day from first to last
　In the Republic's triumph ; nor
　A foot came home to Dante's door.

(RESPUBLICA—a public thing :
　A shameful shameless prostitute,
　Whose lust with one lord may not suit,
So takes by turns its revelling
　A night with each, till each at morn
　Is stripped and beaten forth forlorn,　　　　390

And leaves her, cursing her. If she,
　Indeed, have not some spice-draught, hid
　In scent under a silver lid,
To drench his open throat with—he
　Once hard asleep ; and thrust him not
　At dawn beneath the boards to rot.)

Years filled out their twelve moons, and ceased
　One in another ; and alway
　There were the whole twelve hours each day
And each night as the years increased ;　　　400
　And rising moon and setting sun
　Beheld that Dante's work was done.

What of his work for Florence ? Well
　It was, he knew, and well must be.
　Yet evermore her hate's decree
Dwelt in his thought intolerable :—
　His body to be burned,[1]—his soul
　To beat its wings at hope's vain goal.

What of his work for Beatrice ?
　Now well-nigh was the third song writ,—　　410
　The stars a third time sealing it
With sudden music of pure peace :
　For echoing thrice the threefold song,
　The unnumbered stars the tone prolong.[2]

---

[1] Such was the last sentence passed by Florence against Dante, as a recalcitrant exile.

[2] ' E quindi uscimmo a riveder le *stelle*.'—*Inferno*.
　' Puro e disposto a salire alle *stelle*.'—*Purgatorio*.
　' L'amor che muove il sole e l'altre *stelle*.'—*Paradiso*.

Each hour, as then the Vision pass'd,
  He heard the utter harmony
  Of the nine trembling spheres, till she
Bowed her eyes towards him in the last,
  So that all ended with her eyes,
  Hell, Purgatory, Paradise.   420

' It is my trust, as the years fall,
  To write more worthily of her
  Who now, being made God's minister,
Looks on His visage and knows all.'
  Such was the hope that love did blend
  With grief's slow fires, to make an end

Of the ' New Life ', his youth's dear book :
  Adding thereunto : ' In such trust
  I labour, and believe I must
Accomplish this which my soul took   430
  In charge, if God, my Lord and hers,
  Leave my life with me a few years.'

The trust which he had borne in youth
  Was all at length accomplished. He
  At length had written worthily—
Yea even of her ; no rhymes uncouth
  'Twixt tongue and tongue ; but by God's aid
  The first words Italy had said.

Ah ! haply now the heavenly guide
  Was not the last form seen by him :   440
  But there that Beatrice stood slim
And bowed in passing at his side,
  For whom in youth his heart made moan
  Then when the city sat alone.[1]

Clearly herself ; the same whom he
  Met, not past girlhood, in the street,
  Low-bosomed and with hidden feet ;

---

[1] ' *Quomodo sedet sola civitas !* '—the words quoted by Dante in the *Vita Nuova* when he speaks of the death of Beatrice.

DANTE AT VERONA

And then as woman perfectly,
  In years that followed, many an once,—
  And now at last among the suns   450
In that high vision. But indeed
  It may be memory did recall
  Last to him then the first of all,—
The child his boyhood bore in heed
  Nine years. At length the voice brought peace,—
  ' Even I, even I am Beatrice.'

All this, being there, we had not seen.
  Seen only was the shadow wrought
  On the strong features bound in thought ;
The vagueness gaining gait and mien ;   460
  The white streaks gathering clear to view
  In the burnt beard the women knew.

For a tale tells that on his track,
  As through Verona's streets he went,
  This saying certain women sent :—
' Lo, he that strolls to Hell and back
  At will ! Behold him, how Hell's reek
  Has crisped his beard and singed his cheek.'

' Whereat ' (Boccaccio's words) ' he smil'd
  For pride in fame.' It might be so :   470
  Nevertheless we cannot know
If haply he were not beguil'd
  To bitterer mirth, who scarce could tell
  If he indeed were back from Hell.

So the day came, after a space,
  When Dante felt assured that there
  The sunshine must lie sicklier
Even than in any other place,
  Save only Florence. When that day
  Had come, he rose and went his way.   480

He went and turned not. From his shoes
  It may be that he shook the dust,
  As every righteous dealer must

Once and again ere life can close :
  And unaccomplished destiny
  Struck cold his forehead, it may be.

No book keeps record how the Prince
  Sunned himself out of Dante's reach,
  Nor how the Jester stank in speech ;
While courtiers, used to smile and wince,   490
  Poets and harlots, all the throng,
  Let loose their scandal and their song.

No book keeps record if the seat
  Which Dante held at his host's board
  Were sat in next by clerk or lord,—
If leman lolled with dainty feet
  At ease, or hostage brooded there,
  Or priest lacked silence for his prayer.

Eat and wash hands, Can Grande ;—scarce
  We know their deeds now ; hands which fed
  Our Dante with that bitter bread ;   501
And thou the watch-dog of those stairs
  Which, of all paths his feet knew well,
  Were steeper found than Heaven or Hell.

JENNY

'Vengeance of Jenny's case ! Fie on her ! Never name her, child !'
  —(*Mrs. Quickly.*)

LAZY laughing languid Jenny,
Fond of a kiss and fond of a guinea,
Whose head upon my knee to-night
Rests for a while, as if grown light
With all our dances and the sound
To which the wild tunes spun you round :
Fair Jenny mine, the thoughtless queen
Of kisses which the blush between
Could hardly make much daintier ;

JENNY

Whose eyes are as blue skies, whose hair 10
Is countless gold incomparable :
Fresh flower, scarce touched with signs that tell
Of Love's exuberant hotbed :—Nay,
Poor flower left torn since yesterday
Until to-morrow leave you bare ;
Poor handful of bright spring-water
Flung in the whirlpool's shrieking face ;
Poor shameful Jenny, full of grace
Thus with your head upon my knee ;—
Whose person or whose purse may be 20
The lodestar of your reverie ?

This room of yours, my Jenny, looks
A change from mine so full of books,
Whose serried ranks hold fast, forsooth,
So many captive hours of youth,—
The hours they thieve from day and night
To make one's cherished work come right,
And leave it wrong for all their theft,
Even as to-night my work was left :
Until I vowed that since my brain 30
And eyes of dancing seemed so fain,
My feet should have some dancing too :—
And thus it was I met with you.
Well, I suppose 'twas hard to part,
For here I am. And now, sweetheart,
You seem too tired to get to bed

It was a careless life I led
When rooms like this were scarce so strange
Not long ago. What breeds the change,—
The many aims or the few years ? 40
Because to-night it all appears
Something I do not know again.

The cloud's not danced out of my brain,—
The cloud that made it turn and swim
While hour by hour the books grew dim.

Why, Jenny, as I watch you there,—
For all your wealth of loosened hair,
Your silk ungirdled and unlac'd
And warm sweets open to the waist,
All golden in the lamplight's gleam,—
You know not what a book you seem,
Half-read by lightning in a dream!
How should you know, my Jenny? Nay,
And I should be ashamed to say :—
Poor beauty, so well worth a kiss!
But while my thought runs on like this
With wasteful whims more than enough,
I wonder what you're thinking of.

If of myself you think at all,
What is the thought?—conjectural
On sorry matters best unsolved?—
Or inly is each grace revolved
To fit me with a lure?—or (sad
To think!) perhaps you're merely glad
That I'm not drunk or ruffianly
And let you rest upon my knee.

For sometimes, were the truth confess'd,
You're thankful for a little rest,—
Glad from the crush to rest within,
From the heart-sickness and the din
Where envy's voice at virtue's pitch
Mocks you because your gown is rich;
And from the pale girl's dumb rebuke,
Whose ill-clad grace and toil-worn look
Proclaim the strength that keeps her weak
And other nights than yours bespeak;
And from the wise unchildish elf
To schoolmate lesser than himself
Pointing you out, what thing you are :—
Yes, from the daily jeer and jar,
From shame and shame's outbraving too,
Is rest not sometimes sweet to you?—
But most from the hatefulness of man
Who spares not to end what he began,

JENNY

Whose acts are ill and his speech ill,
Who, having used you at his will,
Thrusts you aside, as when I dine
I serve the dishes and the wine.

Well, handsome Jenny mine, sit up,
I've filled our glasses, let us sup,   90
And do not let me think of you,
Lest shame of yours suffice for two.
What, still so tired ? Well, well then, keep
Your head there, so you do not sleep ;
But that the weariness may pass
And leave you merry, take this glass.
Ah ! lazy lily hand, more bless'd
If ne'er in rings it had been dress'd
Nor ever by a glove conceal'd !

Behold the lilies of the field,   100
They toil not neither do they spin ;
(So doth the ancient text begin,—
Not of such rest as one of these
Can share.) Another rest and ease
Along each summer-sated path
From its new lord the garden hath,
Than that whose spring in blessings ran
Which praised the bounteous husbandman,
Ere yet, in days of hankering breath,
The lilies sickened unto death.   110

What, Jenny, are your lilies dead ?
Aye, and the snow-white leaves are spread
Like winter on the garden-bed.
But you had roses left in May,—
They were not gone too. Jenny, nay,
But must your roses die, and those
Their purfled buds that should unclose ?
Even so ; the leaves are curled apart,
Still red as from the broken heart,
And here 's the naked stem of thorns.   120

Nay, nay, mere words. Here nothing warns
As yet of winter. Sickness here
Or want alone could waken fear,—
Nothing but passion wrings a tear.
Except when there may rise unsought
Haply at times a passing thought
Of the old days which seem to be
Much older than any history
That is written in any book;
When she would lie in fields and look 130
Along the ground through the blown grass,
And wonder where the city was,
Far out of sight, whose broil and bale
They told her then for a child's tale.

Jenny, you know the city now.
A child can tell the tale there, how
Some things which are not yet enroll'd
In market-lists are bought and sold
Even till the early Sunday light,
When Saturday night is market-night 140
Everywhere, be it dry or wet,
And market-night in the Haymarket.
Our learned London children know,
Poor Jenny, all your pride and woe;
Have seen your lifted silken skirt
Advertise dainties through the dirt;
Have seen your coach-wheels splash rebuke
On virtue; and have learned your look
When, wealth and health slipped past, you stare
Along the streets alone, and there, 150
Round the long park, across the bridge,
The cold lamps at the pavement's edge
Wind on together and apart,
A fiery serpent for your heart.

Let the thoughts pass, an empty cloud!
Suppose I were to think aloud,—
What if to her all this were said?
Why, as a volume seldom read

Being opened halfway shuts again,
So might the pages of her brain
Be parted at such words, and thence
Close back upon the dusty sense.
For is there hue or shape defin'd
In Jenny's desecrated mind,
Where all contagious currents meet,
A Lethe of the middle street ?
Nay, it reflects not any face,
Nor sound is in its sluggish pace,
But as they coil those eddies clot,
And night and day remember not.

   Why, Jenny, you're asleep at last !—
Asleep, poor Jenny, hard and fast,—
So young and soft and tired ; so fair,
With chin thus nestled in your hair,
Mouth quiet, eyelids almost blue
As if some sky of dreams shone through !

   Just as another woman sleeps !
Enough to throw one's thoughts in heaps
Of doubt and horror,—what to say
Or think,—this awful secret sway,
The potter's power over the clay !
Of the same lump (it has been said)
For honour and dishonour made,
Two sister vessels. Here is one.

   My cousin Nell is fond of fun,
And fond of dress, and change, and praise,
So mere a woman in her ways :
And if her sweet eyes rich in youth
Are like her lips that tell the truth,
My cousin Nell is fond of love.
And she's the girl I'm proudest of.
Who does not prize her, guard her well ?
The love of change, in cousin Nell,
Shall find the best and hold it dear :
The unconquered mirth turn quieter

Not through her own, through others' woe :
The conscious pride of beauty glow
Beside another's pride in her,
One little part of all they share.
For Love himself shall ripen these 200
In a kind soil to just increase
Through years of fertilizing peace.

Of the same lump (as it is said)
For honour and dishonour made,
Two sister vessels. Here is one.

It makes a goblin of the sun.

So pure,—so fall'n ! How dare to think
Of the first common kindred link ?
Yet, Jenny, till the world shall burn
It seems that all things take their turn ; 210
And who shall say but this fair tree
May need, in changes that may be,
Your children's children's charity ?
Scorned then, no doubt, as you are scorn'd !
Shall no man hold his pride forewarn'd
Till in the end, the Day of Days,
At Judgement, one of his own race,
As frail and lost as you, shall rise,—
His daughter, with his mother's eyes ?

How Jenny's clock ticks on the shelf ! 220
Might not the dial scorn itself
That has such hours to register ?
Yet as to me, even so to her
Are golden sun and silver moon,
In daily largesse of earth's boon,
Counted for life-coins to one tune.
And if, as blindfold fates are toss'd,
Through some one man this life be lost,
Shall soul not somehow pay for soul ?

Fair shines the gilded aureole 230
In which our highest painters place
Some living woman's simple face.

JENNY

And the stilled features thus descried
As Jenny's long throat droops aside,—
The shadows where the cheeks are thin,
And pure wide curve from ear to chin,—
With Raffael's or Da Vinci's hand
To show them to men's souls, might stand,
Whole ages long, the whole world through,
For preachings of what God can do. 240
What has man done here ? How atone,
Great God, for this which man has done ?
And for the body and soul which by
Man's pitiless doom must now comply
With lifelong hell, what lullaby
Of sweet forgetful second birth
Remains ? All dark. No sign on earth
What measure of God's rest endows
The many mansions of his house.

    If but a woman's heart might see 250
Such erring heart unerringly
For once ! But that can never be.

    Like a rose shut in a book
In which pure women may not look,
For its base pages claim control
To crush the flower within the soul ;
Where through each dead rose-leaf that clings,
Pale as transparent psyche-wings,
To the vile text, are traced such things
As might make lady's cheek indeed 260
More than a living rose to read ;
So nought save foolish foulness may
Watch with hard eyes the sure decay ;
And so the life-blood of this rose,
Puddled with shameful knowledge, flows
Through leaves no chaste hand may unclose :
Yet still it keeps such faded show
Of when 'twas gathered long ago,
That the crushed petals' lovely grain,
The sweetness of the sanguine stain, 270

Seen of a woman's eyes, must make
Her pitiful heart, so prone to ache,
Love roses better for its sake :—
Only that this can never be :—
Even so unto her sex is she.

Yet, Jenny, looking long at you,
The woman almost fades from view.
A cipher of man's changeless sum
Of lust, past, present, and to come,
Is left. A riddle that one shrinks   280
To challenge from the scornful sphinx.

Like a toad within a stone
Seated while Time crumbles on ;
Which sits there since the earth was curs'd
For Man's transgression at the first ;
Which, living through all centuries,
Not once has seen the sun arise ;
Whose life, to its cold circle charmed,
The earth's whole summers have not warmed ;
Which always—whitherso the stone   290
Be flung—sits there, deaf, blind, alone ;—
Aye, and shall not be driven out
Till that which shuts him round about
Break at the very Master's stroke,
And the dust thereof vanish as smoke,
And the seed of Man vanish as dust :—
Even so within this world is Lust.

Come, come, what use in thoughts like this ?
Poor little Jenny, good to kiss,—
You'd not believe by what strange roads   300
Thought travels, when your beauty goads
A man to-night to think of toads !
Jenny, wake up. . . . Why, there's the dawn !

And there's an early waggon drawn
To market, and some sheep that jog
Bleating before a barking dog ;

JENNY

And the old streets come peering through
Another night that London knew;
And all as ghostlike as the lamps.

So on the wings of day decamps
My last night's frolic. Glooms begin
To shiver off as lights creep in
Past the gauze curtains half drawn-to,
And the lamp's doubled shade grows blue,—
Your lamp, my Jenny, kept alight,
Like a wise virgin's, all one night!
And in the alcove coolly spread
Glimmers with dawn your empty bed;
And yonder your fair face I see
Reflected lying on my knee,
Where teems with first foreshadowings
Your pier-glass scrawled with diamond rings.

And now without, as if some word
Had called upon them that they heard,
The London sparrows far and nigh
Clamour together suddenly;
And Jenny's cage-bird grown awake
Here in their song his part must take,
Because here too the day doth break.

And somehow in myself the dawn
Among stirred clouds and veils withdrawn
Strikes greyly on her. Let her sleep.
But will it wake her if I heap
These cushions thus beneath her head
Where my knee was? No,—there's your bed,
My Jenny, while you dream. And there
I lay among your golden hair
Perhaps the subject of your dreams,
These golden coins.
                      For still one deems
That Jenny's flattering sleep confers
New magic on the magic purse,—
Grim web, how clogged with shrivelled flies!

Between the threads fine fumes arise
And shape their pictures in the brain.
There roll no streets in glare and rain,
Nor flagrant man-swine whets his tusk;
But delicately sighs in musk
The homage of the dim boudoir;
Or like a palpitating star
Thrilled into song, the opera-night   350
Breathes faint in the quick pulse of light;
Or at the carriage-window shine
Rich wares for choice; or, free to dine,
Whirls through its hour of health (divine
For her) the concourse of the Park.
And though in the discounted dark
Her functions there and here are one,
Beneath the lamps and in the sun
There reigns at least the acknowledged belle
Apparelled beyond parallel.   360
Ah Jenny, yes, we know your dreams.

For even the Paphian Venus seems
A goddess o'er the realms of love,
When silver-shrined in shadowy grove:
Aye, or let offerings nicely placed
But hide Priapus to the waist,
And whoso looks on him shall see
An eligible deity.

Why, Jenny, waking here alone
May help you to remember one,   370
Though all the memory's long outworn
Of many a double-pillowed morn.
I think I see you when you wake,
And rub your eyes for me, and shake
My gold, in rising, from your hair,
A Danaë for a moment there.

Jenny, my love rang true! for still
Love at first sight is vague, until
That tinkling makes him audible.

And must I mock you to the last, 380
Ashamed of my own shame,—aghast
Because some thoughts not born amiss
Rose at a poor fair face like this?
Well, of such thoughts so much I know:
In my life, as in hers, they show,
By a far gleam which I may near,
A dark path I can strive to clear.

Only one kiss. Good-bye, my dear.

THE PORTRAIT

This is her picture as she was:
   It seems a thing to wonder on,
As though mine image in the glass
   Should tarry when myself am gone.
I gaze until she seems to stir,—
Until mine eyes almost aver
   That now, even now, the sweet lips part
   To breathe the words of the sweet heart:—
And yet the earth is over her.

Alas! even such the thin-drawn ray 10
   That makes the prison-depths more rude,—
The drip of water night and day
   Giving a tongue to solitude.
Yet this, of all love's perfect prize,
Remains; save what in mournful guise
   Takes counsel with my soul alone,—
   Save what is secret and unknown,
Below the earth, above the skies.

In painting her I shrined her face
   Mid mystic trees, where light falls in 20
Hardly at all; a covert place
   Where you might think to find a din

Of doubtful talk, and a live flame
Wandering, and many a shape whose name
  Not itself knoweth, and old dew,
  And your own footsteps meeting you,
And all things going as they came.

A deep dim wood ; and there she stands
  As in that wood that day : for so
Was the still movement of her hands
  And such the pure line's gracious flow.
And passing fair the type must seem,
Unknown the presence and the dream.
  'Tis she : though of herself, alas !
  Less than her shadow on the grass
Or than her image in the stream.

That day we met there, I and she
  One with the other all alone ;
And we were blithe ; yet memory
  Saddens those hours, as when the moon
Looks upon daylight. And with her
I stooped to drink the spring-water,
  Athirst where other waters sprang ;
  And where the echo is, she sang,—
My soul another echo there.

But when that hour my soul won strength
  For words whose silence wastes and kills,
Dull raindrops smote us, and at length
  Thundered the heat within the hills.
That eve I spoke those words again
Beside the pelted window-pane ;
  And there she hearkened what I said,
  With under-glances that surveyed
The empty pastures blind with rain.

Next day the memories of these things,
  Like leaves through which a bird has flown,
Still vibrated with Love's warm wings ;
  Till I must make them all my own

THE PORTRAIT

And paint this picture. So, 'twixt ease
Of talk and sweet long silences,
   She stood among the plants in bloom
   At windows of a summer room,
To feign the shadow of the trees.

And as I wrought, while all above
   And all around was fragrant air,
In the sick burthen of my love
   It seemed each sun-thrilled blossom there
Beat like a heart among the leaves.
O heart that never beats nor heaves,
   In that one darkness lying still,
   What now to thee my love's great will
Or the fine web the sunshine weaves?

For now doth daylight disavow
   Those days,—nought left to see or hear.
Only in solemn whispers now
   At night-time these things reach mine ear,
When the leaf-shadows at a breath
Shrink in the road, and all the heath,
   Forest and water, far and wide,
   In limpid starlight glorified,
Lie like the mystery of death.

Last night at last I could have slept,
   And yet delayed my sleep till dawn,
Still wandering. Then it was I wept:
   For unawares I came upon
Those glades where once she walked with me:
And as I stood there suddenly,
   All wan with traversing the night,
   Upon the desolate verge of light
Yearned loud the iron-bosomed sea.

Even so, where Heaven holds breath and hears
   The beating heart of Love's own breast,—
Where round the secret of all spheres
   All angels lay their wings to rest,—

How shall my soul stand rapt and awed,
When, by the new birth borne abroad
   Throughout the music of the suns,
    It enters in her soul at once
And knows the silence there for God !

Here with her face doth memory sit
   Meanwhile, and wait the day's decline,
Till other eyes shall look from it,
   Eyes of the spirit's Palestine,
Even than the old gaze tenderer :
While hopes and aims long lost with her
   Stand round her image side by side,
    Like tombs of pilgrims that have died
About the Holy Sepulchre.

SISTER HELEN

'WHY did you melt your waxen man,
         Sister Helen ?
To-day is the third since you began.'
'The time was long, yet the time ran,
         Little brother.'
        (O Mother, Mary Mother,
Three days to-day, between Hell and Heaven !)

'But if you have done your work aright,
         Sister Helen,
You'll let me play, for you said I might.'
'Be very still in your play to-night,
         Little brother.'
        (O Mother, Mary Mother,
Third night, to-night, between Hell and Heaven !)

'You said it must melt ere vesper-bell,
         Sister Helen ;
If now it be molten, all is well.'
'Even so,—nay, peace ! you cannot tell,
         Little brother.'
        (O Mother, Mary Mother,
O what is this, between Hell and Heaven ?)

SISTER HELEN

'Oh the waxen knave was plump to-day,
         Sister Helen ;
How like dead folk he has dropped away ! '
' Nay now, of the dead what can you say,
         Little brother ? '
        (O Mother, Mary Mother,
What of the dead, between Hell and Heaven ?)

' See, see, the sunken pile of wood,
         Sister Helen,   30
Shines through the thinned wax red as blood ! '
' Nay now, when looked you yet on blood,
         Little brother ? '
        (O Mother, Mary Mother,
How pale she is, between Hell and Heaven !)

' Now close your eyes, for they're sick and sore,
         Sister Helen,
And I'll play without the gallery door.'
' Aye, let me rest,—I'll lie on the floor,
         Little brother.'   40
        (O Mother, Mary Mother,
What rest to-night, between Hell and Heaven ?)

' Here high up in the balcony,
         Sister Helen,
The moon flies face to face with me.'
' Aye, look and say whatever you see,
         Little brother.'
        (O Mother, Mary Mother,
What sight to-night, between Hell and Heaven ?)

' Outside it 's merry in the wind's wake,   50
         Sister Helen ;
In the shaken trees the chill stars shake.'
' Hush, heard you a horse-tread as you spake,
         Little brother ? '
        (O Mother, Mary Mother,
What sound to-night, between Hell and Heaven ?)

'I hear a horse-tread, and I see,
                    Sister Helen,
Three horsemen that ride terribly.'
'Little brother, whence come the three,   60
                    Little brother?'
            (O Mother, Mary Mother,
Whence should they come, between Hell and Heaven?)

'They come by the hill-verge from Boyne Bar,
                    Sister Helen,
And one draws nigh, but two are afar.'
'Look, look, do you know them who they are,
                    Little brother?'
            (O Mother, Mary Mother,
Who should they be, between Hell and Heaven?)

'Oh, it's Keith of Eastholm rides so fast,   71
                    Sister Helen,
For I know the white mane on the blast.'
'The hour has come, has come at last,
                    Little brother!'
            (O Mother, Mary Mother,
Her hour at last, between Hell and Heaven!)

'He has made a sign and called Halloo!
                    Sister Helen,
And he says that he would speak with you.'   80
'Oh tell him I fear the frozen dew,
                    Little brother.'
            (O Mother, Mary Mother,
Why laughs she thus, between Hell and Heaven?)

'The wind is loud, but I hear him cry,
                    Sister Helen,
That Keith of Ewern's like to die.'
'And he and thou, and thou and I,
                    Little brother.'
            (O Mother, Mary Mother,   90
And they and we, between Hell and Heaven!)

SISTER HELEN

'For three days now he has lain abed,
    Sister Helen,
And he prays in torment to be dead.'
'The thing may chance, if he have prayed,
    Little brother!'
  (O Mother, Mary Mother,
If he have prayed, between Hell and Heaven!)

'But he has not ceased to cry to-day,
    Sister Helen,   100
That you should take your curse away.'
'*My* prayer was heard,—he need but pray,
    Little brother!'
  (O Mother, Mary Mother,
Shall God not hear, between Hell and Heaven?)

'But he says, till you take back your ban,
    Sister Helen,
His soul would pass, yet never can.'
'Nay then, shall I slay a living man,
    Little brother?'   110
  (O Mother, Mary Mother,
A living soul, between Hell and Heaven!)

'But he calls for ever on your name,
    Sister Helen,
And says that he melts before a flame.'
'My heart for his pleasure fared the same,
    Little brother.'
  (O Mother, Mary Mother,
Fire at the heart, between Hell and Heaven!)

'Here's Keith of Westholm riding fast, 120
    Sister Helen,
For I know the white plume on the blast.'
'The hour, the sweet hour I forecast,
    Little brother!'
  (O Mother, Mary Mother,
Is the hour sweet, between Hell and Heaven?)

'He stops to speak, and he stills his horse,
                    Sister Helen;
But his words are drowned in the wind's course.'
'Nay hear, nay hear, you must hear perforce,
                    Little brother!'   131
            (*O Mother, Mary Mother,*
A word ill heard, between Hell and Heaven!)

'Oh he says that Keith of Ewern's cry,
                    Sister Helen,
Is ever to see you ere he die.'
'He sees me in earth, in moon and sky,
                    Little brother!'
            (*O Mother, Mary Mother,*
Earth, moon and sky, between Hell and Heaven!)

'He sends a ring and a broken coin,   141
                    Sister Helen,
And bids you mind the banks of Boyne.'
'What else he broke will he ever join,
                    Little brother?'
            (*O Mother, Mary Mother,*
Oh, never more, between Hell and Heaven!)

'He yields you these and craves full fain,
                    Sister Helen,
You pardon him in his mortal pain.'   150
'What else he took will he give again,
                    Little brother?'
            (*O Mother, Mary Mother,*
No more, no more, between Hell and Heaven!)

'He calls your name in an agony,
                    Sister Helen,
That even dead Love must weep to see.'
'Hate, born of Love, is blind as he,
                    Little brother!'
            (*O Mother, Mary Mother,*   160
Love turned to hate, between Hell and Heaven!)

SISTER HELEN

'Oh it's Keith of Keith now that rides fast,
  Sister Helen,
For I know the white hair on the blast.'
'The short short hour will soon be past,
  Little brother!'
    (O Mother, Mary Mother,
Will soon be past, between Hell and Heaven!)

'He looks at me and he tries to speak,
  Sister Helen,
But oh! his voice is sad and weak!'
'What here should the mighty Baron seek,
  Little brother?'
    (O Mother, Mary Mother,
Is this the end, between Hell and Heaven?)

'Oh his son still cries, if you forgive,
  Sister Helen,
The body dies but the soul shall live.'
'Fire shall forgive me as I forgive,
  Little brother!'
    (O Mother, Mary Mother,
As she forgives, between Hell and Heaven!)

'Oh he prays you, as his heart would rive,
  Sister Helen,
To save his dear son's soul alive.'
'Nay, flame cannot slay it, it shall thrive,
  Little brother!'
    (O Mother, Mary Mother,
Alas, alas, between Hell and Heaven!)

'He cries to you, kneeling in the road,
  Sister Helen,
To go with him for the love of God!'
'The way is long to his son's abode,
  Little brother.'
    (O Mother, Mary Mother,
The way is long, between Hell and Heaven!)

'O Sister Helen, you heard the bell,
        Sister Helen!
More loud than the vesper-chime it fell.'
'No vesper-chime, but a dying knell,   200
        Little brother!'
        (O Mother, Mary Mother,
His dying knell, between Hell and Heaven!)

'Alas! but I fear the heavy sound,
        Sister Helen;
Is it in the sky or in the ground?'
'Say, have they turned their horses round,
        Little brother?'
        (O Mother, Mary Mother,   209
What would she more, between Hell and Heaven?)

'They have raised the old man from his knee,
        Sister Helen,
And they ride in silence hastily.'
'More fast the naked soul doth flee,
        Little brother!'
        (O Mother, Mary Mother,
The naked soul, between Hell and Heaven!)

'Oh the wind is sad in the iron chill,
        Sister Helen,
And weary sad they look by the hill.'   220
'But Keith of Ewern's sadder still,
        Little brother!'
        (O Mother, Mary Mother,
Most sad of all, between Hell and Heaven!)

'See, see, the wax has dropped from its place,
        Sister Helen,
And the flames are winning up apace!'
'Yet here they burn but for a space,
        Little brother!'
        (O Mother, Mary Mother,   230
Here for a space, between Hell and Heaven!)

'Ah! what white thing at the door has cross'd,
        Sister Helen?
Ah! what is this that sighs in the frost?'
'A soul that's lost as mine is lost,
        Little brother!'
        (*O Mother, Mary Mother,
Lost, lost, all lost, between Hell and Heaven!)

STRATTON WATER

'O HAVE you seen the Stratton flood
  That's great with rain to-day?
It runs beneath your wall, Lord Sands,
  Full of the new-mown hay.

'I led your hounds to Hutton bank
  To bathe at early morn:
They got their bath by Borrowbrake
  Above the standing corn.'

Out from the castle-stair Lord Sands
  Looked up the western lea;   10
The rook was grieving on her nest,
  The flood was round her tree.

Over the castle-wall Lord Sands
  Looked down the eastern hill:
The stakes swam free among the boats,
  The flood was rising still.

'What's yonder far below that lies
  So white against the slope?'
'O it's a sail o' your bonny barks
  The waters have washed up.'   20

'But I have never a sail so white,
  And the water's not yet there.'
'O it's the swans o' your bonny lake
  The rising flood doth scare.'

STRATTON WATER

'The swans they would not hold so still,
  So high they would not win.'
'O it's Joyce my wife has spread her smock
  And fears to fetch it in.'

'Nay, knave, it's neither sail nor swans,
  Nor aught that you can say;
For though your wife might leave her smock,
  Herself she'd bring away.'

Lord Sands has passed the turret-stair,
  The court, and yard, and all;
The kine were in the byre that day,
  The nags were in the stall.

Lord Sands has won the weltering slope
  Whereon the white shape lay:
The clouds were still above the hill,
  And the shape was still as they.

Oh pleasant is the gaze of life
  And sad is death's blind head;
But awful are the living eyes
  In the face of one thought dead!

'In God's name, Janet, is it me
  Thy ghost has come to seek?'
'Nay, wait another hour, Lord Sands,—
  Be sure my ghost shall speak.'

A moment stood he as a stone,
  Then grovelled to his knee.
'O Janet, O my love, my love,
  Rise up and come with me!'
'O once before you bade me come,
  And it's here you have brought me!

'O many's the sweet word, Lord Sands,
  You've spoken oft to me;
But all that I have from you to-day
  Is the rain on my body.

STRATTON WATER

'And many's the good gift, Lord Sands,
  You've promised oft to me;
But the gift of yours I keep to-day
  Is the babe in my body.

'O it's not in any earthly bed
  That first my babe I'll see;
For I have brought my body here
  That the flood may cover me.'

His face was close against her face,
  His hands of hers were fain:
O her wet cheeks were hot with tears,
  Her wet hands cold with rain.

'They told me you were dead, Janet,—
  How could I guess the lie?'
'They told me you were false, Lord Sands,—
  What could I do but die?'

'Now keep you well, my brother Giles,—
  Through you I deemed her dead!
As wan as your towers be to-day
  To-morrow they'll be red.

'Look down, look down, my false mother,
  That bade me not to grieve:
You'll look up when our marriage fires
  Are lit to-morrow eve.

'O more than one and more than two
  The sorrow of this shall see:
But it's to-morrow, love, for them,—
  To-day's for thee and me.'

He's drawn her face between his hands
  And her pale mouth to his:
No bird that was so still that day
  Chirps sweeter than his kiss.

STRATTON WATER

The flood was creeping round their feet.
  'O Janet, come away!
The hall is warm for the marriage-rite,
  The bed for the birthday.'

'Nay, but I hear your mother cry,
  "Go bring this bride to bed!
And would she christen her babe unborn
  So wet she comes to wed?"'

'I'll be your wife to cross your door
  And meet your mother's e'e.
We plighted troth to wed i' the kirk,
  And it's there I'll wed with ye.'

He's ta'en her by the short girdle
  And by the dripping sleeve:
'Go fetch Sir Jock my mother's priest,—
  You'll ask of him no leave.

'O it's one half-hour to reach the kirk
  And one for the marriage-rite;
And kirk and castle and castle-lands
  Shall be our babe's to-night.'

'The flood's in the kirkyard, Lord Sands,
  And round the belfry-stair.'
'I bade ye fetch the priest,' he said,
  'Myself shall bring him there.

'It's for the lilt of wedding bells
  We'll have the hail to pour,
And for the clink of bridle-reins
  The plashing of the oar.'

Beneath them on the nether hill
  A boat was floating wide:
Lord Sands swam out and caught the oars
  And rowed to the hill-side.

STRATTON WATER

He's wrapped her in a green mantle
  And set her softly in;
Her hair was wet upon her face,
  Her face was grey and thin;
And 'Oh!' she said, 'lie still, my babe,
  It's out you must not win!'

But woe's my heart for Father John!
  As hard as he might pray,
There seemed no help but Noah's ark
  Or Jonah's fish that day.

The first strokes that the oars struck
  Were over the broad leas;
The next strokes that the oars struck
  They pushed beneath the trees;

The last stroke that the oars struck,
  The good boat's head was met,
And there the gate of the kirkyard
  Stood like a ferry-gate.

He's set his hand upon the bar
  And lightly leaped within:
He's lifted her to his left shoulder,
  Her knees beside his chin.

The graves lay deep beneath the flood
  Under the rain alone;
And when the foot-stone made him slip,
  He held by the head-stone.

The empty boat thrawed i' the wind
  Against the postern tied.
'Hold still, you've brought my love with me,
  You shall take back my bride.'

But woe's my heart for Father John
  And the saints he clamoured to!
There's never a saint but Christopher
  Might hale such buttocks through!

And 'Oh!' she said, 'on men's shoulders
    I well had thought to wend,
And well to travel with a priest,
    But not to have cared or ken'd.   160

'And oh!' she said, 'it's well this way
    That I thought to have fared,—
Not to have lighted at the kirk
    But stopped in the kirkyard.

'For it's oh and oh I prayed to God,
    Whose rest I hoped to win,
That when to-night at your board-head
    You'd bid the feast begin,
This water past your window-sill
    Might bear my body in.'   170

Now make the white bed warm and soft
    And greet the merry morn.
The night the mother should have died
    The young son shall be born.

THE STREAM'S SECRET

WHAT thing unto mine ear
Wouldst thou convey,—what secret thing,
O wandering water ever whispering?
Surely thy speech shall be of her.
Thou water, O thou whispering wanderer,
        What message dost thou bring?

        Say, hath not Love leaned low
This hour beside thy far well-head,
And there through jealous hollowed fingers said
    The thing that most I long to know,—   10
Murmuring with curls all dabbled in thy flow
        And washed lips rosy red?

THE STREAM'S SECRET

He told it to thee there
  Where thy voice hath a louder tone;
But where it welters to this little moan
  His will decrees that I should hear.
Now speak: for with the silence is no fear,
  And I am all alone.

Shall Time not still endow
  One hour with life, and I and she
Slake in one kiss the thirst of memory?
  Say, stream; lest Love should disavow
Thy service, and the bird upon the bough
  Sing first to tell it me.

What whisperest thou? Nay, why
  Name the dead hours? I mind them well:
Their ghosts in many darkened doorways dwell
  With desolate eyes to know them by.
The hour that must be born ere it can die,—
  Of that I'd have thee tell.

But hear, before thou speak!
  Withhold, I pray, the vain behest
That while the maze hath still its bower for quest
  My burning heart should cease to seek.
Be sure that Love ordained for souls more meek
  His roadside dells of rest.

Stream, when this silver thread
  In flood-time is a torrent brown,
May any bulwark bind thy foaming crown?
  Shall not the waters surge and spread
And to the crannied boulders of their bed
  Still shoot the dead leaves down?

Let no rebuke find place
  In speech of thine: or it shall prove
That thou dost ill expound the words of Love,
  Even as thine eddy's rippling race
Would blur the perfect image of his face.
  I will have none thereof.

O learn and understand
   That 'gainst the wrongs himself did wreak
Love sought her aid ; until her shadowy cheek
   And eyes beseeching gave command ;
And compassed in her close compassionate hand
      My heart must burn and speak.

   For then at last we spoke
What eyes so oft had told to eyes
Through that long-lingering silence whose half-sighs
   Alone the buried secret broke,
Which with snatched hands and lips' reverberate stroke
      Then from the heart did rise.

   But she is far away
Now ; nor the hours of night grown hoar
Bring yet to me, long gazing from the door,
   The wind-stirred robe of roseate grey
And rose-crown of the hour that leads the day
      When we shall meet once more.

   Dark as thy blinded wave
When brimming midnight floods the glen,—
Bright as the laughter of thy runnels when
   The dawn yields all the light they crave ;
Even so these hours to wound and that to save
      Are sisters in Love's ken.

   Oh sweet her bending grace
Then when I kneel beside her feet ;
And sweet her eyes' o'erhanging heaven ; and sweet
   The gathering folds of her embrace ;
And her fall'n hair at last shed round my face
      When breaths and tears shall meet.

   Beneath her sheltering hair,
In the warm silence near her breast,
Our kisses and our sobs shall sink to rest ;
   As in some still trance made aware
That day and night have wrought to fulness there
      And Love has built our nest.

THE STREAM'S SECRET

And as in the dim grove,
When the rains cease that hushed them long,
'Mid glistening boughs the song-birds wake to song,—
So from our hearts deep-shrined in love,
While the leaves throb beneath, around, above,
    The quivering notes shall throng.

Till tenderest words found vain
Draw back to wonder mute and deep,
And closed lips in closed arms a silence keep,
    Subdued by memory's circling strain,—
The wind-rapt sound that the wind brings again
    While all the willows weep.

Then by her summoning art
Shall memory conjure back the sere
Autumnal Springs, from many a dying year
    Born dead; and, bitter to the heart,
The very ways where now we walk apart
    Who then shall cling so near.

And with each thought new-grown,
Some sweet caress or some sweet name
Low-breathed shall let me know her thought the same;
    Making me rich with every tone
And touch of the dear heaven so long unknown
    That filled my dreams with flame.

Pity and love shall burn
In her pressed cheek and cherishing hands;
And from the living spirit of love that stands
    Between her lips to soothe and yearn,
Each separate breath shall clasp me round in turn
    And loose my spirit's bands.

Oh passing sweet and dear,
Then when the worshipped form and face
Are felt at length in darkling close embrace;
    Round which so oft the sun shone clear,
With mocking light and pitiless atmosphere,
    In many an hour and place.

Ah me! with what proud growth
Shall that hour's thirsting race be run;
While, for each several sweetness still begun
Afresh, endures love's endless drouth:
Sweet hands, sweet hair, sweet cheeks, sweet eyes,
sweet mouth,
Each singly wooed and won.

Yet most with the sweet soul
Shall love's espousals then be knit;
For very passion of peace shall breathe from it
O'er tremulous wings that touch the goal,   130
As on the unmeasured height of Love's control
The lustral fires are lit.

Therefore, when breast and cheek
Now part, from long embraces free,—
Each on the other gazing shall but see
A self that has no need to speak:
All things unsought, yet nothing more to seek,—
One love in unity.

O water wandering past,—
Albeit to thee I speak this thing,   140
O water, thou that wanderest whispering,
Thou keep'st thy counsel to the last.
What spell upon thy bosom should Love cast,
His message thence to wring?

Nay, must thou hear the tale
Of the past days,—the heavy debt
Of life that obdurate time withholds,—ere yet
To win thine ear these prayers prevail,
And by thy voice Love's self with high All-hail
Yield up the love-secret?   150

How should all this be told?—
All the sad sum of wayworn days;—
Heart's anguish in the impenetrable maze;
And on the waste uncoloured wold
The visible burthen of the sun grown cold
And the moon's labouring gaze?

THE STREAM'S SECRET

    Alas! shall hope be nurs'd
On life's all-succouring breast in vain,
And made so perfect only to be slain?
    Or shall not rather the sweet thirst
Even yet rejoice the heart with warmth dispers'd
        And strength grown fair again?

    Stands it not by the door—
Love's Hour—till she and I shall meet;
With bodiless form and unapparent feet
    That cast no shadow yet before,
Though round its head the dawn begins to pour
        The breath that makes day sweet?

    Its eyes invisible
Watch till the dial's thin-thrown shade
Be born,—yea, till the journeying line be laid
    Upon the point that wakes the spell,
And there in lovelier light than tongue can tell
        Its presence stand array'd.

    Its soul remembers yet
Those sunless hours that passed it by;
And still it hears the night's disconsolate cry,
    And feels the branches wringing wet
Cast on its brow, that may not once forget,
        Dumb tears from the blind sky.

    But oh! when now her foot
Draws near, for whose sake night and day
Were long in weary longing sighed away,—
    The Hour of Love, 'mid airs grown mute,
Shall sing beside the door, and Love's own lute
        Thrill to the passionate lay.

    Thou know'st, for Love has told
Within thine ear, O stream, how soon
That song shall lift its sweet appointed tune.
    O tell me, for my lips are cold,
And in my veins the blood is waxing old
        Even while I beg the boon.

So, in that hour of sighs
　Assuaged, shall we beside this stone
Yield thanks for grace ; while in thy mirror shown
　　The twofold image softly lies,
Until we kiss, and each in other's eyes
　　Is imaged all alone.

　　Still silent ? Can no art
Of Love's then move thy pity ? Nay, 200
To thee let nothing come that owns his sway :
　　Let happy lovers have no part
With thee ; nor even so sad and poor a heart
　　As thou hast spurned to-day.

　　To-day ? Lo ! night is here.
The glen grows heavy with some veil
Risen from the earth or fall'n to make earth pale ;
　　And all stands hushed to eye and ear,
Until the night-wind shake the shade like fear
　　And every covert quail. 210

　　Ah ! by a colder wave
On deathlier airs the hour must come
Which to thy heart, my love, shall call me home.
　　Between the lips of the low cave
Against that night the lapping waters lave,
　　And the dark lips are dumb.

　　But there Love's self doth stand,
And with Life's weary wings far-flown,
And with Death's eyes that make the water moan,
　　Gathers the water in his hand : 220
And they that drink know nought of sky or land
　　But only love alone.

　　O soul-sequestered face
Far off,—O were that night but now !
So even beside that stream even I and thou
　　Through thirsting lips should draw Love's grace,
And in the zone of that supreme embrace
　　Bind aching breast and brow.

O water whispering
  Still through the dark into mine ears,— 230
As with mine eyes, is it not now with hers ?—
  Mine eyes that add to thy cold spring,
Wan water, wandering water weltering,
    This hidden tide of tears.

THE CARD-DEALER

COULD you not drink her gaze like wine ?
  Yet though its splendour swoon
Into the silence languidly
  As a tune into a tune,
Those eyes unravel the coiled night
  And know the stars at noon.

The gold that 's heaped beside her hand,
  In truth rich prize it were ;
And rich the dreams that wreathe her brows
  With magic stillness there ; 10
And he were rich who should unwind
  That woven golden hair.

Around her, where she sits, the dance
  Now breathes its eager heat ;
And not more lightly or more true
  Fall there the dancers' feet
Than fall her cards on the bright board
  As 'twere an heart that beat.

Her fingers let them softly through,
  Smooth polished silent things ; 20
And each one as it falls reflects
  In swift light-shadowings,
Blood-red and purple, green and blue,
  The great eyes of her rings.

Whom plays she with? With thee, who lov'st
  Those gems upon her hand;
With me, who search her secret brows;
  With all men, bless'd or bann'd.
We play together, she and we,
  Within a vain strange land: 30

A land without any order,—
  Day even as night, (one saith,)—
Where who lieth down ariseth not
  Nor the sleeper awakeneth;
A land of darkness as darkness itself
  And of the shadow of death.

What be her cards, you ask? Even these:—
  The heart, that doth but crave
More, having fed; the diamond,
  Skilled to make base seem brave;   40
The club, for smiting in the dark;
  The spade, to dig a grave.

And do you ask what game she plays?
  With me 'tis lost or won;
With thee it is playing still; with him
  It is not well begun;
But 'tis a game she plays with all
  Beneath the sway o' the sun.

Thou seest the card that falls,—she knows
  The card that followeth: 50
Her game in thy tongue is called Life,
  As ebbs thy daily breath:
When she shall speak, thou'lt learn her tongue
  And know she calls it Death.

MY SISTER'S SLEEP [1]

She fell asleep on Christmas Eve :
    At length the long-ungranted shade
    Of weary eyelids overweigh'd
The pain nought else might yet relieve.

Our mother, who had leaned all day
    Over the bed from chime to chime,
    Then raised herself for the first time,
And as she sat her down, did pray.

Her little work-table was spread
    With work to finish. For the glare   10
    Made by her candle, she had care
To work some distance from the bed.

Without, there was a cold moon up,
    Of winter radiance sheer and thin ;
    The hollow halo it was in
Was like an icy crystal cup.

Through the small room, with subtle sound
    Of flame, by vents the fireshine drove
    And reddened. In its dim alcove
The mirror shed a clearness round.   20

I had been sitting up some nights,
    And my tired mind felt weak and blank ;
    Like a sharp strengthening wine it drank
The stillness and the broken lights.

Twelve struck. That sound, by dwindling years
    Heard in each hour, crept off ; and then
    The ruffled silence spread again,
Like water that a pebble stirs.

---

[1] This little poem, written in 1847, was printed in a periodical at the outset of 1850. The metre, which is used by several old English writers, became celebrated a month or two later on the publication of *In Memoriam*.

MY SISTER'S SLEEP

Our mother rose from where she sat:
  Her needles, as she laid them down,   30
  Met lightly, and her silken gown
Settled: no other noise than that.

'Glory unto the Newly Born!'
  So, as said angels, she did say;
  Because we were in Christmas Day,
Though it would still be long till morn.

Just then in the room over us
  There was a pushing back of chairs,
  As some who had sat unawares
So late, now heard the hour, and rose.   40

With anxious softly-stepping haste
  Our mother went where Margaret lay,
  Fearing the sounds o'erhead—should they
Have broken her long watched-for rest!

She stooped an instant, calm, and turned;
  But suddenly turned back again;
  And all her features seemed in pain
With woe, and her eyes gazed and yearned.

For my part, I but hid my face,
  And held my breath, and spoke no word: 50
  There was none spoken; but I heard
The silence for a little space.

Our mother bowed herself and wept:
  And both my arms fell, and I said,
  'God knows I knew that she was dead.'
And there, all white, my sister slept.

Then kneeling, upon Christmas morn
  A little after twelve o'clock
  We said, ere the first quarter struck,
'Christ's blessing on the newly born!'   60

A NEW YEAR'S BURDEN

ALONG the grass sweet airs are blown
  Our way this day in Spring.
Of all the songs that we have known
  Now which one shall we sing?
        Not that, my love, ah no!—
        Not this, my love? why, so!—
Yet both were ours, but hours will come and go.

The grove is all a pale frail mist,
  The new year sucks the sun.
Of all the kisses that we kissed
  Now which shall be the one?
        Not that, my love, ah no!—
        Not this, my love?—heigh-ho
For all the sweets that all the winds can blow!

The branches cross above our eyes,
  The skies are in a net:
And what's the thing beneath the skies
  We two would most forget?
        Not birth, my love, no, no,—
        Not death, my love, no, no,--
The love once ours, but ours long hours ago.

EVEN SO

    So it is, my dear.
All such things touch secret strings
    For heavy hearts to hear.
    So it is, my dear.

    Very like indeed:
Sea and sky, afar, on high,
    Sand and strewn seaweed,—
    Very like indeed.

            But the sea stands spread
As one wall with the flat skies,
Where the lean black craft like flies
            Seem well-nigh stagnated
            Soon to drop off dead.

            Seemed it so to us
When I was thine and thou wast mine,
            And all these things were thus,
            But all our world in us?

            Could we be so now?
Not if all beneath heaven's pall
            Lay dead but I and thou,
            Could we be so now!

AN OLD SONG ENDED

*'How should I your true love know
        From another one?'
'By his cockle-hat and staff
        And his sandal-shoon.'*

'And what signs have told you now
        That he hastens home?'
'Lo! the spring is nearly gone,
        He is nearly come.'

'For a token is there nought,
        Say, that he should bring?'
'He will bear a ring I gave
        And another ring.'

'How may I, when he shall ask,
        Tell him who lies there?'
'Nay, but leave my face unveiled
        And unbound my hair.'

'Can you say to me some word
        I shall say to him?'
'Say I'm looking in his eyes
        Though my eyes are dim.'

ASPECTA MEDUSA

ANDROMEDA, by Perseus saved and wed,
Hankered each day to see the Gorgon's head:
Till o'er a fount he held it, bade her lean,
And mirrored in the wave was safely seen
That death she lived by.

                Let not thine eyes know
Any forbidden thing itself, although
It once should save as well as kill : but be
Its shadow upon life enough for thee.

THREE TRANSLATIONS FROM FRANÇOIS VILLON, 1450

I

THE BALLAD OF DEAD LADIES

TELL me now in what hidden way is
   Lady Flora the lovely Roman ?
Where 's Hipparchia, and where is Thais,
   Neither of them the fairer woman ?
   Where is Echo, beheld of no man,
Only heard on river and mere,—
   She whose beauty was more than human ? . . .
But where are the snows of yester-year ?

Where 's Héloise, the learned nun,
   For whose sake Abeillard, I ween,
Lost manhood and put priesthood on ?
   (From Love he won such dule and teen !)
   And where, I pray you, is the Queen
Who willed that Buridan should steer
   Sewed in a sack's mouth down the Seine ? . . .
But where are the snows of yester-year ?

White Queen Blanche, like a queen of lilies,
  With a voice like any mermaiden —
Bertha Broadfoot, Beatrice, Alice,
  And Ermengarde the lady of Maine,—
  And that good Joan whom Englishmen
At Rouen doomed and burned her there,—
  Mother of God, where are they then? . . .
But where are the snows of yester-year?

Nay, never ask this week, fair lord,
  Where they are gone, nor yet this year,
Except with this for an overword,—
  But where are the snows of yester-year?

II

To Death, of His Lady

Death, of thee do I make my moan,
  Who hadst my lady away from me,
  Nor wilt assuage thine enmity
Till with her life thou hast mine own;
For since that hour my strength has flown.
Lo! what wrong was her life to thee,
                    Death?

Two we were, and the heart was one;
  Which now being dead, dead I must be,
  Or seem alive as lifelessly
As in the choir the painted stone,
                    Death!

III

His Mother's Service to Our Lady

Lady of Heaven and earth, and therewithal
  Crowned Empress of the nether clefts of Hell,—
I, thy poor Christian, on thy name do call,
  Commending me to thee, with thee to dwell,

Albeit in nought I be commendable.
But all mine undeserving may not mar
Such mercies as thy sovereign mercies are;
   Without the which (as true words testify)
No soul can reach thy Heaven so fair and far.
   Even in this faith I choose to live and die.   10

Unto thy Son say thou that I am His,
   And to me graceless make Him gracious.
Sad Mary of Egypt lacked not of that bliss,
   Nor yet the sorrowful clerk Theophilus,
   Whose bitter sins were set aside even thus
Though to the Fiend his bounden service was.
Oh help me, lest in vain for me should pass
   (Sweet Virgin that shalt have no loss thereby!)
The blessed Host and sacring of the Mass.
   Even in this faith I choose to live and die.   20

A pitiful poor woman, shrunk and old,
   I am, and nothing learn'd in letter-lore.
Within my parish-cloister I behold
   A painted Heaven where harps and lutes adore,
   And eke an Hell whose damned folk seethe full sore:
One bringeth fear, the other joy to me.
That joy, great Goddess, make thou mine to be,—
   Thou of whom all must ask it even as I;
And that which faith desires, that let it see.
   For in this faith I choose to live and die.   30

O excellent Virgin Princess! thou didst bear
King Jesus, the most excellent comforter,
Who even of this our weakness craved a share
   And for our sake stooped to us from on high,
Offering to death His young life sweet and fair.
Such as He is, Our Lord, I Him declare,
   And in this faith I choose to live and die.

JOHN OF TOURS

(Old French)

John of Tours is back with peace,
But he comes home ill at ease.

'Good-morrow, mother.' 'Good-morrow, son;
Your wife has borne you a little one.'

'Go now, mother, go before,
Make me a bed upon the floor;

'Very low your foot must fall,
That my wife hear not at all.'

As it neared the midnight toll,
John of Tours gave up his soul.   10

'Tell me now, my mother my dear,
What's the crying that I hear?'

'Daughter, it's the children wake
Crying with their teeth that ache.'

'Tell me though, my mother my dear,
What's the knocking that I hear?'

'Daughter, it's the carpenter
Mending planks upon the stair.'

'Tell me too, my mother my dear,
What's the singing that I hear?'   20

'Daughter, it's the priests in rows
Going round about our house.'

'Tell me then, my mother my dear,
What's the dress that I should wear?'

'Daughter, any reds or blues,
But the black is most in use.'

'Nay, but say, my mother my dear,
Why do you fall weeping here?'

'Oh! the truth must be said,—
It's that John of Tours is dead.' 30

'Mother, let the sexton know
That the grave must be for two;

'Aye, and still have room to spare,
For you must shut the baby there.'

MY FATHER'S CLOSE

(Old French)

INSIDE my father's close,
    (Fly away O my heart away!)
Sweet apple-blossom blows
    So sweet.

Three kings' daughters fair,
    (Fly away O my heart away!)
They lie below it there
    So sweet.

'Ah!' says the eldest one,
    (Fly away O my heart away!) 10
'I think the day's begun
    So sweet.'

'Ah!' says the second one,
    (Fly away O my heart away!)
'Far off I hear the drum
    So sweet.'

'Ah!' says the youngest one,
    (Fly away O my heart away!)
'It's my true love, my own,
    So sweet. 20

'Oh! if he fight and win,'
   (Fly away O my heart away!)
'I keep my love for him,
   So sweet:
Oh! let him lose or win,
   He hath it still complete.'

ONE GIRL

(A combination from Sappho)

I

LIKE the sweet apple which reddens upon the topmost bough,
A-top on the topmost twig,—which the pluckers forgot, somehow,—
Forgot it not, nay, but got it not, for none could get it till now.

II

Like the wild hyacinth flower which on the hills is found,
Which the passing feet of the shepherds for ever tear and wound,
Until the purple blossom is trodden into the ground.

SONNETS AND SONGS

Towards a Work to be called 'The House of Life'

[The first twenty-eight sonnets and the seven first songs treat of love. These and the others would belong to separate sections of the projected work.]

Sonnet I

BRIDAL BIRTH

As when desire, long darkling, dawns, and first
  The mother looks upon the newborn child,
  Even so my Lady stood at gaze and smiled
When her soul knew at length the Love it nursed.
Born with her life, creature of poignant thirst
  And exquisite hunger, at her heart Love lay
  Quickening in darkness, till a voice that day
Cried on him, and the bonds of birth were burst.

Now, shielded in his wings, our faces yearn
  Together, as his fullgrown feet now range
  The grove, and his warm hands our couch prepare:
Till to his song our bodiless souls in turn
  Be born his children, when Death's nuptial change
  Leaves us for light the halo of his hair.

Sonnet II

LOVE'S REDEMPTION

O THOU who at Love's hour ecstatically
  Unto my lips dost evermore present
  The body and blood of Love in sacrament ;
Whom I have neared and felt thy breath to be
The inmost incense of his sanctuary ;
  Who without speech hast owned him, and intent
  Upon his will, thy life with mine hast blent,
And murmured o'er the cup, Remember me !—

O what from thee the grace, for me the prize,
  And what to Love the glory,—when the whole
  Of the deep stair thou tread'st to the dim shoal
And weary water of the place of sighs,
And there dost work deliverance, as thine eyes
  Draw up my prisoned spirit to thy soul !

Sonnet III

LOVESIGHT

WHEN do I see thee most, beloved one ?
  When in the light the spirits of mine eyes
  Before thy face, their altar, solemnize
The worship of that Love through thee made known ?
Or when in the dusk hours, (we two alone,)
  Close-kissed and eloquent of still replies
  Thy twilight-hidden glimmering visage lies,
And my soul only sees thy soul its own ?

O love, my love ! if I no more should see
Thyself, nor on the earth the shadow of thee,
  Nor image of thine eyes in any spring,—
How then should sound upon Life's darkening slope
The ground-whirl of the perished leaves of Hope,
  The wind of Death's imperishable wing ?

THE HOUSE OF LIFE

Sonnet IV

THE KISS

What smouldering senses in death's sick delay
   Or seizure of malign vicissitude
   Can rob this body of honour, or denude
This soul of wedding-raiment worn to-day ?
For lo ! even now my lady's lips did play
   With these my lips such consonant interlude
   As laurelled Orpheus longed for when he wooed
The half-drawn hungering face with that last lay.

I was a child beneath her touch,—a man
   When breast to breast we clung, even I and she,—
   A spirit when her spirit looked through me,—
A god when all our life-breath met to fan
Our life-blood, till love's emulous ardours ran,
   Fire within fire, desire in deity.

Sonnet V

NUPTIAL SLEEP

At length their long kiss severed, with sweet smart :
   And as the last slow sudden drops are shed
   From sparkling eaves when all the storm has fled,
So singly flagged the pulses of each heart.
Their bosoms sundered, with the opening start
   Of married flowers to either side outspread
   From the knit stem ; yet still their mouths, burnt red,
Fawned on each other where they lay apart.

Sleep sank them lower than the tide of dreams,
   And their dreams watched them sink, and slid away.
Slowly their souls swam up again, through gleams
   Of watered light and dull drowned waifs of day ;
Till from some wonder of new woods and streams
   He woke, and wondered more : for there she lay.

Sonnet VI

SUPREME SURRENDER

To all the spirits of love that wander by
   Along the love-sown fallowfield of sleep
   My lady lies apparent ; and the deep
Calls to the deep ; and no man sees but I.
The bliss so long afar, at length so nigh,
   Rests there attained. Methinks proud Love must weep
   When Fate's control doth from his harvest reap
The sacred hour for which the years did sigh.

First touched, the hand now warm around my neck
   Taught memory long to mock desire : and lo !
   Across my breast the abandoned hair doth flow,
Where one shorn tress long stirred the longing ache :
And next the heart that trembled for its sake
   Lies the queen-heart in sovereign overthrow.

Sonnet VII

LOVE'S LOVERS

Some ladies love the jewels in Love's zone
   And gold-tipped darts he hath for painless play
   In idle scornful hours he flings away ;
And some that listen to his lute's soft tone
Do love to vaunt the silver praise their own ;
   Some prize his blindfold sight ; and there be they
   Who kissed his wings which brought him yesterday
And thank his wings to-day that he is flown.

My lady only loves the heart of Love :
   Therefore Love's heart, my lady, hath for thee
   His bower of unimagined flower and tree :
There kneels he now, and all-anhungered of
Thine eyes grey-lit in shadowing hair above,
   Seals with thy mouth his immortality.

Sonnet VIII

PASSION AND WORSHIP

One flame-winged brought a white-winged harp-player
  Even where my lady and I lay all alone ;
  Saying : ' Behold, this minstrel is unknown ;
Bid him depart, for I am minstrel here :
Only my strains are to Love's dear ones dear.'
  Then said I : ' Through thine hautboy's rapturous tone
  Unto my lady still this harp makes moan,
And still she deems the cadence deep and clear.'

Then said my lady : ' Thou art Passion of Love,
  And this Love's Worship : both he plights to me.
  Thy mastering music walks the sunlit sea :
But where wan water trembles in the grove
And the wan moon is all the light thereof,
  This harp still makes my name its voluntary.'

Sonnet IX

THE PORTRAIT

O Lord of all compassionate control,
  O Love ! let this my lady's picture glow
  Under my hand to praise her name, and show
Even of her inner self the perfect whole :
That he who seeks her beauty's furthest goal,
  Beyond the light that the sweet glances throw
  And refluent wave of the sweet smile, may know
The very sky and sea-line of her soul.

Lo ! it is done. Above the long lithe throat
  The mouth's mould testifies of voice and kiss,
    The shadowed eyes remember and foresee.
Her face is made her shrine. Let all men note
  That in all years (O Love, thy gift is this !)
    They that would look on her must come to me.

Sonnet X

THE LOVE-LETTER

Warmed by her hand and shadowed by her hair
  As close she leaned and poured her heart through thee,
  Whereof the articulate throbs accompany
The smooth black stream that makes thy whiteness
    fair,—
Sweet fluttering sheet, even of her breath aware,—
  Oh let thy silent song disclose to me
  That soul wherewith her lips and eyes agree
Like married music in Love's answering air.

Fain had I watched her when, at some fond thought,
  Her bosom to the writing closelier press'd,
  And her breast's secrets peered into her breast;
When, through eyes raised an instant, her soul sought
My soul, and from the sudden confluence caught
  The words that made her love the loveliest.

Sonnet XI

THE BIRTH-BOND

Have you not noted, in some family
  Where two were born of a first marriage-bed,
  How still they own their gracious bond, though fed
And nursed on the forgotten breast and knee?—
How to their father's children they shall be
  In act and thought of one goodwill; but each
  Shall for the other have, in silence speech,
And in a word complete community?

Even so, when first I saw you, seemed it, love,
  That among souls allied to mine was yet
One nearer kindred than life hinted of.
  O born with me somewhere that men forget,
  And though in years of sight and sound unmet,
Known for my soul's birth-partner well enough!

Sonnet XII
A DAY OF LOVE

Those envied places which do know her well,
   And are so scornful of this lonely place,
   Even now for once are emptied of her grace :
Nowhere but here she is : and while Love's spell
From his predominant presence doth compel
   All alien hours, an outworn populace,
   The hours of Love fill full the echoing space
With sweet confederate music favourable.

Now many memories make solicitous
   The delicate love-lines of her mouth, till, lit
   With quivering fire, the words take wing from it ;
As here between our kisses we sit thus
   Speaking of things remembered, and so sit
Speechless while things forgotten call to us.

Sonnet XIII
LOVE-SWEETNESS

Sweet dimness of her loosened hair's downfall
   About thy face ; her sweet hands round thy head
   In gracious fostering union garlanded ;
Her tremulous smiles ; her glances' sweet recall
Of love ; her murmuring sighs memorial ;
   Her mouth's culled sweetness by thy kisses shed
   On cheeks and neck and eyelids, and so led
Back to her mouth which answers there for all :—

What sweeter than these things, except the thing
   In lacking which all these would lose their sweet :—
   The confident heart's still fervour ; the swift beat
And soft subsidence of the spirit's wing,
Then when it feels, in cloud-girt wayfaring,
   The breath of kindred plumes against its feet ?

Sonnet XIV

LOVE'S BAUBLES

I STOOD where Love in brimming armfuls bore
   Slight wanton flowers and foolish toys of fruit:
   And round him ladies thronged in warm pursuit,
Fingered and lipped and proffered the strange store:
And from one hand the petal and the core
   Savoured of sleep; and cluster and curled shoot
   Seemed from another hand like shame's salute,—
Gifts that I felt my cheek was blushing for.

At last Love bade my Lady give the same:
   And as I looked, the dew was light thereon;
   And as I took them, at her touch they shone
With inmost heaven-hue of the heart of flame.
   And then Love said: 'Lo! when the hand is hers,
   Follies of love are love's true ministers.'

Sonnet XV

WINGED HOURS

EACH hour until we meet is as a bird
   That wings from far his gradual way along
   The rustling covert of my soul,—his song
Still loudlier trilled through leaves more deeply stirr'd:
But at the hour of meeting, a clear word
   Is every note he sings, in Love's own tongue;
   Yet, Love, thou know'st the sweet strain suffers wrong,
Through our contending kisses oft unheard.

What of that hour at last, when for her sake
   No wing may fly to me nor song may flow;
   When, wandering round my life unleaved, I know
The bloodied feathers scattered in the brake,
   And think how she, far from me, with like eyes
   Sees through the untuneful bough the wingless skies?

Sonnet XVI

LIFE-IN-LOVE

Not in thy body is thy life at all
  But in this lady's lips and hands and eyes ;
  Through these she yields thee life that vivifies
What else were sorrow's servant and death's thrall.
Look on thyself without her, and recall
  The waste remembrance and forlorn surmise
  That lived but in a dead-drawn breath of sighs
O'er vanished hours and hours eventual.

Even so much life hath the poor tress of hair
  Which, stored apart, is all love hath to show
  For heart-beats and for fire-heats long ago ;
Even so much life endures unknown, even where,
  'Mid change the changeless night environeth,
  Lies all that golden hair undimmed in death.

Sonnet XVII

THE LOVE-MOON

' When that dead face, bowered in the furthest years,
  Which once was all the life years held for thee,
  Can now scarce bid the tides of memory
Cast on thy soul a little spray of tears,—
How canst thou gaze into these eyes of hers
  Whom now thy heart delights in, and not see
  Within each orb Love's philtred euphrasy
Make them of buried troth remembrancers ? '

' Nay, pitiful Love, nay, loving Pity ! Well
  Thou knowest that in these twain I have confess'd
Two very voices of thy summoning bell.
  Nay, Master, shall not Death make manifest
In these the culminant changes which approve
The love-moon that must light my soul to Love ? '

Sonnet XVIII

THE MORROW'S MESSAGE

'Thou Ghost,' I said, ' and is thy name To-day ?—
    Yesterday's son, with such an abject brow !—
    And can To-morrow be more pale than thou ? '
While yet I spoke, the silence answered : ' Yea,
Henceforth our issue is all grieved and grey,
    And each beforehand makes such poor avow
    As of old leaves beneath the budding bough
Or night-drift that the sundawn shreds away.'

Then cried I : ' Mother of many malisons,
    O Earth, receive me to thy dusty bed ! '
    But therewithal the tremulous silence said :
' Lo ! Love yet bids thy lady greet thee once :—
Yea, twice,—whereby thy life is still the sun's ;
    And thrice,—whereby the shadow of death is dead.'

Sonnet XIX

SLEEPLESS DREAMS

Girt in dark growths, yet glimmering with one star,
    O night desirous as the nights of youth !
    Why should my heart within thy spell, forsooth,
Now beat, as the bride's finger-pulses are
Quickened within the girdling golden bar ?
    What wings are these that fan my pillow smooth ?
    And why does Sleep, waved back by Joy and Ruth,
Tread softly round and gaze at me from far ?

Nay, night deep-leaved ! And would Love feign in thee
    Some shadowy palpitating grove that bears
    Rest for man's eyes and music for his ears ?
O lonely night ! art thou not known to me,
A thicket hung with masks of mockery
    And watered with the wasteful warmth of tears ?

Sonnet XX
SECRET PARTING

BECAUSE our talk was of the cloud-control
   And moon-track of the journeying face of Fate,
   Her tremulous kisses faltered at love's gate
And her eyes dreamed against a distant goal:
But soon, remembering her how brief the whole
   Of joy, which its own hours annihilate,
   Her set gaze gathered, thirstier than of late,
And as she kissed, her mouth became her soul.

Thence in what ways we wandered, and how strove
   To build with fire-tried vows the piteous home
   Which memory haunts and whither sleep may roam,—
They only know for whom the roof of Love
Is the still-seated secret of the grove,
   Nor spire may rise nor bell be heard therefrom.

Sonnet XXI
PARTED LOVE

WHAT shall be said of this embattled day
   And armed occupation of this night
   By all thy foes beleaguered,—now when sight
Nor sound denotes the loved one far away?
Of these thy vanquished hours what shalt thou say,—
   As every sense to which she dealt delight
   Now labours lonely o'er the stark noon-height
To reach the sunset's desolate disarray?

Stand still, fond fettered wretch! while Memory's art
   Parades the Past before thy face, and lures
   Thy spirit to her passionate portraitures:
Till the tempestuous tide-gates flung apart
Flood with wild will the hollows of thy heart,
   And thy heart rends thee, and thy body endures.

Sonnet XXII

BROKEN MUSIC

The mother will not turn, who thinks she hears
　Her nursling's speech first grow articulate ;
　But breathless with averted eyes elate
She sits, with open lips and open ears,
That it may call her twice. 'Mid doubts and fears
　Thus oft my soul has hearkened ; till the song,
　A central moan for days, at length found tongue.
And the sweet music welled and the sweet tears.

But now, whatever while the soul is fain
　To list that wonted murmur, as it were
The speech-bound sea-shell's low importunate strain,—
　No breath of song, thy voice alone is there,
O bitterly beloved ! and all her gain
　Is but the pang of unpermitted prayer.

Sonnet XXIII

DEATH-IN-LOVE

There came an image in Life's retinue
　That had Love's wings and bore his gonfalon :
　Fair was the web, and nobly wrought thereon,
O soul-sequestered face, thy form and hue !
Bewildering sounds, such as Spring wakens to,
　Shook in its folds ; and through my heart its power
　Sped trackless as the immemorable hour
When birth's dark portal groaned and all was new.

But a veiled woman followed, and she caught
　The banner round its staff, to furl and cling,—
　Then plucked a feather from the bearer's wing,
And held it to his lips that stirred it not,
　And said to me, ' Behold, there is no breath :
　I and this Love are one, and I am Death.'

THE HOUSE OF LIFE

Sonnets XXIV, XXV, XXVI, XXVII

WILLOWWOOD

I

I SAT with Love upon a woodside well,
  Leaning across the water, I and he ;
  Nor ever did he speak nor looked at me,
But touched his lute wherein was audible
The certain secret thing he had to tell :
  Only our mirrored eyes met silently
  In the low wave ; and that sound came to be
The passionate voice I knew ; and my tears fell.

And at their fall, his eyes beneath grew hers ;
And with his foot and with his wing-feathers
  He swept the spring that watered my heart's drouth.
Then the dark ripples spread to waving hair,
And as I stooped, her own lips rising there
  Bubbled with brimming kisses at my mouth.

II

AND now Love sang : but his was such a song,
  So meshed with half-remembrance hard to free,
  As souls disused in death's sterility
May sing when the new birthday tarries long.
And I was made aware of a dumb throng
  That stood aloof, one form by every tree,
  All mournful forms, for each was I or she,
The shades of those our days that had no tongue.

They looked on us, and knew us and were known ;
  While fast together, alive from the abyss,
  Clung the soul-wrung implacable close kiss ;
And pity of self through all made broken moan
Which said, ' For once, for once, for once alone ! '
  And still Love sang, and what he sang was this :—

III

'O YE, all ye that walk in Willowwood,
  That walk with hollow faces burning white;
What fathom-depth of soul-struck widowhood,
  What long, what longer hours, one lifelong night,
Ere ye again, who so in vain have wooed
  Your last hope lost, who so in vain invite
Your lips to that their unforgotten food,
  Ere ye, ere ye again shall see the light!

Alas! the bitter banks in Willowwood,
  With tear-spurge wan, with blood-wort burning red:
Alas! if ever such a pillow could
  Steep deep the soul in sleep till she were dead,—
Better all life forget her than this thing,
That Willowwood should hold her wandering!'

IV

So sang he: and as meeting rose and rose
  Together cling through the wind's wellaway,
  Nor change at once, yet near the end of day
The leaves drop loosened where the heart-stain glows,—
So when the song died did the kiss unclose;
  And her face fell back drowned, and was as grey
  As its grey eyes; and if it ever may
Meet mine again I know not if Love knows.

Only I know that I leaned low and drank
A long draught from the water where she sank,
  Her breath and all her tears and all her soul:
And as I leaned, I know I felt Love's face
Pressed on my neck with moan of pity and grace,
  Till both our heads were in his aureole.

Sonnet XXVIII

STILLBORN LOVE

The hour which might have been yet might not be,
  Which man's and woman's heart conceived and bore
  Yet whereof life was barren,—on what shore
Bides it the breaking of Time's weary sea ?
Bondchild of all consummate joys set free,
  It somewhere sighs and serves, and mute before
  The house of Love, hears through the echoing door
His hours elect in choral consonancy.

But lo ! what wedded souls now hand in hand
Together tread at last the immortal strand
  With eyes where burning memory lights love home ?
Lo ! how the little outcast hour has turned
And leaped to them and in their faces yearned :—
  'I am your child : O parents, ye have come !'

Sonnet XXIX

INCLUSIVENESS

The changing guests, each in a different mood,
  Sit at the roadside table and arise :
  And every life among them in likewise
Is a soul's board set daily with new food.
What man has bent o'er his son's sleep, to brood
  How that face shall watch his when cold it lies ?—
  Or thought, as his own mother kissed his eyes,
Of what her kiss was when his father wooed ?

May not this ancient room thou sit'st in dwell
  In separate living souls for joy or pain ?
  Nay, all its corners may be painted plain
Where Heaven shows pictures of some life spent well ;
  And may be stamped, a memory all in vain,
Upon the sight of lidless eyes in Hell.

Sonnet XXX

KNOWN IN VAIN

As two whose love, first foolish, widening scope,
   Knows suddenly, with music high and soft,
   The Holy of holies ; who because they scoff'd
Are now amazed with shame, nor dare to cope
With the whole truth aloud, lest heaven should ope ;
   Yet, at their meetings, laugh not as they laugh'd
   In speech ; nor speak, at length ; but sitting oft
Together, within hopeless sight of hope
   For hours are silent :—So it happeneth
   When Work and Will awake too late, to gaze
After their life sailed by, and hold their breath.
   Ah ! who shall dare to search through what sad maze
   Thenceforth their incommunicable ways
Follow the desultory feet of Death ?

Sonnet XXXI

THE LANDMARK

Was *that* the landmark ? What,—the foolish well
   Whose wave, low down, I did not stoop to drink,
   But sat and flung the pebbles from its brink
In sport to send its imaged skies pell-mell,
(And mine own image, had I noted well !)—
   Was that my point of turning ?—I had thought
   The stations of my course should rise unsought,
As altar-stone or ensigned citadel.

But lo ! the path is missed, I must go back,
   And thirst to drink when next I reach the spring
Which once I stained, which since may have grown black.
   Yet though no light be left nor bird now sing
   As here I turn, I'll thank God, hastening,
That the same goal is still on the same track.

Sonnet XXXII

A DARK DAY

The gloom that breathes upon me with these airs
  Is like the drops which strike the traveller's brow
  Who knows not, darkling, if they bring him now
Fresh storm, or be old rain the covert bears.
Ah ! bodes this hour some harvest of new tares,
  Or hath but memory of the day whose plough
  Sowed hunger once,—the night at length when thou,
O prayer found vain, didst fall from out my prayers ?

How prickly were the growths which yet how smooth,
  Along the hedgerows of this journey shed,
Lie by Time's grace till night and sleep may soothe !
  Even as the thistledown from pathsides dead
Gleaned by a girl in autumns of her youth,
  Which one new year makes soft her marriage-bed.

Sonnet XXXIII

THE HILL SUMMIT

This feast-day of the sun, his altar there
  In the broad west has blazed for vesper-song ;
  And I have loitered in the vale too long
And gaze now a belated worshipper.
Yet may I not forget that I was 'ware,
  So journeying, of his face at intervals
  Transfigured where the fringed horizon falls,—
A fiery bush with coruscating hair.

And now that I have climbed and won this height,
  I must tread downward through the sloping shade
And travel the bewildered tracks till night.
  Yet for this hour I still may here be stayed
  And see the gold air and the silver fade
And the last bird fly into the last light.

Sonnet XXXIV

BARREN SPRING

Once more the changed year's turning wheel returns:
   And as a girl sails balanced in the wind,
   And now before and now again behind
Stoops as it swoops, with cheek that laughs and burns,—
So Spring comes merry towards me now, but earns
   No answering smile from me, whose life is twin'd
   With the dead boughs that winter still must bind,
And whom to-day the Spring no more concerns.

Behold, this crocus is a withering flame;
   This snowdrop, snow; this apple-blossom's part
   To breed the fruit that breeds the serpent's art.
Nay, for these Spring-flowers, turn thy face from them,
Nor gaze till on the year's last lily-stem
   The white cup shrivels round the golden heart.

Sonnets XXXV, XXXVI, XXXVII

THE CHOICE

I

Eat thou and drink; to-morrow thou shalt die.
   Surely the earth, that's wise being very old,
   Needs not our help. Then loose me, love, and hold
Thy sultry hair up from my face; that I
May pour for thee this golden wine, brim-high,
   Till round the glass thy fingers glow like gold.
   We'll drown all hours: thy song, while hours are toll'd,
Shall leap, as fountains veil the changing sky.

Now kiss, and think that there are really those,
   My own high-bosomed beauty, who increase
      Vain gold, vain lore, and yet might choose our way!
      Through many days they toil; then comes a day
   They die not,—never having lived,—but cease;
And round their narrow lips the mould falls close.

II

WATCH thou and fear : to-morrow thou shalt die.
  Or art thou sure thou shalt have time for death ?
  Is not the day which God's word promiseth
To come man knows not when ?   In yonder sky,
Now while we speak, the sun speeds forth : can I
  Or thou assure him of his goal ?   God's breath
  Even at the moment haply quickeneth
The air to a flame ; till spirits, always nigh
Though screened and hid, shall walk the daylight here.
  And dost thou prate of all that man shall do ?
    Canst thou, who hast but plagues, presume to be
    Glad in his gladness that comes after thee ?
  Will *his* strength slay *thy* worm in Hell ?   Go to :
Cover thy countenance, and watch, and fear.

III

THINK thou and act ; to-morrow thou shalt die.
  Outstretched in the sun's warmth upon the shore,
  Thou say'st : ' Man's measured path is all gone o'er :
Up all his years, steeply, with strain and sigh,
Man clomb until he touched the truth ; and I,
  Even I, am he whom it was destined for.'
  How should this be ?   Art thou then so much more
Than they who sowed, that thou shouldst reap thereby?

Nay, come up hither.   From this wave-washed mound
  Unto the furthest flood-brim look with me ;
Then reach on with thy thought till it be drown'd.
  Miles and miles distant though the grey line be,
And though thy soul sail leagues and leagues beyond,—
  Still, leagues beyond those leagues, there is more sea.

Sonnet XXXVIII

HOARDED JOY

I said : ' Nay, pluck not,—let the first fruit be :
   Even as thou sayest, it is sweet and red,
   But let it ripen still. The tree's bent head
Sees in the stream its own fecundity
And bides the day of fulness. Shall not we
   At the sun's hour that day possess the shade,
   And claim our fruit before its ripeness fade,
And eat it from the branch and praise the tree ? '

I say : ' Alas ! our fruit hath wooed the sun
   Too long,—'tis fallen and floats adown the stream.
Lo, the last clusters ! Pluck them every one,
   And let us sup with summer ; ere the gleam
Of autumn set the year's pent sorrow free,
And the woods wail like echoes from the sea.'

Sonnet XXXIX

VAIN VIRTUES

What is the sorriest thing that enters Hell ?
   None of the sins,—but this and that fair deed
   Which a soul's sin at length could supersede.
These yet are virgins, whom death's timely knell
Might once have sainted ; whom the fiends compel
   Together now, in snake-bound shuddering sheaves
   Of anguish, while the scorching bridegroom leaves
Their refuse maidenhood abominable.

Night sucks them down, the garbage of the pit,
   Whose names, half entered in the book of Life,
   Were God's desire at noon. And as their hair
And eyes sink last, the Torturer deigns no whit
   To gaze, but, yearning, waits his worthier wife,
   The Sin still blithe on earth that sent them there.

SONNET XL

LOST DAYS

The lost days of my life until to-day,
  What were they, could I see them on the street
  Lie as they fell ? Would they be ears of wheat
Sown once for food but trodden into clay ?
Or golden coins squandered and still to pay ?
  Or drops of blood dabbling the guilty feet ?
  Or such spilt water as in dreams must cheat
The throats of men in Hell, who thirst alway ?

I do not see them here ; but after death
  God knows I know the faces I shall see,
Each one a murdered self, with low last breath.
  ' I am thyself,—what hast thou done to me ? '
' And I—and I—thyself,' (lo ! each one saith,)
  ' And thou thyself to all eternity ! '

SONNET XLI

DEATH'S SONGSTERS

When first that horse, within whose populous womb
  The birth was death, o'ershadowed Troy with fate,
  Her elders, dubious of its Grecian freight,
Brought Helen there to sing the songs of home :
She whispered, ' Friends, I am alone ; come, come ! '
  Then, crouched within, Ulysses waxed afraid,
  And on his comrades' quivering mouths he laid
His hands, and held them till the voice was dumb.

The same was he who, lashed to his own mast,
  There where the sea-flowers screen the charnel-caves,
Beside the sirens' singing island pass'd,
  Till sweetness failed along the inveterate waves. . . .
Say, soul,—are songs of Death no heaven to thee,
Nor shames her lip the cheek of Victory ?

Sonnet XLII

'RETRO ME, SATHANA!'

Get thee behind me. Even as, heavy-curled,
  Stooping against the wind, a charioteer
  Is snatched from out his chariot by the hair,
So shall Time be; and as the void car, hurled
Abroad by reinless steeds, even so the world:
  Yea, even as chariot-dust upon the air,
  It shall be sought and not found anywhere.
Get thee behind me, Satan. Oft unfurled,
Thy perilous wings can beat and break like lath
  Much mightiness of men to win thee praise.
  Leave these weak feet to tread in narrow ways.
Thou still, upon the broad vine-sheltered path,
Mayst wait the turning of the phials of wrath
  For certain years, for certain months and days.

Sonnet XLIII

LOST ON BOTH SIDES

As when two men have loved a woman well,
  Each hating each, through Love's and Death's deceit;
  Since not for either this stark marriage-sheet
And the long pauses of this wedding-bell;
Yet o'er her grave the night and day dispel
  At last their feud forlorn, with cold and heat;
  Nor other than dear friends to death may fleet
The two lives left that most of her can tell:—

So separate hopes, which in a soul had wooed
  The one same Peace, strove with each other long,
    And Peace before their faces perished since:
So through that soul, in restless brotherhood,
  They roam together now, and wind among
    Its bye-streets, knocking at the dusty inns.

Sonnet XLIV

THE SUN'S SHAME

BEHOLDING youth and hope in mockery caught
　From life ; and mocking pulses that remain
　When the soul's death of bodily death is fain ;
Honour unknown, and honour known unsought ;
And penury's sedulous self-torturing thought
　On gold, whose master therewith buys his bane ;
　And longed-for woman longing all in vain
For lonely man with love's desire distraught ;
And wealth, and strength, and power, and pleasantness,
　Given unto bodies of whose souls men say,
　None poor and weak, slavish and foul, as they :—
Beholding these things, I behold no less
The blushing morn and blushing eve confess
　The shame that loads the intolerable day.

Sonnet XLV

THE VASE OF LIFE

AROUND the vase of Life at your slow pace
　He has not crept, but turned it with his hands,
　And all its sides already understands.
There, girt, one breathes alert for some great race ;
Whose road runs far by sands and fruitful space ;
　Who laughs, yet through the jolly throng has pass'd ;
　Who weeps, nor stays for weeping ; who at last,
A youth, stands somewhere crowned, with silent face.

And he has filled this vase with wine for blood,
　With blood for tears, with spice for burning vow,
　　With watered flowers for buried love most fit ;
And would have cast it shattered to the flood,
　Yet in Fate's name has kept it whole ; which now
　　Stands empty till his ashes fall in it.

Sonnet XLVI

A SUPERSCRIPTION

Look in my face ; my name is Might-have-been ;
   I am also called No-more, Too-late, Farewell ;
   Unto thine ear I hold the dead-sea shell
Cast up thy Life's foam-fretted feet between ;
Unto thine eyes the glass where that is seen
   Which had Life's form and Love's, but by my spell
   Is now a shaken shadow intolerable,
Of ultimate things unuttered the frail screen.

Mark me, how still I am ! But should there dart
   One moment through thy soul the soft surprise
   Of that winged Peace which lulls the breath of sighs,—
Then shalt thou see me smile, and turn apart
Thy visage to mine ambush at thy heart
   Sleepless with cold commemorative eyes.

Sonnet XLVII

HE AND I

Whence came his feet into my field, and why ?
   How is it that he sees it all so drear ?
   How do I see his seeing, and how hear
The name his bitter silence knows it by ?
This was the little fold of separate sky
   Whose pasturing clouds in the soul's atmosphere
   Drew living light from one continual year :
How should he find it lifeless ? He, or I ?

Lo ! this new Self now wanders round my field,
   With plaints for every flower, and for each tree
   A moan, the sighing wind's auxiliary :
And o'er sweet waters of my life, that yield
Unto his lips no draught but tears unseal'd,
   Even in my place he weeps. Even I, not he.

THE HOUSE OF LIFE

Sonnets XLVIII, XLIX

NEWBORN DEATH

I

To-day Death seems to me an infant child
  Which her worn mother Life upon my knee
  Has set to grow my friend and play with me;
If haply so my heart might be beguil'd
To find no terrors in a face so mild,—
  If haply so my weary heart might be
  Unto the newborn milky eyes of thee,
O Death, before resentment reconcil'd.

How long, O Death? And shall thy feet depart
  Still a young child's with mine, or wilt thou stand
Fullgrown the helpful daughter of my heart,
  What time with thee indeed I reach the strand
Of the pale wave which knows thee what thou art,
  And drink it in the hollow of thy hand?

II

And thou, O Life, the lady of all bliss,
  With whom, when our first heart beat full and fast,
  I wandered till the haunts of men were pass'd,
And in fair places found all bowers amiss
Till only woods and waves might hear our kiss,
  While to the winds all thought of Death we cast:—
  Ah, Life! and must I have from thee at last
No smile to greet me and no babe but this?

Lo! Love, the child once ours; and Song, whose hair
  Blew like a flame and blossomed like a wreath;
And Art, whose eyes were worlds by God found fair;
  These o'er the book of Nature mixed their breath
With neck-twined arms, as oft we watched them there:
  And did these die that thou mightst bear me Death?

Sonnet L

THE ONE HOPE

When vain desire at last and vain regret
  Go hand in hand to death, and all is vain,
  What shall assuage the unforgotten pain
And teach the unforgetful to forget?
Shall Peace be still a sunk stream long unmet,—
  Or may the soul at once in a green plain
  Stoop through the spray of some sweet life-fountain
And cull the dew-drenched flowering amulet?

Ah! when the wan soul in that golden air
  Between the scriptured petals softly blown
  Peers breathless for the gift of grace unknown,—
Ah! let none other written spell soe'er
But only the one Hope's one name be there,—
  Not less nor more, but even that word alone.

Song I

LOVE-LILY

Between the hands, between the brows,
  Between the lips of Love-Lily,
A spirit is born whose birth endows
  My blood with fire to burn through me;
Who breathes upon my gazing eyes,
  Who laughs and murmurs in mine ear,
At whose least touch my colour flies,
  And whom my life grows faint to hear.

Within the voice, within the heart,
  Within the mind of Love-Lily,
A spirit is born who lifts apart
  His tremulous wings and looks at me;
Who on my mouth his finger lays,
  And shows, while whispering lutes confer,
That Eden of Love's watered ways
  Whose winds and spirits worship her.

THE HOUSE OF LIFE

Brows, hands, and lips, heart, mind, and voice,
    Kisses and words of Love-Lily,—
Oh! bid me with your joy rejoice
    Till riotous longing rest in me!
Ah! let not hope be still distraught,
    But find in her its gracious goal,
Whose speech Truth knows not from her thought
    Nor Love her body from her soul.

Song II

FIRST LOVE REMEMBERED

PEACE in her chamber, wheresoe'er
    It be, a holy place:
The thought still brings my soul such grace
    As morning meadows wear.

Whether it still be small and light,
    A maid's who dreams alone,
As from her orchard-gate the moon
    Its ceiling showed at night:

Or whether, in a shadow dense
    As nuptial hymns invoke,
Innocent maidenhood awoke
    To married innocence:

There still the thanks unheard await
    The unconscious gift bequeathed;
For there my soul this hour has breathed
    An air inviolate.

Song III

PLIGHTED PROMISE

In a soft-complexioned sky,
    Fleeting rose and kindling grey,
Have you seen Aurora fly
    At the break of day?

So my maiden, so my plighted may
   Blushing cheek and gleaming eye
      Lifts to look my way.

Where the inmost leaf is stirred
   With the heart-beat of the grove,
Have you heard a hidden bird
   Cast her note above?
So my lady, so my lovely love,
   Echoing Cupid's prompted word,
      Makes a tune thereof.

Have you seen, at heaven's mid-height,
   In the moon-rack's ebb and tide,
Venus leap forth burning white,
   Dian pale and hide?
So my bright breast-jewel, so my bride,
   One sweet night, when fear takes flight,
      Shall leap against my side.

Song IV

SUDDEN LIGHT

I HAVE been here before,
   But when or how I cannot tell:
I know the grass beyond the door,
   The sweet keen smell,
The sighing sound, the lights around the shore.

You have been mine before,—
   How long ago I may not know:
But just when at that swallow's soar
   Your neck turned so,
Some veil did fall,—I knew it all of yore.

Then, now,—perchance again! . . .
   O round mine eyes your tresses shake!
Shall we not lie as we have lain
   Thus for Love's sake,
And sleep, and wake, yet never break the chain?

THE HOUSE OF LIFE

Song V

A LITTLE WHILE

A LITTLE while a little love
　　The hour yet bears for thee and me
　　Who have not drawn the veil to see
If still our heaven be lit above.
Thou merely, at the day's last sigh,
　　Hast felt thy soul prolong the tone;
And I have heard the night-wind cry
　　And deemed its speech mine own.

A little while a little love
　　The scattering autumn hoards for us
　　Whose bower is not yet ruinous
Nor quite unleaved our songless grove.
Only across the shaken boughs
　　We hear the flood-tides seek the sea,
And deep in both our hearts they rouse
　　One wail for thee and me.

A little while a little love
　　May yet be ours who have not said
　　The word it makes our eyes afraid
To know that each is thinking of.
Not yet the end : be our lips dumb
　　In smiles a little season yet :
I'll tell thee, when the end is come,
　　How we may best forget.

Song VI

THE SONG OF THE BOWER

SAY, is it day, is it dusk in thy bower,
　　Thou whom I long for, who longest for me ?
Oh ! be it light, be it night, 'tis Love's hour,
　　Love's that is fettered as Love's that is free.

Free Love has leaped to that innermost chamber,
　　Oh! the last time, and the hundred before:
Fettered Love, motionless, can but remember,
　　Yet something that sighs from him passes the door.

Nay, but my heart when it flies to thy bower,
　　What does it find there that knows it again?
There it must droop like a shower-beaten flower,
　　Red at the rent core and dark with the rain.
Ah! yet what shelter is still shed above it,—
　　What waters still image its leaves torn apart?
Thy soul is the shade that clings round it to love it,
　　And tears are its mirror deep down in thy heart.

What were my prize, could I enter thy bower,
　　This day, to-morrow, at eve or at morn?
Large lovely arms and a neck like a tower,
　　Bosom then heaving that now lies forlorn.
Kindled with love-breath, (the sun's kiss is colder!)
　　Thy sweetness all near me, so distant to-day;
My hand round thy neck and thy hand on my shoulder,
　　My mouth to thy mouth as the world melts away.

What is it keeps me afar from thy bower,—
　　My spirit, my body, so fain to be there?
Waters engulfing or fires that devour?—
　　Earth heaped against me or death in the air?
Nay, but in day-dreams, for terror, for pity,
　　The trees wave their heads with an omen to tell;
Nay, but in night-dreams, throughout the dark city,
　　The hours, clashed together, lose count in the bell.

Shall I not one day remember thy bower,
　　One day when all days are one day to me?—
Thinking, 'I stirred not, and yet had the power,'—
　　Yearning, 'Ah God, if again it might be!'
Peace, peace! such a small lamp illumes, on this highway,
　　So dimly so few steps in front of my feet,—
Yet shows me that her way is parted from my way....
　　Out of sight, beyond light, at what goal may we meet?

Song VII

PENUMBRA

I DID not look upon her eyes
(Though scarcely seen, with no surprise,
'Mid many eyes a single look),
Because they should not gaze rebuke,
At night, from stars in sky and brook.

I did not take her by the hand
(Though little was to understand
From touch of hand all friends might take),
Because it should not prove a flake
Burnt in my palm to boil and ache.

I did not listen to her voice
(Though none had noted, where at choice
All might rejoice in listening),
Because no such a thing should cling
In the wood's moan at evening.

I did not cross her shadow once
(Though from the hollow west the sun's
Last shadow runs along so far),
Because in June it should not bar
My ways, at noon when fevers are.

They told me she was sad that day
(Though wherefore tell what love's soothsay,
Sooner than they, did register?),
And my heart leapt and wept to her,
And yet I did not speak nor stir.

So shall the tongues of the sea's foam
(Though many voices therewith come
From drowned hope's home to cry to me),
Bewail one hour the more, when sea
And wind are one with memory.

Song VIII

THE WOODSPURGE

The wind flapped loose, the wind was still,
Shaken out dead from tree and hill :
I had walked on at the wind's will,—
I sat now, for the wind was still.

Between my knees my forehead was,—
My lips, drawn in, said not Alas !
My hair was over in the grass,
My naked ears heard the day pass.

My eyes, wide open, had the run
Of some ten weeds to fix upon ;
Among those few, out of the sun,
The woodspurge flowered, three cups in one.

From perfect grief there need not be
Wisdom or even memory :
One thing then learnt remains to me,—
The woodspurge has a cup of three.

Song IX

THE HONEYSUCKLE

I plucked a honeysuckle where
  The hedge on high is quick with thorn,
  And climbing for the prize, was torn,
And fouled my feet in quag-water ;
  And by the thorns and by the wind
  The blossom that I took was thinn'd
And yet I found it sweet and fair.

Thence to a richer growth I came,
  Where, nursed in mellow intercourse,
  The honeysuckles sprang by scores,
Not harried like my single stem,
  All virgin lamps of scent and dew.
  So from my hand that first I threw,
Yet plucked not any more of them.

Song X

A YOUNG FIR-WOOD

THESE little firs to-day are things
    To clasp into a giant's cap,
    Or fans to suit his lady's lap.
From many winters many springs
    Shall cherish them in strength and sap,
    Till they be marked upon the map,
A wood for the wind's wanderings.

All seed is in the sower's hands :
    And what at first was trained to spread
    Its shelter for some single head,—
Yea, even such fellowship of wands,—
    May hide the sunset, and the shade
    Of its great multitude be laid
Upon the earth and elder sands.

Song XI

THE SEA-LIMITS

CONSIDER the sea's listless chime :
    Time's self it is, made audible,—
    The murmur of the earth's own shell.
Secret continuance sublime
    Is the sea's end : our sight may pass
    No furlong further. Since time was,
This sound hath told the lapse of time.

No quiet, which is death's,—it hath
    The mournfulness of ancient life,
    Enduring always at dull strife.
As the world's heart of rest and wrath,
    Its painful pulse is in the sands.
    Last utterly, the whole sky stands,
Grey and not known, along its path.

Listen alone beside the sea,
  Listen alone among the woods;
  Those voices of twin solitudes
Shall have one sound alike to thee:
  Hark where the murmurs of thronged men
  Surge and sink back and surge again,—
Still the one voice of wave and tree.

Gather a shell from the strown beach
  And listen at its lips: they sigh
  The same desire and mystery,
The echo of the whole sea's speech.
  And all mankind is thus at heart
  Not anything but what thou art:
And Earth, Sea, Man, are all in each.

SONNETS FOR PICTURES

AND OTHER SONNETS

FOR

'OUR LADY OF THE ROCKS'

By Leonardo da Vinci

Mother, is this the darkness of the end,
  The Shadow of Death ? and is that outer sea
  Infinite imminent Eternity ?
And does the death-pang by man's seed sustain'd
In Time's each instant cause thy face to bend
  Its silent prayer upon the Son, while he
  Blesses the dead with his hand silently
To his long day which hours no more offend ?

Mother of grace, the pass is difficult,
  Keen as these rocks, and the bewildered souls
    Throng it like echoes, blindly shuddering through.
  Thy name, O Lord, each spirit's voice extols,
    Whose peace abides in the dark avenue
Amid the bitterness of things occult.

FOR

A VENETIAN PASTORAL

BY GIORGIONE

(*In the Louvre*)

WATER, for anguish of the solstice :—nay,
  But dip the vessel slowly,—nay, but lean
  And hark how at its verge the wave sighs in
Reluctant. Hush ! Beyond all depth away
The heat lies silent at the brink of day :
  Now the hand trails upon the viol-string
  That sobs, and the brown faces cease to sing,
Sad with the whole of pleasure. Whither stray
Her eyes now, from whose mouth the slim pipes creep
  And leave it pouting, while the shadowed grass
    Is cool against her naked side ? Let be :—
Say nothing now unto her lest she weep,
  Nor name this ever. Be it as it was,—
    Life touching lips with Immortality.

FOR

AN ALLEGORICAL DANCE OF WOMEN

BY ANDREA MANTEGNA

(*In the Louvre*)

SCARCELY, I think ; yet it indeed *may* be
  The meaning reached him, when this music rang
  Clear through his frame, a sweet possessive pang,
And he beheld these rocks and that ridged sea.
But I believe that, leaning tow'rds them, he
  Just felt their hair carried across his face
  As each girl passed him ; nor gave ear to trace
How many feet ; nor bent assuredly
His eyes from the blind fixedness of thought
  To know the dancers. It is bitter glad
    Even unto tears. Its meaning filleth it,
    A secret of the wells of Life : to wit :—
The heart's each pulse shall keep the sense it had
With all, though the mind's labour run to nought.

FOR
'RUGGIERO AND ANGELICA'
By Ingres

I

A REMOTE sky, prolonged to the sea's brim:
   One rock-point standing buffeted alone,
   Vexed at its base with a foul beast unknown,
Hell-birth of geomaunt and teraphim:
A knight, and a winged creature bearing him,
   Reared at the rock: a woman fettered there,
   Leaning into the hollow with loose hair
And throat let back and heartsick trail of limb.

The sky is harsh, and the sea shrewd and salt:
   Under his lord the griffin-horse ramps blind
     With rigid wings and tail. The spear's lithe stem
   Thrills in the roaring of those jaws: behind,
That evil length of body chafes at fault.
     She doth not hear nor see—she knows of them.

II

CLENCH thine eyes now,—'tis the last instant, girl:
   Draw in thy senses, set thy knees, and take
   One breath for all: thy life is keen awake,—
Thou mayst not swoon. Was that the scattered whirl
Of its foam drenched thee?—or the waves that curl
   And split, bleak spray wherein thy temples ache?
   Or was it his the champion's blood to flake
Thy flesh?—or thine own blood's anointing, girl?

Now, silence: for the sea's is such a sound
   As irks not silence; and except the sea,
     All now is still. Now the dead thing doth cease
   To writhe, and drifts. He turns to her: and she,
Cast from the jaws of Death, remains there, bound,
     Again a woman in her nakedness.

FOR

'THE WINE OF CIRCE'

BY EDWARD BURNE JONES

DUSK-HAIRED and gold-robed o'er the golden wine
   She stoops, wherein, distilled of death and shame,
   Sink the black drops ; while, lit with fragrant flame,
Round her spread board the golden sunflowers shine.
Doth Helios here with Hecatè combine
   (O Circe, thou their votaress !) to proclaim
   For these thy guests all rapture in Love's name,
Till pitiless Night gave Day the countersign ?

Lords of their hour, they come. And by her knee
   Those cowering beasts, their equals heretofore,
Wait ; who with them in new equality
   To-night shall echo back the unchanging roar
   Which sounds for ever from the tide-strown shore
Where the dishevelled seaweed hates the sea.

MARY'S GIRLHOOD

(*For a Picture*)

THIS is that blessed Mary, pre-elect
   God's Virgin. Gone is a great while, and she
   Dwelt young in Nazareth of Galilee.
Unto God's will she brought devout respect,
Profound simplicity of intellect,
   And supreme patience. From her mother's knee
   Faithful and hopeful ; wise in charity ;
Strong in grave peace ; in pity circumspect.

So held she through her girlhood ; as it were
   An angel-watered lily, that near God
     Grows and is quiet. Till, one dawn at home,
She woke in her white bed, and had no fear
   At all,—yet wept till sunshine, and felt awed :
     Because the fulness of the time was come.

THE PASSOVER IN THE HOLY FAMILY
(*For a Drawing*) [1]

Here meet together the prefiguring day
  And day prefigured. 'Eating, thou shalt stand,
Feet shod, loins girt, thy road-staff in thine hand,
With blood-stained door and lintel,'—did God say
By Moses' mouth in ages passed away.
  And now, where this poor household doth comprise
  At Paschal-Feast two kindred families,—
Lo! the slain lamb confronts the Lamb to slay.

The pyre is piled. What agony's crown attained,
  What shadow of death the Boy's fair brow subdues
Who holds that blood wherewith the porch is stained
  By Zachary the priest? John binds the shoes
  He deemed himself not worthy to unloose;
And Mary culls the bitter herbs ordained.

MARY MAGDALENE
AT THE DOOR OF SIMON THE PHARISEE
(*For a Drawing*) [2]

Why wilt thou cast the roses from thine hair?
Nay, be thou all a rose,—wreath, lips, and cheek.
Nay, not this house,—that banquet-house we seek;
See how they kiss and enter; come thou there.
This delicate day of love we two will share
  Till at our ear love's whispering night shall speak.
  What, sweet one,—hold'st thou still the foolish freak?
Nay, when I kiss thy feet they'll leave the stair.'

'Oh loose me! See'st thou not my Bridegroom's face
  That draws me to Him? For His feet my kiss,
  My hair, my tears He craves to-day:—and oh!
What words can tell what other day and place
  Shall see me clasp those blood-stained feet of His?
  He needs me, calls me, loves me: let me go!'

---

[1] The scene is in the house-porch, where Christ holds a bowl of blood from which Zacharias is sprinkling the posts and lintel. Joseph has brought the lamb and Elisabeth lights the pyre. The shoes which John fastens and the bitter herbs which Mary is gathering form part of the ritual.

[2] In the drawing Mary has left a festal procession, and is ascending by a sudden impulse the steps of the house where she sees Christ. Her lover has followed her and is trying to turn her back.

SAINT LUKE THE PAINTER

(For a Drawing)

GIVE honour unto Luke Evangelist;
  For he it was (the aged legends say)
  Who first taught Art to fold her hands and pray.
Scarcely at once she dared to rend the mist
Of devious symbols; but soon having wist
  How sky-breadth and field-silence and this day
  Are symbols also in some deeper way,
She looked through these to God and was God's priest.

And if, past noon, her toil began to irk,
And she sought talismans, and turned in vain
  To soulless self-reflections of man's skill,—
  Yet now, in this the twilight, she might still
Kneel in the latter grass to pray again,
Ere the night cometh and she may not work.

LILITH

(For a Picture)

OF Adam's first wife, Lilith, it is told
  (The witch he loved before the gift of Eve,)
  That, ere the snake's, her sweet tongue could deceive,
And her enchanted hair was the first gold.
And still she sits, young while the earth is old,
  And, subtly of herself contemplative,
  Draws men to watch the bright net she can weave,
Till heart and body and life are in its hold.

The rose and poppy are her flowers; for where
  Is he not found, O Lilith, whom shed scent
And soft-shed kisses and soft sleep shall snare?
  Lo! as that youth's eyes burned at thine, so went
  Thy spell through him, and left his straight neck bent,
And round his heart one strangling golden hair.

SIBYLLA PALMIFERA

(For a Picture)

UNDER the arch of Life, where love and death,
　Terror and mystery, guard her shrine, I saw
　Beauty enthroned ; and though her gaze struck awe,
I drew it in as simply as my breath.
Hers are the eyes which, over and beneath,
　The sky and sea bend on thee,—which can draw,
　By sea or sky or woman, to one law,
The allotted bondman of her palm and wreath.

This is that Lady Beauty, in whose praise
　Thy voice and hand shake still,—long known to thee
　　By flying hair and fluttering hem,—the beat
　　Following her daily of thy heart and feet,
　How passionately and irretrievably,
In what fond flight, how many ways and days!

VENUS

(For a Picture)

SHE hath the apple in her hand for thee,
　Yet almost in her heart would hold it back ;
　She muses, with her eyes upon the track
Of that which in thy spirit they can see.
Haply, 'Behold, he is at peace,' saith she ;
　'Alas ! the apple for his lips,—the dart
　That follows its brief sweetness to his heart,—
The wandering of his feet perpetually ! '

A little space her glance is still and coy ;
　But if she give the fruit that works her spell,
Those eyes shall flame as for her Phrygian boy.
　Then shall her bird's strained throat the woe foretell,
　And her far seas moan as a single shell,
And her grove glow with love-lit fires of Troy.

CASSANDRA

(For a Drawing) [1]

I

Rend, rend thine hair, Cassandra: he will go.
  Yea, rend thy garments, wring thine hands, and cry
  From Troy still towered to the unreddened sky.
See, all but she that bore thee mock thy woe :—
He most whom that fair woman arms, with show
  Of wrath on her bent brows ; for in this place
  This hour thou bad'st all men in Helen's face
The ravished ravishing prize of Death to know.

What eyes, what ears hath sweet Andromache,
  Save for her Hector's form and step ; as tear
    On tear make salt the warm last kiss he gave ?
He goes. Cassandra's words beat heavily
  Like crows above his crest, and at his ear
    Ring hollow in the shield that shall not save.

II

' O Hector, gone, gone, gone ! O Hector, thee
  Two chariots wait, in Troy long bless'd and curs'd ;
  And Grecian spear and Phrygian sand athirst
Crave from thy veins the blood of victory.
Lo ! long upon our hearth the brand had we,
  Lit for the roof-tree's ruin : and to-day
  The ground-stone quits the wall,—the wind hath way,—
And higher and higher the wings of fire are free.

O Paris, Paris ! O thou burning brand,
  Thou beacon of the sea whence Venus rose,
Lighting thy race to shipwreck ! Even that hand
  Wherewith she took thine apple let her close
  Within thy curls at last, and while Troy glows
Lift thee her trophy to the sea and land.'

[1] The subject shows Cassandra prophesying among her kindred, as Hector leaves them for his last battle. They are on the platform of a fortress, from which the Trojan troops are marching out. Helen is arming Paris ; Priam soothes Hecuba ; and Andromache holds the child to her bosom.

PANDORA

(For a Picture)

WHAT of the end, Pandora ? Was it thine,
 The deed that set these fiery pinions free ?
 Ah ! wherefore did the Olympian consistory
In its own likeness make thee half divine ?
Was it that Juno's brow might stand a sign
 For ever ? and the mien of Pallas be
 A deadly thing ? and that all men might see
In Venus' eyes the gaze of Proserpine ?

What of the end ? These beat their wings at will,
The ill-born things, the good things turned to ill,—
 Powers of the impassioned hours prohibited.
Aye, hug the casket now ! Whither they go
Thou mayst not dare to think : nor canst thou know
 If Hope still pent there be alive or dead.

ON REFUSAL OF AID BETWEEN NATIONS

NOT that the earth is changing, O my God !
 Nor that the seasons totter in their walk,—
 Not that the virulent ill of act and talk
Seethes ever as a winepress ever trod,—
Not therefore are we certain that the rod
 Weighs in thine hand to smite thy world ; though now
 Beneath thine hand so many nations bow,
So many kings :—not therefore, O my God !—

But because Man is parcelled out in men
 Even thus ; because, for any wrongful blow,
 No man not stricken asks, ' I would be told
Why thou dost strike ; ' but his heart whispers then,
' He is he, I am I.' By this we know
 That the earth falls asunder, being old.

ON THE 'VITA NUOVA' OF DANTE

As he that loves oft looks on the dear form
   And guesses how it grew to womanhood,
   And gladly would have watched the beauties **bud**
And the mild fire of precious life wax warm :—
So I, long bound within the threefold charm
   Of Dante's love sublimed to heavenly mood,
   Had marvelled, touching his Beatitude,
How grew such presence from man's shameful **swarm.**

At length within this book I found pourtrayed
   Newborn that Paradisal Love of his,
And simple like a child ; with whose clear aid
   I understood. To such a child as this,
Christ, charging well his chosen ones, forbade
   Offence : ' for lo ! of such my kingdom is.'

DANTIS TENEBRÆ

(In Memory of my Father)

AND did'st thou know indeed, when at the font
   Together with thy name thou gav'st me his,
   That also on thy son must Beatrice
Decline her eyes according to her wont,
Accepting me to be of those that haunt
   The vale of magical dark mysteries
   Where to the hills her poet's foot-track lies
And wisdom's living fountain to his chaunt
Trembles in music ? This is that steep land
   Where he that holds his journey stands at gaze
     Tow'rd sunset, when the clouds like a new **height**
Seem piled to climb. These things I understand :
   For here, where day still soothes my lifted face,
     On thy bowed head, my father, fell the night.

BEAUTY AND THE BIRD

She fluted with her mouth as when one sips,
  And gently waved her golden head, inclin'd
  Outside his cage close to the window-blind;
Till her fond bird, with little turns and dips,
Piped low to her of sweet companionships.
  And when he made an end, some seed took she
  And fed him from her tongue, which rosily
Peeped as a piercing bud between her lips.

And like the child in Chaucer, on whose tongue
  The Blessed Mary laid, when he was dead,
A grain,—who straightway praised her name in song:
  Even so, when she, a little lightly red,
Now turned on me and laughed, I heard the throng
  Of inner voices praise her golden head.

A MATCH WITH THE MOON

Weary already, weary miles to-night
  I walked for bed: and so, to get some ease,
  I dogged the flying moon with similes.
And like a wisp she doubled on my sight
In ponds; and caught in tree-tops like a kite;
  And in a globe of film all vapourish
  Swam full-faced like a silly silver fish;—
Last like a bubble shot the welkin's height
Where my road turned, and got behind me, and sent
  My wizened shadow craning round at me,
  And jeered, ' So, step the measure,—one two three!'—
And if I faced on her, looked innocent.
  But just at parting, halfway down a dell,
  She kissed me for goodnight. So you'll not tell.

AUTUMN IDLENESS

This sunlight shames November where he grieves
  In dead red leaves, and will not let him shun
  The day, though bough with bough be over-run:
But with a blessing every glade receives
High salutation; while from hillock-eaves
  The deer gaze calling, dappled white and dun,
  As if, being foresters of old, the sun
Had marked them with the shade of forest-leaves.

Here dawn to-day unveiled her magic glass;
  Here noon now gives the thirst and takes the dew;
Till eve bring rest when other good things pass.
  And here the lost hours the lost hours renew
While I still lead my shadow o'er the grass,
  Nor know, for longing, that which I should do.

FAREWELL TO THE GLEN

Sweet stream-fed glen, why say 'farewell' to thee
  Who far'st so well and find'st for ever smooth
  The brow of Time where man may read no ruth?
Nay, do thou rather say 'farewell' to me,
Who now fare forth in bitterer fantasy
  Than erst was mine where other shade might soothe
  By other streams, what while in fragrant youth
The bliss of being sad made melancholy.

And yet, farewell! For better shalt thou fare
  When children bathe sweet faces in thy flow
And happy lovers blend sweet shadows there
  In hours to come, than when an hour ago
Thine echoes had but one man's sighs to bear
  And thy trees whispered what he feared to know.

THE MONOCHORD

(*Written during Music*)

Is it the moved air or the moving sound
   That is Life's self and draws my life from me,
   And by instinct ineffable decree
Holds my breath quailing on the bitter bound?
Nay, is it Life or Death, thus thunder-crown'd,
   That 'mid the tide of all emergency
   Now notes my separate wave, and to what sea
Its difficult eddies labour in the ground?

Oh! what is this that knows the road I came,
The flame turned cloud, the cloud returned to flame,
   The lifted shifted steeps and all the way?—
That draws round me at last this wind-warm space,
And in regenerate rapture turns my face
   Upon the devious coverts of dismay?

POEMS AND A PROSE STORY
FROM *The Germ*, 1850

SONNETS FOR PICTURES

I

A Virgin and Child, by Hans Memmeling ; in the Academy of Bruges

MYSTERY : God, Man's Life, born into man
  Of woman. There abideth on her brow
  The ended pang of knowledge, the which now
Is calm assured. Since first her task began,
She hath known all. What more of anguish than
  Endurance oft hath lived through, the whole space
  Through night till night, passed weak upon her face
While like a heavy flood the darkness ran ?
All hath been told her touching her dear Son,
  And all shall be accomplished. Where he sits
    Even now, a babe, he holds the symbol fruit
  Perfect and chosen. Until God permits,
    His soul's elect still have the absolute
Harsh nether darkness, and make painful moan.

II

A Marriage of St. Katharine, by the same ; in the Hospital of St. John at Bruges

MYSTERY : Katharine, the bride of Christ.
  She kneels, and on her hand the holy Child
  Setteth the ring. Her life is sad and mild,
Laid in God's knowledge—ever unenticed
From Him, and in the end thus fitly priced.
  Awe, and the music that is near her, wrought
  Of Angels, hath possessed her eyes in thought :
Her utter joy is her's, and hath sufficed.
There is a pause while Mary Virgin turns
  The leaf, and reads. With eyes on the spread book,
    That damsel at her knees reads after her.
    John whom He loved and John His harbinger
  Listen and watch. Whereon soe'er thou look,
The light is starred in gems, and the gold burns.

THE CARILLON

Antwerp and Bruges

₊ In these and others of the Flemish towns, the *Carillon*, or chimes which have a most fantastic and delicate music, are played almost continually. The custom is very ancient.

    At Antwerp, there is a low wall
        Binding the city, and a moat
        Beneath, that the wind keeps afloat.
    You pass the gates in a slow drawl
    Of wheels. If it is warm at all
        The Carillon will give you thought.

    I climbed the stair in Antwerp church,
        What time the urgent weight of sound
        At sunset seems to heave it round.
    Far up, the Carillon did search
    The wind ; and the birds came to perch
        Far under, where the gables wound.

    In Antwerp harbour on the Scheldt
        I stood along, a certain space
        Of night. The mist was near my face :
    Deep on, the flow was heard and felt.
    The Carillon kept pause, and dwelt
        In music through the silent place.

    At Bruges, when you leave the train,
        —A singing numbness in your ears,—
        The Carillon's first sound appears
    Only the inner moil. Again
    A little minute though—your brain
        Takes quiet, and the whole sense hears.

    John Memmeling and John Van Eyck
        Hold state at Bruges. In sore shame
        I scanned the works that keep their name.
    The Carillon, which then did strike
    Mine ears, was heard of theirs alike :
        It set me closer unto them.

THE CARILLON

I climbed at Bruges all the flight
　The Belfry has of ancient stone.
　　For leagues I saw the east wind blown:
The earth was grey, the sky was white.
I stood so near upon the height
　That my flesh felt the Carillon.

October, 1849.

PAX VOBIS

'Tis of the Father Hilary.
　He strove, but could not pray; so took
　The darkened stair, where his feet shook
A sad blind echo. He kept up
　Slowly. 'Twas a chill sway of air
　That autumn noon within the stair,
Sick, dizzy, like a turning cup.
　His brain perplexed him, void and thin:
　He shut his eyes and felt it spin;
　The obscure deafness hemmed him in.
He said: 'The air is calm outside.'

He leaned unto the gallery
　Where the chime keeps the night and day:
　It hurt his brain,—he could not pray.
He had his face upon the stone:
　Deep 'twixt the narrow shafts, his eye
　Passed all the roofs unto the sky
Whose greyness the wind swept alone.
　Close by his feet he saw it shake
　With wind in pools that the rains make:
　The ripple set his eyes to ache.
He said: 'Calm hath its peace outside.'

He stood within the mystery
　Girding God's blessed Eucharist:
　The organ and the chaunt had ceased:

A few words paused against his ear,
　　Said from the altar : drawn round him,
　　The silence was at rest and dim.
He could not pray. The bell shook clear
　　And ceased. All was great awe,—the breath
　　Of God in man, that warranteth
　　Wholly the inner things of Faith.
He said : ' There is the world outside.'

Ghent : Church of St. Bavon.

HAND AND SOUL

> Rivolsimi in quel lato
> Là 'nde venia la voce,
> E parvemi una luce
> Che lucea quanto stella :
> La mia mente era quella.
> 　　　*Bonaggiunta Urbiciani* (1250).

BEFORE any knowledge of painting was brought to Florence, there were already painters in Lucca, and Pisa, and Arezzo, who feared God and loved the art. The keen, grave workmen from Greece, whose trade it was to sell their own works in Italy and teach Italians to imitate them, had already found rivals of the soil with skill that could forestall their lessons and cheapen their crucifixes and *addolorate*, more years than is supposed before the art came at all into Florence. The pre-eminence to which Cimabue was raised at once by his contemporaries, and which he still retains to a wide extent even in the modern mind, is to be accounted for, partly by the circumstances under which he arose, and partly by that extraordinary *purpose of fortune* born with the lives of some few, and through which it is not a little thing for any who went before, if they are even remembered as the shadows of the coming of such an one, and the voices which prepared his way in the wilderness. It is thus, almost exclusively, that the painters of whom I speak are now known. They have left little, and but little heed is taken of that which men hold to have been surpassed; it is gone like time gone, —a track of dust and dead leaves that merely led to the fountain.

Nevertheless, of very late years and in very rare instances, some signs of a better understanding have become manifest. A case in point is that of the triptyc and two cruciform pictures at Dresden, by Chiaro di Messer Bello dell' Erma, to which the eloquent pamphlet of Dr. Aemmster has at length succeeded in attracting the students. There is another still more solemn and beautiful work, now proved to be by the same hand, in the gallery at Florence. It is the one to which my narrative will relate.

This Chiaro dell' Erma was a young man of very honourable family in Arezzo; where, conceiving art almost, as it were, for himself, and loving it deeply, he endeavoured from early boyhood towards the imitation of any objects offered in nature. The extreme longing after a visible embodiment of his thoughts strengthened as his years increased, more even than his sinews or the blood of his life; until he would feel faint in sunsets and at the sight of stately persons. When he had lived nineteen years, he heard of the famous Giunta Pisano; and, feeling much of admiration, with, perhaps, a little of that envy which youth always feels until it has learned to measure success by time and opportunity, he determined that he would seek out Giunta, and, if possible, become his pupil.

Having arrived in Pisa, he clothed himself in humble apparel, being unwilling that any other thing than the desire he had for knowledge should be his plea with the great painter; and then, leaving his baggage at a house of entertainment, he took his way along the street, asking whom he met for the lodging of Giunta. It soon chanced that one of that city, conceiving him to be a stranger and poor, took him into his house, and refreshed him; afterwards directing him on his way.

When he was brought to speech of Giunta, he said

HAND AND SOUL

merely that he was a student, and that nothing in the world was so much at his heart as to become that which he had heard told of him with whom he was speaking. He was received with courtesy and consideration, and shown into the study of the famous artist. But the forms he saw there were lifeless and incomplete; and a sudden exultation possessed him as he said within himself, 'I am the master of this man.' The blood came at first into his face, but the next moment he was quite pale and fell to trembling. He was able, however, to conceal his emotion; speaking very little to Giunta, but, when he took his leave, thanking him respectfully.

After this, Chiaro's first resolve was, that he would work out thoroughly some one of his thoughts, and let the world know him. But the lesson which he had now learned, of how small a greatness might win fame, and how little there was to strive against, served to make him torpid, and rendered his exertions less continual. Also Pisa was a larger and more luxurious city than Arezzo; and when, in his walks, he saw the great gardens laid out for pleasure, and the beautiful women who passed to and fro, and heard the music that was in the groves of the city at evening, he was taken with wonder that he had never claimed his share of the inheritance of those years in which his youth was cast. And women loved Chiaro; for, in despite of the burthen of study, he was well-favoured and very manly in his walking; and, seeing his face in front, there was a glory upon it, as upon the face of one who feels a light round his hair.

So he put thought from him, and partook of his life. But, one night, being in a certain company of ladies, a gentleman that was there with him began to speak of the paintings of a youth named Bonaventura, which he had seen in Lucca; adding that Giunta Pisano might now look for a rival. When Chiaro heard this, the lamps shook before him and the music beat in his ears and made him giddy. He rose up, alleging a sudden sickness, and went out of that house with his teeth set.

He now took to work diligently; not returning to
Arezzo, but remaining in Pisa, that no day more might
be lost; only living entirely to himself. Sometimes,
after nightfall, he would walk abroad in the most
solitary places he could find; hardly feeling the ground
under him, because of the thoughts of the day which
held him in fever.

The lodging he had chosen was in a house that looked
upon gardens fast by the Church of San Rocco. During
the offices, as he sat at work, he could hear the music
of the organ and the long murmur that the chanting
left; and if his window were open, sometimes, at those
parts of the mass where there is silence throughout the
church, his ear caught faintly the single voice of the
priest. Beside the matters of his art and a very few
books, almost the only object to be noticed in Chiaro's
room was a small consecrated image of St. Mary Virgin
wrought out of silver, before which stood always, in
summer-time, a glass containing a lily and a rose.

It was here, and at this time, that Chiaro painted the
Dresden pictures; as also, in all likelihood, the one—
inferior in merit, but certainly his—which is now at
Munich. For the most part, he was calm and regular
in his manner of study; though often he would remain
at work through the whole of a day, not resting once so
long as the light lasted; flushed, and with the hair
from his face. Or, at times, when he could not paint,
he would sit for hours in thought of all the greatness
the world had known from of old; until he was weak
with yearning, like one who gazes upon a path of stars.

He continued in this patient endeavour for about
three years, at the end of which his name was spoken
throughout all Tuscany. As his fame waxed, he began
to be employed, besides easel-pictures, upon paintings
in fresco; but I believe that no traces remain to us of
any of these latter. He is said to have painted in the
Duomo; and D'Agincourt mentions having seen some
portions of a fresco by him which originally had its
place above the high altar in the Church of the Certosa;
but which, at the time he saw it, being very dilapidated,

had been hewn out of the wall, and was preserved in the stores of the convent. Before the period of Dr. Aemmster's researches, however, it had been entirely destroyed.

Chiaro was now famous. It was for the race of fame that he had girded up his loins; and he had not paused until fame was reached: yet now, in taking breath, he found that the weight was still at his heart. The years of his labour had fallen from him, and his life was still in its first painful desire.

With all that Chiaro had done during these three years, and even before, with the studies of his early youth, there had always been a feeling of worship and service. It was the peace-offering that he made to God and to his own soul for the eager selfishness of his aim. There was earth, indeed, upon the hem of his raiment; but *this* was of the heaven, heavenly. He had seasons when he could endure to think of no other feature of his hope than this: and sometimes, in the ecstasy of prayer, it had even seemed to him to behold that day when his mistress—his mystical lady (now hardly in her ninth year, but whose solemn smile at meeting had already lighted on his soul like the dove of the Trinity) —even she, his own gracious and holy Italian Art— with her virginal bosom, and her unfathomable eyes, and the thread of sunlight round her brows—should pass, through the sun that never sets, into the circle of the shadow of the tree of life, and be seen of God, and found good: and then it had seemed to him that he, with many who, since his coming, had joined the band of whom he was one (for, in his dream, the body he had worn on earth had been dead an hundred years), were permitted to gather round the blessed maiden, and to worship with her through all ages and ages of ages, saying, Holy, holy, holy. This thing he had seen with the eyes of his spirit; and in this thing had trusted, believing that it would surely come to pass.

But now (being at length led to inquire closely into himself), even as, in the pursuit of fame, the unrest abiding after attainment had proved to him that he had misinterpreted the craving of his own spirit—so also, now that he would willingly have fallen back on devotion, he became aware that much of that reverence which he had mistaken for faith had been no more than the worship of beauty. Therefore, after certain days passed in perplexity, Chiaro said within himself, 'My life and my will are yet before me: I will take another aim to my life.'

From that moment Chiaro set a watch on his soul, and put his hand to no other works but only to such as had for their end the presentment of some moral greatness that should impress the beholder: and, in doing this, he did not choose for his medium the action and passion of human life, but cold symbolism and abstract impersonation. So the people ceased to throng about his pictures as heretofore; and, when they were carried through town and town to their destination, they were no longer delayed by the crowds eager to gaze and admire: and no prayers or offerings were brought to them on their path, as to his Madonnas, and his Saints, and his Holy Children. Only the critical audience remained to him; and these, in default of more worthy matter, would have turned their scrutiny on a puppet or a mantle. Meanwhile, he had no more of fever upon him; but was calm and pale each day in all that he did and in his goings in and out. The works he produced at this time have perished—in all likelihood, not unjustly. It is said (and we may easily believe it), that, though more laboured than his former pictures, they were cold and unemphatic; bearing marked out upon them, as they must certainly have done, the measure of that boundary to which they were made to conform.

And the weight was still close at Chiaro's heart: but he held in his breath, never resting (for he was afraid), and would not know it.

Now it happened, within these days, that there fell a great feast in Pisa, for holy matters: and each man left his occupation; and all the guilds and companies of the city were got together for games and rejoicings.

And there were scarcely any that stayed in the houses, except ladies who lay or sat along their balconies between open windows which let the breeze beat through the rooms and over the spread tables from end to end. And the golden cloths that their arms lay upon drew all eyes upward to see their beauty; and the day was long; and every hour of the day was bright with the sun.

So Chiaro's model, when he awoke that morning on the hot pavement of the Piazza Nunziata, and saw the hurry of people that passed him, got up and went along with them; and Chiaro waited for him in vain.

For the whole of that morning, the music was in Chiaro's room from the Church close at hand; and he could hear the sounds that the crowd made in the streets; hushed only at long intervals while the processions for the feast-day chanted in going under his windows. Also, more than once, there was a high clamour from the meeting of factious persons: for the ladies of both leagues were looking down; and he who encountered his enemy could not choose but draw upon him. Chiaro waited a long time idle; and then knew that his model was gone elsewhere. When at his work, he was blind and deaf to all else; but he feared sloth: for then his stealthy thoughts would begin, as it were, to beat round and round him, seeking a point for attack. He now rose, therefore, and went to the window. It was within a short space of noon; and underneath him a throng of people was coming out through the porch of San Rocco.

The two greatest houses of the feud in Pisa had filled the church for that mass. The first to leave had been the Gherghiotti; who, stopping on the threshold, had fallen back in ranks along each side of the archway: so that now, in passing outward, the Marotoli had to walk between two files of men whom they hated, and whose fathers had hated theirs. All the chiefs were there and their whole adherence; and each knew the name of each. Every man of the Marotoli, as he came forth and saw his foes, laid back his hood and gazed about him, to show the badge upon the close cap that held his hair. And of the Gherghiotti there were some who tightened their girdles; and some shrilled and threw up their wrists scornfully, as who flies a falcon; for that was the crest of their house.

On the walls within the entry were a number of tall narrow frescoes, presenting a moral allegory of Peace, which Chiaro had painted that year for the Church. The Gherghiotti stood with their backs to these frescoes; and among them Golzo Ninuccio, the youngest noble of the faction, called by the people Golaghiotta, for his debased life. This youth had remained for some while talking listlessly to his fellows, though with his sleepy sunken eyes fixed on them who passed: but now, seeing that no man jostled another, he drew the long silver shoe off his foot, and struck the dust out of it on the cloak of him who was going by, asking him how far the tides rose at Viderza. And he said so because it was three months since, at that place, the Gherghiotti had beaten the Marotoli to the sands, and held them there while the sea came in; whereby many had been drowned. And, when he had spoken, at once the whole archway was dazzling with the light of confused swords; and they who had left turned back; and they who were still behind made haste to come forth: and there was so much blood cast up the walls on a sudden, that it ran in long streams down Chiaro's paintings.

Chiaro turned himself from the window; for the light felt dry between his lids, and he could not look. He sat down, and heard the noise of contention driven out of the church-porch and a great way through the streets; and soon there was a deep murmur that heaved and waxed from the other side of the city, where those of both parties were gathering to join in the tumult.

Chiaro sat with his face in his open hands. Once again he had wished to set his foot on a place that looked green and fertile; and once again it seemed to him that the thin rank mask was about to spread away, and that this time the chill of the water must leave leprosy in his flesh. The light still swam in his head, and bewildered him at first; but when he knew his thoughts, they were these :—

'Fame failed me : faith failed me : and now this also,—the hope that I nourished in this my generation of men,—shall pass from me, and leave my feet and my hands groping. Yet, because of this, are my feet become slow and my hands thin. I am as one who, through the whole night, holding his way diligently, hath smitten the steel unto the flint, to lead some whom he knew darkling; who hath kept his eyes always on the sparks that himself made, lest they should fail; and who, towards dawn, turning to bid them that he had guided God speed, sees the wet grass untrodden except of his own feet. I am as the last hour of the day, whose chimes are a perfect number; whom the next followeth not, nor light ensueth from him; but in the same darkness is the old order begun afresh. Men say, "This is not God nor man; he is not as we are, neither above us: let him sit beneath us, for we are many." Where I write Peace, in that spot is the drawing of swords, and there men's footprints are red. When I would sow, another harvest is ripe. Nay, it is much worse with me than thus much. Am I not as a cloth drawn before the light, that the looker may not be blinded? but which showeth thereby the grain of its own coarseness; so that the light seems defiled, and men say, "We will not walk by it." Wherefore through me they shall be doubly accursed, seeing that through me they reject the light. May one be a devil and not know it?'

As Chiaro was in these thoughts, the fever encroached slowly on his veins, till he could sit no longer and would have risen; but suddenly he found awe within him, and held his head bowed, without stirring. The warmth of the air was not shaken; but there seemed a pulse in the light, and a living freshness, like rain. The silence was a painful music, that made the blood ache in his temples; and he lifted his face and his deep eyes.

A woman was present in his room, clad to the hands and feet with a green and grey raiment, fashioned to that time. It seemed that the first thoughts he had ever known were given him as at first from her eyes, and he knew her hair to be the golden veil through which he beheld his dreams. Though her hands were joined, her face was not lifted, but set forward; and though the gaze was austere, yet her mouth was supreme in gentleness. And as he looked, Chiaro's spirit appeared abashed of its own intimate presence, and his lips shook with the thrill of tears; it seemed such a bitter while till the spirit might be indeed alone.

She did not move closer towards him, but he felt her to be as much with him as his breath. He was like one who, scaling a great steepness, hears his own voice echoed in some place much higher than he can see, and the name of which is not known to him. As the woman stood, her speech was with Chiaro: not, as it were, from her mouth or in his ears; but distinctly between them.

'I am an image, Chiaro, of thine own soul within thee. See me, and know me as I am. Thou sayest that fame has failed thee, and faith failed thee; but because at least thou hast not laid thy life unto riches, therefore, though thus late, I am suffered to come into thy knowledge. Fame sufficed not, for that thou didst seek fame: seek thine own conscience (not thy mind's conscience, but thine heart's), and all shall approve and suffice. For Fame, in noble soils, is a fruit of the Spring: but not therefore should it be said: "Lo! my garden that I planted is barren: the crocus is here, but the lily is dead in the dry ground, and shall not lift the earth that covers it: therefore I will fling my garden together, and give it unto the builders." Take heed rather that thou trouble not the wise secret earth; for in the mould that thou throwest up shall the first tender growth lie to waste; which else had been strong in its season. Yea, and even if the year fall past in all its months, and the soil be indeed, to thee, peevish and incapable, and though thou indeed gather all thy harvest, and it suffice for others, and thou remain vext with emptiness; and others drink of thy streams, and the drouth rasp thy throat;—let it be enough that these have found the feast good, and thanked the giver : remembering that, when the winter is striven through, there is another year, whose wind is meek, and whose sun fulfilleth all.'

While he heard, Chiaro went slowly on his knees. It was not to her that spoke, for the speech seemed within him and his own. The air brooded in sunshine, and though the turmoil was great outside, the air within was at peace. But when he looked in her eyes, he wept. And she came to him, and cast her hair over him, and took her hands about his forehead, and spoke again :—

'Thou hast said,' she continued, gently, 'that faith failed thee. This cannot be so. Either thou hadst it not, or thou hast it. But who bade thee strike the point betwixt love and faith ? Wouldst thou sift the warm breeze from the sun that quickens it ? Who bade thee turn upon God and say : "Behold, my offering is of earth, and not worthy : thy fire comes not upon it ; therefore, though I slay not my brother whom thou acceptest, I will depart before thou smite me." Why shouldst thou rise up and tell God He is not content ? Had He, of His warrant, certified so to thee ? Be not nice to seek out division ; but possess thy love in sufficiency : assuredly this is faith, for the heart must believe first. What He hath set in thine heart to do, that do thou ; and even though thou do it without thought of Him, it shall be well done ; it is this sacrifice that He asketh of thee, and His flame is upon it for a sign. Think not of Him ; but of His love and thy love. For God is no morbid exactor : He hath no hand to bow beneath, nor a foot, that thou shouldst kiss it.'

And Chiaro held silence, and wept into her hair which covered his face ; and the salt tears that he shed ran through her hair upon his lips ; and he tasted the bitterness of shame.

Then the fair woman, that was his soul, spoke again to him, saying :

'And for this thy last purpose, and for those unprofitable truths of thy teaching,—thine heart hath already put them away, and it needs not that I lay my bidding upon thee. How is it that thou, a man, wouldst say coldly to the mind what God hath said to the heart warmly? Thy will was honest and wholesome; but look well lest this also be folly,—to say, "I, in doing this, do strengthen God among men." When at any time hath he cried unto thee, saying, "My son, lend me thy shoulder, for I fall?" Deemest thou that the men who enter God's temple in malice, to the provoking of blood, and neither for his love nor for his wrath will abate their purpose,—shall afterwards stand with thee in the porch, midway between Him and themselves, to give ear unto thy thin voice, which merely the fall of their visors can drown, and to see thy hands, stretched feebly, tremble among their swords? Give thou to God no more than he asketh of thee; but to man also, that which is man's. In all that thou doest, work from thine own heart, simply; for his heart is as thine, when thine is wise and humble; and he shall have understanding of thee. One drop of rain is as another, and the sun's prism in all: and shalt not thou be as he, whose lives are the breath of One? Only by making thyself his equal can he learn to hold communion with thee, and at last own thee above him. Not till thou lean over the water shalt thou see thine image therein: stand erect, and it shall slope from thy feet and be lost. Know that there is but this means whereby thou may'st serve God with man:—Set thine hand and thy soul to serve man with God.'

And when she that spoke had said these words within Chiaro's spirit, she left his side quietly, and stood up as he had first seen her: with her fingers laid together, and her eyes steadfast, and with the breadth of her long dress covering her feet on the floor. And, speaking again, she said:

'Chiaro, servant of God, take now thine Art unto thee, and paint me thus, as I am, to know me: weak, as I am, and in the weeds of this time; only with eyes which seek out labour, and with a faith, not learned, yet jealous of prayer. Do this; so shall thy soul stand before thee always, and perplex thee no more.'

And Chiaro did as she bade him. While he worked,

his face grew solemn with knowledge : and before the shadows had turned, his work was done. Having finished, he lay back where he sat, and was asleep immediately ; for the growth of that strong sunset was heavy about him, and he felt weak and haggard ; like one just come out of a dusk, hollow country, bewildered with echoes, where he had lost himself, and who has not slept for many days and nights. And when she saw him lie back, the beautiful woman came to him, and sat at his head, gazing, and quieted his sleep with her voice.

The tumult of the factions had endured all that day through all Pisa, though Chiaro had not heard it : and the last service of that Feast was a mass sung at midnight from the windows of all the churches for the many dead who lay about the city, and who had to be buried before morning, because of the extreme heats.

In the Spring of 1847 I was at Florence. Such as were there at the same time with myself—those, at least, to whom Art is something—will certainly recollect how many rooms of the Pitti Gallery were closed through that season, in order that some of the pictures they contained might be examined and repaired without the necessity of removal. The hall, the staircases, and the vast central suite of apartments, were the only accessible portions ; and in these such paintings as they could admit from the sealed *penetralia* were profanely huddled together, without respect of dates, schools, or persons.

I fear that, through this interdict, I may have missed seeing many of the best pictures. I do not mean *only* the most talked of : for these, as they were restored, generally found their way somehow into the open rooms, owing to the clamours raised by the students ; and I remember how old Ercoli's, the curator's, spectacles used to be mirrored in the reclaimed surface, as he leaned mysteriously over these works with some of the visitors, to scrutinize and elucidate.

One picture that I saw that Spring, I shall not easily forget. It was among those, I believe, brought from the other rooms, and had been hung, obviously out of all chronology, immediately beneath that head by Raphael so long known as the 'Berrettino', and now said to be the portrait of Cecco Ciulli.

The picture I speak of is a small one, and represents merely the figure of a woman, clad to the hands and feet with a green and grey raiment, chaste and early in its fashion, but exceedingly simple. She is standing: her hands are held together lightly, and her eyes set earnestly open.

The face and hands in this picture, though wrought with great delicacy, have the appearance of being painted at once, in a single sitting: the drapery is unfinished. As soon as I saw the figure, it drew an awe upon me, like water in shadow. I shall not attempt to describe it more than I have already done; for the most absorbing wonder of it was its literality. You knew that figure, when painted, had been seen; yet it was not a thing to be seen of men. This language will appear ridiculous to such as have never looked on the work; and it may be even to some among those who have. On examining it closely, I perceived in one corner of the canvas the words *Manus Animam pinxit*, and the date 1239.

I turned to my Catalogue, but that was useless, for the pictures were all displaced. I then stepped up to the Cavaliere Ercoli, who was in the room at the moment, and asked him regarding the subject and authorship of the painting. He treated the matter, I thought, somewhat slightingly, and said that he could show me the reference in the Catalogue, which he had compiled. This, when found, was not of much value, as it merely said, 'Schizzo d'autore incerto,' adding the inscription.[1] I could willingly have prolonged my inquiry, in the

[1] I should here say, that in the catalogue for the year just over, (owing, as in cases before mentioned, to the zeal and enthusiasm of Dr. Aemmster) this, and several other pictures, have been more competently entered. The work in question is now placed in the Sala Sessagona, a room I did not see—under the number 161. It is described as 'Figura mistica di Chiaro dell' Erma', and there is a brief notice of the author appended.

hope that it might somehow lead to some result; but I had disturbed the curator from certain yards of Guido, and he was not communicative. I went back therefore, and stood before the picture till it grew dusk.

The next day I was there again; but this time a circle of students was round the spot, all copying the 'Berrettino'. I contrived, however, to find a place whence I could see *my* picture, and where I seemed to be in nobody's way. For some minutes I remained undisturbed; and then I heard, in an English voice: 'Might I beg of you, sir, to stand a little more to this side, as you interrupt my view?'

I felt vext, for, standing where he asked me, a glare struck on the picture from the windows, and I could not see it. However, the request was reasonably made, and from a countryman; so I complied, and turning away, stood by his easel. I knew it was not worth while; yet I referred in some way to the work underneath the one he was copying. He did not laugh, but he smiled as we do in England. '*Very* odd, is it not?' said he.

The other students near us were all continental; and seeing an Englishman select an Englishman to speak with, conceived, I suppose, that he could understand no language but his own. They had evidently been noticing the interest which the little picture appeared to excite in me.

One of them, an Italian, said something to another who stood next to him. He spoke with a Genoese accent, and I lost the sense in the villainous dialect. 'Che so?' replied the other, lifting his eyebrows towards the figure; 'roba mistica: 'st' Inglesi son matti sul misticismo: somiglia alle nebbie di là. Li fa pensare alla patria,

"E intenerisce il core
Lo dì ch' han detto ai dolci amici adio."'

'La notte, vuoi dire,' said a third.

There was a general laugh. My compatriot was evidently a novice in the language, and did not take in what was said. I remained silent, being amused.

'Et toi donc ?' said he who had quoted Dante, turning to a student, whose birthplace was unmistakable, even had he been addressed in any other language: 'que dis-tu de ce genre-là ?'

'Moi ?' returned the Frenchman, standing back from his easel, and looking at me and at the figure, quite politely, though with an evident reservation: 'Je dis, mon cher, que c'est une spécialité dont je me fiche pas mal. Je tiens que quand on ne comprend pas une chose, c'est qu'elle ne signifie rien.'

My reader thinks possibly that the French student was right.

THE
EARLY ITALIAN POETS

FROM CIULLO D'ALCAMO TO
DANTE ALIGHIERI

(1100—1200—1300)

IN THE ORIGINAL METRES
TOGETHER WITH DANTE'S VITA NUOVA

PART I.—POETS CHIEFLY BEFORE DANTE
PART II.—DANTE AND HIS CIRCLE

WHATEVER IS MINE IN THIS BOOK IS INSCRIBED
TO MY WIFE
D. G. R., 1861.

PREFACE

I NEED not dilate here on the characteristics of the first epoch of Italian Poetry; since the extent of my translated selections is sufficient to afford a complete view of it. Its great beauties may often remain unapproached in the versions here attempted; but, at the same time, its imperfections are not all to be charged to the translator. Among these I may refer to its limited range of subject and continual obscurity, as well as to its monotony in the use of rhymes or frequent substitution of assonances. But to compensate for much that is incomplete and inexperienced, these poems possess, in their degree, beauties of a kind which can never again exist in art; and offer, besides, a treasure of grace and variety in the formation of their metres. Nothing but a strong impression, first of their poetic value, and next of the biographical interest of some of them (chiefly of those in my second division), would have inclined me to bestow the time and trouble which have resulted in this collection.

Much has been said, and in many respects justly, against the value of metrical translation. But I think it would be admitted that the tributary art might find a not illegitimate use in the case of poems which come down to us in such a form as do these early Italian ones. Struggling originally with corrupt dialect and imperfect expression, and hardly kept alive through centuries of neglect, they have reached that last and worst state in which the *coup-de-grâce* has almost been dealt them by clumsy transcription and pedantic superstructure. At this stage the task of talking much more about them in any language is hardly to be entered upon; and a translation (involving as it does the necessity of settling many points without discussion) remains perhaps the most direct form of commentary.

The life-blood of rhymed translation is this,—that a good poem shall not be turned into a bad one. The only true motive for putting poetry into a fresh language must be to endow a fresh nation, as far as possible, with one more possession of beauty. Poetry not being an exact science, literality of rendering is altogether secondary to this chief aim. I say *literality*,—not fidelity, which is by no means the same thing. When literality can be combined with what is thus the primary condition of success, the translator is fortunate, and must strive his utmost to unite them; when such object can only be attained by paraphrase, that is his only path.

Any merit possessed by these translations is derived from an effort to follow this principle; and, in some degree, from the fact that such painstaking in arrangement and descriptive heading as is often indispensable to old and especially to 'occasional' poetry, has here been bestowed on these poets for the first time.

That there are many defects in these translations, or that the above merit is their defect, or that they have no merits but only defects, are discoveries so sure to be made if necessary (or perhaps here and there in any case), that I may safely leave them in other hands. The collection has probably a wider scope than some readers might look for, and includes now and then (though I believe in rare instances) matter which may not meet with universal approval; and whose introduction, needed as it is by the literary aim of my work, is I know inconsistent with the principles of pretty bookmaking. My wish has been to give a full and truthful view of early Italian poetry; not to make it appear to consist only of certain elements to the exclusion of others equally belonging to it.

Of the difficulties I have had to encounter,—the causes of imperfections for which I have no other excuse,—it is the reader's best privilege to remain ignorant; but I may perhaps be pardoned for briefly referring to such among these as concern the exigencies of translation. The task of the translator (and with all humility be it spoken) is one of some self-denial.

Often would he avail himself of any special grace of his own idiom and epoch, if only his will belonged to him ; often would some cadence serve him but for his author's structure—some structure but for his author's cadence ; often the beautiful turn of a stanza must be weakened to adopt some rhyme which will tally, and he sees the poet revelling in abundance of language where himself is scantily supplied. Now he would slight the matter for the music, and now the music for the matter ; but no, he must deal to each alike. Sometimes, too, a flaw in the work galls him, and he would fain remove it, doing for the poet that which his age denied him ; but no,— it is not in the bond. His path is like that of Aladdin through the enchanted vaults : many are the precious fruits and flowers which he must pass by unheeded in search for the lamp alone ; happy if at last, when brought to light, it does not prove that his old lamp has been exchanged for a new one,—glittering indeed to the eye, but scarcely of the same virtue nor with the same genius at its summons.

In relinquishing this work (which, small as it is, is the only contribution I expect to make to our English knowledge of old Italy), I feel, as it were, divided from my youth. The first associations I have are connected with my father's devoted studies, which, from his own point of view, have done so much towards the general investigation of Dante's writings. Thus, in those early days, all around me partook of the influence of the great Florentine ; till, from viewing it as a natural element, I also, growing older, was drawn within the circle. I trust that from this the reader may place more confidence in a work not carelessly undertaken, though produced in the spare-time of other pursuits more closely followed. He should perhaps be told that it has occupied the leisure moments of not a few years ; thus affording, often at long intervals, every opportunity for consideration and revision ; and that on the score of care, at least, he has no need to mistrust it.

Nevertheless, I know there is no great stir to be made by launching afresh, on high-seas busy with new traffic, the ships which have been long outstripped and the ensigns which are grown strange. The feeling of self-doubt inseparable from such an attempt has been admirably expressed by a great living poet, in words which may be applied exactly to my humbler position, though relating in his case to a work all his own.

> Still, what if I approach the august sphere
> Named now with only one name,—disentwine
> That under current soft and argentine
> From its fierce mate in the majestic mass
> Leaven'd as the sea whose fire was mix'd with glass
> In John's transcendent vision,—launch once more
> That lustre? Dante, pacer of the shore
> Where glutted Hell disgorges filthiest gloom,
> Unbitten by its whirring sulphur-spume—
> Or whence the grieved and obscure waters slope
> Into a darkness quieted by hope—
> Plucker of amaranths grown beneath God's eye
> In gracious twilights where His chosen lie,—
> I would do this! If I should falter now! ...
>
> (*Sordello*, by ROBERT BROWNING, B. 1.)

It may be well to conclude this short preface with a list of the works which have chiefly contributed to the materials of the present volume.

I. Poeti del primo secolo della Lingua Italiana. 2 vol. (Firenze. 1816.)

II. Raccolta di Rime antiche Toscane. 4 vol. (Palermo, 1817.)

III. Manuale della Letteratura del primo Secolo, del Prof. V. Nannucci. 3 vol. (Firenze. 1843.)

IV. Poesie Italiane inedite di dugento autori : raccolte da Francesco Trucchi. 4 vol. (Prato. 1846.) [1]

V. Opere Minori di Dante. Edizione di P. I. Fraticelli. (Firenze. 1843, &c.)

VI. Rime di Guido Cavalcanti ; raccolte da A. Cicciaporci. (Firenze. 1813.)

---

[1] This work contains, in its first and second volumes, by far the best edited collection I know of early Italian poetry. Unfortunately it is only a supplement to the previous ones, giving poems till then unpublished. A reprint of the whole mass by the same editor, with such revision and further additions as he could give it, would be very desirable.

VII. Vita e Poesie di Messer Cino da Pistoia. Edizione di S. Ciampi. (Pisa. 1813.)

VIII. Documenti d'Amore; di Francesco da Barberino. Annotati da F. Ubaldini. (Roma. 1640.)

IX. Del Reggimento e dei Costumi delle Donne; di Francesco da Barberino. (Roma. 1815.)

X. Il Dittamondo di Fazio degli Uberti. (Milano. 1826.)

TABLE OF POETS IN PART I

I. CIULLO D'ALCAMO, 1172-8.

Ciullo is a popular form of the name Vincenzo, and Alcamo an Arab fortress some miles from Palermo. The Dialogue which is the only known production of this poet holds here the place generally accorded to it as the earliest Italian poem (exclusive of one or two dubious inscriptions) which has been preserved to our day. Arguments have sometimes been brought to prove that it must be assigned to a later date than the poem by Folcachiero, which follows it in this volume; thus ascribing the first honours of Italian poetry to Tuscany, and not to Sicily, as is commonly supposed. Trucchi, however (in the preface to his valuable collection), states his belief that the two poems are about contemporaneous, fixing the date of that by Ciullo between 1172 and 1178—chiefly from the fact that the fame of Saladin, to whom this poet alludes, was most in men's mouths during that interval. At first sight, any casual reader of the original would suppose that this poem must be unquestionably the earliest of all, as its language is far the most unformed and difficult; but much of this might, of course, be dependent on the inferior dialect of Sicily, mixed however in this instance (as far as I can judge) with mere nondescript *patois*.

II. FOLCACHIERO DE' FOLCACHIERI, KNIGHT OF SIENA, 1177.

The above date has been assigned with probability to Folcachiero's Canzone, on account of its first line, where the whole world is said to be 'living without war'; an assertion which seems to refer its production to the period of the celebrated peace concluded at Venice between Frederick Barbarossa and Pope Alexander III.

III. LODOVICO DELLA VERNACCIA, 1200.

IV. SAINT FRANCIS OF ASSISI; BORN, 1182; DIED, 1226.

His baptismal name was Giovanni, and his father was Bernardone Moriconi, whose mercantile pursuits he shared till the age of twenty-five; after which his life underwent the extraordinary change which resulted in his canonization, by Gregory IX, three years after his death, and in the formation of the Religious Order called Franciscans.

TABLE OF POETS IN PART I

V. FREDERICK II, EMPEROR ; BORN, 1194 ; DIED, 1250.

The life of Frederick II, and his excommunication and deposition from the Empire by Innocent IV, to whom, however, he did not succumb, are matters of history which need no repetition. Intellectually, he was in all ways a highly-gifted and accomplished prince ; and lovingly cultivated the Italian language, in preference to the many others with which he was familiar. The poem of his which I give has great passionate beauty ; yet I believe that an allegorical interpretation may here probably be admissible ; and that the lady of the poem may be the Empire, or perhaps the Church herself, held in bondage by the Pope.

VI. ENZO, KING OF SARDINIA ; BORN, 1225 ; DIED, 1272.

The unfortunate Enzo was a natural son of Frederick II, and was born at Palermo. By his own warlike enterprise, at an early age (it is said at fifteen !) he subjugated the Island of Sardinia, and was made king of it by his father. Afterwards he joined Frederick in his war against the Church, and displayed the highest promise as a leader ; but at the age of twenty-five was taken prisoner by the Bolognese, whom no threats or promises from the Emperor could induce to set him at liberty. He died in prison at Bologna, after a confinement of nearly twenty-three years. A hard fate indeed for one who, while moving among men, excited their hopes and homage, still on record, by his great military genius and brilliant gifts of mind and person.

VII. GUIDO GUINICELLI, 1220.

This poet, certainly the greatest of his time, belonged to a noble and even princely Bolognese family. Nothing seems known of his life, except that he was married to a lady named Beatrice, and that in 1274, having adhered to the Imperial cause, he was sent into exile, but whither cannot be learned. He died two years afterwards. The highest praise has been bestowed by Dante on Guinicelli, in the *Commedia* (*Purg.* C. xxvi), in the *Convito*, and in the *De Vulgari Eloquio* ; and many instances might be cited in which the works of the great Florentine contain reminiscences of his Bolognese predecessor ; especially the third canzone of Dante's *Convito* may be compared with Guido's most famous one *On the Gentle Heart*.

VIII. GUERZO DI MONTECANTI, 1220.

IX. INGHILFREDI, SICILIANO, 1220.

X. RINALDO D'AQUINO, 1250.

I have placed this poet, belonging to a Neapolitan family, under the date usually assigned to him ; but Trucchi states his belief that he flourished much earlier, and was a contemporary of Folcachiero; partly on account of two lines in one of his poems which say:—

> Lo Imperadore con pace
> Tutto il mondo mantene.

If so, the mistake would be easily accounted for, as there seem to have been various members of the family named Rinaldo, at different dates.

XI. JACOPO DA LENTINO, 1250.

This Sicilian poet is generally called 'The Notary of Lentino'. The low estimate expressed of him, as well as of Bonaggiunta and Guittone, by Dante (*Purg.* C. xxiv), must be understood as referring in great measure to their want of grammatical purity and nobility of style, as we may judge when the passage is taken in conjunction with the principles of the *De Vulgari Eloquio*. However, Dante also attributes his own superiority to the fact of his writing only when love (or natural impulse) really prompted him,—the highest certainly of all laws relating to art:—

> Io mi son un che quando
> Amor mi spira, noto, ed in quel modo
> Ch' ei detta dentro, vo significando.

A translation does not suffer from such offences of dialect as may exist in its original; and I think my readers will agree that, chargeable as he is with some conventionality of sentiment, the Notary of Lentino is often not without his claims to beauty and feeling. There is a peculiar charm in the sonnet which stands first among my specimens.

XII. MAZZEO DI RICCO, DA MESSINA, 1250.

XIII. PANNUCCIO DAL BAGNO, PISANO, 1250.

XIV. GIACOMINO PUGLIESI, KNIGHT OF PRATO, 1250.

Of this poet there seems nothing to be learnt; but he deserves special notice as possessing rather more poetic individuality than usual, and also as furnishing the only instance, among Dante's predecessors, of a poem (and a very beautiful one) written on a lady's death.

XV. FRA GUITTONE D'AREZZO, 1250.

Guittone was not a monk, but derived the prefix to his name from the fact of his belonging to the religious and military order of *Cavalieri di Santa Maria*. He seems to have enjoyed a greater literary reputation than almost any writer of his day; but certainly his poems, of which many have been preserved, cannot be said to possess merit of a prominent kind; and Dante shows

TABLE OF POETS IN PART I

by various allusions that he considered them much over-rated. The sonnet I have given is somewhat remarkable, from Petrarch's having transplanted its last line into his *Trionfi d'Amore* (cap. III). Guittone is the author of a series of Italian letters to various eminent persons, which are the earliest known epistolary writings in the language.

XVI. BARTOLOMEO DI SANT' ANGELO, 1250.

XVII. SALADINO DA PAVIA, 1250.

XVIII. BONAGGIUNTA URBICIANI, DA LUCCA, 1250.

XIX. MEO ABBRACCIAVACCA, DA PISTOIA, 1250.

XX. UBALDO DI MARCO, 1250.

XXI. SIMBUONO GIUDICE, 1250.

XXII. MASOLINO DA TODI, 1250.

XXIII. ONESTO DI BONCIMA, BOLOGNESE, 1250.

Onesto was a doctor of laws, and an early friend of Cino da Pistoia. He was living as late as 1301, though his career as a poet may be fixed somewhat further back.

XXIV. TERINO DA CASTEL FIORENTINO, 1250.

XXV. MAESTRO MIGLIORE, DA FIORENZA, 1250.

XXVI. DELLO DA SIGNA, 1250.

XXVII. FOLGORE DA SAN GEMINIANO, 1250.

XXVIII. GUIDO DELLE COLONNE, 1250.

This Sicilian poet has few equals among his contemporaries, and is ranked high by Dante in his treatise *De Vulgari Eloquio*. He visited England, and wrote in Latin a *Historia de regibus et rebus Angliae*, as well as a *Historia destructionis Trojae*.

XXIX. PIER MORONELLI, DI FIORENZA, 1250.

XXX. CIUNCIO FIORENTINO, 1250.

XXXI. RUGGIERI DI AMICI, SICILIANO, 1250.

XXXII. CARNINO GHIBERTI, DA FIORENZA, 1250.

XXXIII. PRINZIVALLE DORIA, 1250.

Prinzivalle commenced by writing Italian poetry, but afterwards composed verses entirely in Provençal, for the love of Beatrice, Countess of Provence. He wrote also, in Provençal prose, a treatise ' On the dainty Madness of Love ', and another ' On the War of Charles, King of Naples, against the tyrant Manfredi '. He held various high offices, and died at Naples in 1276.

XXXIV. RUSTICO DI FILIPPO; BORN ABOUT 1200; DIED, 1270.

The writings of this Tuscan poet (called also Rustico Barbuto) show signs of more vigour and versatility than was common in his day, and he probably began writing in Italian verse even before many of those already mentioned. In his old age, he, though a Ghibelline, received the dedication of the *Tesoretto* from the Guelf Brunetto Latini, who there pays him unqualified homage for surpassing worth in peace and war. It is strange that more should not be known regarding this doubtless remarkable man. His compositions have sometimes much humour, and on the whole convey the impression of an active and energetic nature. Moreover, Trucchi pronounces some of them to be as pure in language as the poems of Dante or Guido Cavalcanti, though written thirty or forty years earlier.

XXXV. PUCCIARELLO DI FIORENZA, 1260.

XXXVI. ALBERTUCCIO DELLA VIOLA, 1260.

XXXVII. TOMMASO BUZZUOLA, DA FAENZA, 1280.

XXXVIII. NOFFO BONAGUIDA, 1280.

XXXIX. LIPPO PASCHI DE' BARDI, 1280.

XL. SER PACE, NOTAIO DA FIORENZA, 1280.

XLI. NICCOLÒ DEGLI ALBIZZI, 1300.

The noble Florentine family of Albizzi produced writers of poetry in more than one generation. The vivid and admirable sonnet which I have translated is the only one I have met with by Niccolò. I must confess my inability to trace the circumstances which gave rise to it.

XLII. FRANCESCO DA BARBERINO; BORN, 1264; DIED, 1348.

With the exception of Brunetto Latini (whose poems are neither very poetical nor well adapted for extract), Francesco da Barberino shows by far the most sustained productiveness among the poets who preceded Dante, or were contemporaries of his youth. Though born only one year in advance of Dante, Barberino seems to have undertaken, if not completed, his two long poetic treatises, some years before the commencement of the *Commedia*.

This poet was born at Barberino di Valdelsa, of a noble family, his father being Neri di Rinuccio da Barberino. Up to the year of his father's death, 1296, he pursued the study of law chiefly in Bologna and Padua; but afterwards removed to Florence for the same purpose, and seems to have been there, even earlier, one of the many distinguished disciples of Brunetto Latini, who probably had more influence than any other one man in forming the youth of his time to the great things they accomplished. After this he travelled in France and elsewhere; and on his return to Italy in 1313, was the first who, by special favour of Pope Clement V, received the grade of Doctor of Laws in Florence. Both as lawyer and as citizen, he held great trusts and discharged them honourably. He was twice married, the name of his second wife being Barna di Tano, and had several children. At the age of eighty-four he died in the great Plague of Florence. Of the two works which Barberino has left, one bears the title of *Documenti d'Amore*, literally 'Documents of Love', but perhaps more properly rendered as 'Laws of Courtesy'; while the other is called *Del Reggimento e dei Costumi delle Donne*,—'Of the Government and Conduct of Women'. They may be described, in the main, as manuals of good breeding, or social chivalry, the one for men and the other for women. Mixed with vagueness, tediousness, and not seldom with artless absurdity, they contain much simple wisdom, much curious record of manners, and (as my specimens show) occasional poetic sweetness or power, though these last are far from being their most prominent merits. The first-named treatise, however, has much more of such qualities than the second; and contains, moreover, passages of homely humour which startle by their truth as if written yesterday. At the same time, the second book is quite as well worth reading, for the sake of its authoritative minuteness in matters which ladies, nowadays, would probably consider their own undisputed region; and also for the quaint gravity of certain surprising prose anecdotes of real life, with which it is interspersed. Both these works remained long unprinted, the first edition of the *Documenti d'Amore* being that edited by Ubaldini in 1640, at which time he reports the *Reggimento, &c.*, to be only possessed by his age 'in name and in desire'. This treatise was afterwards brought to light, but never printed till 1815. I should not forget to state that Barberino attained some knowledge of drawing, and that Ubaldini had seen his original MS. of the *Documenti*, containing, as he says, skilful miniatures by the author.

Barberino never appears to have taken a very active part in politics, but he inclined to the Imperial and Ghibelline party. This contributes with other things to render it rather singular that we find no poetic correspondence or apparent communication of any kind between him and his many great countrymen, contemporaries of his long life, and with whom he had more than one bond of sympathy. His career stretched from Dante, Guido Cavalcanti, and Cino da Pistoia, to Petrarca and Boccaccio; yet only in one respectful but not enthusiastic notice of him by the last-named writer (*Genealogia degli Dei*), do we ever meet with an allusion to him by any of the greatest men of his time. Nor in his own writings, as far as I remember, are they ever referred to. His epitaph is said to have been written by Boccaccio, but this is doubtful. On reviewing the present series, I am sorry, on the whole, not to have included more specimens of Barberino, whose writings, though not very easy to tackle in the mass, would afford an excellent field for selection and summary.

XLIII. FAZIO DEGLI UBERTI, 1326–60.

The dates of this poet's birth and death are not ascertainable, but I have set against his name two dates which result from his writings as belonging to his lifetime. He was a member of that great house of the Uberti which was driven from Florence on the expulsion of the Ghibellines in 1267, and which was ever afterwards specially excluded by name from the various amnesties offered from time to time to the exiled Florentines. His grandfather was Farinata degli Uberti, whose stern nature, unyielding even amid penal fires, has been recorded by Dante in the tenth canto of the *Inferno*. Farinata's son Lapo, himself a poet, was the father of Fazio (i.e. Bonifazio), who was no doubt born in the lifetime of Dante, and in some place of exile, but where is not known. In his youth he was enamoured of a certain Veronese lady named Angiola, and was afterwards married, but whether to her or not is again among the uncertainties. Certain it is that he had a son named Leopardo, who, after his father's death at Verona, settled in Venice, where his descendants maintained an honourable rank for the space of two succeeding centuries. Though Fazio appears to have suffered sometimes from poverty, he enjoyed high reputation as a poet, and is even said, on the authority of various early writers, to have publicly received the laurel crown; but in what city of Italy this took place we do not learn.

There is much beauty in several of Fazio's lyrical poems, of which, however, no great number have been preserved. The finest of all is the Canzone which I have translated; whose excellence is such as to have procured it the high honour of being attributed to Dante, so that it is to be found in most editions of the *Canzoniere*; and as far as poetic beauty is concerned, it must be allowed to hold even there an eminent place. Its style, however (as Monti was the first to point out in our own day, though Ubaldini, in his Glossary to Barberino had already quoted it as the work of Fazio), is more particularizing than accords with the practice of Dante; while, though certainly more perfect than any other poem by Fazio, its manner is quite his; bearing

especially a strong resemblance throughout in structure to one
canzone, where he speaks of his love with minute reference to
the seasons of the year. Moreover, Fraticelli tells us that it is
not attributed to Dante in any one of the many ancient MSS.
he had seen, but has been fathered on him solely on the authority
of a printed collection of 1518. This contested Canzone is well
worth fighting for; and the victor would deserve to receive his
prize at the hands of a peerless Queen of Beauty, for never was
beauty better described. I believe we may decide that the triumph
belongs by right to Fazio.

An exile by inheritance, Fazio seems to have acquired restless
tastes; and in the latter years of his life (which was prolonged
to old age), he travelled over a great part of Europe, and composed his long poem entitled *Il Dittamondo*—'The Song of the
World'. This work, though by no means contemptible in point
of execution, certainly falls far short of its conception, which is
a grand one; the topics of which it treats in great measure—
geography and natural history—rendering it in those days the
native home of all credulities and monstrosities. In scheme it
was intended as an earthly parallel to Dante's Sacred Poem,
doing for this world what he did for the other. At Fazio's death
it remained unfinished, but I should think by very little; the
plan of the work seeming in the main accomplished. The whole
earth (or rather all that was then known of it) is traversed—its
surface and its history—ending with the Holy Land, and thus
bringing Man's world as near as may be to God's; that is, to
the point at which Dante's office begins. No conception could
well be nobler, or worthier even now of being dealt with by
a great master. To the work of such a man, Fazio's work might
afford such first materials as have usually been furnished before-
hand to the greatest poets by some unconscious steward.

XLIV. FRANCO SACCHETTI; BORN, 1335; DIED, SHORTLY
AFTER 1400.

This excellent writer is the only member of my gathering who
was born after the death of Dante, which event (in 1321) preceded Franco's birth by some fourteen years. I have introduced
a few specimens of his poetry, partly because their attraction
was irresistible, but also because he is the earliest Italian poet
with whom playfulness is the chief characteristic; for even with
Boccaccio, in his poetry, this is hardly the case, and we can but
ill accept as playfulness the cynical humour of Cecco Angiolieri:
perhaps Rustico di Filippo alone might put in claims to priority
in this respect. However, Franco Sacchetti wrote poems also on
political subjects; and had he belonged more strictly to the
period of which I treat, there is no one who would better have

deserved abundant selection. Besides his poetry, he is the author of a well-known series of three hundred stories; and Trucchi gives a list of prose works by him which are still in MS., and whose subjects are genealogical, historical, natural-historical, and even theological. He was a prolific writer, and one who well merits complete and careful publication. The pieces which I have translated, like many others of his, are written for music.

Franco Sacchetti was a Florentine noble by birth, and was the son of Benci di Uguccione Sacchetti. Between this family and the Alighieri there had been a *vendetta* of long standing (spoken of here in the *Appendix to Part II*), but which was probably set at rest before Franco's time, by the deaths of at least one Alighieri and two Sacchetti. After some years passed in study, Franco devoted himself to commerce, like many nobles of the republic, and for that purpose spent some time in Sclavonia, whose uncongenial influences he has recorded in an amusing poem. As his literary fame increased, he was called to many important offices; was one of the *Priori* in 1383, and for some time was deputed to the government of Faenza, in the absence of its lord, Astorre Manfredi. He was three times married; to Felice degli Strozzi, to Ghita Gherardini, and to Nannina di Santi Bruni.

XLV. ANONYMOUS POEMS.

POETS CHIEFLY BEFORE DANTE

CIULLO D'ALCAMO

Dialogue: *Lover and Lady*

He: Thou sweetly-smelling fresh red rose
  That near thy summer art,
 Of whom each damsel and each dame
  Would fain be counterpart;
 O! from this fire to draw me forth
  Be it in thy good heart:
For night or day there is no rest with me,
Thinking of none, my lady, but of thee.
She: If thou hast set thy thoughts on me,
  Thou hast done a foolish thing.
 Yea, all the pine-wood of this world
  Together might'st thou bring,
 And make thee ships, and plough the sea
  Therewith for corn-sowing,
Ere any way to win me could be found:
For I am going to shear my locks all round.
He: Lady, before thou shear thy locks
  I hope I may be dead:
 For I should lose such joy thereby
  And gain such grief instead.
 Merely to pass and look at thee,
  Rose of the garden-bed,
Has comforted me much, once and again.
Oh! if thou wouldst but love, what were it then!
She: Nay, though my heart were prone to love,
  I would not grant it leave.
 Hark! should my father or his kin
  But find thee here this eve,

>   Thy loving body and lost breath
>   Our moat may well receive.
>   Whatever path to come here thou dost know,
>   By the same path I counsel thee to go.
> *He :* And if thy kinsfolk find me here,
>   Shall I be drowned then ?   Marry,
>   I'll set, for price against my head,
>   Two thousand agostari.
>   I think thy father would not do't
>   For all his lands in Bari.
>   Long life to the Emperor !   Be God's the praise !
>   Thou hear'st, my beauty, what thy servant says.
> *She :* And am I then to have no peace
>   Morning or evening ?
>   I have strong coffers of my own
>   And much good gold therein ;
>   So that if thou couldst offer me
>   The wealth of Saladin,
>   And add to that the Soldan's money-hoard,
>   Thy suit would not be anything toward.
> *He :* I have known many women, love,
>   Whose thoughts were high and proud,
>   And yet have been made gentle by
>   Man's speech not over-loud.
>   If we but press ye long enough,
>   At length ye will be bow'd ;
>   For still a woman's weaker than a man.
>   When the end comes, recall how this began.
> *She :* God grant that I may die before
>   Any such end do come,—
>   Before the sight of a chaste maid
>   Seem to me troublesome !
>   I marked thee here all yestereve
>   Lurking about my home,
>   And now I say, Leave climbing, lest thou fall,
>   For these thy words delight me not at all.
> *He :* How many are the cunning chains
>   Thou hast wound round my heart !
>   Only to think upon thy voice
>   Sometimes I groan apart.

For I did never love a maid
  Of this world, as thou art,   70
So much as I love thee, thou crimson rose.
Thou wilt be mine at last: this my soul knows.
She: If I could think it would be so,
  Small pride it were of mine
That all my beauty should be meant
  But to make thee to shine.
  Sooner than stoop to that, I'd shear
  These golden tresses fine,
And make one of some holy sisterhood;
Escaping so thy love, which is not good.   80
He: If thou unto the cloister fly,
  Thou cruel lady and cold,
Unto the cloister I will come
  And by the cloister hold;
For such a conquest liketh me
  Much better than much gold;
At matins and at vespers I shall be
Still where thou art. Have I not conquered thee?
She: Out and alack! wherefore am I
  Tormented in suchwise?   90
Lord Jesus Christ the Saviour,
  In whom my best hope lies,
O give me strength that I may hush
  This vain man's blasphemies!
Let him seek through the earth; 'tis long and broad:
He will find fairer damsels, O my God!
He: I have sought through Calabria,
  Lombardy, and Tuscany,
Rome, Pisa, Lucca, Genoa,
  All between sea and sea: 100
Yea, even to Babylon I went
  And distant Barbary:
But not a woman found I anywhere
Equal to thee, who art indeed most fair.
She: If thou have all this love for me,
  Thou canst no better do
Than ask me of my father dear
  And my dear mother too:

  They willing, to the abbey-church
   We will together go,
 And, before Advent, thou and I will wed;
 After the which, I'll do as thou hast said.
He : These thy conditions, lady mine,
   Are altogether nought :
  Despite of them, I'll make a net
   Wherein thou shalt be caught.
  What, wilt thou put on wings to fly ?
   Nay, but of wax they're wrought,—
 They'll let thee fall to earth, not rise with thee :
 So, if thou canst, then keep thyself from me.
She : Think not to fright me with thy nets
   And suchlike childish gear ;
  I am safe pent within the walls
   Of this strong castle here ;
  A boy before he is a man
   Could give me as much fear.
 If suddenly thou get not hence again,
 It is my prayer thou mayst be found and slain.
He : Wouldst thou in very truth that I
   Were slain, and for thy sake ?
  Then let them hew me to such mince
   As a man's limbs may make !
  But meanwhile I shall not stir hence
   Till of that fruit I take
 Which thou hast in thy garden, ripe enough :
 All day and night I thirst to think thereof.
She : None have partaken of that fruit,
   Not Counts nor Cavaliers :
  Though many have reached up for it,
   Barons and great Seigneurs,
  They all went hence in wrath because
   They could not make it theirs.
 Then how canst *thou* think to succeed alone
 Who hast not a thousand ounces of thine own ?
He : How many nosegays I have sent
   Unto thy house, sweet soul !
  At least till I am put to proof,
   This scorn of thine control.

  For if the wind, so fair for thee,
   Turn ever and wax foul,
 Be sure that thou shalt say when all is done,
 ' Now is my heart heavy for him that 's gone.'
She: If by my grief thou couldst be grieved,
   God send me a grief soon !
  I tell thee that though all my friends
   Prayed me as for a boon,
  Saying, ' Even for the love of us,
   Love thou this worthless loon,'
 Thou shouldst not have the thing that thou dost hope.
 No, verily ; not for the realm o' the Pope.
He: Now could I wish that I in truth
   Were dead here in thy house :
  My soul would get its vengeance then ;
   Once known, the thing would rouse
  A rabble, and they'd point and say,—
   ' Lo ! she that breaks her vows,
 And, in her dainty chamber, stabs ! ' Love, see :
 One strikes just thus : it is soon done, pardie !
She: If now thou do not hasten hence,
   (My curse companioning,)
  That my stout friends will find thee here
   Is a most certain thing :
  After the which, my gallant sir,
   Thy points of reasoning
 May chance, I think, to stand thee in small stead,
 Thou hast no friend, sweet friend, to bring thee aid.
He: Thou sayest truly, saying that
   I have not any friend :
  A landless stranger, lady mine,
   None but his sword defend.
  One year ago, my love began,
   And now, is this the end ?
 Oh ! the rich dress thou worest on that day
 Since when thou art walking at my side alway !
She: So 'twas my dress enamoured thee !
   What marvel ? I did wear
  A cloth of samite silver-flowered,
   And gems within my hair.

But one more word ; if on Christ's Book
    To wed me thou didst swear, 190
There's nothing now could win me to be thine :
I had rather make my bed in the sea-brine.
He : And if thou make thy bed therein,
    Most courteous lady and bland,
I'll follow all among the waves,
    Paddling with foot and hand ;
Then, when the sea hath done with thee,
    I'll seek thee on the sand.
For I will not be conquered in this strife :
I'll wait, but win ; or losing, lose my life. 200
She : For Father, Son, and Holy Ghost,
    Three times I cross myself.
Thou art no godless heretic,
    Nor Jew, whose God's his pelf :
Even as I know it then, meseems,
    Thou needs must know thyself
That woman, when the breath in her doth cease,
Loseth all savour and all loveliness.
He : Woe's me ! Perforce it must be said
    No craft could then avail : 210
So that if thou be thus resolved,
    I know my suit must fail.
Then have some pity, of thy grace !
    Thou may'st, love, very well ;
For though thou love not me, my love is such
That 'tis enough for both—yea overmuch.
She : Is it even so ? Learn then that I
    Do love thee from my heart.
To-morrow, early in the day,
    Come here, but now depart. 220
By thine obedience in this thing
    I shall know what thou art,
And if thy love be real or nothing worth ;
Do but go now, and I am thine henceforth.
He : Nay, for such promise, my own life,
    I will not stir a foot.
I've said, if thou wouldst tear away
    My love even from its root,

    I have a dagger at my side
        Which thou mayst take to do't ;
    But as for going hence, it will not be.
    O hate me not ! my heart is burning me.
She : Think'st thou I know not that thy heart
        Is hot and burns to death ?
    Of all that thou or I can say,
        But one word succoureth.
    Till thou upon the Holy Book
        Give me thy bounden faith,
    God is my witness that I will not yield :
    For with thy sword 'twere better to be kill'd.
He : Then on Christ's Book, borne with me still
        To read from and to pray,
    (I took it, fairest, in a church,
        The priest being gone away,)
    I swear that my whole self shall be
        Thine always from this day.
    And now at once give joy for all my grief,
    Lest my soul fly, that's thinner than a leaf.
She : Now that this oath is sworn, sweet lord,
        There is no need to speak :
    My heart, that was so strong before,
        Now feels itself grow weak.
    If any of my words were harsh,
        Thy pardon : I am meek
    Now, and will give thee entrance presently.
    It is best so, sith so it was to be.

FOLCACHIERO DE' FOLCACHIERI, KNIGHT OF SIENA

Canzone

He speaks of his Condition through Love

ALL the whole world is living without war,
   And yet I cannot find out any peace.
      O God! that this should be!
O God! what does the earth sustain me for?
   My life seems made for other lives' ill-ease:
      All men look strange to me;
      Nor are the wood-flowers now
      As once, when up above
      The happy birds in love
Made such sweet verses, going from bough to bough.

And if I come where other gentlemen
   Bear arms, or say of love some joyful thing—
      Then is my grief most sore,
And all my soul turns round upon me then:
   Folk also gaze upon me, whispering,
      Because I am not what I was before.
      I know not what I am.
      I know how wearisome
      My life is now become,
And that the days I pass seem all the same.

I think that I shall die; yea, death begins;
   Though 'tis no set-down sickness that I have,
      Nor are my pains set down.
But to wear raiment seems a burden since
   This came, nor ever any food I crave;
      Not any cure is known
      To me, nor unto whom
      I might commend my case:
      This evil therefore stays
Still where it is, and hope can find no room.

I know that it must certainly be Love :
  No other Lord, being thus set over me,
    Had judged me to this curse ;
With such high hand he rules, sitting above
  That of myself he takes two parts in fee,
    Only the third being hers.
    Yet if through service I
    Be justified with God,
    He shall remove this load,
Because my heart with inmost love doth sigh.   40

Gentle my lady, after I am gone,
  There will not come another, it may be,
    To show thee love like mine :
For nothing can I do, neither have done,
  Except what proves that I belong to thee
    And am a thing of thine.
    Be it not said that I
    Despaired and perished, then ;
    But pour thy grace, like rain,
On him who is burned up, yea, visibly.   50

LODOVICO DELLA VERNACCIA

Sonnet

He exhorts the State to vigilance

THINK a brief while on the most marvellous arts
  Of our high-purposed labour, citizens ;
  And having thought, draw clear conclusion thence ;
And say, do not ours seem but childish parts ?
Also on these intestine sores and smarts
  Ponder advisedly ; and the deep sense
  Thereof shall bow your heads in penitence,
And like a thorn shall grow into your hearts.
If, of our foreign foes, some prince or lord
  Is now, perchance, some whit less troublesome,
    Shall the sword therefore drop into the sheath ?
    Nay, grasp it as the friend that warranteth :
  For unto this vile rout, our foes at home,
Nothing is high or awful save the sword.

SAINT FRANCIS OF ASSISI

Cantica

Our Lord Christ: of order [1]

SET Love in order, thou that lovest Me.
  Never was virtue out of order found ;
And though I fill thy heart desirously,
  By thine own virtue I must keep My ground :
When to My love thou dost bring charity,
  Even she must come with order girt and gown'd.
    Look how the trees are bound
    To order, bearing fruit ;
    And by one thing compute,
In all things earthly, order's grace or gain.   10

All earthly things I had the making of
  Were numbered and were measured then by Me ;
And each was ordered to its end by Love,
  Each kept, through order, clean for ministry.
Charity most of all, when known enough,
  Is of her very nature orderly.
    Lo, now ! what heat in thee,
    Soul, can have bred this rout ?
    Thou putt'st all order out.
Even this love's heat must be its curb and rein.   20

---

[1] This speech occurs in a long poem on Divine Love, half ecstatic, half scholastic, and hardly appreciable now. The passage stands well by itself, and is the only one spoken by our Lord.

FREDERICK II. EMPEROR

Canzone

Of his Lady in bondage

For grief I am about to sing,
  Even as another would for joy;
  Mine eyes which the hot tears destroy
Are scarce enough for sorrowing:
To speak of such a grievous thing
  Also my tongue I must employ,
Saying: Woe's me, who am full of woes!
  Not while I live shall my sighs cease
  For her in whom my heart found peace:
I am become like unto those   10
  That cannot sleep for weariness,
Now I have lost my crimson rose.

And yet I will not call her lost;
  She is not gone out of the earth;
  She is but girded with a girth
Of hate, that clips her in like frost.
Thus says she every hour almost:—
  'When I was born, 'twas an ill birth!
O that I never had been born.
  If I am still to fall asleep   20
  Weeping, and when I wake to weep;
If he whom I most loathe and scorn
  Is still to have me his, and keep
Smiling about me night and morn!

'O that I never had been born
  A woman! a poor, helpless fool,
  Who can but stoop beneath the rule
Of him she needs must loathe and scorn!
If ever I feel less forlorn,
  I stand all day in fear and dule,   30
Lest he discern it, and with rough
  Speech mock at me, or with his smile

So hard you scarce could call it guile :
No man is there to say, " Enough."
  O, but if God waits a long while,
Death cannot always stand aloof !

' Thou, God the Lord, dost know all this :
  Give me a little comfort then,
  Him who is worst among bad men
Smite thou for me.   Those limbs of his
Once hidden where the sharp worm is,
  Perhaps I might see hope again.
Yet for a certain period
  Would I seem like as one that saith
  Strange things for grief, and murmureth
With smitten palms and hair abroad :
  Still whispering under my held breath,
" Shall I not praise Thy name, O God ? "

' Thou, God the Lord, dost know all this :
  It is a very weary thing
  Thus to be always trembling :
And till the breath of his life cease,
The hate in him will but increase,
  And with his hate my suffering.
Each morn I hear his voice bid them
  That watch me, to be faithful spies
  Lest I go forth and see the skies ;
Each night, to each, he saith the same :—
  And in my soul and in mine eyes
There is a burning heat like flame.'

Thus grieves she now ; but she shall wear
  This love of mine, whereof I spoke,
  About her body for a cloak,
And for a garland in her hair,
Even yet : because I mean to prove,
Not to speak only, this my love.

ENZO, KING OF SARDINIA

Sonnet

On the Fitness of Seasons

There is a time to mount ; to humble thee
  A time ; a time to talk, and hold thy peace ;
  A time to labour, and a time to cease ;
A time to take thy measures patiently ;
A time to watch what Time's next step may be ;
  A time to make light count of menaces,
  And to think over them a time there is ;
There is a time when to seem not to see.
Wherefore I hold him well-advised and sage
  Who evermore keeps prudence facing him,
    And lets his life slide with occasion ;
And so comports himself, through youth to age,
  That never any man at any time
    Can say, Not thus, but thus thou shouldst have done.

GUIDO GUINICELLI

I. Sonnet

Concerning Lucy

When Lucy draws her mantle round her face,
  So sweeter than all else she is to see,
  That hence unto the hills there lives not he
Whose whole soul would not love her for her grace.
Then seems she like a daughter of some race
  That holds high rule in France or Germany :
  And a snake's head stricken off suddenly
Throbs never as then throbs my heart to embrace
Her body in these arms, even were she loth ;—
  To kiss her lips, to kiss her cheeks, to kiss
    The lids of her two eyes which are two flames.
    Yet what my heart so longs for, my heart blames :
  For surely sorrow might be bred from this
Where some man's patient love abides its growth.

II. Canzone

Of the gentle Heart

Within the gentle heart Love shelters him
  As birds within the green shade of the grove.
Before the gentle heart, in nature's scheme,
  Love was not, nor the gentle heart ere Love.
    For with the sun, at once,
So sprang the light immediately; nor was
    Its birth before the sun's.
And Love hath his effect in gentleness
    Of very self; even as
Within the middle fire the heat's excess.   10

The fire of Love comes to the gentle heart
  Like as its virtue to a precious stone;
To which no star its influence can impart
  Till it is made a pure thing by the sun:
    For when the sun hath smit
From out its essence that which there was vile,
    The star endoweth it.
And so the heart created by God's breath
    Pure, true, and clean from guile,
A woman, like a star, enamoureth.   20

In gentle heart Love for like reason is
  For which the lamp's high flame is fanned and bow'd:
Clear, piercing bright, it shines for its own bliss;
  Nor would it burn there else, it is so proud.
    For evil natures meet
With Love as it were water met with flame,
    As cold abhorring heat.
Through gentle heart Love doth a track divine,—
    Like knowing like; the same
As diamond runs through iron in the mine.   30

The sun strikes full upon the mud all day:
　　It remains vile, nor the sun's worth is less.
' By race I am gentle,' the proud man doth say:
　　He is the mud, the sun is gentleness.
　　　　Let no man predicate
That aught the name of gentleness should have,
　　　　Even in a king's estate,
Except the heart there be a gentle man's.
　　　　The star-beam lights the wave,—
Heaven holds the star and the star's radiance.　　　　40

God, in the understanding of high Heaven,
　　Burns more than in our sight the living sun:
There to behold His Face unveiled is given;
　　And Heaven, whose will is homage paid to One
　　　　Fulfils the things which live
In God, from the beginning excellent.
　　　　So should my lady give
That truth which in her eyes is glorified,
　　　　On which her heart is bent,
To me whose service waiteth at her side.　　　　50

My lady, God shall ask, ' What daredst thou ? '
　　(When my soul stands with all her acts review'd ;)
' Thou passedst Heaven, into My sight, as now,
　　To make Me of vain love similitude.
　　　　To Me doth praise belong,
And to the Queen of all the realm of grace
　　　　Who slayeth fraud and wrong.'
Then may I plead : ' As though from Thee he came,
　　　　Love wore an angel's face :
Lord, if I loved her, count it not my shame.'　　　60

III. Sonnet

He will praise his Lady

Yea, let me praise my lady whom I love :
  Likening her unto the lily and rose :
  Brighter than morning star her visage glows ;
She is beneath even as her Saint above ;
She is as the air in summer which God wove
  Of purple and of vermilion glorious ;
  As gold and jewels richer than man knows.
Love's self, being love for her, must holier prove.
Ever as she walks she hath a sober grace,
  Making bold men abashed and good men glad ;
    If she delight thee not, thy heart must err.
No man dare look on her, his thoughts being base :
  Nay, let me say even more than I have said ;—
    No man could think base thoughts who looked on her.

IV. Canzone

He perceives his Rashness in Love, but has no choice

I hold him, verily, of mean emprise,
  Whose rashness tempts a strength too great to bear ;
As I have done, alas ! who turned mine eyes
  Upon those perilous eyes of the most fair.
    Unto her eyes I bow'd ;
No need her other beauties in that hour
    Should aid them, cold and proud :
As when the vassals of a mighty lord,
    What time he needs his power,
Are all girt round him to make strong his sword.   10

With such exceeding force the stroke was dealt
  That by mine eyes its path might not be stay'd ;
But deep into the heart it pierced, which felt
  The pang of the sharp wound, and waxed afraid ;
    Then rested in strange wise,
As when some creature utterly outworn
    Sinks into bed and lies.
And she the while doth in no manner care,
    But goes her way in scorn,
Beholding herself alway proud and fair.   20

And she may be as proud as she shall please,
  For she is still the fairest woman found :
A sun she seems among the rest ; and these
  Have all their beauties in her splendour drown'd.
    In her is every grace,—
Simplicity of wisdom, noble speech,
    Accomplished loveliness ;
All earthly beauty is her diadem,
    This truth my song would teach,—
My lady is of ladies chosen gem.   30

Love to my lady's service yieldeth me,—
  Will I, or will I not, the thing is so,—
Nor other reason can I say or see,
  Except that where it lists the wind doth blow.
    He rules and gives no sign ;
Nor once from her did show of love upbuoy
    This passion which is mine.
It is because her virtue's strength and stir
    So fill her full of joy
That I am glad to die for love of her.   40

V. Sonnet

Of Moderation and Tolerance

He that has grown to wisdom hurries not,
   But thinks and weighs what Reason bids him do
And after thinking he retains his thought
   Until as he conceived the fact ensue.
Let no man to o'erweening pride be wrought,
   But count his state as Fortune's gift and due.
He is a fool who deems that none has sought
   The truth, save he alone, or knows it true.
Many strange birds are on the air abroad,
   Nor all are of one flight or of one force,
     But each after his kind dissimilar :
To each was portioned of the breath of God,
   Who gave them divers instincts from one source.
     Then judge not thou thy fellows what they are.

VI. Sonnet

Of Human Presumption

Among my thoughts I count it wonderful,
   How foolishness in man should be so rife
   That masterly he takes the world to wife
As though no end were set unto his rule :
In labour alway that his ease be full,
   As though there never were another life ;
   Till Death throws all his order into strife,
And round his head his purposes doth pull.
And evermore one sees the other die,
   And sees how all conditions turn to change,
     Yet in no wise may the blind wretch be heal'd.
I therefore say, that sin can even estrange
Man's very sight, and his heart satisfy
   To live as lives a sheep upon the field.

GUERZO DI MONTECANTI

Sonnet

He is out of Heart with his Time

If any man would know the very cause
   Which makes me to forget my speech in rhyme,
   All the sweet songs I sang in other time,—
I'll tell it in a sonnet's simple clause.
I hourly have beheld how good withdraws
   To nothing, and how evil mounts the while:
   Until my heart is gnawed as with a file,
Nor aught of this world's worth is what it was.
At last there is no other remedy
   But to behold the universal end;
     And so upon this hope my thoughts are urged:
To whom, since truth is sunk and dead at sea,
   There has no other part or prayer remain'd,
     Except of seeing the world's self submerged.

INGHILFREDI, SICILIANO

Canzone

He rebukes the Evil of that Time

Hard is it for a man to please all men:
   I therefore speak in doubt,
     And as one may that looketh to be chid.
But who can hold his peace in these days?—when
   Guilt cunningly slips out,
     And Innocence atones for what he did;
     When worth is crushed, even if it be not hid;
When on crushed worth, guile sets his foot to rise;
And when the things wise men have counted wise
     Make fools to smile and stare and lift the lid.   10

Let none who have not wisdom govern you :
   For he that was a fool
     At first shall scarce grow wise under the sun.
And as it is, my whole heart bleeds anew
   To think how hard a school
     Young hope grows old at, as these seasons run.
     Behold, sirs, we have reached this thing for one :—
The lord before his servant bends the knee,
And service puts on lordship suddenly.
     Ye speak o' the end ? Ye have not yet begun.   20

I would not have ye without counsel ta'en
   Follow my words ; nor meant,
     If one should talk and act not, to praise him
But who, being much opposed, speaks not again,
   Confesseth himself shent
     And put to silence,—by some loud-mouthed mime,
     Perchance, for whom I speak not in this rhyme.
Strive what ye can ; and if ye cannot all,
Yet should not your hearts fall :
     The fruit commends the flower in God's good time.

(For without fruit, the flower delights not God :)   31
   Wherefore let him whom Hope
     Puts off, remember time is not gone by.
Let him say calmly : ' Thus far on this road
   A foolish trust buoyed up
     My soul, and made it like the summer fly
     Burned in the flame it seeks : even so was I :
But now I'll aid myself : for still this trust,
I find, falleth to dust :
     The fish gapes for the bait-hook, and doth die.'   40

And yet myself, who bid ye do this thing,—
   Am I not also spurn'd
     By the proud feet of Hope continually ;
Till that which gave me such good comforting
   Is altogether turn'd
     Unto a fire whose heat consumeth me ?
     I am so girt with grief that my thoughts be

Tired of themselves, and from my soul I loathe
Silence and converse both ;
    And my own face is what I hate to see.   50

Because no act is meet now nor unmeet.
    He that does evil, men applaud his name,
    And the well-doer must put up with shame :
Yea, and the worst man sits in the best seat.

RINALDO D'AQUINO

I. CANZONE

He is resolved to be joyful in Love

A THING is in my mind,—
    To have my joy again,
Which I had almost put away from me.
    It were in foolish kind
    For ever to refrain
From song, and renounce gladness utterly.
Seeing that I am given into the rule
  Of Love, whom only pleasure makes alive,
    Whom pleasure nourishes and brings to growth :
      The wherefore sullen sloth   10
    Will he not suffer in those serving him ;
      But pleasant they must seem,
  That good folk love them and their service thrive ;
Nor even their pain must make them sorrowful.

    So bear he him that thence
      The praise of men be gain'd,—
He that would put his hope in noble Love ;
      For by great excellence
      Alone can be attain'd
That amorous joy which wisdom may approve.   20

The way of Love is this, righteous and just ;
　　Then whoso would be held of good account,
　　　　To seek the way of Love must him befit,—
　　　　　　Pleasure, to wit.
　　　Through pleasure, man attains his worthiness :
　　　　　　For he must please
All men, so bearing him that Love may mount
In their esteem ; Love's self being in his trust.

　　　Trustful in servitude
　　　　　　I have been and will be,　　　　　　　　30
And loyal unto Love my whole life through ;
　　　A hundred-fold of good
　　　　　Hath he not guerdoned me
For what I have endured of grief and woe ?
Since he hath given me unto one of whom
　　Thus much he said,—thou mightest seek for aye
　　　Another of such worth so beauteous.
　　　　　Joy therefore may keep house
　　　In this my heart, that it hath loved so well.
　　　　　Meseems I scarce could dwell　　　　　40
　　Ever in weary life or in dismay
If to true service still my heart gave room.

　　　Serving at her pleasaunce
　　　　　Whose service pleasureth,
I am enriched with all the wealth of Love.
　　　Song hath no utterance
　　　　For my life's joyful breath
Since in this lady's grace my homage throve.
Yea, for I think it would be difficult
　　One should conceive my former abject case :—　　50
　　　Therefore have knowledge of me from this rhyme.
　　　　　My penance-time
　　　Is all accomplished now, and all forgot,
　　　　　So that no jot
Do I remember of mine evil days.
It is my lady's will that I exult.

>   Exulting let me take
>   My joyful comfort, then,
> Seeing myself in so much blessedness.
>   Mine ease even as mine ache
>   Accepting, let me gain
> No pride towards Love ; but with all humbleness,
> Even still, my pleasurable service pay.
>   For a good servant ne'er was left to pine :
>   Great shall his guerdon be who greatly bears.
>   But, because he that fears
>   To speak too much, by his own silence shent,
>   Hath sometimes made lament,—
> I am thus boastful, lady ; being thine
> For homage and obedience night and day.

II. CANZONE

A Lady, in Spring, repents of her Coldness

>   Now, when it flowereth,
>   And when the banks and fields
>   Are greener every day,
>   And sweet is each bird's breath,
>   In the tree where he builds
>   Singing after his way,—
> Spring comes to us with hasty step and brief,
>   Everywhere in leaf,
> And everywhere makes people laugh and play.
>
>   Love is brought unto me
>   In the scent of the flower
>   And in the bird's blithe noise.
>   When day begins to be,
>   I hear in every bower
>   New verses finding voice :
> From every branch around me and above,
>   A minstrels' court of love,
> The birds contend in song about love's joys.

What time I hear the lark
    And nightingale keep Spring,
        My heart will pant and yearn
For love. (Ye all may mark
    The unkindly comforting
        Of fire that will not burn.)
And, being in the shadow of the fresh wood,
        How excellently good
A thing love is, I cannot choose but learn.

Let me ask grace ; for I,
    Being loved, loved not again.
        Now springtime makes me love,
And bids me satisfy
    The lover whose fierce pain
        I thought too lightly of :
For that the pain is fierce I do feel now.
        And yet this pride is slow
To free my heart, which pity would fain move.

Wherefore I pray thee, Love,
    That thy breath turn me o'er,
        Even as the wind a leaf ;
And I will set thee above
    This heart of mine, that's sore
        Perplexed, to be its chief.
Let also the dear youth, whose passion must
        Henceforward have good trust,
Be happy without words : for words bring grief.

JACOPO DA LENTINO

I. Sonnet

Of his Lady in Heaven

I HAVE it in my heart to serve God so
  That into Paradise I shall repair,—
  The holy place through the which everywhere
I have heard say that joy and solace flow.
Without my lady I were loth to go,—
  She who has the bright face and the bright hair;
  Because if she were absent, I being there,
My pleasure would be less than nought, I know.
Look you, I say not this to such intent
  As that I there would deal in any sin:
  I only would behold her gracious mien,
  And beautiful soft eyes, and lovely face,
That so it should be my complete content
  To see my lady joyful in her place.

II. Canzonetta

Of his Lady, and of her Portrait

MARVELLOUSLY elate,
  Love makes my spirit warm
  With noble sympathies:
As one whose mind is set
  Upon some glorious form,
  To paint it as it is;—
I verily who bear
Thy face at heart, most fair,
  Am like to him in this

Not outwardly declared,
  Within me dwells enclosed
  Thine image as thou art.
Ah! strangely hath it fared!
  I know not if thou know'st
  The love within my heart.
Exceedingly afraid,
My hope I have not said,
  But gazed on thee apart.

Because desire was strong,
  I made a portraiture   20
    In thine own likeness, love:
When absence has grown long,
  I gaze, till I am sure
    That I behold thee move;
As one who purposeth
To save himself by faith,
    Yet sees not, nor can prove.

Then comes the burning pain:
  As with the man that hath
    A fire within his breast,—   30
When most he struggles, then
  Most boils the flame in wrath,
    And will not let him rest.
So still I burned and shook,
To pass, and not to look
    In thy face, loveliest.

For where thou art I pass,
  And do not lift mine eyes,
    Lady, to look on thee:
But, as I go, alas!   40
  With bitterness of sighs
    I mourn exceedingly.
Alas! the constant woe!
Myself I do not know,
    So sore it troubles me.

And I have sung thy praise,
  Lady, and many times
    Have told thy beauties o'er.
Hast heard in anyways,
  Perchance, that these my rhymes   50
    Are song-craft and no more?
Nay, rather deem, when thou
Shalt see me pass and bow,
    These words I sicken for.

Delicate song of mine,
    Go sing thou a new strain:
Seek, with the first sunshine,
    Our lady, mine and thine,—
    The rose of Love's domain,
Than red gold comelier.   60
    'Lady, in Love's name hark
    To Jacopo the clerk,
Born in Lentino here.'

III. SONNET

No Jewel is worth his Lady

SAPPHIRE, nor diamond, nor emerald,
    Nor other precious stones past reckoning,
    Topaz, nor pearl, nor ruby like a king,
Nor that most virtuous jewel, jasper call'd,
Nor amethyst, nor onyx, nor basalt,
    Each counted for a very marvellous thing,
    Is half so excellently gladdening
As is my lady's head uncoronall'd.
All beauty by her beauty is made dim;
    Like to the stars she is for loftiness;
        And with her voice she taketh away grief.
        She is fairer than a bud, or than a leaf.
Christ have her well in keeping, of His grace,
And make her holy and beloved, like Him!

IV. CANZONETTA

He will neither boast nor lament to his Lady

Love will not have me cry
    For grace, as others do;
Nor as they vaunt, that I
    Should vaunt my love to you.
For service, such as all
Can pay, is counted small;
Nor is it much to praise
    The thing which all must know;—
    Such pittance to bestow
On you my love gainsays.   10

Love lets me not turn shape
  As chance or use may strike ;
As one may see an ape
  Counterfeit all alike.
Then, lady, unto you
Be it not mine to sue,
For grace or pitying.
  Many the lovers be
  That of such suit are free,—
It is a common thing.

A gem, the more 'tis rare,
  The more its cost will mount :
And, be it not so fair,
  It is of more account.
So, coming from the East,
The sapphire is increased
In worth, though scarce so bright ;
  I therefore seek thy face
  Not to solicit grace,
Being cheapened and made slight.

So is the colosmine
  Now cheapened, which in fame
Was once so brave and fine,
  But now is a mean gem.
So be such prayers for grace
Not heard in any place ;
Would they indeed hold fast
  Their worth, be they not said,
  Nor by true lovers made
Before nine years be past.

Lady, sans sigh or groan,
  My longing thou canst see ;
Much better am I known
  Than to myself, to thee.
And is there nothing else
That in my heart avails
For love but groan and sigh ?
  And wilt thou have it thus,
  This love betwixen us ?—
Much rather let me die.

JACOPO DA LENTINO

V. Canzonetta

Of his Lady, and of his making her Likeness

My Lady mine,[1] I send
  These sighs in joy to thee
Though, loving till the end,
  There were no hope for me
That I should speak my love;
  And I have loved indeed,
  Though, having fearful heed,
It was not spoken of.

Thou art so high and great
  That whom I love I fear;
Which thing to circumstate
  I have no messenger:
Wherefore to Love I pray,
  On whom each lover cries,
  That these my tears and sighs
Find unto thee a way.

Well have I wished, when I
  At heart with sighs have ach'd,
That there were in each sigh
  Spirit and intellect,
The which, where thou dost sit,
  Should kneel and sue for aid,
  Since I am thus afraid
And have no strength for it.

Thou, lady, killest me,
  Yet keepest me in pain,
For thou must surely see
  How, fearing, I am fain.
Ah! why not send me still
  Some solace, small and slight,
  So that I should not quite
Despair of thy good will?

[1] Madonna mia.

Thy grace, all else above,
  Even now while I implore,
Enamoureth my love
  To love thee still the more.
Yet scarce should I know well—
  A greater love to gain,
  Even if a greater pain,
Lady, were possible.   40

Joy did that day relax
  My grief's continual stress,
When I essayed in wax
  Thy beauty's life-likeness.
Ah! much more beautiful
  Than golden-haired Yseult,—
  Who mak'st all men exult,
Who bring'st all women dule

And certes without blame
  Thy love might fall to me,   50
Though it should chance my name
  Were never heard of thee.
Yea, for thy love, in fine,
  Lentino gave me birth,
  Who am not nothing worth
If worthy to be thine.

VI. Sonnet

Of his Lady's Face

HER face has made my life most proud and glad;
  Her face has made my life quite wearisome;
  It comforts me when other troubles come,
And amid other joys it strikes me sad.
Truly I think her face can drive me mad;
  For now I am too loud, and anon dumb.
  There is no second face in Christendom
Has a like power, nor shall have, nor has had.

JACOPO DA LENTINO

What man in living face has seen such eyes,
   Or such a lovely bending of the head,
   Or mouth that opens to so sweet a smile ?
In speech, my heart before her faints and dies,
   And into Heaven seems to be spirited ;
   So that I count me blest a certain while.

VII. CANZONE

At the End of his Hope

REMEMBERING this—how Love
   Mocks me, and bids me hoard
Mine ill reward that keeps me nigh to death,—
   How it doth still behove
   I suffer the keen sword,
Whence undeplor'd I may not draw my breath
   In memory of this thing
   Sighing and sorrowing,
   I am languid at the heart
     For her to whom I bow,
     Craving her pity now,
   And who still turns apart.

I am dying, and through her—
   This flower, from paradise
Sent in some wise, that I might have no rest.
   Truly she did not err
   To come before his eyes
Who fails and dies, by her sweet smile possess'd ;
   For, through her countenance
   (Fair brows and lofty glance !)
   I live in constant dule.
     Of lovers' hearts the chief
     For sorrow and much grief,
   My heart is sorrowful.

    For Love has made me weep
        With sighs that do him wrong,
Since, when most strong my joy, he gave this woe.
        I am broken, as a ship
            Perishing of the song,
Sweet, sweet and long, the songs the sirens know.   30
        The mariner forgets,
        Voyaging in those straits,
        And dies assuredly.
            Yea, from her pride perverse,
            Who hath my heart as hers,
        Even such my death must be.

    I deemed her not so fell
        And hard but she would greet,
From her high seat, at length, the love I bring;
        For I have loved her well;—   40
            Nor that her face so sweet
In so much heat would keep me languishing;
        Seeing that she I serve
        All honour doth deserve
        For worth unparallel'd.
            Yet what availeth moan
            But for more grief alone?
        O God! that it avail'd!

    Thou, my new song, shalt pray
        To her, who for no end   50
Each day doth tend her virtues that they grow,—
        Since she to love saith nay;—
            (More charms she had attain'd
Than sea hath sand, and wisdom even so);—
        Pray thou to her that she
        For my love pity me,
        Since with my love I burn,—
            That of the fruit of love,
            While help may come thereof,
        She give to me in turn.   60

MAZZEO DI RICCO DA MESSINA

I. CANZONE

He solicits his Lady's Pity

THE lofty worth and lovely excellence,
    Dear lady, that thou hast,
  Hold me consuming in the fire of love:
That I am much afeared and wildered thence,
    As who, being meanly plac'd,
  Would win unto some height he dreameth of.
      Yet, if it be decreed,
  After the multiplying of vain thought,
  By Fortune's favour he at last is brought
To his far hope, the mighty bliss indeed.

Thus, in considering thy loveliness,
    Love maketh me afear'd,—
  So high art thou, joyful, and full of good;—
And all the more, thy scorn being never less.
    Yet is this comfort heard,—
  That underneath the water fire doth brood,
      Which thing would seem unfit
  By law of nature. So may thy scorn prove
  Changed at the last, through pity into love,
If favourable Fortune should permit.

Lady, though I do love past utterance,
    Let it not seem amiss,
  Neither rebuke thou the enamoured eyes.
Look thou thyself on thine own countenance,
    From that charm unto this,
  All thy perfections of sufficiencies.
      So shalt thou rest assured
  That thine exceeding beauty lures me on
  Perforce, as by the passive magnet-stone
The needle, of its nature's self, is lured.

Certes, it was of Love's dispiteousness
    That I must set my life
  On thee, proud lady, who accept'st it not.
And how should I attain unto thy grace,
    That falter, thus at strife
  To speak to thee the thing which is my thought?
      Thou, lovely as thou art,
    I pray for God, when thou dost pass me by,
    Look upon me: so shalt thou certify,
By my cheek's ailing, that which ails my heart.   40

So thoroughly my love doth tend toward
    Thy love its lofty scope,
  That I may never think to ease my pain;
Because the ice, when it is frozen hard
    May have no further hope
  That it should ever become snow again.
      But, since Love bids me bend
      Unto thy seigniory,
      Have pity thou on me,
That so upon thyself all grace descend.   50

II. Canzone

After six years' Service he renounces his Lady

I LABOURED these six years
    For thee, thou bitter sweet;
    Yea, more than it is meet
That speech should now rehearse
    Or song should rhyme to thee;
But love gains never aught
    From thee, by depth or length;
    Unto thine eyes such strength
And calmness thou hast taught,
      That I say wearily:—   10
      'The child is most like me,
Who thinks in the clear stream
  To catch the round flat moon
And draw it all a-dripping unto him,—

MAZZEO DI RICCO

Who fancies he can take into his hand
   The flame o' the lamp, but soon
     Screams and is nigh to swoon
At the sharp heat his flesh may not withstand.'

Though it be late to learn
  How sore I was possest,
   Yet do I count me blest,
Because I still can spurn
    This thrall which is so mean.
For when a man, once sick,
  Has got his health anew,
   The fever which boiled through
His veins, and made him weak,
    Is as it had not been.
    For all that I had seen,
Thy spirit, like thy face,
   More excellently shone
Than precious crystal in an untrod place.
Go to: thy worth is but as glass, the cheat,
   Which, to gaze thereupon,
    Seems crystals, even as one,
But only is a cunning counterfeit.

Foil'd hope has made me mad,
  As one who, playing high,
   Thought to grow rich thereby,
And loses what he had.
    Yet I can now perceive
How true the saying is
  That says: 'If one turn back
   Out of an evil track
Through loss which has been his,
    He gains, and need not grieve.'
    To me now, by your leave,
It chances as to him
   Who of his purse is free
To one whose memory for such debts is dim.
Long time he speaks no word thereof, being loth.
   But having asked, when he
    Is answered slightingly,
Then shall he lose his patience and be wroth.

III Sonnet

Of Self-seeing

If any his own foolishness might see
  As he can see his fellow's foolishness,
  His evil speakings could not but prove less,
For his own fault would vex him inwardly.
But, by old custom, each man deems that he
  Has to himself all this world's worthiness;
  And thou, perchance, in blind contentedness,
Scorn'st *him*, yet know'st not what *I* think of *thee*.
Wherefore I wish it were so ordered
  That each of us might know the good that's his,
    And also the ill,—his honour and his shame.
For oft a man has on his proper head
  Such weight of sins, that, did he know but this,
    He could not for his life give others blame.

PANNUCCIO DAL BAGNO PISANO

Canzone

Of his Change through Love

My lady, thy delightful high command,
  Thy wisdom's great intent,
    The worth which ever rules thee in thy sway,
(Whose righteousness of strength hath ta'en in hand
    Such full accomplishment
  As height makes worthy of more height alway,)
Have granted to thy servant some poor due
    Of thy perfection; who
From them has gained a proper will so fix'd,
    With other thought unmix'd,   10
That nothing save thy service now impels
His life, and his heart longs for nothing else.

Beneath thy pleasure, lady mine, I am:
    The circuit of my will,
  The force of all my life, to serve thee so:
Never but only this I think or name,
    Nor ever can I fill
  My heart with other joy that man may know.
And hence a sovereign blessedness I draw,
    Who soon most clearly saw
That not alone my perfect pleasure is
    In this my life-service:
But Love has made my soul with thine to touch
Till my heart feels unworthy of so much.

For all that I could strive, it were not worth
    That I should be uplift
  Into thy love, as certainly I know:
Since one to thy deserving should stretch forth
    His love for a free gift,
  And be full fain to serve and sit below.
And forasmuch as this is verity,
    It came to pass with thee
That seeing how my love was not loud-tongued
    Yet for thy service long'd—
As only thy pure wisdom brought to pass,—
Thou knew'st my heart for only what it was.

Also because thou thus at once didst learn
    This heart of mine and thine,
  With all its love for thee, which was and is;
Thy lofty sense that could so well discern
    Wrought even in me some sign
  Of thee, and of itself some emphasis,
Which evermore might hold my purpose fast.
    For lo! thy law is pass'd
That this my love should manifestly be
    To serve and honour thee:
And so I do: and my delight is full,
Accepted for the servant of thy rule.

Without almost, I am all rapturous,
   Since thus my will was set   50
 To serve, thou flower of joy, thine excellence:
Nor ever seems it anything could rouse
   A pain or a regret,
 But on thee dwells mine every thought and sense;
Considering that from thee all virtues spread
   As from a fountain-head,—
That in thy gift is wisdom's best avail
   And honour without fail;
With whom each sovereign good dwells separate,
Fulfilling the perfection of thy state.   60

   Lady, since I conceived
Thy pleasurable aspect in my heart,
My life has been apart
In shining brightness and the place of truth;
   Which till that time, good sooth,
Groped among shadows in a darken'd place
   Where many hours and days
It hardly ever had remembered good.
   But now my servitude
Is thine, and I am full of joy and rest.   70
   A man from a wild beast
Thou madest me, since for thy love I lived.

GIACOMINO PUGLIESI, KNIGHT OF PRATO

I. Canzonetta

Of his Lady in Absence

The sweetly-favoured face
   She has, and her good cheer,
Have filled me full of grace
   When I have walked with her.
They did upon that day:
   And everything that pass'd
   Comes back from first to last
Now that I am away.

There went from her meek mouth
  A poor low sigh which made   10
My heart sink down for drouth.
  She stooped, and sobbed, and said,
' Sir, I entreat of you
  Make little tarrying:
  It is not a good thing
To leave one's love and go.'

But when I turned about
  Saying, ' God keep you well!'
As she look'd up, I thought
  Her lips that were quite pale   20
Strove much to speak, but she
  Had not half strength enough:
  My own dear graceful love
Would not let go of me.

I am not so far, sweet maid,
  That now the old love's unfelt:
I believe Tristram had
  No such love for Yseult:
And when I see your eyes
  And feel your breath again,   30
  I shall forget this pain
And my whole heart will rise.

II. CANZONETTA

To his Lady, in Spring

To see the green returning
  To stream-side, garden, and meadow,—
To hear the birds give warning,
  (The laughter of sun and shadow
Awakening them full of revel,)
  It puts me in strength to carol
A music measured and level,
  This grief in joy to apparel;
For the deaths of lovers are evil.

Love is a foolish riot, 10
　　And to be loved is a burden ;
Who loves and is loved in quiet
　　Has all the world for his guerdon.
Ladies on him take pity
　　Who for their sake hath trouble :
Yet, if any heart be a city
　　From love embarrèd double,
Thereof is a joyful ditty.

That heart shall be always joyful ;—
　　But I in the heart, my lady, 20
Have jealous doubts unlawful,
　　And stubborn pride stands ready.
Yet love is not with a measure,
　　But still is willing to suffer
Service at his good pleasure :
　　The whole Love hath to offer
Tends to his perfect treasure.

Thine be this prelude-music
　　That was of thy commanding ;
Thy gaze was not delusive,— 30
　　Of my heart thou hadst understanding.
Lady, by thine attemp'rance
　　Thou heldst my life from pining :
This tress thou gav'st, in semblance
　　Like gold of the third refining,
Which I do keep for remembrance.

III.   CANZONE

Of his Dead Lady

DEATH, why hast thou made life so hard to bear,
　　Taking my lady hence ?   Hast thou no whit
Of shame ?   The youngest flower and the most fair
　　Thou hast plucked away, and the world wanteth it.
O leaden Death, hast thou no pitying ?
Our warm love's very spring

Thou stopp'st, and endest what was holy and meet ;
And of my gladdening
Mak'st a most woful thing,
And in my heart dost bid the bird not sing
  That sang so sweet.

Once the great joy and solace that I had
  Was more than is with other gentlemen :—
Now is my love gone hence, who made me glad.
  With her that hope I lived in she hath ta'en
And left me nothing but these sighs and tears,—
Nothing of the old years
  That come not back again,
Wherein I was so happy, being hers.
Now to mine eyes her face no more appears,
Nor doth her voice make music in mine ears,
  As it did then.

O God, why hast thou made my grief so deep ?
  Why set me in the dark to grope and pine ?
Why parted me from her companionship,
  And crushed the hope which was a gift of thine ?
To think, dear, that I never any more
Can see thee as before !
  Who is it shuts thee in ?
Who hides that smile for which my heart is sore,
And drowns those words that I am longing for,
  Lady of mine ?

Where is my lady, and the lovely face
  She had, and the sweet motion when she walk'd ?—
Her chaste, mild favour—her so delicate grace—
  Her eyes, her mouth, and the dear way she talk'd ?—
Her courteous bending—her most noble air—
The soft fall of her hair ? . . .
My lady—she to whom my soul
  A gladness brought !
Now I do never see her anywhere,
And may not, looking in her eyes, gain there
  The blessing which I sought.

So if I had the realm of Hungary,
  With Greece, and all the Almayn even to France,
Or Saint Sophia's treasure-hoard, you see
  All could not give me back her countenance.
For since the day when my dear lady died
From us, (with God being born and glorified,)
  No more pleasaunce 50
Her image bringeth, seated at my side,
But only tears. Ay me! the strength and pride
  Which it brought once.

Had I my will, beloved, I would say
  To God, unto whose bidding all things bow,
That we were still together night and day:
  Yet be it done as His behests allow.
I do remember that while she remain'd
With me, she often called me her sweet friend;
  But does not now, 60
Because God drew her towards Him, in the end.
Lady, that peace which none but He can send
  Be thine. Even so.

FRA GUITTONE D'AREZZO

Sonnet

To the Blessed Virgin Mary

Lady of Heaven, the mother glorified
  Of glory, which is Jesus,—He whose death
  Us from the gates of Hell delivereth
And our first parents' error sets aside:—
Behold this earthly Love, how his darts glide—
  How sharpened—to what fate—throughout this earth!
  Pitiful Mother, partner of our birth,
Win these from following where his flight doth guide.
And O, inspire in me that holy love
  Which leads the soul back to its origin,
    Till of all other love the link do fail.
This water only can this fire reprove,—
  Only such cure suffice for suchlike sin;
    As nail from out a plank is struck by nail.

BARTOLOMEO DI SANT' ANGELO

Sonnet

He jests concerning his Poverty

I AM so passing rich in poverty
  That I could furnish forth Paris and Rome,
  Pisa and Padua and Byzantium,
Venice and Lucca, Florence and Forlì ;
For I possess in actual specie,
  Of nihil and of nothing a great sum ;
  And unto this my hoard whole shiploads come,
What between nought and zero, annually.
In gold and precious jewels I have got
  A hundred ciphers' worth, all roundly writ ;
    And therewithal am free to feast my friend.
    Because I need not be afraid to spend,
  Nor doubt the safety of my wealth a whit :—
No thief will ever steal thereof, God wot.

SALADINO DA PAVIA

Dialogue

Lover and Lady

She

    FAIR sir, this love of ours,
      In joy begun so well,
I see at length to fail upon thy part :
Wherefore my heart sinks very heavily.
    Fair sir, this love of ours
Began with amorous longing, well I ween :
Yea, of one mind, yea, of one heart and will
    This love of ours hath been.
    Now these are sad and still ;
For on thy part at length it fails, I see.   10
    And now thou art gone from me,
    Quite lost to me thou art ;
Wherefore my heart in this pain languisheth,
Which sinks it unto death thus heavily.

He

Lady, for will of mine
Our love had never changed in anywise,
    Had not the choice been thine
With so much scorn my homage to despise.
    I swore not to yield sign
Of holding 'gainst all hope my heart-service.   20
    Nay, let thus much suffice :—
    From thee whom I have serv'd,
All undeserved contempt is my reward,—
Rich prize prepar'd to guerdon fealty!

She

Fair sir, it oft is found
That ladies who would try their lovers so,
    Have for a season frown'd,
Not from their heart but in mere outward show.
    Then chide not on such ground,
Since ladies oft have tried their lovers so.   30
    Alas, but I will go,
    If now it be thy will.
Yet turn thee still, alas! for I do fear
Thou lov'st elsewhere, and therefore fly'st from me.

He

Lady, there needs no doubt
Of my good faith, nor any nice suspense
    Lest love be elsewhere sought.
For thine did yield me no such recompense,—
    Rest thou assured in thought,—
That now, within my life's circumference,   40
    I should not quite dispense
    My heart from woman's laws,
Which for no cause give pain and sore annoy,
And for one joy a world of misery.

BONAGGIUNTA URBICIANI, DA LUCCA

I. Canzone

Of the True End of Love ; with a Prayer to his Lady

NEVER was joy or good that did not soothe
    And beget glorying,
  Neither a glorying without perfect love.
Wherefore, if one would compass of a truth
    The flight of his soul's wing,
  To bear a loving heart must him behove.
Since from the flower man still expects the fruit,
  And, out of love, that he desireth ;
    Seeing that by good faith
  Alone hath love its comfort and its joy ;
For, suffering falsehood, love were at the root
Dead of all worth, which living must aspire ;
    Nor could it breed desire
  If its reward were less than its annoy.

Even such the joy, the triumph, and pleasaunce,
    Whose issue honour is,
  And grace, and the most delicate teaching sent
To amorous knowledge, its inheritance ;
    Because Love's properties
  Alter not by a true accomplishment ;
But it were scarcely well if one should gain,
  Without much pain so great a blessedness ;
    He errs, when all things bless,
  Whose heart had else been humbled to implore.
He gets not joy who gives no joy again ;
Nor can win love whose love hath little scope ;
    Nor fully can know hope
  Who leaves not of the thing most languished for.

Wherefore his choice must err immeasurably
    Who seeks the image when
  He might behold the thing substantial.
I at the noon have seen dark night to be,
    Against earth's natural plan,
  And what was good to worst abasement fall.

Then be thus much sufficient, lady mine ;
 If of thy mildness pity may be born,
  Count thou my grief outworn,
 And turn into sweet joy this bitter ill ;
Lest I might change, if left too long to pine :
As one who, journeying, in mid path should stay   40
  And not pursue his way,
 But should go back against his proper will.

Natheless I hope, yea trust, to make an end
  Of the beginning made,
 Even by this sign—that yet I triumph not.
And if in truth, against my will constrain'd,
  To turn my steps essay'd,
 No courage have I, neither strength, God wot.
Such is Love's rule, who thus subdueth me
 By thy sweet face, lovely and delicate ;   50
  Through which I live elate,
 But in such longing that I die for love.
Ah ! and these words as nothing seem to be :
For love to such a constant fear has chid
  My heart that I keep hid
 Much more than I have dared to tell thee of.

II. CANZONETTA

How he dreams of his Lady

 LADY, my wedded thought,
 When to thy shape 'tis wrought,
 Can think of nothing else
  But only of thy grace,
  And of those gentle ways
 Wherein thy life excels.
 For ever, sweet one, dwells
 Thine image on my sight,
  (Even as it were the gem
  Whose name is as thy name) [1]   10
 And fills the sense with light.

[1] The lady was probably called Diamante, Margherita, or some similar name.

Continual ponderings
That brood upon these things
Yield constant agony :
   Yea, the same thoughts have crept
   About me as I slept.
My spirit looks at me,
And asks, ' Is sleep for thee ?
Nay, mourner, do not sleep,
   But fix thine eyes, for lo !
   Love's fullness thou shalt know
By steadfast gaze and deep.'

Then, burning, I awake,
Sore tempted to partake
Of dreams that seek thy sight :
   Until, being greatly stirr'd,
   I turn to where I heard
That whisper in the night ;
And there a breath of light
Shines like a silver star.
   The same is mine own soul,
   Which lures me to the goal
Of dreams that gaze afar.

But now my sleep is lost ;
And through this uttermost
Sharp longing for thine eyes
   At length it may be said
   That I indeed am mad
With love's extremities.
Yet when in such sweet wise
Thou passest and dost smile,
   My heart so fondly burns,
   That unto sweetness turns
Its bitter pang the while.

Even so Love rends apart
My spirit and my heart,
Lady, in loving thee ;
   Till when I see thee now,
   Life beats within my brow
And would be gone from me.

So hear I ceaselessly,
Love's whisper well fulfill'd—
*Even I am he, even so,
Whose flame thy heart doth know:*
And while I strive I yield.

III. SONNET

Of Wisdom and Foresight

SUCH wisdom as a little child displays
  Were not amiss in certain lords of fame :
For where he fell, thenceforth he shuns the place,
  And having suffered blows, he feareth them.
Who knows not this may forfeit all he sways
  At length, and find his friends go as they came.
O therefore on the past time turn thy face,
  And, if thy will do err, forget the same.
Because repentance brings not back the past:
  Better thy will should bend than thy life break :
    Who owns not this, by him shall it appear.
  And, because even from fools the wise may make
Wisdom, the first should count himself the last,
  Since a dog scourged can bid the lion fear.

IV. SONNET

Of Continence in Speech

WHOSO abandons peace for war-seeking,
  'Tis of all reason he should bear the smart.
Whoso hath evil speech, his medicine
  Is silence, lest it seem a hateful art.
To vex the wasps' nest is not a wise thing ;
  Yet who rebukes his neighbour in good part,
A hundred years shall show his right therein.
  Too prone to fear, one wrongs another's heart.
If ye but knew what may be known to me,
  Ye would fall sorry sick, nor be thus bold
    To cry among your fellows your ill thought.
Wherefore I would that every one of ye
  Who thinketh ill, his ill thought should withhold :
    If that ye would not hear it, speak it not.

MEO ABBRACCIAVACCA DA PISTOIA

I. Canzone

He will be silent and watchful in his Love

Your joyful understanding, lady mine,
    Those honours of fair life
  Which all in you agree to pleasantness,
Long since to service did my heart assign;
    That never it has strife,
  Nor once remembers other means of grace;
But this desire alone gives light to it.
    Behold, my pleasure, by your favour, drew
      Me, lady, unto you,
All beauty's and all joy's reflection here:
  From whom good women also have thought fit
    To take their life's example every day;
      Whom also to obey
My wish and will have wrought, with love and fear.

With love and fear to yield obedience, I
    Might never half deserve:
  Yet you must know, merely to look on me,
How my heart holds its love and lives thereby;
    Though, well intent to serve,
  It can accept Love's arrow silently.
'Twere late to wait, ere I would render plain
  My heart, (thus much I tell you, as I should,)
    Which, to be understood,
Craves therefore the fine quickness of your glance.
So shall you know my love of such high strain
  As never yet was shown by its own will;
    Whose proffer is so still,
That love in heart hates love in countenance.

In countenance oft the heart is evident
    Full clad in mirth's attire,
      Wherein at times it overweens to waste:
Which yet of selfish joy or foul intent
    Doth hide the deep desire,
    And is, of heavy surety, double-faced;
Upon things double therefore look ye twice.
    O ye that love! not what is fair alone
      Desire to make your own,
But a wise woman, fair in purity;
    Nor think that any, without sacrifice
      Of his own nature, suffers service still;
      But out of high free-will;
In honour propped, though bowed in dignity.

In dignity as best I may, must I
    The guerdon very grand,
      The whole of it, secured in purpose, sing?
Lady, whom all my heart doth magnify,
    You took me in your hand,
    Ah! not ungraced with other guerdoning:
For you of your sweet reason gave me rest
    From yearning, from desire, from potent pain;
      Till, now, if Death should gain
Me to his kingdom, it would pleasure me,
    Having obeyed the whole of your behest.
      Since you have drawn, and I am yours by lot,
      I pray you doubt me not
Lest my faith swerve, for this could never be.

Could never be; because the natural heart
    Will absolutely build
      Her dwelling-place within the gates of truth;
And, if it be no grief to bear her part,
    Why, then by change were fill'd
    The measure of her shame beyond all truth.
And therefore no delay shall once disturb
  My bounden service, nor bring grief to it:
    Nor unto you deceit.
True virtue her provision first affords,

MEO ABBRACCIAVACCA

Ere she yield grace, lest afterward some curb
Or check should come, and evil enter in:
   For alway shame and sin
Stand cover'd, ready, full of faithful words.   70

II. BALLATA

His Life is by Contraries

By the long sojourning
  That I have made with grief,
    I am quite changed, you see:—
    If I weep, 'tis for glee;
  I smile at a sad thing;
    Despair is my relief.

Good hap makes me afraid;
Ruin seems rest and shade;
    In May the year is old;
    With friends I am ill at ease: 10
  Among foes I find peace;
    At noonday I feel cold.

The thing that strengthens others, frightens me.
    If I am grieved, I sing;
    I chafe at comforting;
Ill fortune makes me smile exultingly.

And yet, though all my days are thus,—despite
    A shaken mind, and eyes
    Which see by contraries,—
I know that without wings is an ill flight.   20

UBALDO DI MARCO

Sonnet

Of a Lady's Love for him

My body resting in a haunt of mine,
   I ranged among alternate memories;
   What while an unseen noble lady's eyes
Were fixed upon me, yet she gave no sign;
To stay and go she sweetly did incline,
   Always afraid lest there were any spies;
   Then reached to me,—and smelt it in sweet wise,
And reached to me—some sprig of bloom or bine.
Conscious of perfume, on my side I leant,
   And rose upon my feet, and gazed around
     To see the plant whose flower could so beguile.
Finding it not, I sought it by the scent;
   And by the scent, in truth, the plant I found,
     And rested in its shadow a great while.

SIMBUONO GIUDICE

Canzone

He finds that Love has beguiled him, but will trust in his Lady

Often the day had a most joyful morn
   That bringeth grief at last
Unto the human heart which deemed all well:
Of a sweet seed the fruit was often born
   That hath a bitter taste:
Of mine own knowledge, oft it thus befell.
I say it for myself, who, foolishly
   Expectant of all joy,
     Triumphing undertook
To love a lady proud and beautiful,
For one poor glance vouchsafed in mirth to me:
   Wherefrom sprang all annoy:
     For, since the day Love shook
My heart, she ever hath been cold and cruel.

SIMBUONO GIUDICE

Well thought I to possess my joy complete
    When that sweet look of hers
  I felt upon me, amorous and kind :
Now is my hope even underneath my feet.
    And still the arrow stirs
  Within my heart—(oh hurt no skill can bind !)—   20
Which through mine eyes found entrance cunningly !
    In manner as through glass
      Light pierces from the sun,
And breaks it not, but wins its way beyond,—
As into an unaltered mirror, free
    And still, some shape may pass.
      Yet has my heart begun
  To break, methinks, for I on death grow fond.

But, even though death were longed for, the sharp wound
  I have might yet be heal'd,   30
  And I not altogether sink to death.
In mine own foolishness the curse I found,
    Who foolish faith did yield
Unto mine eyes, in hope that sickeneth.
Yet might love still exult and not be sad—
    (For some such utterance
      Is at my secret heart)—
  If from herself the cure it could obtain,—
Who hath indeed the power Achilles had,
    To wit, that of his lance   40
      The wound could by no art
Be closed till it were touched therewith again.

So must I needs appeal for pity now
    From her on her own fault,
  And in my prayer put meek humility :
For certes her much worth will not allow
    That anything be call'd
Treacherousness in such an one as she,
In whom is judgement and true excellence.
    Wherefore I cry for grace ;   50
      Not doubting that all good,
  Joy, wisdom, pity, must from her be shed ;

For scarcely should it deal in death's offence,
    The so-belovèd face
      So watched for ; rather should
All death and ill be thereby subjected.

And since, in hope of mercy, I have bent
    Unto her ordinance
Humbly my heart, my body, and my life,
Giving her perfect power acknowledgement,—   60
    I think some kinder glance
She'll deign, and, in mere pity, pause from strife.
She surely shall enact the good lord's part :
    When one whom force compels
      Doth yield, he is pacified,
Forgiving him therein where he did err.
Ah ! well I know she hath the noble heart
    Which in the lion quells
      Obduracy of pride ;
Whose nobleness is for a crown on her.   70

MASOLINO DA TODI

Sonnet

Of Work and Wealth

A MAN should hold in very dear esteem
    The first possession that his labours gain'd ;
    For, though great riches be at length attain'd,
From that first mite they were increased to him.
Who followeth after his own wilful whim
    Shall see himself outwitted in the end ;
    Wherefore I still would have him apprehend
His fall, who toils not being once supreme.
Thou seldom shalt find folly, of the worst,
    Holding companionship with poverty,
      Because it is distracted of much care.
Howbeit, if one that hath been poor at first
    Is brought at last to wealth and dignity,
      Still the worst folly thou shalt find it there.

ONESTO DI BONCIMA, BOLOGNESE

I. SONNET

Of the Last Judgement

UPON that cruel season when our Lord
  Shall come to judge the world eternally ;
When to no man shall anything afford
  Peace in the heart, how pure soe'er it be ;
When heaven shall break asunder at His word,
  With a great trembling of the earth and sea ;
When even the just shall fear the dreadful sword,—
  The wicked crying, ' Where shall I cover me ? '—
When no one angel in His presence stands
  That shall not be affrighted of that wrath,
    Except the Virgin Lady, she our guide ;—
How shall I then escape, whom sin commands ?
  Out and alas on me ! There is no path,
    If in her prayers I be not justified.

II. SONNET

He wishes that he could meet his Lady alone

WHETHER all grace have fail'd I scarce may scan,
  Be it of mere mischance, or art's ill sway,
  That this-wise, Monday, Tuesday, every day,
Afflicts me, through her means, with bale and ban.
Now are my days but as a painful span ;
  Nor once ' Take heed of dying ' did she say.
I thank thee for my life thus cast away,
Thou who hast wearied out a living man.
Yet, oh ! my Lord, if I were blest no more
  Than thus much,—clothed with thy humility,
    To find her for a single hour alone,—
Such perfectness of joy would triumph o'er
  This grief wherein I waste, that I should be
    As a new image of Love to look upon.

TERINO DA CASTEL FIORENTINO

Sonnet

To Onesto di Boncima, in Answer to the Foregoing

If, as thou say'st, thy love tormenteth thee,
   That thou thereby wast in the fear of death,
Messer Onesto, couldst thou bear to be
   Far from Love's self, and breathing other breath?
Nay, thou wouldst pass beyond the greater sea
   (I do not speak of the Alps, an easy path),
For thy life's gladdening; if so to see
   That light which for *my* life no comfort hath,
But rather makes my grief the bitterer:
   For I have neither ford nor bridge—no course
To reach my lady, or send word to her.
And there is not a greater pain, I think,
   Than to see waters at the limpid source,
And to be much athirst, and not to drink.

MAESTRO MIGLIORE, DA FIORENZA

Sonnet

He declares all Love to be Grief

Love taking leave, my heart then leaveth me,
   And is enamour'd even while it would shun;
   For I have looked so long upon the sun
That the sun's glory is now in all I see.
To its first will unwilling may not be
   This heart (though by its will its death be won),
   Having remembrance of the joy forerun:
Yea, all life else seems dying constantly.
Ay and alas! in love is no relief,
   For any man who loveth in full heart,
      That is not rather grief than gratefulness.
Whoso desires it, the beginning is grief;
   Also the end is grief, most grievous smart;
      And grief is in the middle, and is call'd grace.

DELLO DA SIGNA

Ballata

His Creed of Ideal Love

Prohibiting all hope
Of the fulfilment of the joy of love,
  My lady chose me for her lover still.

So am I lifted up
To trust her heart which piteous pulses move,
  Her face which is her joy made visible.

Nor have I any fear
Lest love and service should be met with scorn,
  Nor doubt that thus I shall rejoice the more.

For ruth is born of prayer ;
Also, of ruth delicious love is born ;
  And service wrought makes glad the servitor.

Behold, I, serving more than others, love
    One lovely more than all :
  And, singing and exulting, look for joy
There where my homage is for ever paid.

And, for I know she does not disapprove
    If on her grace I call,
  My soul's good trust I will not yet destroy,
Though Love's fulfilment stand prohibited.

FOLGORE DA SAN GEMINIANO

I. Sonnet

To the Guelf Faction

Because ye made your backs your shields, it came
  To pass, ye Guelfs, that these your enemies
  From hares grew lions : and because your eyes
Turned homeward, and your spurs e'en did the same,
Full many an one who still might win the game
  In fevered tracts of exile pines and dies.
  Ye blew your bubbles as the falcon flies,
And the wind broke them up and scattered them.
This counsel, therefore. Shape your high resolves
  In good King Robert's humour,[1] and afresh
    Accept your shames, forgive, and go your way.
    And so her peace is made with Pisa ! Yea,
  What cares she for the miserable flesh
That in the wilderness has fed the wolves ?

II. Sonnet

To the Same

Were ye but constant, Guelfs, in war or peace,
  As in divisions ye are constant still !
  There is no wisdom in your stubborn will,
Wherein all good things wane, all harms increase.
But each upon his fellow looks, and sees
  And looks again, and likes his favour ill ;
  And traitors rule ye ; and on his own sill
Each stirs the fire of household enmities.
What, Guelfs ! and is Monte Catini[2] quite
  Forgot,—where still the mothers and sad wives
    Keep widowhood, and curse the Ghibellins ?
    O fathers, brothers, yea, all dearest kins !
  Those men of ye that cherish kindred lives
Even once again must set their teeth and fight.

[1] See what is said in allusion to his government of Florence by Dante (*Parad.* C. VIII).
[2] The Battle of Monte Catini was fought and won by the Ghibelline leader Uguccione della Faggiola against the Florentines, August 29, 1315.

III. Sonnet
Of Virtue

The flower of Virtue is the heart's content ;
  And fame is Virtue's fruit that she doth bear ;
  And Virtue's vase is fair without and fair
Within ; and Virtue's mirror brooks no taint ;
And Virtue by her names is sage and saint ;
  And Virtue hath a steadfast front and clear ;
  And Love is Virtue's constant minister ;
And Virtue's gift of gifts is pure descent.
And Virtue dwells with knowledge, and therein
  Her cherished home of rest is real love ;
    And Virtue's strength is in a suffering will ;
And Virtue's work is life exempt from sin,
  With arms that aid ; and in the sum hereof,
    All Virtue is to render good for ill.

OF THE MONTHS
Twelve Sonnets
Addressed to a Fellowship of Sienese Nobles [1]

DEDICATION

Unto the blithe and lordly Fellowship,
  (I know not where, but wheresoe'er, I know,
  Lordly and blithe,) be greeting ; and thereto,
Dogs, hawks, and a full purse wherein to dip ;
Quails struck i' the flight ; nags mettled to the whip ;
  Hart-hounds, hare-hounds, and blood-hounds even so ;
  And o'er that realm, a crown for Niccolò,
Whose praise in Siena springs from lip to lip.
Tingoccio, Atuin di Togno, and Ancaiàn,
  Bartolo and Mugaro and Faënot,
Who well might pass for children of King Ban,
  Courteous and valiant more than Lancelot,—
To each, God speed ! how worthy every man
  To hold high tournament in Camelot.

---

[1] This fellowship or club (*Brigata*), so highly approved and encouraged by our Folgore, is the same to which, and to some of its members

January

For January I give you vests of skins,
  And mighty fires in hall, and torches lit;
  Chambers and happy beds with all things fit;
Smooth silken sheets, rough furry counterpanes;
And sweetmeats baked; and one that deftly spins
  Warm arras; and Douay cloth, and store of it;
  And on this merry manner still to twit
The wind, when most his mastery the wind wins.
Or issuing forth at seasons in the day,
  Ye'll fling soft handfuls of the fair white snow
Among the damsels standing round, in play:
  And when you all are tired and all aglow,
Indoors again the court shall hold its sway,
  And the free Fellowship continue so.

by name, scornful allusion is made by Dante (*Inferno*, C. xxix, l. 130), where he speaks of the hare-brained character of the Sienese. Mr. Cayley, in his valuable notes on Dante, says of it: 'A dozen extravagant youths of Siena had put together by equal contributions 216,000 florins to spend in pleasuring; they were reduced in about a twelvemonth to the extremes of poverty. It was their practice to give mutual entertainments twice a-month; at each of which, three tables having been sumptuously covered, they would feast at one, wash their hands on another, and throw the last out of window'.

There exists a second curious series of sonnets for the months, addressed also to this club, by Cena della Chitarra d'Arezzo. Here, however, all sorts of disasters and discomforts, in the same pursuits of which Folgore treats, are imagined for the prodigals; each sonnet, too, being composed with the same terminations in its rhymes as the corresponding one among his. They would seem to have been written after the ruin of the club, as a satirical prophecy of the year to succeed the golden one. But this second series, though sometimes laughable, not having the poetical merit of the first, I have not included it.

My translations of Folgore's sonnets were made from the versions given in the forlorn Florentine collection of 1816, where editorial incompetence walks naked and not ashamed, indulging indeed in gambols as of Punch, and words which no voice but his could utter. Not till my book was in the printer's hands, did I meet with Nannucci's *Manuale del Primo Secolo* (1843), and am sorry that it is too late to avail myself of lights cast here and there by him on dark passages through which I had groped as I could. Nor is it only in these sonnets that his suggestions might have done me service, though fortunately the instances are never of much importance.

February

In February I give you gallant sport
  Of harts and hinds and great wild boars ; and all
  Your company good foresters and tall,
With buskins strong, with jerkins close and short ;
And in your leashes, hounds of brave report ;
  And from your purses, plenteous money-fall,
  In very spleen of misers' starveling gall,
Who at your generous customs snarl and snort.
At dusk wend homeward, ye and all your folk,
  All laden from the wilds, to your carouse,
    With merriment and songs accompanied :
And so draw wine and let the kitchen smoke ;
  And so be till the first watch glorious ;
    Then sound sleep to you till the day be wide.

March

In March I give you plenteous fisheries
  Of lamprey and of salmon, eel and trout,
  Dental and dolphin, sturgeon, all the rout
Of fish in all the streams that fill the seas.
With fishermen and fishing-boats at ease,
  Sail-barques and arrow-barques, and galleons stout,
  To bear you, while the season lasts, far out,
And back, through spring, to any port you please.
But with fair mansions see that it be fill'd,
  With everything exactly to your mind,
    And every sort of comfortable folk.
No convent suffer there, nor priestly guild :
  Leave the mad monks to preach after their kind
    Their scanty truth, their lies beyond a joke.

April

I GIVE you meadow-lands in April, fair
  With over-growth of beautiful green grass;
  There among fountains the glad hours shall pass,
And pleasant ladies bring you solace there.
With steeds of Spain and ambling palfreys rare;
  Provençal songs and dances that surpass;
  And quaint French mummings; and through hollow brass
A sound of German music on the air.
And gardens ye shall have, that every one
  May lie at ease about the fragrant place;
    And each with fitting reverence shall bow down
    Unto that youth to whom I gave a crown
  Of precious jewels like to those that grace
The Babylonian Kaiser, Prester John.

May

I GIVE you horses for your games in May,
  And all of them well trained unto the course,—
  Each docile, swift, erect, a goodly horse;
With armour on their chests, and bells at play
Between their brows, and pennons fair and gay;
  Fine nets, and housings meet for warriors,
  Emblazoned with the shields ye claim for yours;
Gules, argent, or, all dizzy at noonday.
And spears shall split, and fruit go flying up
In merry counterchange for wreaths that drop
  From balconies and casements far above;
And tender damsels with young men and youths
Shall kiss together on the cheeks and mouths;
  And every day be glad with joyful love.

JUNE

In June I give you a close-wooded fell,
  With crowns of thicket coiled about its head,
  With thirty villas twelve times turreted,
All girdling round a little citadel ;
And in the midst a springhead and fair well
  With thousand conduits branched and shining speed,
  Wounding the garden and the tender mead,
Yet to the freshened grass acceptable.
And lemons, citrons, dates, and oranges,
  And all the fruits whose savour is most rare,
Shall shine within the shadow of your trees ;
  And every one shall be a lover there ;
Until your life, so filled with courtesies,
  Throughout the world be counted debonair.

JULY

For July, in Siena, by the willow-tree,
  I give you barrels of white Tuscan wine
  In ice far down your cellars stored supine ;
And morn and eve to eat in company
Of those vast jellies dear to you and me ;
  Of partridges and youngling pheasants sweet,
  Boiled capons, sovereign kids : and let their treat
Be veal and garlic, with whom these agree.
Let time slip by, till by-and-by, all day ;
  And never swelter through the heat at all,
But move at ease at home, sound, cool, and gay ;
  And wear sweet-coloured robes that lightly fall ;
And keep your tables set in fresh array,
  Not coaxing spleen to be your seneschal.

AUGUST

For August, be your dwelling thirty towers
  Within an Alpine valley mountainous,
  Where never the sea-wind may vex your house,
But clear life separate, like a star, be yours.
There horses shall wait saddled at all hours,
  That ye may mount at morning or at eve:
  On each hand either ridge ye shall perceive,
A mile apart, which soon a good beast scours.
So alway, drawing homewards, ye shall tread
  Your valley parted by a rivulet
    Which day and night shall flow sedate and smooth.
There all through noon ye may possess the shade,
  And there your open purses shall entreat
    The best of Tuscan cheer to feed your youth.

SEPTEMBER

And in September, O what keen delight!
  Falcons and astors, merlins, sparrowhawks;
  Decoy-birds that shall lure your game in flocks;
And hounds with bells: and gauntlets stout and light;
Wide pouches; crossbows shooting out of sight;
  Arblasts and javelins; balls and ball-cases;
  All birds the best to fly at; moulting these,
Those reared by hand; with finches mean and slight;
And for their chase, all birds the best to fly;
  And each to each of you be lavish still
    In gifts; and robbery find no gainsaying;
And if you meet with travellers going by,
  Their purses from your purse's flow shall fill;
    And avarice be the only outcast thing.

October

Next, for October, to some sheltered coign
  Flouting the winds, I'll hope to find you slunk ;
  Though in bird-shooting (lest all sport be sunk),
Your foot still press the turf, the horse your groin.
At night with sweethearts in the dance you'll join,
  And drink the blessed must, and get quite drunk,
  There's no such life for any human trunk ;
And that's a truth that rings like golden coin !
Then, out of bed again when morning 's come,
  Let your hands drench your face refreshingly,
    And take your physic roast, with flask and knife.
Sounder and snugger you shall feel at home
  Than lake-fish, river-fish, or fish at sea,
    Inheriting the cream of Christian life.

November

Let baths and wine-butts be November's due,
  With thirty mule-loads of broad gold-pieces ;
  And canopy with silk the streets that freeze ;
And keep your drink-horns steadily in view.
Let every trader have his gain of you :
  Clareta shall your lamps and torches send,—
  Caëta, citron-candies without end ;
And each shall drink, and help his neighbour to.
And let the cold be great, and the fire grand :
  And still for fowls, and pastries sweetly wrought,
    For hares and kids, for roast and boiled, be sure
You always have your appetites at hand ;
  And then let night howl and heaven fall, so nought
    Be missed that makes a man's bed-furniture.

DECEMBER

LAST, for December, houses on the plain,
    Ground-floors to live in, logs heaped mountain-high,
    And carpets stretched, and newest games to try,
And torches lit, and gifts from man to man :
(Your host, a drunkard and a Catalan ;)
    And whole dead pigs, and cunning cooks to ply
    Each throat with tit-bits that shall satisfy ;
And wine-butts of Saint Galganus' brave span.
And be your coats well-lined and tightly bound,
    And wrap yourselves in cloaks of strength and weight,
        With gallant hoods to put your faces through.
And make your game of abject vagabond
    Abandoned miserable reprobate
        Misers ; don't let them have a chance with you.

CONCLUSION

AND now take thought, my sonnet, who is he
    That most is full of every gentleness ;
    And say to him (for thou shalt quickly guess
His name) that all his 'hests are law to me.
For if I held fair Paris town in fee,
    And were not called his friend, 'twere surely less.
    Ah ! had he but the emperor's wealth, my place
Were fitted in his love more steadily
Than is Saint Francis at Assisi. Alway
    Commend him unto me and his,—not least
        To Caian, held so dear in the blithe band.
' Folgore da San Geminiano ' (say),
    ' Has sent me, charging me to travel fast,
        Because his heart went with you in your hand.'

OF THE WEEK

Seven Sonnets

DEDICATION

There is among my thoughts the joyous plan
  To fashion a bright-jewelled carcanet,
  Which I upon such worthy brows would set,
To say, it suits them fairly as it can.
And now I have newly found a gentleman,
  Of courtesies and birth commensurate,
  Who better would become the imperial state
Than fits the gem within the signet's span.
Carlo di Messer Guerra Cavicciuoli,[1]
  Of him I speak,—brave, wise, of just award
    And generous service, let who list command:
  And lithelier limbed than ounce or lëopard.
He holds not money-bags, as children, holy;
    For Lombard Esté hath no freer hand.

Monday

The Day of Songs and Love

Now with the moon the day-star Lucifer
  Departs, and night is gone at last, and day
  Brings, making all men's spirits strong and gay,
A gentle wind to gladden the new air.
Lo! this is Monday, the week's harbinger;
  Let music breathe her softest matin-lay,
  And let the loving damsels sing to-day,
And the sun wound with heat at noontide here.
And thou, young lord, arise and do not sleep,
  For now the amorous day inviteth thee
The harvest of thy lady's youth to reap.
  Let coursers round the door, and palfreys, be,
    With squires and pages clad delightfully;
And Love's commandments have thou heed to keep.

[1] That is, according to early Tuscan nomenclature, Carlo, *the son of* Messer Guerra Cavicciuoli.

Tuesday

The Day of Battles

To a new world on Tuesday shifts my song,
  Where beat of drum is heard, and trumpet-blast;
  Where footmen armed and horsemen armed go past,
And bells say ding to bells that answer dong;
Where he the first and after him the throng,
  Armed all of them with coats and hoods of steel,
  Shall see their foes and make their foes to feel,
And so in wrack and rout drive them along.
Then hither, thither, dragging on the field
  His master, empty-seated goes the horse,
'Mid entrails strown abroad of soldiers kill'd;
  Till blow to camp those trumpeters of yours
Who noise awhile your triumph and are still'd,
  And to your tents you come back conquerors.

Wednesday

The Day of Feasts

And every Wednesday, as the swift days move,
  Pheasant and peacock-shooting out of doors
  You'll have, and multitude of hares to course,
And after you come home, good cheer enough;
And sweetest ladies at the board above,
  Children of kings and counts and senators;
  And comely-favoured youthful bachelors
To serve them, bearing garlands, for true love.
  And still let cups of gold and silver ware,
Runlets of vernage-wine and wine of Greece,
  Comfits and cakes be found at bidding there;
And let your gifts of birds and game increase:
  And let all those who in your banquet share
Sit with bright faces perfectly at ease.

Thursday

The Day of Jousts and Tournaments

For Thursday be the tournament prepar'd,
  And gentlemen in lordly jousts compete:
  First man with man, together let them meet,—
By fifties and by hundreds afterward.
Let arms with housings each be fitly pair'd,
  And fitly hold your battle to its heat
  From the third hour to vespers, after meat;
Till the best-winded be at last declared.
Then back unto your beauties, as ye came:
  Where upon sovereign beds, with wise control
    Of leaches, shall your hurts be swathed in bands.
    The ladies shall assist with their own hands,
And each be so well paid in seeing them
  That on the morrow he be sound and whole.

Friday

The Day of Hunting

Let Friday be your highest hunting-tide,—
  No hound nor brach nor mastiff absent thence,—
  Through a low wood, by many miles of dens,
All covert, where the cunning beasts abide:
Which now driven forth, at first you scatter wide,—
  Then close on them, and rip out blood and breath:
  Till all your huntsmen's horns wind at the death,
And you count up how many beasts have died.
Then, men and dogs together brought, you'll say:
  Go fairly greet from us this friend and that,
    Bid each make haste to blithest wassailings.
    Might not one vow that the whole pack had wings?
What! hither, Beauty, Dian, Dragon, what!
  I think we held a royal hunt to-day.

Saturday

The Day of Hawking

I'VE jolliest merriment for Saturday :—
  The very choicest of all hawks to fly
  That crane or heron could be stricken by,
As up and down you course the steep highway.
So shall the wild geese, in your deadly play,
  Lose at each stroke a wing, a tail, a thigh ;
  And man with man and horse with horse shall vie,
Till you all shout for glory and holiday.
Then, going home, you'll closely charge the cook :
  ' All this is for to-morrow's roast and stew.
Skin, lop, and truss : hang pots on every hook.
  And we must have fine wine and white bread too,
Because this time we mean to feast : so look
  We do not think your kitchens lost on you.'

Sunday

The Day of Balls and Deeds of Arms in Florence

AND on the morrow, at first peep o' the day
  Which follows, and which men as Sunday spell,—
  Whom most him liketh, dame or damozel,
Your chief shall choose out of the sweet array.
So in the palace painted and made gay
  Shall he converse with her whom he loves best ;
  And what he wishes, his desire express'd
Shall bring to presence there, without gainsay.
And youths shall dance, and men do feats of arms,
  And Florence be sought out on every side
From orchards and from vineyards and from farms :
  That they who fill her streets from far and wide
In your fine temper may discern such charms
  As shall from day to day be magnified.

GUIDO DELLE COLONNE

Canzone

To Love and to his Lady

O Love, who all this while hast urged me on,
  Shaking the reins, with never any rest,—
  Slacken for pity somewhat of thy haste;
I am oppress'd with languor and foredone,—
Having outrun the power of sufferance,—
  Having much more endured than who, through faith
  That his heart holds, makes no account of death.
Love is assuredly a fair mischance,
And well may it be called a happy ill:
  Yet thou, my lady, on this constant sting,   10
So sharp a thing, have thou some pity still,—
Howbeit a sweet thing too, unless it kill.

O comely-favoured, whose soft eyes prevail,
  More fair than is another on this ground,—
  Lift now my mournful heart out of its stound,
Which thus is bound for thee in great travail:
For a high gale a little rain may end.
  Also, my lady, be not angered thou
  That Love should thee enforce, to whom all bow.
There is but little shame to apprehend   20
If to a higher strength the conquest be;
  And all the more to Love who conquers all.
Why then appal my heart with doubts of thee?
Courage and patience triumph certainly.

I do not say that with such loveliness
  Such pride may not beseem; it suits thee well,
  For in a lovely lady pride may dwell,
Lest homage fail and high esteem grow less:
Yet pride's excess is not a thing to praise.
  Therefore, my lady, let thy harshness gain   30
  Some touch of pity which may still restrain

Thy hand, ere Death cut short these hours and days.
The sun is very high and full of light,
   And the more bright the higher he doth ride:
So let thy pride, my lady, and thy height,
Stand me in stead and turn to my delight.

Still inmostly I love thee, labouring still
   That others may not know my secret smart.
   Oh! what a pain it is for the grieved heart
To hold apart and not to show its ill!   40
Yet by no will the face can hide the soul;
   And ever with the eyes the heart has need
   To be in all things willingly agreed.
It were a mighty strength that should control
The heart's fierce beat, and never speak a word:
   It were a mighty strength, I say again,
To hide such pain, and to be sovran lord
Of any heart that had such love to hoard.

For Love can make the wisest turn astray;
   Love, at its most, of measure still has least;   50
   He is the maddest man who loves the best;
It is Love's jest, to make men's hearts alway
So hot that they by coldness cannot cool.
   The eyes unto the heart bear messages
   Of the beginnings of all pain and ease:
And thou, my lady, in thy hand dost rule
Mine eyes and heart which thou hast made thine own.
   Love rocks my life with tempests on the deep,
Even as a ship round which the winds are blown:
Thou art my pennon that will not go down.   60

PIER MORONELLI DI FIORENZA

Canzonetta

A bitter Song to his Lady

O LADY amorous,
Merciless lady,
Full blithely play'd ye
These your beguilings.
So with an urchin
A man makes merry,—
In mirth grows clamorous,
Laughs and rejoices,—
But when his choice is
To fall aweary,   10
Cheats him with silence.
This is Love's portion:—
In much wayfaring
With many burdens
He loads his servants,
But at the sharing,
The underservice
And overservice
Are alike barren.

As my disaster   20
Your jest I cherish,
And well may perish.
Even so a falcon
Is sometimes taken
And scantly cautell'd;
Till when his master
At length to loose him,
To train and use him,
Is after all gone,—
The creature's throttled   30
And will not waken.
Wherefore, my lady,
If you will own me,
O look upon me!

If I'm not thought on,
At least perceive me!
O do not leave me
So much forgotten!

If, lady, truly
You wish my profit,
What follows of it
Though still you say so?—
For all your well-wishes
I still am waiting.
I grow unruly,
And deem at last I'm
Only your pastime.
A child will play so,
Who greatly relishes
Sporting and petting
With a little wild bird:
Unaware he kills it,—
Then turns it, feels it,
Calls it with a mild word,
Is angry after,—
Then again in laughter
Loud is the child heard.

O my delightful
My own my lady,
Upon the Mayday
Which brought me to you
Was all my haste then
But a fool's venture?
To have my sight full
Of you propitious
Truly my wish was,
And to pursue you
And let love chasten
My heart to the centre.
But warming, lady,
May end in burning.
Of all this yearning

What comes, I beg you?
In all your glances
What is't a man sees?—
Fever and ague.

CIUNCIO FIORENTINO

Canzone

*Of his Love; with the Figures of a Stag, of Water, and
of an Eagle*

Lady, with all the pains that I can take,
  I'll sing my love renewed, if I may, well,
    And only in your praise.
The stag in his old age seeks out a snake
  And eats it, and then drinks, (I have heard tell)
    Fearing the hidden ways
Of the snake's poison, and renews his youth.
    Even such a draught, in truth,
Was your sweet welcome, which cast out of me,
    With whole cure instantly,   10
Whatever pain I felt, for my own good,
When first we met that I might be renew'd.

A thing that has its proper essence changed
  By virtue of some powerful influence,
    As water has by fire,
Returns to be itself, no more estranged,
  So soon as that has ceased which gave offence:
    Yea, now will more aspire
Than ever, as the thing it first was made.
    Thine advent long delay'd   20
Even thus had almost worn me out of love,
    Biding so far above:
But now that thou hast brought love back for me,
It mounts too much,—O lady, up to thee.

I have heard tell, and can esteem it true,
  How that an eagle looking on the sun,
    Rejoicing for his part
And bringing oft his young to look there too,—
  If one gaze longer than another one,
    On him will set his heart.   30
So I am made aware that Love doth lead
  All lovers, by their need,
To gaze upon the brightness of their loves;
  And whosoever moves
His eyes the least from gazing upon her,
The same shall be Love's inward minister.

RUGGIERI DI AMICI, SICILIANO

CANZONETTA

For a Renewal of Favours

I PLAY this sweet prelùde
  For the best heart, and queen
Of gentle womanhood,
  From here unto Messene;
Of flowers the fairest one;
The star that's next the sun;
  The brightest star of all.
What time I look at her,
My thoughts do crowd and stir
  And are made musical.   10

Sweetest my lady, then
  Wilt thou not just permit,
As once I spoke, again
  That I should speak of it?
My heart is burning me
Within, though outwardly
  I seem so brave and gay.
Ah! dost thou not sometimes
Remember the sweet rhymes
  Our lips made on that day?—   20

When I her heart did move
  By kisses and by vows,
Whom I then called my love,
  Fair-haired, with silver brows:
She sang there as we sat;
Nor then withheld she aught
  Which it were right to give;
But said, 'Indeed I will
Be thine through good and ill
  As long as I may live.'   30

And while I live, dear love,
  In gladness and in need
Myself I will approve
  To be thine own indeed.
If any man dare blame
Our loves,—bring him to shame,
  O God! and of this year
Let him not see the May.
Is't not a vile thing, say,
  To freeze at Midsummer?   40

CARNINO GHIBERTI, DA FIORENZA

Canzone

Being absent from his Lady, he fears Death

I AM afar, but near thee is my heart;
    Only soliciting
  That this long absence seem not ill to thee:
For, if thou knew'st what pain and evil smart
    The lack of thy sweet countenance can bring,
  Thou wouldst remember me compassionately.
Even as my case, the stag's is wont to be,
    Which, thinking to escape
His death, escaping whence the pack gives cry,
    Is wounded and doth die.   10
So, in my spirit imagining thy shape,
  I would fly Death, and Death o'ermasters me.

I am o'erpower'd of Death when, telling o'er
    Thy beauties in my thought,
  I seem to have that which I have not : then
I am as he who in each meteor,
Dazzled and wildered, sees the thing he sought.
  In suchwise Love deals with me among men :—
  Thee whom I have not, yet who dost sustain
My life, he bringeth in his arms to me   20
Full oft,—yet I approach not unto thee.
Ah ! if we be not joined i' the very flesh,
  It cannot last but I indeed shall die
    By burden of this love that weigheth so.
As an o'erladen bough, while yet 'tis fresh,
  Breaks, and itself and fruit are lost thereby,—
    So shall I, love, be lost, alas for woe !
And, if this slay indeed that thus doth rive
  My heart, how then shall I be comforted ?
    Thou, as a lioness   30
      Her cub, in sore distress
Might'st toil to bring me out of death alive :
  But couldst thou raise me up, if I were dead ?

Oh ! but an' if thou wouldst, I were more glad
    Of death than life,—thus kept
  From thee and the true life thy face can bring.
So in nowise could death be harsh or bad ;
  But it should seem to me that I had slept
  And was awakened with thy summoning.
Yet, sith the hope thereof is a vain thing,   40
    I, in fast fealty,
      Can like the Assassin [1] be,
Who, to be subject to his lord in all,
  Goes and accepts his death and has no heed :
  Even as he doth so could I do indeed.
Nevertheless, this one memorial—
The last—I send thee, for Love orders it.
He, this last once, wills that thus much be writ

[1] Alluding to the Syrian tribe of Assassins, whose chief was the Old Man of the Mountain.

In prayer that it may fall 'twixt thee and me
    After the manner of 50
    Two birds that feast their love
Even unto anguish, till, if neither quit
  The other, one must perish utterly.

PRINZIVALLE DORIA

Canzone

Of his Love, with the Figure of a sudden Storm

Even as the day when it is yet at dawning
  Seems mild and kind, being fair to look upon,
While the birds carol underneath their awning
  Of leaves, as if they never would have done ;
  Which on a sudden changes, just at noon,
And the broad light is broken into rain
  That stops and comes again ;
Even as the traveller, who had held his way
  Hopeful and glad because of the bright weather,
  Forgetteth then his gladness altogether ; 10
Even so am I, through Love, alas the day !

It plainly is through Love that I am so.
  At first, he let me still grow happier
Each day, and made her kindness seem to grow ;
  But now he has quite changed her heart in her.
  And I, whose hopes throbbed and were all astir
For times when I should call her mine aloud,
  And in her pride be proud
Who is more fair than gems are, ye may say,
  Having that fairness which holds hearts in rule ;—
  I have learnt now to count him but a fool 21
Who before evening says, A goodly day.

It had been better not to have begun,
  Since, having known my error, 'tis too late.
This thing from which I suffer, thou hast done,
  Lady : canst thou restore me my first state ?

The wound thou gavest canst thou medicate?
Not thou, forsooth: thou hast not any art
  To keep death from my heart.
O lady! where is now my life's full meed
  Of peace,—mine once, and which thou took'st away?
  Surely it cannot now be far from day:
Night is already very long indeed.

The sea is much more beautiful at rest
  Than when the storm is trampling over it.
Wherefore, to see the smile which has so bless'd
  This heart of mine, deem'st thou these eyes unfit?
  There is no maid so lovely, it is writ,
That by such stern unwomanly regard
  Her face may not be marr'd.
I therefore pray of thee, my own soul's wife,
  That thou remember me who am forgot.
  How shall I stand without thee? Art thou not
The pillar of the building of my life?

RUSTICO DI FILIPPO

I. SONNET

Of the Making of Master Messerin

WHEN God had finished Master Messerin,
  He really thought it something to have done:
  Bird, man, and beast had got a chance in one,
And each felt flattered, it was hoped, therein.
For he is like a goose i' the windpipe thin,
  And like a cameleopard high i' the loins;
  To which, for manhood, you'll be told, he joins
Some kinds of flesh-hues and a callow chin.
As to his singing, he affects the crow;
  As to his learning, beasts in general;
    And sets all square by dressing like a man.
God made him, having nothing else to do;
  And proved there is not anything at all
    He cannot make, if that's a thing He can.

II. Sonnet

Of the Safety of Messer Fazio [1]

MASTER BERTUCCIO, you are called to account
  That you guard Fazio's life from poison ill :
  And every man in Florence tells me still
He has no horse that he can safely mount.
A mighty war-horse worth a thousand pound
  Stands in Cremona stabled at his will ;
  Which for his honoured person should fulfil
Its use. Nay, sir, I pray you be not found
So poor a steward. For all fame of yours
  Is cared for best, believe me, when I say :—
    Our Florence gives Bertuccio charge of one
Who rides her own proud spirit like a horse ;
  Whom Cocciolo himself must needs obey ;
And whom she loves best, being her strongest son.

III. Sonnet

Of Messer Ugolino [2]

IF any one had anything to say
  To the Lord Ugolino, because he's
  Not staunch, and never minds his promises,
'Twere hardly courteous, for it is his way.
Courteous it were to say such sayings nay :
  As thus : He's true, sir, only takes his ease
  And don't care merely if it plague or please,
And has good thoughts, no doubt, if they would stay.
Now I know he's so loyal every whit
  And altogether worth such a good word
As worst would best and best would worst befit.
  He'd love his party with a dear accord
If only he could once quite care for it,
  But can't run post for any Law or Lord.

[1] I have not been able to trace the Fazio to whom this sonnet refers.
[2] The character here drawn certainly suggests Count Ugolino de' Gherardeschi, though it would seem that Rustico died nearly twenty years before the tragedy of the Tower of Famine.

PUCCIARELLO DI FIORENZA

Sonnet

Of Expediency

Pass and let pass,—this counsel I would give,—
    And wrap thy cloak what way the wind may blow;
    Who cannot raise himself were wise to know
How best, by dint of stooping, he may thrive.
Take for ensample this: when the winds drive
    Against it, how the sapling tree bends low,
    And, once being prone, abideth even so
Till the hard harsh wind cease to rend and rive.
Wherefore, when thou behold'st thyself abased,
    Be blind, deaf, dumb; yet therewith none the less
    Note thou in peace what thou shalt hear and see,
Till from such state by Fortune thou be raised.
    Then hack, lop, buffet, thrust, and so redress
    Thine ill that it may not return on thee.

ALBERTUCCIO DELLA VIOLA

Canzone

Of his Lady dancing

Among the dancers I beheld her dance,
Her who alone is my heart's sustenance.

So, as she danced, I took this wound of her;
    Alas! the flower of flowers, she did not fail.
Woe 's me! I will be Jew and blasphemer
    If the good god of Love do not prevail
To bring me to thy grace, oh! thou most fair.
    My lady and my lord! alas for wail!
How many days and how much sufferance?

Oh! would to God that I had never seen
  Her face, nor had beheld her dancing so!
Then had I missed this wound which is so keen—
  Yea, mortal—for I think not to win through
Unless her love be my sweet medicine;
  Whereof I am in doubt, alas for woe!
Fearing therein but such a little chance.

She was apparelled in a Syrian cloth,
  My lady:—oh! but she did grace the same,
Gladdening all folk, that they were nowise loth
  At sight of her to put their ills from them.
But upon me her power hath had such growth
  That nought of joy thenceforth, but a live flame,
Stirs at my heart,—which is her countenance.

Sweet-smelling rose, sweet, sweet to smell and see,
  Great solace had she in her eyes for all;
But heavy woe is mine; for upon me
  Her eyes, as they were wont, did never fall.
Which thing if it were done advisedly,
  I would choose death, that could no more appal,
Not caring for my life's continuance.

TOMMASO BUZZUOLA, DA FAENZA
Sonnet
He is in awe of his Lady

Even as the moon amid the stars doth shed
  Her lovelier splendour of exceeding light,—
Even so my lady seems the queen and head
  Among all other ladies in my sight.
Her human visage, like an angel's made,
  Is glorious even to beauty's perfect height;
And with her simple bearing soft and staid
  All secret modesties of soul unite.
I therefore feel a dread in loving her;
  Because of thinking on her excellence,
    The wisdom and the beauty which she has.
  I pray her for the sake of God,—whereas
  I am her servant, yet in sore suspense
Have held my peace,—to have me in her care.

NOFFO BONAGUIDA

Sonnet

He is enjoined to pure Love

A SPIRIT of Love, with Love's intelligence,
  Maketh his sojourn alway in my breast,
  Maintaining me in perfect joy and rest ;
Nor could I live an hour, were he gone thence :
Through whom my love hath such full permanence
  That thereby other loves seem dispossess'd.
  I have no pain, nor am with sighs oppress'd,
So calm is the benignant influence.
Because this spirit of Love, who speaks to me
  Of my dear lady's tenderness and worth,
    Says : ' More than thus to love her seek thou not,
    Even as she loves thee in her wedded thought ;
But honour her in thy heart delicately :
  For this is the most blessed joy on earth.'

LIPPO PASCHI DE' BARDI

Sonnet

He solicits a Lady's Favours

WERT thou as prone to yield unto my prayer
  The thing, sweet virgin, which I ask of thee,
  As to repeat, with all humility,
' Pray you go hence, and of your speech forbear ' ;—
Then unto joy might I my heart prepare,
  Having my fellows in subserviency ;
  But, for that thou contemn'st and mockest me,
Whether of life or death I take no care.
Because my heart may not assuage its drouth
  Nor ever may again rejoice at all
    Till the sweet face bend to be felt of man,—
Till tenderly the beautiful soft mouth
  I kiss by thy good leave ; thenceforth to call
    Blessing and triumph Love's extremest ban.

SER PACE, NOTAIO DA FIORENZA

Sonnet

A Return to Love

A FRESH content of fresh enamouring
  Yields me afresh, at length, the sense of song,
  Who had well-nigh forgotten Love so long :
But now my homage he will have me bring.
So that my life is now a joyful thing,
  Having new-found desire, elate and strong,
  In her to whom all grace and worth belong,
On whom I now attend for ministering.
The countenance remembering, with the limbs,
  She was all imaged on my heart at once
    Suddenly by a single look at her :
Whom when I now behold, a heat there seems
  Within, as of a subtle fire that runs
    Unto my heart, and remains burning there.

NICCOLÒ DEGLI ALBIZZI

Prolonged Sonnet

When the Troops were returning from Milan

If you could see, fair brother, how dead beat
  The fellows look who come through Rome to-day,—
  Black yellow smoke dried visages,—you'd say
They thought their haste at going all too fleet.
Their empty victual-waggons up the street
  Over the bridge dreadfully sound and sway ;
  Their eyes, as hanged men's, turning the wrong way ;
And nothing on their backs, or heads, or feet.
One sees the ribs and all the skeletons
  Of their gaunt horses ; and a sorry sight
Are the torn saddles, crammed with straw and stones.
  They are ashamed, and march throughout the night ;
Stumbling, for hunger, on their marrowbones ;
  Like barrels rolling, jolting, in this plight.
Their arms all gone, not even their swords are saved ;
And each as silent as a man being shaved.

FRANCESCO DA BARBERINO

I. Blank Verse [1]

A Virgin declares her Beauties

Do not conceive that I shall here recount
All my own beauty : yet I promise you
That you, by what I tell, shall understand
All that befits and that is well to know.

My bosom, which is very softly made,
Of a white even colour without stain,
Bears two fair apples, fragrant, sweetly-savoured,
Gathered together from the Tree of Life
The which is in the midst of Paradise.
And these no person ever yet has touched ;   10
For out of nurse's and of mother's hands
I was, when God in secret gave them me.
These ere I yield I must know well to whom ;
And for that I would not be robbed of them,
I speak not all the virtue that they have ;
Yet thus far speaking :—blessed were the man
Who once should touch them, were it but a little ;—
See them I say not, for that might not be.
My girdle, clipping pleasure round about,
Over my clear dress even unto my knees   20
Hangs down with sweet precision tenderly ;
And under it Virginity abides.
Faithful and simple and of plain belief
She is, with her fair garland bright like gold ;
And very fearful if she overhears
Speech of herself ; the wherefore ye perceive
That I speak soft lest she be made ashamed.

Lo ! this is she who hath for company
The Son of God and Mother of the Son ;
Lo ! this is she who sits with many in heaven ;   30
Lo ! this is she with whom are few on earth.

---

[1] Extracted from his long treatise, in unrhymed verse and in prose, 'Of the Government and Conduct of Women' (*Del Reggimento e dei Costumi delle Donne*).

II. Sentenze[1]

Of Sloth against Sin

THERE is a vice which oft
   I've heard men praise; and divers forms it has;
   And it is this. Whereas
Some, by their wisdom, lordship, or repute,

When tumults are afoot,
   Might stifle them, or at the least allay,—
   These certain ones will say,
' The wise man bids thee fly the noise of men.'

One says, ' Wouldst thou maintain
   Worship,—avoid where thou mayst not avail;   10
   And do not breed worse ail
By adding one more voice to strife begun.'

Another, with this one,
   Avers, ' I could but bear a small expense,
   Or yield a slight defence.'
A third says this, ' I could but offer words.'

Or one, whose tongue records
   Unwillingly his own base heart, will say,
   ' I'll not be led astray
To bear a hand in others' life or death.'   20

They have it in their teeth!
   For unto this each man is pledged and bound;
   And this thing shall be found
Entered against him at the Judgement Day.

III. Sentenze

Of Sins in Speech

Now these four things, if thou
   Consider, are so bad that none are worse.
   First,—among counsellors
To thrust thyself, when not called absolutely.

---

[1] This and the three following pieces are extracted from his ' Documents of Love ' (*Documenti d' Amore*).

And in the other three
  Many offend by their own evil wit.
  When men in council sit,
One talks because he loves not to be still;

And one to have his will;
  And one f r nothing else but only show.   10
  These rules were well to know,
First for the first, for the others afterward.

Where many are repair'd
  And met together, never go with them
  Unless thou'rt called by name.
This for the first: now for the other three.

What truly thou dost see
  Turn in thy mind, and faithfully report;
  And in the plainest sort
Thy wisdom may, proffer thy counselling.   20

There is another thing
  Belongs hereto, the which is on this wise.
  If one should ask advice
Of thine for his own need whate'er it be,—

This is my word to thee:—
  Deny it if it be not clearly of use:
  Or turn to some excuse
That may avail, and thou shalt have done well.

IV. SENTENZE

Of Importunities and Troublesome Persons

THERE is a vice prevails
  Concerning which I'll set you on your guard;
  And other four, which hard
It were (as may be thought) that I should blame.

Some think that still of *them*—
  Whate'er is said—some ill speech lies beneath;
  And this to them is death:
Whereby we plainly may perceive their sins.

And now let others wince.
  One sort there is, who, thinking that they please,   10
  (Because no wit's in these,)
Where'er you go, will stick to you all day,

And answer, (when you say,
  ' Don't let me tire you out ! ') ' Oh never mind—
  Say nothing of the kind,—
It's quite a pleasure to be where you are ! '

A second,—when, as far
  As he could follow you, the whole day long
  He's sung you his dull song,
And you for courtesy have borne with it,—   20

Will think you've had a treat.
  A third will take his special snug delight,—
  Some day you've come in sight
Of some great thought and got it well in view,—

Just then to drop on you.
  A fourth, for any insult you've received
  Will say he *is so* grieved,
And daily bring the subject up again.

So now I would be fain
  To show you your best course at all such times;   30
  And counsel you in rhymes
That you yourself offend not in likewise.

In these four cases lies
  This help :—to think upon your own affair,
  Just showing here and there
By just a word that you are listening ;

And still to the last thing
  That's said to you attend in your reply,
  And let the rest go by,—
It's quite a chance if he remembers them.   40

Yet do not, all the same,
  Deny your ear to any speech of weight.
  But if importunate
The speaker is, and will not be denied,

Just turn the speech aside
  When you can find some plausible pretence;
  For if you have the sense,
By a quick question or a sudden doubt

You may so put him out
  That he shall not remember where he was,　　　50
  And by such means you'll pass
Upon your way and be well rid of him.

And now it doth beseem
  I give you the advice I promised you.
  Before you have to do
With men whom you must meet continually,

Take notice what they be;
  And so you shall find readily enough
  If you can win their love,
And give yourself for answer Yes or No.　　　60

And finding Yes, do so
  That still the love between you may increase.
  Yet if they be of these
Whom sometimes it is hard to understand,

Let some slight cause be plann'd,
  And seem to go,—so you shall learn their will:
  And if but one sit still
As 'twere in thought,—then go, unless he call.

Lastly, if insult gall
  Your friend, this is the course that you should take.
  At first 'tis well you make　　　71
As much lament thereof as you think fit,—

Then speak no more of it,
  Unless himself should bring it up again;
  And then no more refrain
From full discourse, but say his grief is yours.

V. Sentenze

Of Caution

Say, wouldst thou guard thy son,
That sorrow he may shun?
Begin at the beginning
And let him keep from sinning.
Wouldst guard thy house? One door
Make to it, and no more.
Wouldst guard thine orchard-wall?
Be free of fruit to all

FAZIO DEGLI UBERTI

I. Canzone

His Portrait of his Lady, Angiola of Verona

I look at the crisp golden-threaded hair
  Whereof, to thrall my heart, Love twists a net,
  Using at times a string of pearls for bait,
    And sometimes with a single rose therein.
I look into her eyes which unaware
  Through mine own eyes to my heart penetrate;
  Their splendour, that is excellently great,
    To the sun's radiance seeming near akin,
    Yet from herself a sweeter light to win.
So that I, gazing on that lovely one,
  Discourse in this wise with my secret thought:—
  'Woe's me! why am I not,
Even as my wish, alone with her alone,—
  That hair of hers, so heavily uplaid,
  To shed down braid by braid,
And make myself two mirrors of her eyes
Within whose light all other glory dies?'

I look at the amorous beautiful mouth,
  The spacious forehead which her locks enclose,
  The small white teeth, the straight and shapely nose,
    And the clear brows of a sweet pencilling.

And then the thought within me gains full growth,
  Saying, ' Be careful that thy glance now goes
  Between her lips, red as an open rose,
    Quite full of every dear and precious thing;
    And listen to her gracious answering,
Born of the gentle mind that in her dwells,
  Which from all things can glean the nobler half.
  Look thou when she doth laugh
How much her laugh is sweeter than aught else.'
  Thus evermore my spirit makes avow
  Touching her mouth ; till now
I would give anything that I possess,
Only to hear her mouth say frankly, ' Yes.'

I look at her white easy neck, so well
  From shoulders and from bosom lifted out;
  And at her round cleft chin, which beyond doubt
    No fancy in the world could have design'd.
And then, with longing grown more voluble,
  ' Were it not pleasant now,' pursues my thought,
  ' To have that neck within thy two arms caught
    And kiss it till the mark were left behind ? '
    Then, urgently : ' The eyelids of thy mind
Open thou : if such loveliness be given
  To sight here,—what of that which she doth hide ?
  Only the wondrous ride
Of sun and planets through the visible heaven
Tells us that there beyond is Paradise.
  Thus, if thou fix thine eyes,
Of a truth certainly thou must infer
That every earthly joy abides in her.'

I look at the large arms, so lithe and round,—
  At the hands, which are white and rosy too,—
  At the long fingers, clasped and woven through,
    Bright with the ring which one of them doth wear.
Then my thought whispers : ' Were thy body wound
  Within those arms, as loving women's do,
  In all thy veins were born a life made new
    Which thou couldst find no language to declare.
    Behold if any picture can compare

With her just limbs, each fit in shape and size,
  Or match her angel's colour like a pearl.
  She is a gentle girl
To see; yet when it needs, her scorn can rise.
  Meek, bashful, and in all things temperate,
  Her virtue holds its state;
In whose least act there is that gift express'd
Which of all reverence makes her worthiest.'

Soft as a peacock steps she, or as a stork
  Straight on herself, taller and statelier:
  'Tis a good sight how every limb doth stir
For ever in a womanly sweet way.
'Open thy soul to see God's perfect work,'
  (My thought begins afresh,) 'and look at her
  When with some lady-friend exceeding fair
She bends and mingles arms and locks in play.
  Even as all lesser lights vanish away,
When the sun moves, before his dazzling face,
So is this lady brighter than all these.
  How should she fail to please,—
Love's self being no more than her loveliness?
  In all her ways some beauty springs to view;
  All that she loves to do
Tends alway to her honour's single scope;
And only from good deeds she draws her hope.'

Song, thou canst surely say, without pretence,
  That since the first fair woman ever made,
  Not one can have display'd
    More power upon all hearts than this one doth;
  Because in her are both
Loveliness and the soul's true excellence:—
And yet (woe's me!) is pity absent thence?

II. Extract from the 'Dittamondo'[1]
(Lib. iv. Cap. 23)

Of England, and of its Marvels

Now to Great Britain we must make our way,
Unto which kingdom Brutus gave its name
What time he won it from the giants' rule.
'Tis thought at first its name was Albion,
And Anglia, from a damsel, afterwards.
The island is so great and rich and fair,
It conquers others that in Europe be,
Even as the sun surpasses other stars.
Many and great sheep-pastures bountifully
Nature has set there, and herein more bless'd, 10
That they can hold themselves secure from wolves.
Black amber[2] also doth the land enrich,
(Whose properties my guide Solinus here
Told me, and how its colour comes to it ;)

---

[1] I am quite sorry (after the foregoing love-song, the original of which is not perhaps surpassed by any poem of its class in existence) to endanger the English reader's respect for Fazio by these extracts from the *Dittamondo*, or ' Song of the World ', in which he will find his own country endowed with some astounding properties. However, there are a few fine characteristic sentences, and the rest is no more absurd than other travellers' tales of that day ; while the table of our Norman line of kings is not without some historical interest. It must be remembered that the love-song was the work of Fazio's youth, and the *Dittamondo* that of his old age, when we may suppose his powers to have been no longer at their best. Besides what I have given relating to Great Britain there is a table of the Saxon dynasty, and some surprising facts about Scotland and Ireland ; as well as a curious passage written in French, and purporting to be an account, given by a royal courier, of Edward the Third's invasion of France. I felt half disposed to include these, but was afraid of overloading with such matter a selection made chiefly for the sake of poetic beauty. I should mention that the *Dittamondo*, like Dante's great poem, is written in *terza rima* ; but as perfect literality was of primary importance in the above extracts, I have departed for once from my rule of fidelity to the original metre.

[2] The word is *Gagata*, which I find described in Alberti's Dictionary, as ' A black, solid, hard, and shining bitumen, formed within the earth, and called also black amber '. Is this coal ?

And pearls are found in great abundance too.
The people are as white and comely-faced
As they of Ethiop land are black and foul.
Many hot springs and limpid fountain-heads
We found about this land, and spacious plains,
And divers beasts that dwell within thick woods. 20
Plentiful orchards too and fertile fields
It has, and castle-forts, and cities fair
With palaces and girth of lofty walls.
And proud wide rivers without any fords
We saw, and flesh, and fish, and crops enough.
Justice is strong throughout those provinces.

Now this I saw not ; but so strange a thing
It was to hear, and by all men confirm'd,
That it is fit to note it as I heard ;—
To wit, there is a certain islet here 30
Among the rest, where folk are born with tails,
Short, as are found in stags and such-like beasts.[1]
For this I vouch,—that when a child is freed
From swaddling bands, the mother without stay
Passes elsewhere, and 'scapes the care of it.

I put no faith herein ; but it is said
Among them, how such marvellous trees are there
That they grow birds, and this is their sole fruit.[2]

Forty times eighty is the circuit ta'en,
With ten times fifteen, if I do not err, 40
By our miles reckoning its circumference.
Here every metal may be dug ; and here

[1] Mediæval Britons would seem really to have been credited with this slight peculiarity. At the siege of Damietta, Cœur-de-Lion's bastard brother is said to have pointed out the prudence of deferring the assault, and to have received for rejoinder from the French crusaders, 'See now these faint-hearted English with the tails!' To which the Englishman replied, 'You will need stout hearts to keep near our tails when the assault is made.'

[2] This is the Barnacle-tree, often described in old books of travels and natural history, and which Sir Thomas Browne classes gravely among his 'Vulgar Errors'.

I found the people to be given to God,
Steadfast, and strong, and restive to constraint.
Nor is this strange, when one considereth ;
For courage, beauty, and large-heartedness,
Were there, as it is said, in ancient days.

North Wales, and Orkney, and the banks of Thames,
Land's End and Stonehenge and Northumberland.
I chose with my companion to behold.[1]   50
We went to London, and I saw the Tower
Where Guenevere her honour did defend,
With the Thames river which runs close to it.
I saw the castle which by force was ta'en
With the three shields by gallant Lancelot,
The second year that he did deeds of arms.
I beheld Camelot despoiled and waste ;
And was where one and the other had her birth,
The maids of Corbonek and Astolat.
Also I saw the castle where Geraint   60
Lay with his Enid ; likewise Merlin's stone,
Which for another's love I joyed to see.
I found the tract where is the pine-tree well,
And where of old the knight of the black shield
With weeping and with laughter kept the pass,
What time the pitiless and bitter dwarf
Before Sir Gawaine's eyes discourteously
With many heavy stripes led him away.
I saw the valley which Sir Tristram won
When having slain the giant hand to hand   70
He set the stranger knights from prison free.

---

[1] The words are 'Listenois' and 'Strangorre', for which I have substituted Land's End and Stonehenge, being unable to identify them. What follows relates to the Romances of the Round Table. The only allusion here which I cannot trace to the *Mort d' Arthur* is one where 'Rech' and 'Nida' are spoken of: it seems however that, by a perversion hardly too corrupt for Fazio, these might be the Geraint and Enid whose story occurs in the *Mabinogion*, and has been used by Tennyson in his *Idylls of the King*. Why Fazio should have 'joyed to see' Merlin's stone 'for another's love' seems inscrutable ; unless indeed the words 'per amor altrui' are a mere idiom, and Merlin himself is the person meant.

And last I viewed the field, at Salisbury,
Of that great martyrdom which left the world
Empty of honour, valour, and delight.

So, compassing that Island round and round,
I saw and hearkened many things and more
Which might be fair to tell but which I hide.

III. Extract from the 'Dittamondo'
(Lib. iv. Cap. 25)

Of the Dukes of Normandy, and thence of the Kings of England, from William the First to Edward the Third.

Thou well hast heard that Rollo had two sons,
One William Longsword, and the other Richard,
Whom thou now know'st to the marrow, as I do.[1]
Daring and watchful, as a leopard is,
Was William, fair in body and in face,
Ready at all times, never slow to act.
He fought great battles, but at last was slain
By the earl of Flanders; so that in his place
Richard his son was o'er the people set.
And next in order, lit with blessed flame   10
Of the Holy Spirit, his son followed him,
Who justly lived 'twixt more and less midway,—
His father's likeness, as in shape in name.
So unto him succeeded as his heir
Robert the Frank, high-counselled and august:
And thereon following, I proceed to tell
How William, who was Robert's son, did make
The realm of England his co-heritage.
The same was brave and courteous certainly,
Generous and gracious, humble before God,   20
Master in war and versed in counsel too.
He with great following came from Normandy
And fought with Harold, and so left him slain,

---

[1] The speaker here is the poet's guide Solinus (a historical and geographical writer of the third century), who bears the same relation to him which Virgil bears to Dante in the *Commedia*.

And took the realm, and held it at his will.
Thus did this kingdom change its signiory;
And know that all the kings it since has had
Only from this man take their origin.
Therefore, that thou mayst quite forget its past,
I say this happened when, since our Lord's Love,
Some thousand years and sixty were gone by. 30

While the fourth Henry ruled as emperor,
This king of England fought in many wars,
And waxed through all in honour and account,
And William Rufus next succeeded him;
Tall, strong, and comely-limbed, but therewith proud
And grasping, and a killer of his kind.
In body he was like his father much,
But was in nature more his contrary
Than fire and water when they come together;
Yet so far good that he won fame in arms, 40
And by himself risked many an enterprise,
All which he brought with honour to an end,
Also if he were bad, he gat great ill;
For, chasing once the deer within a wood,
And having wandered from his company,
Him by mischance a servant of his own
Hit with an arrow, that he fell and died.
And after him Henry the First was king,
His brother, but therewith the father's like,
Being well with God and just in peace and war. 50
Next Stephen, on his death, the kingdom seized,
But with sore strife; of whom thus much be said,
That he was frank and good is told of him.
And after him another Henry reigned,
Who, when the war in France was waged and done,
Passed beyond seas with the first Frederick.
Then Richard came, who, after heavy toil
At sea, was captive made in Germany,
Leaving the Sepulchre to join his host.
Who being dead, full heavy was the wrath 60
Of John his brother; and so well he took
Revenge, that still a moan is made of it.

This John in kingly largesse and in war
Delighted, when the kingdom fell to him ;
Hunting and riding ever in hot haste.

Handsome in body and most poor in heart,
Henry his son and heir succeeded him,
Of whom to speak I count it wretchedness.
Yet there's some good to say of him, I grant ;
Because of him was the good Edward born,
Whose valour still is famous in the world.
The same was he who, being without dread
Of the Old Man's Assassins, captured them,
And who repaid the jester if he lied.[1]
The same was he who over seas wrought scathe
So many times to Malekdar, and bent
Unto the Christian rule whole provinces.
He was a giant of his body, and great
And proud to view, and of such strength of soul
As never saddens with adversity.

His reign was long ; and when his death befell,
The second Edward mounted to the throne,
Who was of one kind with his grandfather.
I say from what report still says of him,
That he was evil, of base intellect,
And would not be advised by any man.
Conceive, good heart ! that how to thatch a roof
With straw,—conceive !—he held himself expert,
And therein constantly would take delight !
By fraud he seized the Earl of Lancaster,
And what he did with him I say not here,
But that he left him neither town nor tower.
And thiswise, step by step, thou mayst perceive
That I to the third Edward have advanced,
Who now lives strong and full of enterprise,
And who already has grown manifest
For the best Christian known of in the world.
Thus I have told, as thou wouldst have me tell,
The race of William even unto the end.

[1] This may either refer to some special incident or merely mean generally that he would not suffer lying even in a jester.

FRANCO SACCHETTI

I. Ballata

His Talk with certain Peasant-girls

'Ye graceful peasant-girls and mountain-maids,
  Whence come ye homeward through these evening
    shades?'

'We come from where the forest skirts the hill;
  A very little cottage is our home,
Where with our father and our mother still
  We live, and love our life, nor wish to roam.
  Back every evening from the field we come
And bring with us our sheep from pasturing there.'

'Where, tell me, is the hamlet of your birth,
  Whose fruitage is the sweetest by so much?   10
Ye seem to me as creatures worship-worth,
  The shining of your countenance is such.
  No gold about your clothes, coarse to the touch,
Nor silver; yet with such an angel's air!

I think your beauties might make great complaint
  Of being thus shown over mount and dell;
Because no city is so excellent
  But that your stay therein were honourable.
  In very truth, now, does it like ye well
To live so poorly on the hill-side here?'   20

'Better it liketh one of us, pardiè,
  Behind her flock to seek the pasture-stance,
Far better than it liketh one of ye
  To ride unto your curtained rooms and dance.
  We seek no riches, neither golden chance
Save wealth of flowers to weave into our hair.'

Ballad, if I were now as once I was,
  I'd make myself a shepherd on some hill,
And, without telling any one, would pass
  Where these girls went, and follow at their will;   30
  And 'Mary' and 'Martin' we would murmur still,
And I would be for ever where they were.

II. Catch

On a Fine Day

'Be stirring, girls! we ought to have a run:
　Look, did you ever see so fine a day?
　Fling spindles right away,
　　And rocks and reels and wools:
　　Now don't be fools,—
To-day your spinning's done.
Up with you, up with you!' So, one by one,
　They caught hands, catch who can,
　Then singing, singing, to the river they ran,
　They ran, they ran
To the river, the river;
　And the merry-go-round
　Carries them at a bound
To the mill o'er the river.
'Miller, miller, miller,
　　Weigh me this lady
　　And this other. Now, steady!'
'You weigh a hundred, you,
And this one weighs two.'
'Why, dear, you do get stout!'
'You think so, dear, no doubt:
Are you in a decline?'
'Keep your temper, and I'll keep mine.'
　'Come, girls,' ('Oh, thank you, miller!')
　'We'll go home when you will.'
So, as we crossed the hill,
A clown came in great grief
Crying, 'Stop thief! stop thief!
　Oh, what a wretch I am!'
'Well, fellow, here's a clatter!
Well, what's the matter?'
　'O Lord, O Lord, the wolf has got my lamb!'
Now at that word of woe,
The beauties came and clung about me so
　That if wolf had but shown himself, maybe
　I too had caught a lamb that fled to me.

D. G. R.

III. Catch

On a Wet Day

As I walk'd thinking through a little grove,
  Some girls that gathered flowers came passing me,
  Saying, ' Look here ! look there ! ' delightedly.
' Oh, here it is ! ' ' What's that ? ' ' A lily, love.'
' And there are violets ! '
' Further for roses ! Oh, the lovely pets—
The darling beauties ! Oh, the nasty thorn !
Look here, my hand's all torn ! '
' What's that that jumps ! ' ' Oh, don't ! it's a grass-
    hopper ! '
' Come run, come run,   10
Here's bluebells ! ' ' Oh, what fun ! '
' Not that way ! Stop her ! '
' Yes, this way ! ' ' Pluck them, then ! '
' Oh, I've found mushrooms ! Oh, look here ! ' ' Oh, I'm
Quite sure that further on we'll get wild thyme.'

' Oh, we shall stay too long, it's going to rain !
There's lightning, oh there's thunder ! '
' Oh, shan't we hear the vesper-bell, I wonder ? '
' Why, it's not nones, you silly little thing ;
And don't you hear the nightingales that sing   20
Fly away O die away ? '
' Oh, I hear something ! Hush ! '
' Why, where ? what is it, then ? ' ' Ah ! in that bush ! '
So every girl here knocks it, shakes and shocks it,
Till with the stir they make
Out skurries a great snake.
' O Lord ! O me ! Alack ! Ah me ! alack ! '
They scream, and then all run and scream again,
And then in heavy drops down comes the rain.

Each running at the other in a fright,   30
Each trying to get before the other, and crying,
And flying, stumbling, tumbling, wrong or right ;
One sets her knee

There where her foot should be;
One has her hands and dress
All smothered up with mud in a fine mess;
And one gets trampled on by two or three.
What's gathered is let fall
About the wood and not picked up at all.
The wreaths of flowers are scattered on the ground;   40
And still as screaming hustling without rest
They run this way and that and round and round,
She thinks herself in luck who runs the best.

I stood quite still to have a perfect view,
And never noticed till I got wet through.

ANONYMOUS POEMS

I. Sonnet

A Lady laments for her lost Lover, by similitude of a Falcon

ALAS for me, who loved a falcon well!
  So well I loved him, I was nearly dead:
  Ever at my low call he bent his head,
And ate of mine, not much, but all that fell.
Now he has fled, how high I cannot tell,
  Much higher now than ever he has fled,
  And is in a fair garden housed and fed;
Another lady, alas! shall love him well.
Oh, my own falcon whom I taught and rear'd!
  Sweet bells of shining gold I gave to thee
That in the chase thou shouldst not be afeard.
  Now thou hast risen like the risen sea,
Broken thy jesses loose, and disappear'd,
  As soon as thou wast skilled in falconry.

II. Ballata

One speaks of the Beginning of his Love

This fairest one of all the stars, whose flame,
For ever lit, my inner spirit fills,
Came to me first one day between the hills.

I wondered very much; but God the Lord
Said, 'From Our Virtue, lo! this light is pour'd.'
So in a dream it seemed that I was led
By a great Master to a garden spread
With lilies underfoot and overhead.

III. Ballata

One speaks of his False Lady

When the last greyness dwells throughout the air,
    And the first star appears,
Appeared to me a lady very fair.

I seemed to know her well by her sweet air;
    And, gazing, I was hers.
To honour her, I followed her: and then . . .
Ah! what thou givest, God give thee again,
Whenever thou remain'st as I remain.

IV. Ballata

One speaks of his Feigned and Real Love

    For no love borne by me,
    Neither because I care
    To find that thou art fair,—
To give another pain I gaze on thee.

And now, lest such as thought that thou couldst move
    My heart, should read this verse,
I will say here, another has my love.
    An angel of the spheres
    She seems, and I am hers;
    Who has more gentleness
    And owns a fairer face
Than any woman else,—at least, to me.

Sweeter than any, more in all at ease,
        Lighter and lovelier.
Not to disparage thee ; for whoso sees
        May like thee more than her.
        This vest will one prefer
        And one another vest.
        To me she seems the best,
And I am hers, and let what will be, be

        For no love borne by me,
        Neither because I care
        To find that thou art fair,—
To give another pain, I gaze on thee.

V. Ballata

Of True and False Singing

A LITTLE wild bird sometimes at my ear
  Sings his own verses very clear :
Others sing louder that I do not hear.

For singing loudly is not singing well ;
  But ever by the song that's soft and low
The master-singer's voice is plain to tell.
  Few have it and yet all are masters now,
And each of them can trill out what he calls
His ballads, canzonets, and madrigals.

The world with masters is so covered o'er,
There is no room for pupils any more.

PART II

DANTE AND HIS CIRCLE

  I. *DANTE ALIGHIERI.*
  II. *GUIDO CAVALCANTI.*
  III. *CINO DA PISTOIA.*
  IV. *DANTE DA MAIANO.*
  V. *CECCO ANGIOLIERI.*
  VI. *GUIDO ORLANDI.*
  VII. *BERNARDO DA BOLOGNA.*
  VIII. *GIANNI ALFANI.*
  IX. *DINO COMPAGNI.*
  X. *LAPO GIANNI.*
  XI. *DINO FRESCOBALDI.*
  XII. *GIOTTO DI BONDONE.*
  XIII. *SIMONE DALL' ANTELLA.*
  XIV. *GIOVANNI QUIRINO.*

INTRODUCTION TO PART II

In the second division of this volume are included all the poems I could find which seemed to have value as being personal to the circle of Dante's friends, and as illustrating their intercourse with each other. Those who know the Italian collections from which I have drawn these pieces (many of them most obscure) will perceive how much which is in fact elucidation is here attempted to be embodied in themselves, as to their rendering, arrangement, and heading: since the Italian editors have never yet paid any of them, except of course those by Dante, any such attention; but have printed and reprinted them in a jumbled and disheartening form, by which they can serve little purpose except as *testi di lingua*—dead stock by whose help the makers of dictionaries may smother the language with decayed words. Appearing now I believe for the first time in print, though in a new idiom, from their once living writers to such living readers as they may find, they require some preliminary notice.

The *Vita Nuova* (the Autobiography or Autopsychology of Dante's youth till about his twenty-seventh year) is already well known to many in the original, or by means of essays and of English versions partial or entire. It is, therefore, and on all accounts, unnecessary to say much more of the work here than it says for itself. Wedded to its exquisite and intimate beauties are personal peculiarities which excite wonder and conjecture, best replied to in the words which Beatrice herself is made to utter in the *Commedia*: 'Questi fù tal nella sua vita nuova.'[1] Thus then young Dante *was*. All that seemed possible to be done here for the work was to translate it in as free and clear a form as was

[1] *Purgatorio*, C. xxx.

consistent with fidelity to its meaning; to ease it, as far as possible, from notes and encumbrances; and to accompany it for the first time with those poems from Dante's own lyrical series which have reference to its events, as well as with such native commentary (so to speak) as might be afforded by the writings of those with whom its author was at that time in familiar intercourse. Not chiefly to Dante, then, of whom so much is known to all or may readily be found written, but to the various other members of his circle, these few pages should be devoted.

It may be noted here, however, how necessary a knowledge of the *Vita Nuova* is to the full comprehension of the part borne by Beatrice in the *Commedia*. Moreover, it is only from the perusal of its earliest and then undivulged self-communings that we can divine the whole bitterness of wrong to such a soul as Dante's, its poignant sense of abandonment, or its deep and jealous refuge in memory. Above all, it is here that we find the first manifestations of that wisdom of obedience, that natural breath of duty, which afterwards, in the *Commedia*, lifted up a mighty voice for warning and testimony. Throughout the *Vita Nuova* there is a strain like the first falling murmur which reaches the ear in some remote meadow, and prepares us to look upon the sea.

Boccaccio, in his 'Life of Dante,' tells us that the great poet, in later life, was ashamed of this work of his youth. Such a statement hardly seems reconcilable with the allusions to it made or implied in the *Commedia*; but it is true that the *Vita Nuova* is a book which only youth could have produced, and which must chiefly remain sacred to the young; to each of whom the figure of Beatrice, less lifelike than lovelike, will seem the friend of his own heart. Nor is this, perhaps, its least praise. To tax its author with effeminacy on account of the extreme sensitiveness evinced by this narrative of his love, would be manifestly unjust, when we find that, though love alone is the theme of the *Vita Nuova*, war already ranked among its author's experiences at the period to which it relates. In the year 1289, the one preceding the death of Beatrice, Dante served with the foremost cavalry in the great battle of Campaldino, on the eleventh of June, when the Florentines defeated the people of Arezzo. In the autumn of the next year, 1290, when for him, by the death of Beatrice, the city as he says 'sat solitary', such refuge as he might find from his grief was sought in action and danger: for we learn from the *Commedia* (*Hell*, C. xxi.) that he served in the war then waged by Florence upon Pisa, and was present at the surrender of Caprona. He says, using the reminiscence to give life to a description, in his great way:—

> I've seen the troops out of Caprona go
> On terms, affrighted thus, when on the spot
> They found themselves with foemen compass'd so.
> (CAYLEY'S *Translation*.)

A word should be said here of the title of Dante's autobiography. The adjective *Nuovo, nuova*, or *Novello, novella*, literally *New*, is often used by Dante and other early writers in the sense of *young*. This has induced some editors of the *Vita Nuova* to explain the title as meaning *Early Life*. I should be glad on some accounts to adopt this supposition, as everything is a gain which increases clearness to the modern reader; but on consideration I think the more mystical interpretation of the words, as *New Life* (in reference to that revulsion of his being which Dante so minutely describes as having occurred simultaneously with his first sight of Beatrice), appears the primary one, and therefore the most necessary to be given in a translation. The probability may be that both were meant, but this I cannot convey.[1]

[1] I must hazard here (to relieve the first page of my translation from a long note) a suggestion as to the meaning of the most puzzling passage in the whole *Vita Nuova*—that sentence just at the outset which says, 'La gloriosa donna della mia mente, la quale fù chiamata da molti Beatrice, i quali non sapeano che si chiamare.' On this passage all the commentators seem helpless, turning it about and sometimes adopting alterations not to be found in any ancient manuscript of the work. The words mean literally, 'The glorious

Among the poets of Dante's circle, the first in order, the first in power, and the one whom Dante has styled his 'first friend', is GUIDO CAVALCANTI, born about 1250, and thus Dante's senior by some fifteen years. It is therefore probable that there is some inaccuracy about the statement, often repeated, that he was Dante's fellow-pupil under Brunetto Latini; though it seems certain that they both studied, probably Guido before Dante, with the same teacher. The Cavalcanti family was among the most ancient in Florence; and its importance may be judged by the fact that in 1280, on the occasion of one of the various missions sent from Rome with the view of pacifying the Florentine factions, the name of 'Guido the son of Messer Cavalcante de' Cavalcanti' appears as one of the sureties offered by the city for the quarter of San Piero Scheraggio. His father must have been notoriously a sceptic in matters of religion, since we find him placed by Dante in the sixth circle of Hell, in one of the fiery tombs of the unbelievers. That Guido shared this heresy was the popular belief, as is

lady of my mind who was called Beatrice by many who knew not how she was called.' This presents the obvious difficulty that the lady's name really *was* Beatrice, and that Dante throughout uses that name himself. In the text of my version I have adopted, as a rendering, the one of the various compromises which seemed to give the most beauty to the meaning. But it occurs to me that a less irrational escape out of the difficulty than any I have seen suggested may possibly be found by linking this passage with the close of the sonnet at page 361 of the *Vita Nuova*, beginning, 'I felt a spirit of love begin to stir', in the last line of which sonnet Love is made to assert that the name of Beatrice is *Love*. Dante appears to have dwelt on this fancy with some pleasure, from what is said in an earlier sonnet (page 332) about 'Love in his proper form' (by which Beatrice seems to be meant) bending over a dead lady. And it is in connection with the sonnet where the name of Beatrice is said to be Love, that Dante, as if to show us that the Love he speaks of is only his own emotion, enters into an argument as to Love being merely an accident in substance—in other words, 'Amore e il cor gentil son una cosa'. This conjecture may be pronounced extravagant; but the *Vita Nuova*, when examined, proves so full of intricate and fantastic analogies, even in the mere arrangement of its parts (much more than appears on any but the closest scrutiny), that it seems admissible to suggest even a whimsical solution of a difficulty which remains unconquered.

plain from an anecdote in Boccaccio which I shall give; and some corroboration of such reports, at any rate as applied to Guido's youth, seems capable of being gathered from an extremely obscure poem, which I have translated on that account (at p. 420) as clearly as I found possible. It must be admitted, however, that there is to the full as much devotional as sceptical tendency implied here and there in his writings; while the presence of either is very rare. We may also set against such a charge the fact that Dino Compagni refers, as will be seen, to his having undertaken a religious pilgrimage. But indeed he seems to have been in all things of that fitful and vehement nature which would impress others always strongly, but often in opposite ways. Self-reliant pride gave its colour to all his moods; making his exploits as a soldier frequently abortive through the headstrong ardour of partisanship, and causing the perversity of a logician to prevail in much of his amorous poetry. The writings of his contemporaries, as well as his own, tend to show him rash in war, fickle in love, and presumptuous in belief; but also, by the same concurrent testimony, he was distinguished by great personal beauty, high accomplishments of all kinds, and daring nobility of soul. Not unworthy, for all the weakness of his strength, to have been the object of Dante's early emulation, the first friend of his youth, and his precursor and fellow-labourer in the creation of Italian Poetry.

In the year 1267, when Guido cannot have been much more than seventeen years of age, a last attempt was made in Florence to reconcile the Guelfs and Ghibellines. With this view several alliances were formed between the leading families of the two factions; and among others, the Guelf Cavalcante de' Cavalcanti wedded his son Guido to a daughter of the Ghibelline Farinata degli Uberti. The peace was of short duration; the utter expulsion of the Ghibellines (through French intervention solicited by the Guelfs) following almost immediately. In the subdivision, which afterwards took place, of the victorious Guelfs into so-called 'Blacks' and 'Whites', Guido embraced the White party, which tended strongly to Ghibellinism, and whose chief was Vieri de' Cerchi, while Corso Donati headed the opposite faction. Whether his wife was still living at the time when the events of the *Vita Nuova* occurred is probably not ascertainable ; but about that time Dante tells us that Guido was enamoured of a lady named *Giovanna* or Joan, and whose Christian name is absolutely all that we know of her. However, on the occasion of his pilgrimage to Thoulouse, recorded by Dino Compagni, he seems to have conceived a fresh passion for a lady of that city named Mandetta, who first attracted him by a striking resemblance to his Florentine mistress. Thoulouse had become a place of pilgrimage from its laying claim to the possession of the body, or part of the body, of St. James the Greater ; though the same supposed distinction had already made the shrine of Compostella in Galicia one of the most famous throughout all Christendom. That this devout journey of Guido's had other results besides a new love will be seen by the passage from Compagni's Chronicle. He says :—

'A young and noble knight named Guido, son of Messer Cavalcante Cavalcanti,—full of courage and courtesy, but disdainful, solitary, and devoted to study, —was a foe to Messer Corso (Donati), and had many times cast about to do him hurt. Messer Corso feared him exceedingly, as knowing him to be of a great spirit, and sought to assassinate him on a pilgrimage which Guido made to the shrine of St. James ; but he might not compass it. Wherefore, having returned to Florence and being made aware of this, Guido incited many youths against Messer Corso, and these promised to stand by him. Who being one day on horseback with certain of the house of the Cerchi, and having a javelin in his hand, spurred his horse against Messer Corso, thinking to be followed by the Cerchi that so their companies might engage each other ; and he running in on his horse cast the javelin, which missed its aim. And with Messer Corso were Simon, his son, a strong and daring youth, and Cecchino de' Bardi, who with

many others pursued Guido with drawn swords; but
not overtaking him they threw stones after him, and
also others were thrown at him from the windows,
whereby he was wounded in the hand. And by this
matter hate was increased. And Messer Corso spoke
great scorn of Messer Vieri, calling him the Ass of the
Gate; because, albeit a very handsome man, he was but
of blunt wit and no great speaker. And therefore Messer
Corso would say often, "To-day the Ass of the Gate has
brayed," and so greatly disparage him; and Guido he
called *Cavicchia*.[1] And thus it was spread abroad of
the *jongleurs*; and especially one named Scampolino
reported worse things than were said, that so the Cerchi
might be provoked to engage the Donati.'

The praise which Compagni, his contemporary, awards
to Guido at the commencement of the foregoing extract,
receives additional value when viewed in connection
with the sonnet addressed to him by the same writer
(see p. 410), where we find that he could tell him of his
faults.

Such scenes as the one related above had become
common things in Florence, which kept on its course
from bad to worse till Pope Boniface VIII resolved on
sending a legate to propose certain amendments in its
scheme of government by *Priori*, or representatives of
the various arts and companies. These proposals, however, were so ill received, that the legate, who arrived in
Florence in the month of June 1300, departed shortly

[1] A nickname chiefly chosen, no doubt, for its resemblance to
Cavalcanti. The word *cavicchia, cavicchio,* or *caviglia*, means a
wooden peg or pin. A passage in Boccaccio says, ' He had tied his
ass to a strong wooden pin ' (*caviglia*). Thus Guido, from his mental
superiority, might be said to be the Pin to which the Ass, Messer
Vieri, was tethered at the Gate (that is, the gate of San Pietro, near
which he lived). However, it seems quite as likely that the nickname
was founded on a popular phrase by which one who fails in any
undertaking is said ' to run his rear on a peg ' (*dare del culo in un
cavicchio*). The haughty Corso Donati himself went by the name
of *Malefammi* or ' Do-me-harm '. For an account of his death in
1307, which proved in keeping with his turbulent life, see Dino
Compagni's *Chronicle*, or the *Pecorone* of Giovanni Fiorentin (Gior.
xxiv. Nov. 2).

afterwards greatly incensed, leaving the city under a papal interdict. In the ill-considered tumults which ensued we again hear of Guido Cavalcanti.

'It happened' (says Giovanni Villani in his *History of Florence*) 'that in the month of December (1300) Messer Corso Donati with his followers, and also those of the house of the Cerchi and their followers, going armed to the funeral of a lady of the Frescobaldi family, this party defying that by their looks would have assailed the one the other; whereby all those who were at the funeral having risen up tumultuously and fled each to his house, the whole city got under arms, both factions assembling in great numbers, at their respective houses. Messer Gentile de' Cerchi, Guido Cavalcanti, Baldinuccio and Corso Adimari, Baschiero della Tosa and Naldo Gherardini, with their comrades and adherents on horse and on foot, hastened to St. Peter's Gate to the house of the Donati. Not finding them there they went on to San Pier Maggiore, where Messer Corso was with his friends and followers; by whom they were encountered and put to flight, with many wounds and with much shame to the party of the Cerchi and to their adherents.'

By this time we may conjecture as probable that Dante, in the arduous position which he then filled as chief of the nine *Priori* on whom the Government of Florence devolved, had resigned for far other cares the sweet intercourse of thought and poetry which he once held with that first friend of his who had now become so factious a citizen. Yet it is impossible to say how much of the old feeling may still have survived in Dante's mind when, at the close of the year 1300 or beginning of 1301, it became his duty, as a faithful magistrate of the republic, to add his voice to those of his colleagues in pronouncing a sentence of banishment on the heads of both the Black and White factions, Guido Cavalcanti being included among the latter. The Florentines had been at last provoked almost to demand this course from their governors, by the discovery of a conspiracy, at the head of which was Corso Donati (while among its leading members was Simone de' Bardi, once the husband

INTRODUCTION TO PART II

of Beatrice Portinari), for the purpose of inducing the Pope to subject the republic to a French peace-maker (*Paciere*), and so shamefully free it from its intestine broils. It appears therefore that the immediate cause of the exile to which both sides were subjected lay entirely with the 'Black' party, the leaders of which were banished to the Castello della Pieve in the wild district of Massa Traberia, while those of the 'White' faction were sent to Sarzana, probably (for more than one place bears the name) in the Genovesato. 'But this party' (writes Villani) 'remained a less time in exile, being recalled on account of the unhealthiness of the place, which made that Guido Cavalcanti returned with a sickness, whereof he died. And of him was a great loss; seeing that he was a man, as in philosophy, so in many things deeply versed; but therewithal too fastidious and prone to take offence.' His death apparently took place in 1301.

When the discords of Florence ceased, for Guido, in death, Dante also had seen their native city for the last time. Before Guido's return he had undertaken that embassy to Rome which bore him the bitter fruit of unjust and perpetual exile: and it will be remembered that a chief accusation against him was that of favour shown to the White party on the banishment of the factions.

Besides the various affectionate allusions to Guido in the *Vita Nuova*, Dante has unmistakably referred to him in at least two passages of the *Commedia*. One of these references is to be found in those famous lines of the Purgatory (C. xi) where he awards him the palm of poetry over Guido Guinicelli (though also of the latter he speaks elsewhere with high praise), and implies at the same time, it would seem, a consciousness of his own supremacy over both.

'Lo, Cimabue thought alone to tread
  The lists of painting; now doth Giotto gain
The praise, and darkness on his glory shed.
  Thus hath one Guido from another ta'en
The praise of speech, and haply one hath pass'd
  Through birth, who from their nest will chase the twain.'
                         (CAYLEY'S *Translation*.)

The other mention of Guido is in that pathetic passage of the Hell (C. x.) where Dante meets among the lost souls Cavalcante de' Cavalcanti :—

> All roundabout he looked, as though he had
> Desire to see if one was with me else.
> But after his surmise was all extinct,
> He weeping said : 'If through this dungeon blind
> Thou goest by loftiness of intellect,—
> Where is my son, and wherefore not with thee ? '
> And I to him : ' Of myself come I not :
> He who there waiteth leads me thoro' here,
> Whom haply in disdain your Guido had.'[1]
> *   *   *   *   *
> Raised upright of a sudden, cried he : ' How
> Didst say *He had ?* Is he not living still ?
> Doth not the sweet light strike upon his eyes ? '
> When he perceived a certain hesitance
> Which I was making ere I should reply,
> He fell supine, and forth appeared no more.

Dante, however, conveys his answer afterwards to the spirit of Guido's father, through another of the condemned also related to Guido, Farinata degli Uberti, with whom he has been speaking meanwhile :—

> Then I, as in compunction for my fault,
> Said : ' Now then shall ye tell that fallen one
> His son is still united with the quick.
> And, if I erst was dumb to the response,
> I did it, make him know, because I thought
> Yet on the error you have solved for me.'
>
> (*Translated by* W. M. ROSSETTI.)[2]

[1] Virgil, Dante's guide through Hell. Any prejudice which Guido entertained against Virgil depended, no doubt, only on his strong desire to see the Latin language give place, in poetry and literature, to a perfected Italian idiom.

[2] These passages are extracted from a literal blank verse translation of the *Inferno* made by my brother, which is as yet in MS., but which I trust may before long see the light; as I believe such a work not to be superfluous even now, notwithstanding the many existing versions of the *Commedia*. It is long since Mr. Cary led the way with a good but rather free rendering, more perhaps in the spirit of that day than of this, and accompanied by notes and other editorial matter which are among the clearest and most complete that Dante's work has ever received. Mr. Cayley's version, of much more recent date, seems to me to have now occupied (and

INTRODUCTION TO PART II

The date which Dante fixed for his vision is Good Friday of the year 1300. A year later, his answer must have been different. The love and friendship of his *Vita Nuova* had then both left him. For ten years Beatrice Portinari had been dead, or (as Dante says in the *Convito*) ' lived in heaven with the angels and on earth with his soul '. And now, distant and probably estranged from him, Guido Cavalcanti was gone too.

Among the Tales of Franco Sacchetti, and in the Decameron of Boccaccio, are two anecdotes relating to Guido. Sacchetti tells us how, one day that he was intent on a game at chess, Guido (who is described as ' one who perhaps had not his equal in Florence ') was disturbed by a child playing about, and threatened punishment if the noise continued. The child, however, managed slily to nail Guido's coat to the chair on which he sat, and so had the laugh against him when he rose soon afterwards to fulfil his threat. This may serve as an amusing instance of Guido's hasty temper, but is rather a disappointment after its magniloquent heading, which sets forth how ' Guido Cavalcanti, being a man of great valour and a philosopher, is defeated by the cunning of a child '.

The ninth Tale of the sixth Day of the Decameron relates a repartee of Guido's, which has all the profound platitude of mediaeval wit. As the anecdote, however, is interesting on other grounds, I translate it here.

that without much likelihood of its being superseded) the post which is the first in all such cases,—that of a fine English poem rendering a great foreign one in its own metre, with all essential fidelity, for the use of English readers who read for the sake of poetry. Dr. Carlyle's prose translation takes other ground, that of word-for-word literality, for which it presupposes prose to be indispensable. I will venture to assert that my brother's work yields nothing to his, however, in minute precision of this kind; and if so, it can hardly be doubtful that its being in blank verse is a great gain, even as adding the last refinement to exactness by showing the division of the lines; but of course also on the higher poetic ground. I do not forget that a version already exists, by Mr. Pollock, professing a like aim with my brother's; and must again express a hope that publicity will shortly afford to all an opportunity of judging the claims of the new attempt. I may here also acknowledge my obligations to my brother for valuable suggestions and assistance in the course of my present work.

'You must know that in past times there were in our city certain goodly and praiseworthy customs no one of which is now left, thanks to avarice, which has so increased with riches that it has driven them all away. Among the which was one whereby the gentlemen of the outskirts were wont to assemble together in divers places throughout Florence, and to limit their fellowships to a certain number, having heed to compose them of such as could fitly discharge the expense. Of whom to-day one, and to-morrow another, and so all in turn, laid tables each on his own day for all the fellowship. And in such wise often they did honour to strangers of worship and also to citizens. They all dressed alike at least once in the year, and the most notable among them rode together through the city; also at seasons they held passages of arms, and specially on the principal feast-days, or whenever any news of victory or other glad tidings had reached the city. And among these fellowships was one headed by Messer Betto Brunelleschi, into the which Messer Betto and his companions had often intrigued to draw Guido di Messer Cavalcante de' Cavalcanti; and this not without cause, seeing that not only he was one of the best logicians that the world held, and a surpassing natural philosopher (for the which things the fellowship cared little), but also he exceeded in beauty and courtesy, and was of great gifts as a speaker; and everything that it pleased him to do, and that best became a gentleman, he did better than any other; and was exceeding rich and knew well to solicit with honourable words whomsoever he deemed worthy. But Messer Betto had never been able to succeed in enlisting him; and he and his companions believed that this was through Guido's much pondering which divided him from other men. Also because he held somewhat of the opinion of the Epicureans, it was said among the vulgar sort that his speculations were only to cast about whether he might find that there was no God. Now on a certain day Guido having left Or San Michele, and held along the Corso degli Adimari as far as San Giovanni (which oftentimes was his walk); and coming to the great marble tombs which now are in the Church of Santa Reparata, but were then with many others in San Giovanni; he being between the porphyry columns which are there among those tombs, and the gate of San Giovanni which was locked;—it so chanced that Messer Betto and his fellowship came riding up by the Piazza di Santa Reparata, and seeing Guido among the sepulchres, said, " Let us go and engage him." Whereupon, spurring their horses in the fashion of a pleasant assault, they were on him almost before he was aware, and began to say to him, " Thou, Guido, wilt none of our fellowship; but lo now! when thou shalt have found that there is no God, what wilt thou have done?" To whom Guido, seeing himself hemmed in among them, readily replied, " Gentlemen, ye are at home here, and may say what ye please to me." Wherewith, setting his hand on one of those high tombs, being very light of his person, he took a leap and was over on the other side; and so having freed himself from them, went his way. And they all remained bewildered, looking on one another; and began to say that he was but a shallow-witted fellow, and that the answer he made was as though one should say nothing; seeing that where they were, they had not more to do than other citizens, and Guido not less than they. To whom Messer Betto turned and said thus: " Ye yourselves are shallow-witted if ye have not understood him. He has civilly and in a few words said to us the most uncivil thing in the world; for if ye look well to it, these tombs are the homes of the dead, seeing that in them the dead are set to dwell; and here he says that we are at home; giving us to know that we and all other simple unlettered men, in comparison of him and the learned, are even as dead men; wherefore, being here, we are at home." Thereupon each of them understood what Guido had meant, and was ashamed; nor ever again did they set themselves to engage him. Also from that day forth they held Messer Betto to be a subtle and understanding knight.'

In the above story mention is made of Guido Cavalcanti's wealth, and there seems no doubt that at that time the family was very rich and powerful. On this account I am disposed to question whether the Canzone at page 418 (where the author speaks of his poverty) can really be Guido's work, though I have included it as being interesting if rightly attributed to him; and it is possible that, when exiled, he may have suffered for the time in purse as well as person. About three years after his death, on the 10th June, 1304, the Black party plotted together and set fire to the quarter of Florence chiefly held by their adversaries. In this conflagration the houses and possessions of the Cavalcanti were almost entirely destroyed; the flames in that neighbourhood (as Dino Compagni records) gaining rapidly in consequence of the great number of waxen images in the Virgin's shrine at Or San Michele; one of which, no doubt, was the very image resembling his lady to which Guido refers in a sonnet (see p. 398). After this, their enemies succeeded in finally expelling from Florence the Cavalcanti family,[1] greatly impoverished by this monstrous fire, in which nearly two thousand houses were consumed.

Guido appears, by various evidence, to have written, besides his poems, a treatise on Philosophy, and another on Oratory, but his poems only have survived to our day. As a poet, he has more individual life of his own than belongs to any of his predecessors; by far the best of his pieces being those which relate to himself, his loves and hates. The best known, however, and perhaps the one for whose sake the rest have been preserved, is the metaphysical canzone on the Nature of Love, beginning 'Donna mi priega', and intended, it is said, as an answer to a sonnet by Guido Orlandi, written as though coming from a lady, and beginning, 'Onde si muove e donde nasce Amore?' On this canzone of

[1] With them were expelled the still more powerful Gherardini, also great sufferers by the conflagration; who, on being driven from their own country, became the founders of the ancient Geraldine family in Ireland. The Cavalcanti reappear now and then in later European history; and especially we hear of a second Guido Cavalcanti, who also cultivated poetry, and travelled to collect books for the Ambrosian Library; and who, in 1563, visited England as Ambassador to the court of Elizabeth from Charles IX of France.

Guido's there are known to exist no fewer than eight commentaries, some of them very elaborate, and written by prominent learned men of the middle ages and *renaissance* ; the earliest being that by Egidio Colonna, a beatified churchman who died in 1316 ; while most of the too numerous Academic writers on Italian literature speak of this performance with great admiration as Guido's crowning work. A love-song which acts as such a fly-catcher for priests and pedants looks very suspicious ; and accordingly, on examination, it proves to be a poem beside the purpose of poetry, filled with metaphysical jargon, and perhaps the very worst of Guido's productions. Its having been written by a man whose life and works include so much that is impulsive and real, is easily accounted for by scholastic pride in those early days of learning. I have not translated it, as being of little true interest ; but was pleased lately, nevertheless, to meet with a remarkably complete translation of it by the Rev. Charles T. Brooks, of Cambridge, United States.[1] The stiffness and cold conceits which prevail in this poem may be found disfiguring much of what Guido Cavalcanti has left, while much besides is blunt, obscure, and abrupt : nevertheless, if it need hardly be said how far he falls short of Dante in variety and personal directness, it may be admitted that he worked worthily at his side, and perhaps before him, in adding those qualities to Italian poetry. That Guido's poems dwelt in the mind of Dante is evident by his having appropriated lines from them (as well as from those of Guinicelli) with little alteration, more than once, in the *Commedia*.

Towards the close of his life, Dante, in his Latin treatise *De Vulgari Eloquio*, again speaks of himself as the friend of a poet—this time of CINO DA PISTOIA. In

[1] This translation occurs in the Appendix to an Essay on the *Vita Nuova* of Dante, including extracts, by my friend Mr. Charles E. Norton, of Cambridge, U.S.A.—a work of high delicacy and appreciation, which originally appeared by portions in the *Atlantic Monthly*, but has since been augmented by the author and privately printed in a volume which is a beautiful specimen of American typography.

an early passage of that work he says that 'those who have most sweetly and subtly written poems in modern Italian are Cino da Pistoia and a friend of his'. This friend we afterwards find to be Dante himself; as among the various poetical examples quoted are several by Cino followed in three instances by lines from Dante's own lyrics, the author of the latter being again described merely as 'Amicus ejus'. In immediate proximity to these, or coupled in two instances with examples from Dante alone, are various quotations taken from Guido Cavalcanti; but in none of these cases is anything said to connect Dante with him who was once 'the first of his friends'.[1] As commonly between old and new, the change of Guido's friendship for Cino's seems doubtful gain. Cino's poetry, like his career, is for the most part smoother than that of Guido, and in some instances it rises into truth and warmth of expression; but it conveys no idea of such powers, for life or for work, as seem to have distinguished the 'Cavicchia' of Messer Corso Donati. However, his one talent (reversing the parable) appears generally to be made the most of, while Guido's two or three remain uncertain through the manner of their use.

[1] It is also noticeable that in this treatise Dante speaks of Guido Guinicelli on one occasion as *Guido Maximus*, thus seeming to contradict the preference of Cavalcanti which is usually supposed to be implied in the passage I have quoted from the *Purgatory*. It has been sometimes surmised (perhaps for this reason) that the two Guidos there spoken of may be Guittone d'Arezzo and Guido Guinicelli, the latter being said to surpass the former, of whom Dante elsewhere in the *Purgatory* has expressed a low opinion. But I should think it doubtful whether the name Guittone, which (if not a nickname, as some say) is substantially the same as Guido, could be so absolutely identified with it: at that rate Cino da Pistoia even might be classed as one Guido, his full name, Guittoncino, being the diminutive of Guittone. I believe it more probable that Guinicelli and Cavalcanti were then really meant, and that Dante afterwards either altered his opinion, or may (conjecturably) have chosen to imply a change of preference in order to gratify Cino da Pistoia, whom he so markedly distinguishes as his friend throughout the treatise, and between whom and Cavalcanti some jealousy appears to have existed, as we may gather from one of Cino's sonnets (at page 433); nor is Guido mentioned anywhere with praise by Cino, as other poets are.

Cino's Canzone addressed to Dante on the death of Beatrice, as well as his answer to the first sonnet of the *Vita Nuova*, indicate that the two poets must have become acquainted in youth, though there is no earlier mention of Cino in Dante's writings than those which occur in his treatise on the Vulgar Tongue. It might perhaps be inferred with some plausibility that their acquaintance was revived after an interruption by the sonnet and answer at p. 392, and that they afterwards corresponded as friends till the period of Dante's death, when Cino wrote his elegy. Of the two sonnets in which Cino expresses disapprobation of what he thinks the partial judgements of Dante's *Commedia*, the first seems written before the great poet's death, but I should think that the second dated after that event, as the *Paradise*, to which it refers, cannot have become fully known in its author's lifetime. Another sonnet sent to Dante elicited a Latin epistle in reply, where we find Cino addressed as 'frater carissime'. Among Cino's lyrical poems are a few more written in correspondence with Dante, which I have not translated as being of little personal interest.

Guittoncino de' Sinibuldi (for such was Cino's full name) was born in Pistoia, of a distinguished family, in the year 1270. He devoted himself early to the study of law, and in 1307 was Assessor of Civil Causes in his native city. In this year, and in Pistoia, the endless contest of the 'Black' and 'White' factions again sprang into activity; the 'Blacks' and Guelfs of Florence and Lucca driving out the 'Whites' and Ghibellines, who had ruled in the city since 1300. With their accession to power came many iniquitous laws in favour of their own party; so that Cino, as a lawyer of Ghibelline opinions, soon found it necessary or advisable to leave Pistoia, for it seems uncertain whether his removal was voluntary or by proscription. He directed his course towards Lombardy, on whose confines the chief of the 'White' party, in Pistoia, Filippo Vergiolesi, still held the fortress of Pitecchio. Hither Vergiolesi had retreated with his family and adherents when resistance in the city became no longer possible ; and it may be supposed that Cino came to join him not on account of political sympathy alone ; as Selvaggia Vergiolesi, his daughter, is the lady celebrated throughout the poet's compositions. Three years later, the Vergiolesi and their followers, finding Pitecchio untenable, fortified themselves on the Monte della Sambuca, a lofty peak on the Apennines ; which again they were finally obliged to abandon, yielding it to the Guelfs of Pistoia at the price of eleven thousand *lire*. Meanwhile the bleak air of the Sambuca had proved fatal to the lady Selvaggia, who remained buried there, or, as Cino expresses it in one of his poems,

> Cast out upon the steep path of the mountains,
> Where Death had shut her in between hard stones.

Over her cheerless tomb Cino bent and mourned, as he has told us, when, after a prolonged absence spent partly in France, he returned through Tuscany on his way to Rome. He had not been with Selvaggia's family at the time of her death ; and it is probable that, on his return to the Sambuca, the fortress was already surrendered, and her grave almost the only record left there of the Vergiolesi.

Cino's journey to Rome was on account of his having received a high office under Louis of Savoy, who preceded the Emperor Henry VII when he went thither to be crowned in 1310. In another three years the last blow was dealt to the hopes of the exiled and persecuted Ghibellines, by the death of the Emperor, caused almost surely by poison. This death Cino has lamented in a canzone. It probably determined him to abandon a cause which seemed dead, and return, when possible, to his native city. This he succeeded in doing before 1319, as in that year we find him deputed, together with six other citizens, by the government of Pistoia to take possession of a stronghold recently yielded to them. He had now been for some time married to Margherita degli Ughi, of a very noble Pistoiese family, who bore him a son named Mino, and four daughters, Diamante, Beatrice, Giovanna, and Lombarduccia. Indeed, this

INTRODUCTION TO PART II

marriage must have taken place before the death of Selvaggia in 1310, as in 1325-6 his son Mino was one of those by whose aid from within the Ghibelline Castruccio Antelminelli obtained possession of Pistoia, which he held in spite of revolts till his death some two or three years afterwards, when it again reverted to the Guelfs.

After returning to Pistoia, Cino's whole life was devoted to the attainment of legal and literary fame. In these pursuits he reaped the highest honours, and taught at the universities of Siena, Perugia, and Florence; having for his disciples men who afterwards became celebrated, among whom rumour has placed Petrarch, though on examination this seems very doubtful. A sonnet by Petrarch exists, however, commencing 'Piangete donne e con voi pianga Amore', written as a lament on Cino's death, and bestowing the highest praise on him. He and his Selvaggia are also coupled with Dante and Beatrice in the same poet's *Trionfi d'Amore* (cap. 4).

Though established again in Pistoia, Cino resided there but little till about the time of his death, which occurred in 1336-7. His monument, where he is represented as a professor among his disciples, still exists in the Cathedral of Pistoia, and is a mediaeval work of great interest. Messer Cino de' Sinibuldi was a prosperous man, of whom we have ample records, from the details of his examinations as a student, to the inventory of his effects after death, and the curious items of his funeral expenses. Of his claims of a poet it may be said that he filled creditably the interval which elapsed between the death of Dante and the full blaze of Petrarch's success. Most of his poems in honour of Selvaggia are full of an elaborate and mechanical tone of complaint which hardly reads like the expression of a real love; nevertheless there are some, and especially the sonnet on her tomb (at p. 431), which display feeling and power. The finest, as well as the most interesting, of all his pieces, is the very beautiful canzone in which he attempts to console Dante for the death of Beatrice. Though I have found much fewer among

Cino's poems than among Guido's which seem to call for translation, the collection of the former is a larger one. Cino produced legal writings also, of which the chief one that has survived is a Commentary on the Statutes of Pistoia, said to have great merit, and whose production in the short space of two years was accounted an extraordinary achievement.

Having now spoken of the chief poets of this division, it remains to notice the others of whom less is known.

DANTE DA MAIANO (Dante being, as with Alighieri, the short of Durante, and Maiano in the neighbourhood of Fiesole) had attained some reputation as a poet before the career of his great namesake began; his Sicilian lady Nina (herself, it is said, a poetess, and not personally known to him) going by the then unequivocal title of 'La Nina di Dante'. This priority may also be inferred from the contemptuous answer sent by him to Dante Alighieri's dream sonnet in the *Vita Nuova* (see p. 435). All the writers on early Italian poetry seem to agree in specially censuring this poet's rhymes as coarse and trivial in manner; nevertheless, they are sometimes distinguished by a careless force not to be despised, and even by snatches of real beauty. Of Dante da Maiano's life no record whatever has come down to us.

Most literary circles have their prodigal, or what in modern phrase might be called their 'scamp'; and among our Danteans, this place is indisputably filled by CECCO ANGIOLIERI, of Siena. Nearly all his sonnets (and no other pieces by him have been preserved) relate either to an unnatural hatred of his father, or to an infatuated love for the daughter of a shoemaker, a certain married Becchina. It would appear that Cecco was probably enamoured of her before her marriage as well as afterwards, and we may surmise that his rancour against his father may have been partly dependent, in the first instance, on the disagreements arising from such a connection. However, from an amusing and lifelike story in the Decameron (Gior. ix. Nov. 4) we learn that on one occasion Cecco's father paid him six months' allowance in advance, in order that he might proceed to the Marca d'Ancona, and join the suite of a Papal Legate who was his patron ; which looks, after all, as if the father had some care of his graceless son. The story goes on to relate how Cecco (whom Boccaccio describes as a handsome and well-bred man) was induced to take with him as his servant a fellow gamester with whom he had formed an intimacy purely on account of the hatred which each of the two bore his own father, though in other respects they had little in common. The result was that this fellow, during the journey, while Cecco was asleep at Buonconvento, took all his money and lost it at the gaming table, and afterwards managed by an adroit trick to get possession of his horse and clothes, leaving him nothing but his shirt. Cecco then, ashamed to return to Siena, made his way, in a borrowed suit and mounted on his servant's sorry hack, to Corsignano, where he had relations ; and there he stayed till his father once more (surely much to his credit) made him a remittance of money. Boccaccio seems to say in conclusion that Cecco ultimately had his revenge on the thief.

Many both of Cecco's love-sonnets and hate-sonnets are very repulsive from their display of powers perverted often to base uses ; while it is impossible not to feel some pity for the indications they contain of self-sought poverty, unhappiness, and natural bent to ruin. Altogether they have too much curious individuality to allow of their being omitted here : especially as they afford the earliest prominent example of a naturalism without afterthought in the whole of Italian poetry. Their humour is sometimes strong, if not well chosen ; their passion always forcible from its evident reality : nor indeed are several among them devoid of a certain delicacy. This quality is also to be discerned in other pieces which I have not included as having less personal interest ; but it must be confessed that for the most part the sentiments expressed in Cecco's poetry are either impious or licentious. Most of the sonnets of his which are in print are here given;[1] the selections concluding with an extraordinary one in which he proposes a sort of murderous crusade against all those who hate their fathers. This I have placed last (exclusive of the Sonnet to Dante in exile) in order to give the writer the benefit of the possibility that it was written last, and really expressed a still rather blood-thirsty contrition; belonging at best, I fear, to the content of self-indulgence when he came to enjoy his father's inheritance. But most likely it is to be received as an expression of impudence alone, unless perhaps of hypocrisy.

Cecco Angiolieri seems to have had poetical intercourse with Dante early as well as later in life; but even from the little that remains, we may gather that Dante soon put an end to any intimacy which may have existed between them. That Cecco already poetized at the time to which the *Vita Nuova* relates, is evident from a date given in one of his sonnets,—the 20th June 1291, and from his sonnet raising objections to the one at the close of Dante's autobiography. When the latter was written he was probably on good terms with the young Alighieri; but within no great while afterwards they had discovered that they could not agree, as is shown by a sonnet in which Cecco can find no words bad enough for Dante, who has remonstrated with him about Becchina.[2] Much later, as we may judge, he again addresses Dante in an insulting tone, apparently while the latter was living in exile at the court of Can Grande della Scala. No other reason can well be assigned for saying that he had 'turned Lombard';

[1] It may be mentioned (as proving how much of the poetry of this period still remains in MS.) that Ubaldini, in his Glossary to Barberino, published in 1640, cites as grammatical examples no fewer than twenty-three short fragments from Cecco Angiolieri, one of which alone is to be found among the sonnets which I have seen, and which I believe are the only ones in print. Ubaldini quotes them from the Strozzi MSS.

[2] Of this sonnet I have seen two printed versions, in both of which the text is so corrupt as to make them very contradictory in important points; but I believe that by comparing the two I have given its meaning correctly (see p. 442).

while some of the insolent allusions seem also to point to the time when Dante learnt by experience 'how bitter is another's bread and how steep the stairs of his house'.

Why Cecco in this sonnet should describe himself as having become a Roman, is more puzzling. Boccaccio certainly speaks of his luckless journey to join a Papal legate, but does not tell us whether fresh clothes and the wisdom of experience served him in the end to become so far identified with the Church of Rome. However, from the sonnet on his father's death he appears (though the allusion is desperately obscure) to have been then living at an abbey; and also, from the one mentioned above, we may infer that he himself, as well as Dante, was forced to sit at the tables of others: coincidences which almost seem to afford a glimpse of the phenomenal fact that the bosom of the Church was indeed for a time the refuge of this shorn lamb. If so, we may further conjecture that the wonderful crusade-sonnet was an *amende honorable* then imposed on him, accompanied probably with more fleshly penance.

It must be remarked, however, that if Guido Cavalcanti's sonnet at page 413 should happen really to have been addressed to Cecco (a possibility there suggested in a footnote,) he must have become a rich man before the period of Dante's exile, as the death of Guido immediately preceded that event. At the same time, there is of course nothing likelier than that he may have found himself poor again before long, and may then (who knows?) have fled to Rome for good, whether with sacred or profane views.

Though nothing indicates the time of Cecco Angiolieri's death, I will venture to surmise that he outlived the writing and revision of Dante's *Inferno*, if only by the token that he is not found lodged in one of its meaner circles. It is easy to feel sure that no sympathy can ever have existed for long between Dante and a man like Cecco; however arrogantly the latter, in his verses, might attempt to establish a likeness and even an equality. We may accept the testimony of so reverent a biographer as Boccaccio, that the Dante of later years was far other than the silent and awe-struck lover of the *Vita Nuova* ; but he was still (as he proudly called himself) 'the singer of Rectitude', and his that 'indignant soul' which made blessed the mother who had borne him.[1]

Leaving to his fate (whatever that may have been) the Scamp of Dante's Circle, I must risk the charge of a confirmed taste for slang by describing GUIDO ORLANDI as its Bore. No other word could present him so fully. Very few pieces of his exist besides the five I have given. In one of these,[2] he rails against his political adversaries ; in three,[3] falls foul of his brother poets ; and in the remaining one,[4] seems somewhat appeased (I think) by a judicious morsel of flattery. I have already referred to a sonnet of his which is said to have led to the composition of Guido Cavalcanti's Canzone on the Nature of Love. He has another sonnet beginning, 'Per troppa sottiglianza il fil si rompe,'[5] in which he is certainly enjoying a fling at somebody, and I suspect at Cavalcanti in rejoinder to the very poem which he himself had instigated. If so, this stamps him a master-critic of the deepest initiation. Of his life nothing is recorded ; but no wish perhaps need be felt to know much of him, as one would probably have dropped his acquaintance. We may be obliged to him, however, for his character of Guido Cavalcanti (at p. 408), which is boldly and vividly drawn.

Next follow three poets of whom I have given one specimen apiece. By BERNARDO DA BOLOGNA (p. 409) no other is known to exist, nor can anything be learnt of his career. GIANNI ALFANI was a noble and distinguished Florentine, a much graver man, it would seem, than one could judge from this sonnet of his

---

[1] Alma sdegnosa,
Benedetta colei che in te s'incinse!
(*Inferno*, C. VIII.)
[2] Page 449.   [3] Pages 399, 408, 436.   [4] Page 411.
[5] This sonnet, as printed, has a gap in the middle ; let us hope (in so immaculate a censor) from unfitness for publication.

(p. 408), which belongs rather to the school of Sir Pandarus of Troy.

DINO COMPAGNI, the chronicler of Florence, is represented here by a sonnet addressed to Guido Cavalcanti,[1] which is all the more interesting, as the same writer's historical work furnishes so much of the little known about Guido. Dino, though one of the noblest citizens of Florence, was devoted to the popular cause, and held successively various high offices in the state. The date of his birth is not fixed, but he must have been at least thirty in 1289, as he was one of the *Priori* in that year, a post which could not be held by a younger man. He died at Florence in 1323. Dino has rather lately assumed for the modern reader a much more important position than he occupied before among the early Italian poets. I allude to the valuable discovery, in the Magliabecchian Library at Florence, of a poem by him in *nona rima*, containing 309 stanzas. It is entitled ' L'Intelligenza ', and is of an allegorical nature interspersed with historical and legendary abstracts.[2]

I have placed LAPO GIANNI in this second division on account of the sonnet by Dante (p. 402), in which he seems undoubtedly to be the Lapo referred to. It has been supposed by some that Lapo degli Uberti (father of Fazio, and brother-in-law of Guido Cavalcanti) is meant; but this is hardly possible. Dante and Guido seem to have been in familiar intercourse with the Lapo of the sonnet at the time when it and others were written; whereas no Uberti can have been in Florence after the year 1267, when the Ghibellines were expelled; the Uberti family (as I have mentioned elsewhere) being the one of all others which was most jealously kept afar and excluded from every amnesty. The only information which I can find respecting Lapo Gianni is the statement

[1] Crescimbeni (*1st. d. Volg. Poes.*) gives this sonnet from a MS., where it is headed ' To Guido Guinicelli '; but he surmises, and I have no doubt correctly, that Cavalcanti is really the person addressed in it.

[2] See *Documents inédits pour servir à l'histoire littéraire de l'Italie, etc., par A. F. Ozanam* (*Paris*, 1850), where the poem is printed entire.

that he was a notary by profession. I have also seen it somewhere asserted (though where I cannot recollect, and am sure no authority was given), that he was a cousin of Dante. We may equally infer him to have been the Lapo mentioned by Dante in his treatise on the Vulgar Tongue, as being one of the few who up to that time had written verses in pure Italian.

DINO FRESCOBALDI'S claim to the place given him here will not be disputed when it is remembered that by his pious care the seven first cantos of Dante's Hell were restored to him in exile, after the Casa Alighieri in Florence had been given up to pillage; by which restoration Dante was enabled to resume his work. This sounds strange when we reflect that a world without Dante would be a poorer planet. Meanwhile, beyond this great fact of Dino's life, which perhaps hardly occupied a day of it, there is no news to be gleaned of him.

GIOTTO falls by right into Dante's circle, as one great man comes naturally to know another. But he is said actually to have lived in great intimacy with Dante, who was about twelve years older than himself; Giotto having been born in or near the year 1276, at Vespignano, fourteen miles from Florence. He died in 1336, fifteen years after Dante. On the authority of Benvenuto da Imola (an early commentator on the *Commedia*), of Vasari, and others, it is said that Dante visited Giotto while he was painting at Padua; that the great poet furnished the great painter with the conceptions of a series of subjects from the Apocalypse, which he painted at Naples; and that Giotto, finally, passed some time with Dante in the exile's last refuge at Ravenna. There is a tradition that Dante also studied drawing with Giotto's master Cimabue; and that he practised it in some degree is evident from the passage in the *Vita Nuova*, where he speaks of his drawing an angel. The reader will not need to be reminded of Giotto's portrait of the youthful Dante, painted in the Bargello at Florence, then the chapel of the Podesta. This is the author of the *Vita Nuova*. That other portrait shown

INTRODUCTION TO PART II

us in the posthumous mask,—a face dead in exile after the death of hope—should front the first page of the Sacred Poem to which heaven and earth had set their hands, but which might never bring him back to Florence, though it had made him haggard for many years.[1]

Giotto's Canzone on the doctrine of voluntary poverty, —the only poem we have of his—is a protest against a perversion of gospel teaching which had gained ground in his day to the extent of becoming a popular frenzy. People went literally mad upon it; and to the reaction against this madness may also be assigned (at any rate partly) Cavalcanti's poem on Poverty, which, as we have seen, is otherwise not easily explained, if authentic. Giotto's canzone is all the more curious when we remember his noble fresco at Assisi, of Saint Francis wedded to Poverty.[2] It would really almost seem as if the poem had been written as a sort of safety-valve for the painter's true feelings, during the composition of the picture. At any rate, it affords another proof of the strong common-sense and turn for humour which all accounts attribute to Giotto.

I have next introduced, as not inappropriate to the series of poems connected with Dante, SIMONE DALL' ANTELLA's fine sonnet relating to the last enterprises of Henry of Luxembourg, and to his then approaching end—that deathblow to the Ghibelline hopes which Dante so deeply shared. This one sonnet is all we know of its author, besides his name.

GIOVANNI QUIRINO is another name which stands forlorn of any personal history. Fraticelli (in his well-known and valuable edition of Dante's Minor Works) says that there lived about 1250 a bishop of that name, belonging to a Venetian family. It is true that the tone of the sonnet which I give (and which is the only one attributed to this author) seems foreign at least to the

---

[1] Se mai continga che il poema sacro,
   Al quale ha posto mano e cielo e terra,
   Sì che m' ha fatto per più anni macro,
   Vinca la crudeltà che fuor mi serra, &c.
   (*Parad.* C. xxv.)

[2] See Dante's reverential treatment of this subject (*Parad.* C. XI).

confessions of bishops. It might seem credibly thus ascribed, however, from the fact that Dante's sonnet probably dates from Ravenna, and that his correspondent writes from some distance; while the poet might well have formed a friendship with a Venetian bishop at the court of Verona.

For me Quirino's sonnet has great value; as Dante's answer [1] to it enables me to wind up this series with the name of its great chief; and, indeed, with what would almost seem to have been his last utterance in poetry, at that supreme juncture when he

> Slaked in his heart the fervour of desire,

as at last he neared the very home

> Of Love which sways the sun and all the stars.[2]

I am sorry to see that this necessary introduction to my second division is longer than I could have wished. Among the severely-edited books which had to be consulted in forming this collection, I have often suffered keenly from the buttonholders of learned Italy, who will not let one go on one's way; and have contracted a horror of those editions where the text, hampered with numerals for reference, struggles through a few lines at the top of the page only to stick fast at the bottom in a slough of verbal analysis. It would seem unpardonable to make a book which should be even as these; and I have thus found myself led on to what I fear forms, by its length, an awkward *intermezzo* to the volume, in the hope of saying at once the most of what was to say; that so the reader may not find himself perpetually worried with footnotes during the consideration of something which may require a little peace. The glare of too many tapers is apt to render the altar-picture confused and inharmonious, even when their smoke does not obscure or deface it.

[1] In the case of the above two sonnets, and of all others interchanged between two poets, I have thought it best to place them together among the poems of one or the other correspondent, wherever they seemed to have most biographical value; and the same with several epistolary sonnets which have no answer.

[2] The last line of the *Paradise* (CAYLEY'S *Translation*).

DANTE ALIGHIERI

THE NEW LIFE

(*LA VITA NUOVA*)

IN that part of the book of my memory before the which is little that can be read, there is a rubric, saying, *Incipit Vita Nova*.[1] Under such rubric I find written many things; and among them the words which I purpose to copy into this little book; if not all of them, at the least their substance.

Nine times already since my birth had the heaven of light returned to the self-same point almost, as concerns its own revolution, when first the glorious Lady of my mind was made manifest to mine eyes; even she who was called Beatrice by many who knew not wherefore.[2] She had already been in this life for so long as that, within her time, the starry heaven had moved towards the Eastern quarter one of the twelve parts of a degree; so that she appeared to me at the beginning of her ninth year almost and I saw her almost at the end of my ninth year. Her dress, on that day, was of a most noble colour, a subdued and goodly crimson, girdled and adorned in such sort as best suited with her very tender age. At that moment, I say most truly that the spirit of life, which hath its dwelling in the secretest chamber of the heart, began to tremble so violently that the least pulses of my body shook therewith; and in trembling it said these words: *Ecce deus*

---

[1] 'Here beginneth the new life.'

[2] In reference to the meaning of the name, 'She who confers blessing'. We learn from Boccaccio that this first meeting took place at a May Feast, given in the year 1274 by Folco Portinari, father of Beatrice, who ranked among the principal citizens of Florence: to which feast Dante accompanied his father, Alighiero Alighieri.

fortior me, qui veniens dominabitur mihi. [1] At that moment the animate spirit, which dwelleth in the lofty chamber whither all the senses carry their perceptions, was filled with wonder, and speaking more especially unto the spirits of the eyes, said these words : *Apparuit iam beatitudo vestra.* [2] At that moment the natural spirit, which dwelleth there where our nourishment is administered, began to weep, and in weeping said these words : *Heu miser! quia frequenter impeditus ero deinceps.* [3]

I say that, from that time forward, Love quite governed my soul ; which was immediately espoused to him, and with so safe and undisputed a lordship (by virtue of strong imagination) that I had nothing left for it but to do all his bidding continually. He oftentimes commanded me to seek if I might see this youngest of the Angels : wherefore I in my boyhood often went in search of her, and found her so noble and praiseworthy that certainly of her might have been said those words of the poet Homer, ' She seemed not to be the daughter of a mortal man, but of God.' [4] And albeit her image, that was with me always, was an exultation of Love to subdue me, it was yet of so perfect a quality that it never allowed me to be overruled by Love without the faithful counsel of reason, whensoever such counsel was useful to be heard. But seeing that were I to dwell overmuch on the passions and doings of such early youth, my words might be counted something fabulous, I will therefore put them aside ; and passing many things that may be conceived by the pattern of these, I will come to such as are writ in my memory with a better distinctness.

After the lapse of so many days that nine years

---

[1] ' Here is a deity stronger than I; who, coming, shall rule over me.'

[2] ' Your beatitude hath now been made manifest unto you.'

[3] ' Woe is me ! for that often I shall be disturbed from this time forth ! '

[4] Οὐδὲ ἐῴκει
Ἀνδρός γε θνητοῦ παῖς ἔμμεναι, ἀλλὰ θεοῖο.
—(*Iliad*, xxiv. 258.)

THE NEW LIFE

exactly were completed since the above-written appearance of this most gracious being, on the last of those days it happened that the same wonderful lady appeared to me dressed all in pure white, between two gentle ladies elder than she. And passing through a street, she turned her eyes thither where I stood sorely abashed: and by her unspeakable courtesy, which is now guerdoned in the Great Cycle, she saluted me with so virtuous a bearing that I seemed then and there to behold the very limits of blessedness. The hour of her most sweet salutation was exactly the ninth of that day; and because it was the first time that any words from her reached mine ears, I came into such sweetness that I parted thence as one intoxicated. And betaking me to the loneliness of mine own room, I fell to thinking of this most courteous lady, thinking of whom I was overtaken by a pleasant slumber, wherein a marvellous vision was presented for me: for there appeared to be in my room a mist of the colour of fire, within the which I discerned the figure of a lord of terrible aspect to such as should gaze upon him, but who seemed therewithal to rejoice inwardly that it was a marvel to see. Speaking he said many things, among the which I could understand but few; and of these, this: *Ego dominus tuus*.[1] In his arms it seemed to me that a person was sleeping, covered only with a blood-coloured cloth; upon whom looking very attentively, I knew that it was the lady of the salutation who had deigned the day before to salute me. And he who held her held also in his hand a thing that was burning in flames; and he said to me, *Vide cor tuum*.[2] But when he had remained with me a little while, I thought that he set himself to awaken her that slept; after the which he made her to eat that thing which flamed in his hand; and she ate as one fearing. Then, having waited again a space, all his joy was turned into most bitter weeping; and as he wept he gathered the lady into his arms, and it seemed to me that he went with her up towards heaven: whereby such a great anguish came upon me that my

[1] 'I am thy master.'   [2] 'Behold thy heart.'

light slumber could not endure through it, but was suddenly broken. And immediately having considered, I knew that the hour wherein this vision had been made manifest to me was the fourth hour (which is to say, the first of the nine last hours) of the night.

Then, musing on what I had seen, I proposed to relate the same to many poets who were famous in that day: and for that I had myself in some sort the art of discoursing with rhyme, I resolved on making a sonnet, in the which, having saluted all such as are subject unto Love, and entreated them to expound my vision, I should write unto them those things which I had seen in my sleep. And the sonnet I made was this:—

To every heart which the sweet pain doth move,
    And unto which these words may now be brought
    For true interpretation and kind thought,
Be greeting in our Lord's name, which is Love.
Of those long hours wherein the stars, above,
    Wake and keep watch, the third was almost nought,
    When Love was shown me with such terrors fraught
As may not carelessly be spoken of.
He seemed like one who is full of joy, and had
    My heart within his hand, and on his arm
    My lady, with a mantle round her, slept;
Whom (having wakened her) anon he made
    To eat that heart; she ate, as fearing harm.
    Then he went out; and as he went, he wept.

This sonnet is divided into two parts. In the first part I give greeting, and ask an answer; in the second I signify what thing has to be answered to. The second part commences here: 'Of those long hours.'

To this sonnet I received many answers, conveying many different opinions; of the which one was sent by him whom I now call the first among my friends, and it began thus, 'Unto my thinking thou beheld'st all worth.'[1] And indeed, it was when he learned that I was he who had sent those rhymes to him, that our

[1] The friend of whom Dante here speaks was Guido Cavalcanti. For this answer, and those of Cino da Pistoia and Dante da Maiano, see their poems further on.

friendship commenced. But the true meaning of that vision was not then perceived by any one, though it be now evident to the least skilful.

From that night forth, the natural functions of my body began to be vexed and impeded, for I was given up wholly to thinking of this most gracious creature: whereby in short space I became so weak and so reduced that it was irksome to many of my friends to look upon me; while others, being moved by spite, went about to discover what it was my wish should be concealed. Wherefore I (perceiving the drift of their unkindly questions), by Love's will, who directed me according to the counsels of reason, told them how it was Love himself who had thus dealt with me: and I said so, because the thing was so plainly to be discerned in my countenance that there was no longer any means of concealing it. But when they went on to ask, 'And by whose help hath Love done this?' I looked in their faces smiling, and spake no word in return.

Now it fell on a day, that this most gracious creature was sitting where words were to be heard of the Queen of Glory;[1] and I was in a place whence mine eyes could behold their beatitude: and betwixt her and me, in a direct line, there sat another lady of a pleasant favour; who looked round at me many times, marvelling at my continued gaze which seemed to have *her* for its object. And many perceived that she thus looked; so that departing thence, I heard it whispered after me, 'Look you to what a pass *such a lady* hath brought him;' and in saying this they named her who had been midway between the most gentle Beatrice and mine eyes. Therefore I was reassured, and knew that for that day my secret had not become manifest. Then immediately it came into my mind that I might make use of this lady as a screen to the truth: and so well did I play my part that the most of those who had hitherto watched and wondered at me, now imagined they had found me out. By her means I kept my secret concealed till some years were gone over; and for my better security, I even

[1] i.e. in a church.

made divers rhymes in her honour; whereof I shall here write only as much as concerneth the most gentle Beatrice, which is but a very little. Moreover, about the same time while this lady was a screen for so much love on my part, I took the resolution to set down the name of this most gracious creature accompanied with many other women's names, and especially with hers whom I spake of. And to this end I put together the names of sixty of the most beautiful ladies in that city where God had placed mine own lady; and these names I introduced in an epistle in the form of a *sirvent*, which it is not my intention to transcribe here. Neither should I have said anything of this matter, did I not wish to take note of a certain strange thing, to wit: that having written the list, I found my lady's name would not stand otherwise than ninth in order among the names of these ladies.

Now it so chanced with her by whose means I had thus long time concealed my desire, that it behoved her to leave the city I speak of, and to journey afar: wherefore I, being sorely perplexed at the loss of so excellent a defence, had more trouble than even I could before have supposed. And thinking that if I spoke not somewhat mournfully of her departure, my former counterfeiting would be the more quickly perceived, I determined that I would make a grievous sonnet [1] thereof; the which I will write here, because it hath certain words in it whereof my lady was the immediate cause, as will be plain to him that understands. And the sonnet was this:—

> ALL ye that pass along Love's trodden way,
> Pause ye awhile and say
>   If there be any grief like unto mine:
> I pray you that you hearken a short space
> Patiently, if my case
>   Be not a piteous marvel and a sign.

[1] It will be observed that this poem is not what we now call a sonnet. Its structure, however, is analogous to that of the sonnet, being two sextetts followed by two quatrains, instead of two quatrains followed by two triplets. Dante applies the term sonnet to both these forms of composition, and to no other.

THE NEW LIFE

Love (never, certes, for my worthless part,
But of his own great heart),
   Vouchsafed to me a life so calm and sweet
That oft I heard folk question as I went
What such great gladness meant :—
   They spoke of it behind me in the street.

But now that fearless bearing is all gone
   Which with Love's hoarded wealth was given me ;
   Till I am grown to be
So poor that I have dread to think thereon.

And thus it is that I, being like as one
   Who is ashamed and hides his poverty,
   Without seem full of glee,
And let my heart within travail and moan.

This poem has two principal parts ; for, in the first, I mean to call the Faithful of Love in those words of Jeremias the Prophet, 'O vos omnes qui transitis per viam, attendite et videte si est dolor sicut dolor meus,' and to pray them to stay and hear me. In the second I tell where Love had placed me, with a meaning other than that which the last part of the poem shows, and I say what I have lost. The second part begins here, 'Love (never, certes).'

A certain while after the departure of that lady, it pleased the Master of the Angels to call into His glory a damsel, young and of a gentle presence, who had been very lovely in the city I speak of : and I saw her body lying without its soul among many ladies, who held a pitiful weeping. Whereupon, remembering that I had seen her in the company of excellent Beatrice, I could not hinder myself from a few tears ; and weeping, I conceived to say somewhat of her death, in guerdon of having seen her somewhile with my lady ; which thing I spake of in the latter end of the verses that I writ in this matter, as he will discern who understands. And I wrote two sonnets, which are these :—

I

Weep, Lovers, sith Love's very self doth weep,
  And sith the cause for weeping is so great;
  When now so many dames, of such estate
In worth, show with their eyes a grief so deep.
For Death the churl has laid his leaden sleep
  Upon a damsel who was fair of late,
  Defacing all our earth should celebrate,—
Yea all save virtue, which the soul doth keep.
Now hearken how much Love did honour her.
  I myself saw him in his proper form
    Bending above the motionless sweet dead,
And often gazing into Heaven; for there
  The soul now sits which when her life was warm
    Dwelt with the joyful beauty that is fled.

This first sonnet is divided into three parts. In the first, I call and beseech the Faithful of Love to weep; and I say that their Lord weeps, and that they, hearing the reason why he weeps, shall be more minded to listen to me. In the second, I relate this reason. In the third, I speak of honour done by Love to this Lady. The second part begins here, ' When now so many dames;' **the third here,** *' Now hearken.'*

II

Death, alway cruel, Pity's foe in chief,
Mother who brought forth grief,
  Merciless judgement and without appeal!
  Since thou alone hast made my heart to feel
  This sadness and unweal,
My tongue upbraideth thee without relief.

And now (for I must rid thy name of ruth)
Behoves me speak the truth
  Touching thy cruelty and wickedness:
  Not that they be not known; but ne'ertheless
  I would give hate more stress
With them that feed on love in very sooth.

Out of this world thou hast driven courtesy,
  And virtue, dearly prized in womanhood;
    And out of youth's gay mood
The lovely lightness is quite gone through thee.

Whom now I mourn, no man shall learn from me
  Save by the measure of these praises given.
    Whoso deserves not Heaven
May never hope to have her company.[1]

This poem is divided into four parts. In the first I address Death by certain proper names of hers. In the second, speaking to her, I tell the reason why I am moved to denounce her. In the third, I rail against her. In the fourth, I turn to speak to a person undefined, although defined in my own conception. The second part commences here, 'Since thou alone;' the third here, 'And now (for I must);' the fourth here, 'Whoso deserves not.'

Some days after the death of this lady, I had occasion to leave the city I speak of, and to go thitherwards where she abode who had formerly been my protection; albeit the end of my journey reached not altogether so far. And notwithstanding that I was visibly in the company of many, the journey was so irksome that I had scarcely sighing enough to ease my heart's heaviness; seeing that as I went, I left my beatitude behind me. Wherefore it came to pass that he who ruled me by virtue of my most gentle lady was made visible to my mind, in the light habit of a traveller, coarsely fashioned. He appeared to me troubled, and looked always on the ground; saving only that sometimes his eyes were turned towards a river which was clear and rapid, and

[1] The commentators assert that the last two lines here do not allude to the dead lady, but to Beatrice. This would make the poem very clumsy in construction; yet there must be some covert allusion to Beatrice, as Dante himself intimates. The only form in which I can trace it consists in the implied assertion that such person as *had* enjoyed the dead lady's society was worthy of heaven, and that person was Beatrice. Or indeed the allusion to Beatrice might be in the first poem, where he says that Love '*in forma vera*' (that is, Beatrice) mourned over the corpse, as he afterwards says of Beatrice, '*Quella ha nome Amor.*' Most probably *both* allusions are intended.

which flowed along the path I was taking. And then I thought that Love called me and said to me these words : ' I come from that lady who was so long thy surety ; for the matter of whose return, I know that it may not be. Wherefore I have taken that heart which I made thee leave with her, and do bear it unto another lady, who, as she was, shall be thy surety ; ' (and when he named her I knew her well.) ' And of these words I have spoken if thou shouldst speak any again, let it be in such sort as that none shall perceive thereby that thy love was feigned for her, which thou must now feign for another.' And when he had spoken thus, all my imagining was gone suddenly, for it seemed to me that Love became a part of myself : so that, changed as it were in mine aspect, I rode on full of thought the whole of that day, and with heavy sighing. And the day being over, I wrote this sonnet :—

> A DAY agone, as I rode sullenly
>   Upon a certain path that liked me not,
>   I met Love midway while the air was hot,
> Clothed lightly as a wayfarer might be.
> And for the cheer he showed, he seemed to me
>   As one who hath lost lordship he had got ;
>   Advancing tow'rds me full of sorrowful thought,
> Bowing his forehead so that none should see.
> Then as I went, he called me by my name,
>   Saying : ' I journey since the morn was dim
>   Thence where I made thy heart to be : which now
> I needs must bear unto another dame.'
>   Wherewith so much passed into me of him
>   That he was gone, and I discerned not how.

This sonnet has three parts. In the first part, I tell how I met Love, and of his aspect. In the second, I tell what he said to me, although not in full, through the fear I had of discovering my secret. In the third, I say how he disappeared. The second part commences here, ' Then as I went ;' *the third here,* ' Wherewith so much.'

On my return, I set myself to seek out that lady whom my master had named to me while I journeyed sighing. And because I would be brief, I will now narrate that in a short while I made her my surety, in such sort that the matter was spoken of by many in terms scarcely courteous; through the which I had oftenwhiles many troublesome hours. And by this it happened (to wit: by this false and evil rumour which seemed to misfame me of vice) that she who was the destroyer of all evil and the queen of all good, coming where I was, denied me her most sweet salutation, in the which alone was my blessedness.

And here it is fitting for me to depart a little from this present matter, that it may be rightly understood of what surpassing virtue her salutation was to me. To the which end I say that when she appeared in any place, it seemed to me, by the hope of her excellent salutation, that there was no man mine enemy any longer; and such warmth of charity came upon me that most certainly in that moment I would have pardoned whosoever had done me an injury; and if one should then have questioned me concerning any matter, I could only have said unto him 'Love,' with a countenance clothed in humbleness. And what time she made ready to salute me, the spirit of Love, destroying all other perceptions, thrust forth the feeble spirits of my eyes, saying, 'Do homage unto your mistress,' and putting itself in their place to obey: so that he who would, might then have beheld Love, beholding the lids of my eyes shake. And when this most gentle lady gave her salutation, Love, so far from being a medium beclouding mine intolerable beatitude, then bred in me such an overpowering sweetness that my body, being all subjected thereto, remained many times helpless and passive. Whereby it is made manifest that in her salutation alone was there any beatitude for me, which then very often went beyond my endurance.

And now, resuming my discourse, I will go on to relate that when, for the first time, this beatitude was denied me, I became possessed with such grief that, parting myself from others, I went into a lonely place to bathe the ground with most bitter tears: and when, by this heat of weeping, I was somewhat relieved, I betook myself to my chamber, where I could lament unheard. And there, having prayed to the Lady of all Mercies, and having said also, 'O Love, aid thou thy servant,' I went suddenly asleep, like a beaten sobbing child. And in my sleep, towards the middle of it, I seemed to see in the room, seated at my side, a youth in very white raiment, who kept his eyes fixed on me in deep thought. And when he had gazed some time, I thought that he sighed and called to me in these words: '*Fili mi, tempus est ut praetermittantur simulata nostra.*'[1] And thereupon I seemed to know him; for the voice was the same wherewith he had spoken at other times in my sleep. Then looking at him, I perceived that he was weeping piteously, and that he seemed to be waiting for me to speak. Wherefore, taking heart, I began thus: 'Why weepest thou, Master of all honour?' And he made answer to me: '*Ego tanquam centrum circuli, cui simili modo se habent circumferentiae partes: tu autem non sic.*'[2] And thinking upon his words, they seemed to me obscure; so that again compelling myself unto speech, I asked of him: 'What thing is this, Master, that thou hast spoken thus darkly?' To the which he made answer in the vulgar tongue: 'Demand no more than may be useful to thee.' Whereupon I began to discourse with him concerning her salutation which she had denied me; and when I had questioned him of the cause, he said these words: 'Our Beatrice hath heard

---

[1] 'My son, it is time for us to lay aside our counterfeiting.'

[2] 'I am as the centre of a circle, to the which all parts of the circumference bear an equal relation: but with thee it is not thus.' This phrase seems to have remained as obscure to commentators as Dante found it at the moment. No one, as far as I know, has even fairly tried to find a meaning for it. To me the following appears a not unlikely one. Love is weeping on Dante's account, and not on his own. He says, 'I am the centre of a circle (*Amor che muove il sole e l' altre stelle*); therefore all lovable objects whether in heaven or earth, or any part of the circle's circumference, are equally near to me. Not so thou, who wilt one day lose Beatrice when she goes to heaven'. The phrase would thus contain an intimation of the death of Beatrice, accounting for Dante being next told not to enquire the meaning of the speech—'Demand no more than may be useful to thee'.

THE NEW LIFE

from certain persons, that the lady whom I named to thee while thou journeyedst full of sighs is sorely disquieted by thy solicitations : and therefore this most gracious creature, who is the enemy of all disquiet, being fearful of such disquiet, refused to salute thee. For the which reason (albeit, in very sooth, thy secret must needs have become known to her by familiar observation) it is my will that thou compose certain things in rhyme, in the which thou shalt set forth how strong a mastership I have obtained over thee, through her ; and how thou wast hers even from thy childhood. Also do thou call upon him that knoweth these things to bear witness to them, bidding him to speak with her thereof ; the which I, who am he, will do willingly. And thus she shall be made to know thy desire ; knowing which, she shall know likewise that they were deceived who spake of thee to her. And so write these things, that they shall seem rather to be spoken by a third person ; and not directly by thee to her, which is scarce fitting. After the which, send them, not without me, where she may chance to hear them ; but have them fitted with a pleasant music, into the which I will pass whensoever it needeth.' With this speech he was away, and my sleep was broken up.

Whereupon, remembering me, I knew that I had beheld this vision during the ninth hour of the day ; and I resolved that I would make a ditty, before I left my chamber, according to the words my master had spoken. And this is the ditty that I made :—

> Song, 'tis my will that thou do seek out Love,
>   And go with him where my dear lady is ;
>   That so my cause, the which thy harmonies
> Do plead, his better speech may clearly prove.
>
> Thou goest, my Song, in such a courteous kind,
>   That even companionless
>   Thou mayst rely on thyself anywhere.
> And yet, an thou wouldst get thee a safe mind,
>   First unto Love address

Thy steps ; whose aid, mayhap, 'twere ill to spare,
  Seeing that she to whom thou mak'st thy prayer
Is, as I think, ill-minded unto me, 12
And that if Love do not companion thee,
  Thou'lt have perchance small cheer to tell me of.

With a sweet accent, when thou com'st to her,
  Begin thou in these words,
    First having craved a gracious audience :
'He who hath sent me as his messenger,
  Lady, thus much records,
    An thou but suffer him, in his defence. 20
    Love, who comes with me, by thine influence
Can make this man do as it liketh him :
Wherefore, if this fault *is* or doth but *seem*
  Do thou conceive : for his heart cannot move.'

Say to her also : 'Lady, his poor heart
  Is so confirmed in faith
    That all its thoughts are but of serving thee :
'Twas early thine, and could not swerve apart.'
  Then, if she wavereth,
    Bid her ask Love, who knows if these things be. 30
    And in the end, beg of her modestly
To pardon so much boldness : saying too :—
'If thou declare his death to be thy due,
  The thing shall come to pass, as doth behove.'

Then pray thou of the Master of all ruth,
  Before thou leave her there,
    That he befriend my cause and plead it well.
'In guerdon of my sweet rhymes and my truth'
  (Entreat him) 'stay with her ;
    Let not the hope of thy poor servant fail ; 40
    And if with her thy pleading should prevail,
Let her look on him and give peace to him.'
Gentle my Song, if good to thee it seem,
  Do this : so worship shall be thine and love.

This ditty is divided into three parts. In the first, I tell it whither to go, and I encourage it, that it may go the more confidently, and I tell it whose company to join if it would go with confidence and without any danger. In the

THE NEW LIFE

second, I say that which it behoves the ditty to set forth. In the third, I give it leave to start when it pleases, recommending its course to the arms of Fortune. The second part begins here, ' With a sweet accent ; ' the third here, ' Gentle my Song.' Some might contradict me, and say that they understand not whom I address in the second person, seeing that the ditty is merely the very words I am speaking. And therefore I say that this doubt I intend to solve and clear up in this little book itself, at a more difficult passage, and then let him understand who now doubts, or would now contradict as aforesaid.

After this vision I have recorded, and having written those words which Love had dictated to me, I began to be harassed with many and divers thoughts, by each of which I was sorely tempted; and in especial, there were four among them that left me no rest. The first was this: 'Certainly the lordship of Love is good; seeing that it diverts the mind from all mean things.' The second was this: 'Certainly the lordship of Love is evil; seeing that the more homage his servants pay to him, the more grievous and painful are the torments wherewith he torments them.' The third was this: 'The name of Love is so sweet in the hearing that it would not seem possible for its effects to be other than sweet; seeing that the name must needs be like unto the thing named: as it is written: "*Nomina sunt consequentia rerum.*" '[1] And the fourth was this: 'The lady whom Love hath chosen out to govern thee is not as other ladies, whose hearts are easily moved.'

And by each one of these thoughts I was so sorely assailed that I was like unto him who doubteth which path to take, and wishing to go, goeth not. And if I bethought myself to seek out some point at the which all these paths might be found to meet, I discerned but one way, and that irked me; to wit, to call upon Pity, and to commend myself unto her. And it was then that, feeling a desire to write somewhat thereof in rhyme, I wrote this sonnet:—

---

[1] 'Names are the consequents of things.'

ALL my thoughts always speak to me of Love,
  Yet have between themselves such difference
  That while one bids me bow with mind and sense,
A second saith, 'Go to : look thou above';
The third one, hoping, yields me joy enough ;
  And with the last come tears, I scarce know whence :
  All of them craving pity in sore suspense,
Trembling with fears that the heart knoweth of.
And thus, being all unsure which path to take,
  Wishing to speak I know not what to say,
    And lose myself in amorous wanderings :
Until, (my peace with all of them to make,)
  Unto mine enemy I needs must pray,
    My Lady Pity, for the help she brings.

This sonnet may be divided into four parts. In the first, I say and propound that all my thoughts are concerning Love. In the second, I say that they are diverse, and I relate their diversity. In the third, I say wherein they all seem to agree. In the fourth, I say that, wishing to speak of Love, I know not from which of these thoughts to take my argument ; and that if I would take it from all, I shall have to call upon mine enemy, my Lady Pity. 'Lady,' I say, as in a scornful mode of speech. The second begins here, ' Yet have between themselves ;' the third, ' All of them craving ;' the fourth, ' And thus.'

After this battling with many thoughts, it chanced on a day that my most gracious lady was with a gathering of ladies in a certain place ; to the which I was conducted by a friend of mine ; he thinking to do me a great pleasure by showing me the beauty of so many women. Then I, hardly knowing whereunto he conducted me, but trusting in him (who yet was leading his friend to the last verge of life), made question : ' To what end are we come among these ladies ? ' and he answered : ' To the end that they may be worthily served.' And they were assembled around a gentlewoman who was given in marriage on that day ; the custom of the city being that these should bear her company when she sat down for the first time at table in the house of her husband.

THE NEW LIFE

Therefore I, as was my friend's pleasure, resolved to stay with him and do honour to those ladies.

But as soon as I had thus resolved, I began to feel a faintness and a throbbing at my left side, which soon took possession of my whole body. Whereupon I remember that I covertly leaned my back unto a painting that ran round the walls of that house; and being fearful lest my trembling should be discerned of them, I lifted mine eyes to look on those ladies, and then first perceived among them the excellent Beatrice. And when I perceived her, all my senses were overpowered by the great lordship that Love obtained, finding himself so near unto that most gracious being, until nothing but the spirits of sight remained to me; and even these remained driven out of their own instruments, because Love entered in that honoured place of theirs, that so he might the better behold her. And although I was other than at first, I grieved for the spirits so expelled, which kept up a sore lament, saying: 'If he had not in this wise thrust us forth, we also should behold the marvel of this lady.' By this, many of her friends, having discerned my confusion, began to wonder; and together with herself, kept whispering of me and mocking me. Whereupon my friend, who knew not what to conceive, took me by the hands, and drawing me forth from among them, required to know what ailed me. Then, having first held me at quiet for a space until my perceptions were come back to me, I made answer to my friend: 'Of a surety I have now set my feet on that point of life, beyond the which he must not pass who would return.'[1]

Afterwards, leaving him, I went back to the room

---

[1] It is difficult not to connect Dante's agony at this wedding-feast, with our knowledge that in her twenty-first year Beatrice was wedded to Simone de' Bardi. That she herself was the bride on this occasion might seem out of the question, from the fact of its not being in any way so stated: but on the other hand, Dante's silence throughout the *Vita Nuova* as regards her marriage (which must have brought deep sorrow even to his ideal love) is so startling, that we might almost be led to conceive in this passage the only intimation of it which he thought fit to give.

where I had wept before; and again weeping and ashamed, said: 'If this lady but knew of my condition, I do not think that she would thus mock at me; nay, I am sure that she must needs feel some pity.' And in my weeping I bethought me to write certain words, in the which, speaking to her, I should signify the occasion of my disfigurement, telling her also how I knew that she had no knowledge thereof; which, if it were known, I was certain must move others to pity. And then, because I hoped that peradventure it might come into her hearing, I wrote this sonnet:—

> EVEN as the others mock, thou mockest me;
>   Not dreaming, noble lady, whence it is
>   That I am taken with strange semblances,
> Seeing thy face which is so fair to see:
> For else, compassion would not suffer thee
>   To grieve my heart with such harsh scoffs as these.
>   Lo! Love, when thou art present, sits at ease,
> And bears his mastership so mightily
> That all my troubled senses he thrusts out,
>   Sorely tormenting some, and slaying some,
>   Till none but he is left and has free range
>   To gaze on thee. This makes my face to change
> Into another's; while I stand all dumb,
> And hear my senses clamour in their rout.

This sonnet I divide not into parts, because a division is only made to open the meaning of the thing divided: and this, as it is sufficiently manifest through the reasons given, has no need of division. True it is that, amid the words whereby is shown the occasion of this sonnet, dubious words are to be found; namely, when I say that Love fills all my spirits, but that the visual remain in life only outside of their own instruments. And this difficulty it is impossible for any to solve who is not in equal guise liege unto Love; and, to those who are so, that is manifest which would clear up the dubious words. And therefore it were not well for me to expound this difficulty, inasmuch as my speaking would be either fruitless or else superfluous.

A while after this strange disfigurement, I became

possessed with a strong conception which left me but very seldom, and then to return quickly. And it was this: 'Seeing that thou comest into such scorn by the companionship of this lady, wherefore seekest thou to behold her? If she should ask thee this thing, what answer couldst thou make unto her? yea, even though thou wert master of all thy faculties, and in no way hindered from answering.' Unto the which, another very humble thought said in reply: 'If I were master of all my faculties, and in no way hindered from answering, I would tell her that no sooner do I image to myself her marvellous beauty than I am possessed with the desire to behold her, the which is of so great strength that it kills and destroys in my memory all those things which might oppose it; and it is therefore that the great anguish I have endured thereby is yet not enough to restrain me from seeking to behold her.' And then, because of these thoughts, I resolved to write somewhat, wherein, having pleaded mine excuse, I should tell her of what I felt in her presence. Whereupon I wrote this sonnet:—

THE thoughts are broken in my memory,
   Thou lovely Joy, whene'er I see thy face;
When thou art near me, Love fills up the space,
Often repeating, 'If death irk thee, fly.'
My face shows my heart's colour, verily,
   Which, fainting, seeks for any leaning-place;
   Till, in the drunken terror of disgrace,
The very stones seem to be shrieking, 'Die!'
It were a grievous sin, if one should not
   Strive then to comfort my bewildered mind
    (Though merely with a simple pitying)
For the great anguish which thy scorn has wrought
   In the dead sight o' the eyes grown nearly blind,
    Which look for death as for a blessed thing.

This sonnet is divided into two parts. In the first, I tell the cause why I abstain not from coming to this lady. In the second, I tell what befalls me through coming to her; and this part begins here, 'When thou art near.'

And also this second part divides into five distinct statements. For, in the first, I say what Love, counselled by Reason, tells me when I am near the Lady. In the second, I set forth the state of my heart by the example of the face. In the third, I say how all ground of trust fails me. In the fourth, I say that he sins who shows not pity of me, which would give me some comfort. In the last, I say why people should take pity ; namely, for the piteous look which comes into mine eyes ; which piteous look is destroyed, that is, appeareth not unto others, through the jeering of this lady, who draws to the like action those who peradventure would see this piteousness. The second part begins here, ' My face shows ;' the third, ' Till, in the drunken terror ;' the fourth, ' It were a grievous sin ;' the fifth, ' For the great anguish.'

Thereafter, this sonnet bred in me desire to write down in verse four other things touching my condition, the which things it seemed to me that I had not yet made manifest. The first among these was the grief that possessed me very often, remembering the strangeness which Love wrought in me ; the second was, how Love many times assailed me so suddenly and with such strength that I had no other life remaining except a thought which spake of my lady ; the third was, how, when Love did battle with me in this wise, I would rise up all colourless, if so I might see my lady, conceiving that the sight of her would defend me against the assault of Love, and altogether forgetting that which her presence brought unto me ; and the fourth was, how, when I saw her, the sight not only defended me not, but took away the little life that remained to me. And I said these four things in a sonnet, which is this :—

AT whiles (yea oftentimes) I muse over
  The quality of anguish that is mine
  Through Love : then pity makes my voice to pine,
Saying, ' Is any else thus, anywhere ? '
Love smiteth me, whose strength is ill to bear ;
  So that of all my life is left no sign
  Except one thought ; and that, because 'tis thine,

THE NEW LIFE

Leaves not the body but abideth there.
And then if I, whom other aid forsook,
   Would aid myself, and innocent of art
     Would fain have sight of thee as a last hope,
No sooner do I lift mine eyes to look
   Than the blood seems as shaken from my heart,
     And all my pulses beat at once and stop.

This sonnet is divided into four parts, four things being therein narrated; and as these are set forth above, I only proceed to distinguish the parts by their beginnings. Wherefore I say that the second part begins, ' Love smiteth me;' the third, ' And then if I;' the fourth, ' No sooner do I lift.'

After I had written these three last sonnets, wherein I spake unto my lady, telling her almost the whole of my condition, it seemed to me that I should be silent, having said enough concerning myself. But albeit I spake not to her again, yet it behoved me afterward to write of another matter, more noble than the foregoing. And for that the occasion of what I then wrote may be found pleasant in the hearing, I will relate it as briefly as I may.

Through the sore change in mine aspect, the secret of my heart was now understood of many. Which thing being thus, there came a day when certain ladies to whom it was well known (they having been with me at divers times in my trouble) were met together for the pleasure of gentle company. And as I was going that way by chance (but I think rather by the will of fortune), I heard one of them call unto me, and she that called was a lady of very sweet speech. And when I had come close up with them, and perceived that they had not among them mine excellent lady, I was reassured; and saluted them, asking of their pleasure. The ladies were many; divers of whom were laughing one to another, while divers gazed at me as though I should speak anon. But when I still spake not, one of them, who before had been talking with another, addressed me by my name, saying, ' To what end lovest thou this lady, seeing that thou canst not support her presence ? Now tell us this thing, that we may know it : for certainly the end of such a love must be worthy of knowledge.' And when she had spoken these words, not she only, but all they that were with her, began to observe me, waiting for my reply. Whereupon I said thus unto them :—' Ladies, the end and aim of my Love was but the salutation of that lady of whom I conceive that ye are speaking ; wherein alone I found that beatitude which is the goal of desire. And now that it hath pleased her to deny me this, Love, my Master, of his great goodness, hath placed all my beatitude there where my hope will not fail me.' Then those ladies began to talk closely together ; and as I have seen snow fall among the rain, so was their talk mingled with sighs. But after a little, that lady who had been the first to address me, addressed me again in these words : ' We pray thee that thou wilt tell us wherein abideth this thy beatitude.' And answering, I said but thus much : ' In those words that do praise my lady.' To the which she rejoined : ' If thy speech were true, those words that thou didst write concerning thy condition would have been written with another intent.'

Then I, being almost put to shame because of her answer, went out from among them ; and as I walked, I said within myself : ' Seeing that there is so much beatitude in those words which do praise my lady, wherefore hath my speech of her been different ? ' And then I resolved that thenceforward I would choose for the theme of my writings only the praise of this most gracious being. But when I had thought exceedingly, it seemed to me that I had taken to myself a theme which was much too lofty, so that I dared not begin ; and I remained during several days in the desire of speaking, and the fear of beginning. After which it happened, as I passed one day along a path which lay beside a stream of very clear water, that there came upon me a great desire to say somewhat in rhyme : but when I began thinking how I should say it, methought that to speak of her were unseemly, unless I spoke to other ladies in

THE NEW LIFE

the second person; which is to say, not to *any* other ladies, but only to such as are so called because they are gentle, let alone for mere womanhood. Whereupon I declare that my tongue spake as though by its own impulse, and said, 'Ladies that have intelligence in love.' These words I laid up in my mind with great gladness, conceiving to take them as my commencement. Wherefore, having returned to the city I spake of, and considered thereof during certain days, I began a poem with this beginning, constructed in the mode which will be seen below in its division. The poem begins here:—

LADIES that have intelligence in love,
  Of mine own lady I would speak with you;
  Not that I hope to count her praises through,
    But telling what I may, to ease my mind.
And I declare that when I speak thereof,
Love sheds such perfect sweetness over me
That if my courage failed not, certainly
    To him my listeners must be all resign'd.
  Wherefore I will not speak in such large kind
That mine own speech should foil me, which were base;
But only will discourse of her high grace   11
    In these poor words, the best that I can find,
With you alone, dear dames and damozels:
'Twere ill to speak thereof with any else.

An Angel, of his blessed knowledge, saith
  To God: 'Lord, in the world that Thou hast made,
  A miracle in action is display'd,
    By reason of a soul whose splendours fare
Even hither: and since Heaven requireth
  Nought saving her, for her it prayeth Thee,   20
  Thy Saints crying aloud continually.'
    Yet Pity still defends our earthly share
  In that sweet soul; God answering thus the prayer:
'My well-belovèd, suffer that in peace
Your hope remain, while so My pleasure is,
  There where one dwells who dreads the loss of her:
And who in Hell unto the doomed shall say,
"I have looked on that for which God's chosen pray."'

My lady is desired in the high Heaven :
   Wherefore, it now behoveth me to tell,   30
    Saying : Let any maid that would be well
      Esteemed keep with her : for as she goes by,
Into foul hearts a deathly chill is driven
By Love, that makes ill thought to perish there :
While any who endures to gaze on her
    Must either be ennobled, or else die.
    When one deserving to be raised so high
Is found, 'tis then her power attains its proof,
Making his heart strong for his soul's behoof
    With the full strength of meek humility.   40
Also this virtue owns she, by God's will :
Who speaks with her can never come to ill.

Love saith concerning her : 'How chanceth it
   That flesh, which is of dust, should be thus pure ?'
   Then, gazing always, he makes oath : 'Forsure,
     This is a creature of God till now unknown.'
She hath that paleness of the pearl that's fit
In a fair woman, so much and not more ;
She is as high as Nature's skill can soar ;
   Beauty is tried by her comparison.   50
   Whatever her sweet eyes are turned upon,
Spirits of love do issue thence in flame,
Which through their eyes who then may look on them
   Pierce to the heart's deep chamber every one.
And in her smile Love's image you may see ;
Whence none can gaze upon her steadfastly.

Dear Song, I know thou wilt hold gentle speech
   With many ladies, when I send thee forth :
   Wherefore (being mindful that thou hadst thy birth
     From Love, and art a modest, simple child,)   60
Whomso thou meetest, say thou this to each :
'Give me good speed ! To her I wend along
In whose much strength my weakness is made strong.'
   And if, i' the end, thou wouldst not be beguiled
   Of all thy labour seek not the defiled
And common sort ; but rather choose to be

THE NEW LIFE

Where man and woman dwell in courtesy.
   So to the road thou shalt be reconciled,
And find the lady, and with the lady, Love.
Commend thou me to each, as doth behove.   70

This poem, that it may be better understood, I will divide more subtly than the others preceding; and therefore I will make three parts of it. The first part is a proem to the words following. The second is the matter treated of. The third is, as it were, a handmaid to the preceding words. The second begins here, 'An angel;' the third here, 'Dear Song, I know.' The first part is divided into four. In the first, I say to whom I mean to speak of my Lady, and wherefore I will so speak. In the second, I say what she appears to myself to be when I reflect upon her excellence, and what I would utter if I lost not courage. In the third, I say what it is I purpose to speak so as not to be impeded by faintheartedness. In the fourth, repeating to whom I purpose speaking, I tell the reason why I speak to them. The second begins here, 'And I declare;' the third here, 'Wherefore I will not speak;' the fourth here, 'With you alone.' Then, when I say 'An Angel,' I begin treating of this lady: and this part is divided into two. In the first, I tell what is understood of her in heaven. In the second, I tell what is understood of her on earth: here, 'My lady is desired.' This second part is divided into two; for, in the first, I speak of her as regards the nobleness of her soul, relating some of her virtues proceeding from her soul; in the second, I speak of her as regards the nobleness of her body, narrating some of her beauties: here, 'Love saith concerning her.' This second part is divided into two, for, in the first, I speak of certain beauties which belong to the whole person; in the second, I speak of certain beauties which belong to a distinct part of the person: here, 'Whatever her sweet eyes.' This second part is divided into two; for, in the one, I speak of the eyes, which are the beginning of love; in the second, I speak of the mouth, which is the end of love. And that every vicious thought may be discarded herefrom, let the reader remember that it is above written that the greeting of this lady, which was an act of her mouth,

*was the goal of my desires, while I could receive it. Then,
when I say, 'Dear Song, I know,' I add a stanza as it
were handmaid to the others, wherein I say what I desire
from this my poem. And because this last part is easy to
understand, I trouble not myself with more divisions. I say,
indeed, that the further to open the meaning of this poem,
more minute divisions ought to be used; but nevertheless
he who is not of wit enough to understand it by these which
have been already made is welcome to leave it alone; for
certes, I fear I have communicated its sense to too many
by these present divisions, if it so happened that many
should hear it.*

When this song was a little gone abroad, a certain
one of my friends, hearing the same, was pleased to
question me, that I should tell him what thing love is;
it may be, conceiving from the words thus heard, a hope
of me beyond my desert. Wherefore I, thinking that
after such discourse it were well to say somewhat of the
nature of Love, and also in accordance with my friend's
desire, proposed to myself to write certain words in the
which I should treat of this argument. And the sonnet
that I then made is this:—

> Love and the gentle heart are one same thing,
>   Even as the wise man [1] in his ditty saith:
>   Each, of itself, would be such life in death
> As rational soul bereft of reasoning.
> 'Tis Nature makes them when she loves: a king
>   Love is, whose palace where he sojourneth
>   Is called the Heart; there draws he quiet breath
> At first, with brief or longer slumbering.
> Then beauty seen in virtuous womankind
>   Will make the eyes desire, and through the heart
>   Send the desiring of the eyes again;
> Where often it abides so long enshrin'd
>   That Love at length out of his sleep will start.
>   And women feel the same for worthy men.

This sonnet is divided into two parts. In the first,

[1] Guido Guinicelli, in the canzone which begins, 'Within the
gentle heart Love shelters him' (see *ante*, page 202).

I speak of him according to his power. In the second, I speak of him according as his power translates itself into act. The second part begins here, ' Then beauty seen.' The first is divided into two. In the first, I say in what subject this power exists. In the second, I say how this subject and this power are produced together, and how the one regards the other, as form does matter. The second begins here, ' 'Tis Nature.' Afterwards when I say, ' Then beauty seen in virtuous womankind,' I say how this power translates itself into act ; and, first, how it so translates itself in a man, then how it so translates itself in a woman : here, ' And women feel.'

Having treated of love in the foregoing, it appeared to me that I should also say something in praise of my lady, wherein it might be set forth how love manifested itself when produced by her ; and how not only she could awaken it where it slept, but where it was not she could marvellously create it. To the which end I wrote another sonnet ; and it is this :—

My lady carries love within her eyes ;
   All that she looks on is made pleasanter ;
   Upon her path men turn to gaze at her ;
He whom she greeteth feels his heart to rise,
And droops his troubled visage, full of sighs,
   And of his evil heart is then aware :
   Hate loves, and pride becomes a worshipper.
O women, help to praise her in somewise.
Humbleness, and the hope that hopeth well,
   By speech of hers into the mind are brought,
   And who beholds is blessèd oftenwhiles.
   The look she hath when she a little smiles
Cannot be said, nor holden in the thought ;
'Tis such a new and gracious miracle.

This sonnet has three sections. In the first, I say how this lady brings this power into action by those most noble features, her eyes ; and, in the third, I say this same as to that most noble feature, her mouth. And between these two sections is a little section, which asks, as it were, help for the previous section and the subsequent ; and it begins here, 'O women, help.' The third begins here, 'Humbleness.' The first is divided into three; for, in the first, I say how she with power makes noble that which she looks upon; and this is as much as to say that she brings Love, in power, thither where he is not. In the second, I say how she brings Love, in act, into the hearts of all those whom she sees. In the third, I tell what she afterwards, with virtue, operates upon their hearts. The second begins, 'Upon her path;' the third, 'He whom she greeteth.' Then, when I say 'O women, help,' I intimate to whom it is my intention to speak, calling on women to help me to honour her. Then, when I say, 'Humbleness,' I say that same which is said in the first part, regarding two acts of her mouth, one whereof is her most sweet speech, and the other her marvellous smile. Only, I say not of this last how it operates upon the hearts of others, because memory cannot retain this smile, nor its operation.

Not many days after this (it being the will of the most High God, who also from Himself put not away death), the father of wonderful Beatrice, going out of this life, passed certainly into glory. Thereby it happened, as of very sooth it might not be otherwise, that this lady was made full of the bitterness of grief: seeing that such a parting is very grievous unto those friends who are left, and that no other friendship is like to that between a good parent and a good child; and furthermore considering that this lady was good in the supreme degree, and her father (as by many it hath been truly averred) of exceeding goodness. And because it is the usage of that city that men meet with men in such a grief, and women with women, certain ladies of her companionship gathered themselves unto Beatrice, where she kept alone in her weeping: and as they passed in and out, I could hear them speak concerning her, how she wept. At length two of them went by me, who said: 'Certainly she grieveth in such sort that one might die for pity, beholding her.' Then, feeling the tears upon my face, I put up my hands to hide them: and had it not been that I hoped to hear more concerning her (seeing that where I sat, her friends passed continually in and out), I should assuredly have gone thence to be alone, when I felt the tears come. But as I still sat in that place, certain ladies again passed near me, who were saying among themselves : ' Which of us shall be joyful any more, who have listened to this lady in her piteous sorrow ? ' And there were others who said as they went by me : ' He that sitteth here could not weep more if he had beheld her as we have beheld her ; ' and again : ' He is so altered that he seemeth not as himself.' And still as the ladies passed to and fro, I could hear them speak after this fashion of her and of me.

Wherefore afterwards, having considered and perceiving that there was herein matter for poesy, I resolved that I would write certain rhymes in the which should be contained all that those ladies had said. And because I would willingly have spoken to them if it had not been for discreetness, I made in my rhymes as though I had spoken and they had answered me. And thereof I wrote two sonnets ; in the first of which I addressed them as I would fain have done ; and in the second related their answer, using the speech that I had heard from them, as though it had been spoken unto myself. And the sonnets are these :—

I

You that thus wear a modest countenance
   With lids weigh'd down by the heart's heaviness,
   Whence come you, that among you every face
Appears the same, for its pale troubled glance ?
Have you beheld my lady's face, perchance,
   Bow'd with the grief that Love makes full of grace ?
   Say now, ' This thing is thus ; ' as my heart says,
Marking your grave and sorrowful advance.
And if indeed you come from where she sighs
   And mourns, may it please you (for his heart's relief)
      To tell how it fares with her unto him
Who knows that you have wept, seeing your eyes,
   And is so grieved with looking on your grief
      That his heart trembles and his sight grows dim ?

This sonnet is divided into two parts. In the first, I call and ask these ladies whether they come from her, telling them that I think they do, because they return the nobler. In the second, I pray them to tell me of her; and the second begins here, 'And if indeed.'

II

Canst thou indeed be he that still would sing
  Of our dear lady unto none but us?
  For though thy voice confirms that it is thus,
Thy visage might another witness bring.
And wherefore is thy grief so sore a thing
  That grieving thou mak'st others dolorous?
  Hast thou too seen her weep, that thou from us
Canst not conceal thine inward sorrowing?
Nay, leave our woe to us: let us alone:
  'Twere sin if one should strive to soothe our woe,
    For in her weeping we have heard her speak:
Also her look's so full of her heart's moan
  That they who should behold her, looking so,
    Must fall aswoon, feeling all life grow weak.

This sonnet has four parts, as the ladies in whose person I reply had four forms of answer. And, because these are sufficiently shown above, I stay not to explain the purport of the parts, and therefore I only discriminate them. The second begins here, 'And wherefore is thy grief;' the third here, 'Nay, leave our woe;' the fourth, 'Also her look.'

A few days after this, my body became afflicted with a painful infirmity, whereby I suffered bitter anguish for many days, which at last brought me unto such weakness that I could no longer move. And I remember that on the ninth day, being overcome with intolerable pain, a thought came into my mind concerning my lady: but when it had a little nourished this thought, my mind returned to its brooding over mine enfeebled body. And then perceiving how frail a thing life is, even though health keep with it, the matter seemed to me so pitiful that I could not choose but weep; and weeping I said within myself : ' Certainly it must some time come to pass that the very gentle Beatrice will die.' Then, feeling bewildered, I closed mine eyes ; and my brain began to be in travail as the brain of one frantic, and to have such imaginations as here follow.

And at the first, it seemed to me that I saw certain faces of women with their hair loosened, which called out to me, ' Thou shalt surely die ; ' after the which, other terrible and unknown appearances said unto me, ' Thou art dead.' At length, as my phantasy held on in its wanderings, I came to be I knew not where, and to behold a throng of dishevelled ladies wonderfully sad, who kept going hither and thither weeping. Then the sun went out, so that the stars showed themselves, and they were of such a colour that I knew they must be weeping : and it seemed to me that the birds fell dead out of the sky, and that there were great earthquakes. With that, while I wondered in my trance, and was filled with a grievous fear, I conceived that a certain friend came unto me and said : ' Hast thou not heard ? She that was thine excellent lady hath been taken out of life.' Then I began to weep very piteously ; and not only in mine imagination, but with mine eyes, which were wet with tears. And I seemed to look towards Heaven, and to behold a multitude of angels who were returning upwards, having before them an exceedingly white cloud : and these angels were singing together gloriously, and the words of their song were these : ' *Osanna in excelsis ;* ' and there was no more that I heard. Then my heart that was so full of love said unto me : ' It is true that our lady lieth dead ; ' and it seemed to me that I went to look upon the body wherein that blessed and most noble spirit had had its abiding-place. And so strong was this idle imagining, that it made me to behold my lady in death, whose head certain ladies seemed to be covering with a white veil ; and who was so humble of her aspect that it was as though she had said, ' I have attained to look on the beginning of peace.' And therewithal I came unto such humility by the sight of her, that I cried out upon Death, saying :

'Now come unto me, and be not bitter against me any longer : surely, there where thou hast been, thou hast learned gentleness. Wherefore come now unto me who do greatly desire thee : seest thou not that I wear thy colour already ? ' And when I had seen all those offices performed that are fitting to be done unto the dead, it seemed to me that I went back unto mine own chamber, and looked up towards Heaven. And so strong was my phantasy that I wept again in very truth, and said with my true voice : ' O excellent soul ! how blessed is he that now looketh upon thee ! '

And as I said these words, with a painful anguish of sobbing and another prayer unto Death, a young and gentle lady, who had been standing beside me where I lay, conceiving that I wept and cried out because of the pain of mine infirmity, was taken with trembling and began to shed tears. Whereby other ladies, who were about the room, becoming aware of my discomfort by reason of the moan that she made (who indeed was of my very near kindred), led her away from where I was, and then set themselves to awaken me, thinking that I dreamed, and saying : ' Sleep no longer, and be not disquieted.'

Then, by their words, this strong imagination was brought suddenly to an end, at the moment that I was about to say, ' O Beatrice ! peace be with thee.' And already I had said, ' O Beatrice ! ' when being aroused, I opened mine eyes, and knew that it had been a deception. But albeit I had indeed uttered her name, yet my voice was so broken with sobs, that it was not understood by these ladies ; so that in spite of the sore shame that I felt, I turned towards them by Love's counselling. And when they beheld me, they began to say, ' He seemeth as one dead,' and to whisper among themselves, ' Let us strive if we may not comfort him.' Whereupon they spake to me many soothing words, and questioned me moreover touching the cause of my fear. Then I, being somewhat reassured, and having perceived that it was a mere phantasy, said unto them, ' This thing it was that made me afeard ; ' and told them of all that

THE NEW LIFE

I had seen, from the beginning even unto the end, but without once speaking the name of my lady. Also, after I had recovered from my sickness, I bethought me to write these things in rhyme; deeming it a lovely thing to be known. Whereof I wrote this poem:—

A VERY pitiful lady, very young,
  Exceeding rich in human sympathies,
    Stood by, what time I clamour'd upon Death
And at the wild words wandering on my tongue
  And at the piteous look within mine eyes
    She was affrighted, that sobs choked her breath.
    So by her weeping where I lay beneath,
Some other gentle ladies came to know
My state, and made her go:
Afterward, bending themselves over me,   10
One said, 'Awaken thee!'
  And one, 'What thing thy sleep disquieteth?'
With that, my soul woke up from its eclipse,
The while my lady's name rose to my lips:

But utter'd in a voice so sob-broken,
  So feeble with the agony of tears,
    That I alone might hear it in my heart;
And though that look was on my visage then
  Which he who is ashamed so plainly wears,   19
    Love made that I through shame held not apart,
    But gazed upon them. And my hue was such
That they look'd at each other and thought of death;
Saying under their breath
Most tenderly, 'O let us comfort him:'
Then unto me: 'What dream
  Was thine, that it hath shaken thee so much?'
And when I was a little comforted,
'This, ladies, was the dream I dreamt,' I said.

'I was a-thinking how life fails with us
  Suddenly after such a little while;   30
    When Love sobb'd in my heart, which is his home.
Whereby my spirit wax'd so dolorous

That in myself I said, with sick recoil :
  "Yea, to my lady too this Death must come."
 And therewithal such a bewilderment
Possess'd me, that I shut mine eyes for peace ;
And in my brain did cease
Order of thought, and every healthful thing.
Afterwards, wandering
   Amid a swarm of doubts that came and went,   40
Some certain women's faces hurried by,
And shriek'd to me, "Thou too shalt die, shalt die !"

' Then saw I many broken hinted sights
 In the uncertain state I stepp'd into.
  Meseem'd to be I know not in what place,
Where ladies through the streets, like mournful lights,
 Ran with loose hair, and eyes that frighten'd you,
  By their own terror, and a pale amaze :
  The while, little by little, as I thought,
The sun ceased, and the stars began to gather,   50
And each wept at the other ;
And birds dropp'd in mid-flight out of the sky ;
And earth shook suddenly ;
  And I was 'ware of one, hoarse and tired out,
Who ask'd of me : "Hast thou not heard it said ? . . .
Thy lady, she that was so fair, is dead."

' Then lifting up mine eyes, as the tears came,
 I saw the Angels, like a rain of manna,
 In a long flight flying back Heavenward ;
Having a little cloud in front of them,   60
 After the which they went and said, "Hosanna" ;
  And if they had said more, you should have heard.
  Then Love said, "Now shall all things be made clear :
Come and behold our lady where she lies."
These 'wildering phantasies
Then carried me to see my lady dead.
Even as I there was led,
 Her ladies with a veil were covering her ;
And with her was such very humbleness
That she appeared to say, "I am at peace."   70

And I became so humble in my grief,
  Seeing in her such deep humility,
    That I said : " Death, I hold thee passing good
  Henceforth, and a most gentle sweet relief,
    Since my dear love has chosen to dwell with thee :
      Pity, not hate, is thine, well understood.
      Lo ! I do so desire to see thy face
  That I am like as one who nears the tomb ;
  My soul entreats thee, Come."
Then I departed, having made my moan ;
And when I was alone
  I said, and cast my eyes to the High Place :
" Blessed is he, fair soul, who meets thy glance ! "
. . . Just then you woke me, of your complaisaùnce.'

This poem has two parts. In the first, speaking to a person undefined, I tell how I was aroused from a vain phantasy by certain ladies, and how I promised them to tell what it was. In the second, I say how I told them. The second part begins here, ' I was a-thinking.' The first part divides into two. In the first, I tell that which certain ladies, and which one singly, did and said because of my phantasy, before I had returned into my right senses. In the second, I tell what these ladies said to me after I had left off this wandering : and it begins here, ' But uttered in a voice.' Then, when I say, ' I was a-thinking,' I say how I told them this my imagination ; and concerning this I have two parts. In the first, I tell, in order, this imagination. In the second, saying at what time they called me, I covertly thank them : and this part begins here, ' Just then you woke me.'

After this empty imagining, it happened on a day, as I sat thoughtful, that I was taken with such a strong trembling at the heart, that it could not have been otherwise in the presence of my lady. Whereupon I perceived that there was an appearance of Love beside me, and I seemed to see him coming from my lady ; and he said, not aloud but within my heart : ' Now take heed that thou bless the day when I entered into thee ; for it is fitting that thou shouldst do so.' And with that my heart was so full of gladness, that I could hardly believe it to be of very truth mine own heart and not another.

A short while after these words which my heart spoke to me with the tongue of Love, I saw coming towards me a certain lady who was very famous for her beauty, and of whom that friend whom I have already called the first among my friends had long been enamoured. This lady's right name was Joan; but because of her comeliness (or at least it was so imagined) she was called of many *Primavera* (Spring), and went by that name among them. Then looking again, I perceived that the most noble Beatrice followed after her. And when both these ladies had passed by me, it seemed to me that Love spake again in my heart, saying: 'She that came first was called Spring, only because of that which was to happen on this day. And it was I myself who caused that name to be given her; seeing that as the Spring cometh first in the year, so should she come first on this day,[1] when Beatrice was to show herself after the vision of her servant. And even if thou go about to consider her right name, it is also as one should say, "She shall come first:" inasmuch as her name, Joan, is taken from that John who went before the True Light, saying: "*Ego vox clamantis in deserto: Parate viam Domini.*"'[2] And also it seemed to me that he added other words, to wit: 'He who should inquire delicately touching this matter, could not but call Beatrice by mine own name, which is to say, Love; beholding her so like unto me.'

Then I, having thought of this, imagined to write it with rhymes and send it unto my chief friend; but setting aside certain words [3] which seemed proper to be

---

[1] There is a play in the original upon the words *Primavera* (Spring) and *prima verrà* (she shall come first), to which I have given as near an equivalent as I could.

[2] 'I am the voice of one crying in the wilderness: "Prepare ye the way of the Lord."'

[3] That is (as I understand it), suppressing, from delicacy towards his friend, the words in which Love describes Joan as merely the forerunner of Beatrice. And perhaps in the latter part of this sentence a reproach is gently conveyed to the fickle Guido Caval-

set aside, because I believed that his heart still regarded the beauty of her that was called Spring. And I wrote this sonnet:—

I FELT a spirit of love begin to stir
  Within my heart, long time unfelt till then;
  And saw Love coming towards me fair and fain,
(That I scarce knew him for his joyful cheer),
Saying, 'Be now indeed my worshipper!'
  And in his speech he laugh'd and laugh'd again.
  Then, while it was his pleasure to remain,
I chanced to look the way he had drawn near
And saw the Ladies Joan and Beatrice
  Approach me, this the other following,
  One and a second marvel instantly.
And even as now my memory speaketh this,
  Love spake it then: 'The first is christen'd Spring;
  The second Love, she is so like to me.'

This sonnet has many parts: whereof the first tells how I felt awakened within my heart the accustomed tremor, and how it seemed that Love appeared to me joyful from afar. The second says how it appeared to me that Love spake within my heart, and what was his aspect. The third tells how, after he had in such wise been with me a space, I saw and heard certain things. The second part begins here, 'Saying, "Be now";' the third here, 'Then, while it was his pleasure.' The third part divides into two. In the first, I say what I saw. In the second, I say what I heard; and it begins here, 'Love spake it then'

It might be here objected unto me (and even by one worthy of controversy,) that I have spoken of Love as though it were a thing outward and visible: not only a spiritual essence, but as a bodily substance also. The which thing, in absolute truth, is a fallacy; Love not being of itself a substance, but an accident of substance. Yet that I speak of Love as though it were a thing tangible and even human, appears by three things which I say thereof. And firstly, I say that I perceived Love

canti, who may already have transferred his homage (though Dante had not then learned it) from Joan to Mandetta. (See his Poems.)

coming towards me; whereby, seeing that *to come* bespeaks locomotion, and seeing also how philosophy teacheth us that none but a corporeal substance hath locomotion, it seemeth that I speak of Love as of a corporeal substance. And secondly, I say that Love smiled: and thirdly, that Love spake; faculties (and especially the risible faculty) which appear proper unto man: whereby it further seemeth that I speak of Love as of a man. Now that this matter may be explained, (as is fitting,) it must first be remembered that anciently they who wrote poems of Love wrote not in the vulgar tongue, but rather certain poets in the Latin tongue. I mean, among us, although perchance the same may have been among others, and although likewise, as among the Greeks, they were not writers of spoken language, but men of letters treated of these things.[1] And indeed it is not a great number of years since poetry began to be made in the vulgar tongue; the writing of rhymes in spoken language corresponding to the writing in metre of Latin verse, by a certain analogy. And I say that it is but a little while, because if we examine the language of *oco* and the language of *sì*,[2] we shall not find in those tongues any written thing of an earlier date than the last hundred and fifty years. Also the reason why certain of a very mean sort obtained at the first some fame as poets is, that before them no man has written verses in the language of *sì*: and of these, the first was moved to the writing of such verses by the wish to make himself understood of a certain lady, unto whom Latin poetry was difficult. This thing is against such as rhyme concerning other matters than love; that mode

---

[1] On reading Dante's treatise *De Vulgari Eloquio*, it will be found that the distinction which he intends here is not between one language, or dialect, and another; but between 'vulgar speech' (that is, the language handed down from mother to son without any conscious use of grammar or syntax), and language as regulated by grammarians and the laws of literary composition, and which Dante calls simply 'Grammar'. A great deal might be said on the bearings of the present passage, but it is no part of my plan to enter on such questions.

[2] i.e. the languages of Provence and Tuscany

of speech having been first used for the expression of love alone.[1] Wherefore, seeing that poets have a licence allowed them that is not allowed unto the writers of prose, and seeing also that they who write in rhyme are simply poets in the vulgar tongue, it becomes fitting and reasonable that a larger licence should be given to these than to other modern writers; and that any metaphor or rhetorical similitude which is permitted unto poets, should also be counted not unseemly in the rhymers of the vulgar tongue. Thus, if we perceive that the former have caused inanimate things to speak as though they had sense and reason, and to discourse one with another; yea, and not only actual things, but such also as have no real existence (seeing that they have made things which are not, to speak; and oftentimes written of those which are merely accidents as though they were substances and things human); it should therefore be permitted to the latter to do the like; which is to say, not inconsiderately, but with such sufficient motive as may afterwards be set forth in prose.

That the Latin poets have done thus, appears through Virgil, where he saith that Juno (to wit, a goddess hostile to the Trojans) spake unto Æolus, master of the Winds; as it is written in the first book of the *Æneid*, *Æole, namque tibi, &c.;* and that this master of the Winds made reply: *Tuus o regina, quid optes— Explorare labor, mihi jussa capessere fas est.* And through the same poet, the inanimate thing speaketh unto the animate, in the third book of the *Æneid*, where it is written: *Dardanidæ duri, &c.* With Lucan, the animate thing speaketh to the inanimate; as thus:

---

[1] It strikes me that this curious passage furnishes a reason, hitherto (I believe) overlooked, why Dante put such of his lyrical poems as relate to philosophy into the form of love-poems. He liked writing in Italian rhyme rather than Latin metre; he thought Italian rhyme ought to be confined to love-poems: therefore whatever he wrote (at this age) had to take the form of a love-poem. Thus any poem by Dante not concerning love is later than his twenty-seventh year (1291-2), when he wrote the prose of the *Vita Nuova*; the poetry having been written earlier, at the time of the events referred to.

Multum, Roma, tamen debes civilibus armis. In Horace, man is made to speak to his own intelligence as unto another person ; (and not only hath Horace done this, but herein he followeth the excellent Homer,) as thus in his Poetics : *Dic mihi, Musa, virum, &c.* Through Ovid, Love speaketh as a human creature, in the beginning of his discourse *De Remediis Amoris :* as thus : *Bella mihi, video, bella parantur, ait.* By which ensamples this thing shall be made manifest unto such as may be offended at any part of this my book. And lest some of the common sort should be moved to jeering hereat, I will here add, that neither did these ancient poets speak thus without consideration, nor should they who are makers of rhyme in our day write after the same fashion, having no reason in what they write; for it were a shameful thing if one should rhyme under the semblance of metaphor or rhetorical similitude, and afterwards, being questioned thereof, should be unable to rid his words of such semblance, unto their right understanding. Of whom (to wit, of such as rhyme thus foolishly), myself and the first among my friends do know many.

But returning to the matter of my discourse. This excellent lady of whom I spake in what hath gone before, came at last into such favour with all men, that when she passed anywhere folk ran to behold her ; which thing was a deep joy to me : and when she drew near unto any, so much truth and simpleness entered into his heart, that he dared neither to lift his eyes nor to return her salutation : and unto this, many who have felt it can bear witness. She went along crowned and clothed with humility, showing no whit of pride in all that she heard and saw : and when she had gone by, it was said of many, 'This is not a woman, but one of the beautiful angels of Heaven ; ' and there were some that said : ' This is surely a miracle ; blessed be the Lord, who hath power to work thus marvellously.' I say, of very sooth, that she showed herself so gentle and so full of all perfection, that she bred in those who looked upon her a soothing quiet beyond any speech ; neither

THE NEW LIFE

could any look upon her without sighing immediately. These things, and things yet more wonderful, were brought to pass through her miraculous virtue. Wherefore I, considering thereof and wishing to resume the endless tale of her praises, resolved to write somewhat wherein I might dwell on her surpassing influence; to the end that not only they who had beheld her, but others also, might know as much concerning her as words could give to the understanding. And it was then that I wrote this sonnet:—

My lady looks so gentle and so pure
   When yielding salutation by the way,
   That the tongue trembles and has nought to say,
And the eyes, which fain would see, may not endure.
And still, amid the praise she hears secure,
   She walks with humbleness for her array;
   Seeming a creature sent from Heaven to stay
On earth, and show a miracle made sure.
She is so pleasant in the eyes of men
That through the sight the inmost heart doth gain
   A sweetness which needs proof to know it by:
And from between her lips there seems to move
A soothing essence that is full of love,
   Saying for ever to the spirit, 'Sigh!'

This sonnet is so easy to understand, from what is afore narrated, that it needs no division; and therefore, leaving it, I say also that this excellent lady came into such favour with all men, that not only she herself was honoured and commended, but through her companionship, honour and commendation came unto others. Wherefore I, perceiving this, and wishing that it should also be made manifest to those that beheld it not, wrote the sonnet here following; wherein is signified the power which her virtue had upon other ladies:—

For certain he hath seen all perfectness
   Who among other ladies hath seen mine:
   They that go with her humbly should combine
To thank their God for such peculiar grace.
So perfect is the beauty of her face

That it begets in no wise any sign
  Of envy, but draws round her a clear line
Of love, and blessed faith, and gentleness.
Merely the sight of her makes all things bow:
  Not she herself alone is holier
    Than all; but hers, through her, are raised above.
From all her acts such lovely graces flow
  That truly one may never think of her
    Without a passion of exceeding love.

This sonnet has three parts. In the first, I say in what company this lady appeared most wondrous. In the second, I say how gracious was her society. In the third, I tell of the things which she, with power, worked upon others. The second begins here, 'They that go with her;' the third here, 'So perfect.' This last part divides into three. In the first, I tell what she operated upon women, that is, by their own faculties. In the second, I tell what she operated in them through others. In the third, I say how she not only operated in women, but in all people; and not only while herself present, but, by memory of her, operated wondrously. The second begins here, 'Merely the sight;' the third here, 'From all her acts.'

Thereafter on a day, I began to consider that which I had said of my lady: to wit, in these two sonnets aforegone: and becoming aware that I had not spoken of her immediate effect on me at that especial time, it seemed to me that I had spoken defectively. Whereupon I resolved to write somewhat of the manner wherein I was then subject to her influence, and of what her influence then was. And conceiving that I should not be able to say these things in the small compass of a sonnet, I began therefore a poem with this beginning:—

LOVE hath so long possessed me for his own
  And made his lordship so familiar
That he, who at first irked me, is now grown
  Unto my heart as its best secrets are.
  And thus, when he in such sore wise doth mar

THE NEW LIFE

My life that all its strength seems gone from it,
Mine inmost being then feels throughly quit
    Of anguish, and all evil keeps afar.
Love also gathers to such power in me
    That my sighs speak, each one a grievous thing,
    Always soliciting
My lady's salutation piteously.
Whenever she beholds me, it is so,
Who is more sweet than any words can show.

* * * * * * *

Quomodo sedet sola civitas plena populo! facta est quasi vidua domina gentium![1]

I was still occupied with this poem (having composed thereof only the above written stanza), when the Lord God of justice called my most gracious lady unto Himself, that she might be glorious under the banner of that blessed Queen Mary, whose name had always a deep reverence in the words of holy Beatrice. And because haply it might be found good that I should say somewhat concerning her departure, I will herein declare what are the reasons which make that I shall not do so.

And the reasons are three. The first is, that such matter belongeth not of right to the present argument; if one consider the opening of this little book. The second is, that even though the present argument required it, my pen doth not suffice to write in a fit manner of this thing. And the third is, that were it both possible and of absolute necessity, it would still be unseemly for me to speak thereof, seeing that thereby it must behove me to speak also mine own praises : a thing that in whosoever doeth it is worthy of blame For the which reasons, I will leave this matter to be treated of by some other than myself.

Nevertheless, as the number nine, which number hath often had mention in what hath gone before (and not, as it might appear, without reason), seems also to have borne a part in the manner of her death : it is therefore

[1] 'How doth the city sit solitary, that was full of people! how is she become as a widow, she that was great among the nations!'—*Lamentations of Jeremiah*, i. 1.

right that I should say somewhat thereof. And for this cause, having first said what was the part it bore herein, I will afterwards point out a reason which made that this number was so closely allied unto my lady.

I say, then, that according to the division of time in Italy her most noble spirit departed from among us in the first hour of the ninth day of the month; and according to the division of time in Syria, in the ninth month of the year: seeing that Tismim, which with us is October, is there the first month. Also she was taken from among us in that year of our reckoning (to wit, of the years of our Lord) in which the perfect number was nine times multiplied within that century wherein she was born into the world: which is to say, the thirteenth century of Christians.[1]

And touching the reason why this number was so closely allied unto her, it may peradventure be this. According to Ptolemy (and also to the Christian verity), the revolving heavens are nine; and according to the common opinion among astrologers, these nine heavens together have influence over the earth. Wherefore it would appear that this number was thus allied unto her for the purpose of signifying that, at her birth, all these nine heavens were at perfect unity with each other as to their influence. This is one reason that may be brought: but more narrowly considering, and according to the infallible truth, this number was her own self: that is to say, by similitude. As thus. The number three is the root of the number nine; seeing that without the interposition of any other number, being multiplied merely by itself, it produceth nine, as we manifestly perceive that three times three are nine. Thus, three being of itself the efficient of nine, and the Great Efficient of Miracles being of Himself Three Persons (to wit: the

[1] Beatrice Portinari will thus be found to have died during the first hour of the 9th of June, 1290. And from what Dante says at the commencement of this work (viz. that she was younger than himself by eight or nine months), it may also be gathered that her age, at the time of her death, was twenty-four years and three months. The 'perfect number' mentioned in the present passage is the number ten.

Father, the Son, and the Holy Spirit), which, being Three, are also One :—this lady was accompanied by the number nine to the end that men might clearly perceive her to be a nine, that is, a miracle, whose only root is the Holy Trinity. It may be that a more subtile person would find for this thing a reason of greater subtilty : but such is the reason that I find, and that liketh me best.

After this most gracious creature had gone out from among us, the whole city came to be as it were widowed and despoiled of all dignity. Then I, left mourning in this desolate city, wrote unto the principal persons thereof, in an epistle, concerning its condition; taking for my commencement those words of Jeremias : *Quomodo sedet sola civitas! &c.* And I make mention of this, that none may marvel wherefore I set down these words before, in beginning to treat of her death. Also if any should blame me, in that I do not transcribe that epistle whereof I have spoken, I will make it mine excuse that I began this little book with the intent that it should be written altogether in the vulgar tongue; wherefore, seeing that the epistle I speak of is in Latin, it belongeth not to mine undertaking : more especially as I know that my chief friend, for whom I write this book, wished also that the whole of it should be in the vulgar tongue.

When mine eyes had wept for some while, until they were so weary with weeping that I could no longer through them give ease to my sorrow, I bethought me that a few mournful words might stand me instead of tears. And therefore I proposed to make a poem, that weeping I might speak therein of her for whom so much sorrow had destroyed my spirit ; and I then began 'The eyes that weep.'

That this poem may seem to remain the more widowed at its close, I will divide it before writing it ; and this method I will observe henceforward. I say that this poor little poem has three parts. The first is a prelude. In the second, I speak of her. In the third, I speak pitifully to the poem. The second begins here, 'Beatrice is gone up'; the third here, 'Weep, pitiful Song of mine.' The first divides into three. In the first, I say what moves me to

*speak. In the second, I say to whom I mean to speak.
In the third, I say of whom I mean to speak. The second
begins here, 'And because often, thinking'; the third here,
'And I will say.' Then, when I say, 'Beatrice is gone
up,' I speak of her; and concerning this I have two parts.
First, I tell the cause why she was taken away from us:
afterwards, I say how one weeps her parting; and this
part commences here, 'Wonderfully.' This part divides
into three. In the first, I say who it is that weeps her not.
In the second, I say who it is that doth weep her. In the
third, I speak of my condition. The second begins here,
'But sighing comes, and grief'; the third, 'With sighs.'
Then, when I say, 'Weep, pitiful Song of mine,' I speak
to this my song, telling it what ladies to go to, and stay with.*

THE eyes that weep for pity of the heart
  Have wept so long that their grief languisheth,
    And they have no more tears to weep withal:
And now, if I would ease me of a part
  Of what, little by little, leads to death,
    It must be done by speech, or not at all.
    And because often, thinking, I recall
How it was pleasant, ere she went afar,
  To talk of her with you, kind damozels,
  I talk with no one else,
But only with such hearts as women's are.
  And I will say,—still sobbing as speech fails,—
That she hath gone to Heaven suddenly,
And hath left Love below, to mourn with me.

Beatrice is gone up into high Heaven,
  The kingdom where the angels are at peace;
    And lives with them: and to her friends is dead.
Not by the frost of winter was she driven
  Away, like others; nor by summer-heats;
    But through a perfect gentleness, instead.
    For from the lamp of her meek lowlihead
Such an exceeding glory went up hence
  That it woke wonder in the Eternal Sire
  Until a sweet desire
Entered Him for that lovely excellence,

THE NEW LIFE

So that He bade her to Himself aspire;
Counting this weary and most evil place
Unworthy of a thing so full of grace.

Wonderfully out of the beautiful form
  Soared her clear spirit, waxing glad the while:
    And is in its first home, there where it is.
Who speaks thereof, and feels not the tears warm
  Upon his face, must have become so vile
    As to be dead to all sweet sympathies.
    Out upon him! an abject wretch like this
May not imagine anything of her,—
  He needs no bitter tears for his relief.
    But sighing comes, and grief,
And the desire to find no comforter,
  (Save only Death, who makes all sorrow brief,)
To him who for a while turns in his thought
How she hath been among us, and is not.

With sighs my bosom always laboureth
  In thinking, as I do continually,
    Of her for whom my heart now breaks apace;
And very often when I think of death,
  Such a great inward longing comes to me
    That it will change the colour of my face;
    And, if the idea settles in its place,
All my limbs shake as with an ague-fit:
  Till, starting up in wild bewilderment,
    I do become so shent
That I go forth, lest folk misdoubt of it.
  Afterward, calling with a sore lament
On Beatrice, I ask, 'Canst thou be dead?'
And calling on her, I am comforted.

Grief with its tears, and anguish with its sighs,
  Come to me now whene'er I am alone;
    So that I think the sight of me gives pain.
And what my life hath been, that living dies,
  Since for my lady the New Birth's begun,
    I have not any language to explain.
    And so, dear ladies, though my heart were fain,
I scarce could tell indeed how I am thus.

All joy is with my bitter life at war;
    Yea, I am fallen so far
That all men seem to say, 'Go out from us,'
    Eyeing my cold white lips, how dead they are.
But she, though I be bowed unto the dust,
Watches me; and will guerdon me, I trust.

Weep, pitiful Song of mine, upon thy way,
    To the dames going and the damozels
    For whom and for none else
Thy sisters have made music many a day.
Thou, that art very sad and not as they
    Go dwell thou with them as a mourner dwells.

After I had written this poem, I received the visit of a friend whom I counted as second unto me in the degrees of friendship, and who, moreover, had been united by the nearest kindred to that most gracious creature. And when we had a little spoken together, he began to solicit me that I would write somewhat in memory of a lady who had died; and he disguised his speech, so as to seem to be speaking of another who was but lately dead: wherefore I, perceiving that his speech was of none other than that blessed one herself, told him that it should be done as he required. Then afterwards, having thought thereof, I imagined to give vent in a sonnet to some part of my hidden lamentations; but in such sort that it might seem to be spoken by this friend of mine, to whom I was to give it. And the sonnet saith thus: 'Stay now with me,' &c.

This sonnet has two parts. In the first, I call the Faithful of Love to hear me. In the second, I relate my miserable condition. The second begins here, 'Mark how they force.'

STAY now with me, and listen to my sighs,
    Ye piteous hearts, as pity bids ye do.
    Mark how they force their way out and press through:
If they be once pent up, the whole life dies.
Seeing that now indeed my weary eyes
    Oftener refuse than I can tell to you
    (Even though my endless grief is ever new,)
To weep and let the smothered anguish rise.

THE NEW LIFE

Also in sighing ye shall hear me call
  On her whose blessed presence doth enrich
    The only home that well befitteth her :
And ye shall hear a bitter scorn of all
  Sent from the inmost of my spirit in speech
    That mourns its joy and its joy's minister.

But when I had written this sonnet, bethinking me who he was to whom I was to give it, that it might appear to be his speech, it seemed to me that this was but a poor and barren gift for one of her so near kindred. Wherefore, before giving him this sonnet, I wrote two stanzas of a poem : the first being written in very sooth as though it were spoken by him, but the other being mine own speech, albeit, unto one who should not look closely, they would both seem to be said by the same person. Nevertheless, looking closely, one must perceive that it is not so, inasmuch as one does not call this most gracious creature *his lady,* and the other does, as is manifestly apparent. And I gave the poem and the sonnet unto my friend, saying that I had made them only for him.

The poem begins, ' Whatever while,' and has two parts. In the first, that is, in the first stanza, this my dear friend, her kinsman, laments. In the second, I lament ; that is, in the other stanza, which begins, ' For ever.' And thus it appears that in this poem two persons lament, of whom one laments as a brother, the other as a servant.

WHATEVER while the thought comes over me
  That I may not again
    Behold that lady whom I mourn for now,
About my heart my mind brings constantly
  So much of extreme pain
    That I say, Soul of mine, why stayest thou ?
    Truly the anguish, soul, that we must bow
Beneath, until we win out of this life,
  Gives me full oft a fear that trembleth :
    So that I call on Death
Even as on Sleep one calleth after strife,
Saying, Come unto me. Life showeth grim
And bare ; and if one dies, I envy him.

> For ever, among all my sighs which burn,
>   There is a piteous speech
>   That clamours upon death continually:
> Yea, unto him doth my whole spirit turn
>   Since first his hand did reach
>   My lady's life with most foul cruelty.
>   But from the height of woman's fairness, she,
> Going up from us with the joy we had,
>   Grew perfectly and spiritually fair;
>   That so she spreads even there
> A light of Love which makes the Angels glad,
> And even unto their subtle minds can bring
> A certain awe of profound marvelling.

On that day which fulfilled the year since my lady had been made of the citizens of eternal life, remembering me of her as I sat alone, I betook myself to draw the resemblance of an angel upon certain tablets. And while I did thus, chancing to turn my head, I perceived that some were standing beside me to whom I should have given courteous welcome, and that they were observing what I did: also I learned afterwards that they had been there a while before I perceived them. Perceiving whom, I arose for salutation, and said: 'Another was with me.'[1]

Afterwards, when they had left me, I set myself again to mine occupation, to wit, to the drawing figures of angels: in doing which, I conceived to write of this matter in rhyme, as for her anniversary, and to address my rhymes unto those who had just left me. It was then that I wrote the sonnet which saith, 'That lady': and as this sonnet hath two commencements, it behoveth me to divide it with both of them here.

I say that, according to the first, this sonnet has three parts. In the first, I say that this lady was then in my memory. In the second, I tell what Love therefore did with me. In the third, I speak of the effects of Love. The

---

[1] Thus according to some texts. The majority, however, add the words, 'And therefore was I in thought:' but the shorter speech is perhaps the more forcible and pathetic.

second begins here, 'Love, knowing': the third here, 'Forth went they.' This part divides into two. In the one, I say that all my sighs issued speaking. In the other, I say how some spoke certain words different from the others. The second begins here, 'And still.' In this same manner is it divided with the other beginning, save that, in the first part, I tell when this lady had thus come into my mind, and this I say not in the other.

THAT lady of all gentle memories
  Had lighted on my soul ;—whose new abode
  Lies now, as it was well ordained of God,
Among the poor in heart, where Mary is.
Love, knowing that dear image to be his,
  Woke up within the sick heart sorrow-bow'd,
  Unto the sighs which are its weary load
Saying, ' Go forth.' And they went forth, I wis ;
Forth went they from my breast that throbbed and
    ached ;
  With such a pang as oftentimes will bathe
    Mine eyes with tears when I am left alone.
And still those sighs which drew the heaviest breath
Came whispering thus : ' O noble intellect !
    It is a year to-day that thou art gone.'

SECOND COMMENCEMENT.

THAT lady of all gentle memories
  Had lighted on my soul ;—for whose sake flowed
  The tears of Love ; in whom the power abode
Which led you to observe while I did this.
Love, knowing that dear image to be his, &c.

Then, having sat for some space sorely in thought because of the time that was now past, I was so filled with dolorous imaginings that it became outwardly manifest in mine altered countenance. Whereupon, feeling this and being in dread lest any should have seen me, I lifted mine eyes to look ; and then perceived a young and very beautiful lady, who was gazing upon

me from a window with a gaze full of pity so that the
very sum of pity appeared gathered together in her.
And seeing that unhappy persons, when they beget
compassion in others, are then most moved unto weeping,
as though they also felt pity for themselves, it came to
pass that mine eyes began to be inclined unto tears.
Wherefore, becoming fearful lest I should make manifest
mine abject condition, I rose up, and went where I could
not be seen of that lady; saying afterwards within
myself: 'Certainly with her also must abide most noble
Love.' And with that, I resolved upon writing a sonnet,
wherein, speaking unto her, I should say all that I have
just said. And as this sonnet is very evident, I will
not divide it:—

> MINE eyes beheld the blessed pity spring
> Into thy countenance immediately
> A while agone, when thou beheldst in me
> The sickness only hidden grief can bring;
> And then I knew thou wast considering
> How abject and forlorn my life must be;
> And I became afraid that thou shouldst see
> My weeping, and account it a base thing.
> Therefore I went out from thee; feeling how
> The tears were straightway loosened at my heart
> Beneath thine eyes' compassionate control.
> And afterwards I said within my soul:
> 'Lo! with this lady dwells the counterpart
> Of the same Love who holds me weeping now.'

It happened after this that whensoever I was seen of
this lady, she became pale and of a piteous countenance,
as though it had been with love; whereby she remembered me many times of my own most noble lady, who
was wont to be of a like paleness. And I know that
often, when I could not weep nor in any way give ease
unto mine anguish, I went to look upon this lady, who
seemed to bring the tears into my eyes by the mere
sight of her. Of the which thing I bethought me to
speak unto her in rhyme, and then made this sonnet:

which begins, 'Love's pallor,' and which is plain without being divided, by its exposition aforesaid :—

LOVE'S pallor and the semblance of deep ruth
  Were never yet shown forth so perfectly
  In any lady's face, chancing to see
Grief's miserable countenance uncouth,
As in thine, lady, they have sprung to soothe,
  When in mine anguish thou hast looked on me;
  Until sometimes it seems as if, through thee,
My heart might almost wander from its truth.
Yet so it is, I cannot hold mine eyes
  From gazing very often upon thine
    In the sore hope to shed those tears they keep;
And at such time, thou mak'st the pent tears rise
  Even to the brim, till the eyes waste and pine;
    Yet cannot they, while thou art present, weep.

At length, by the constant sight of this lady, mine eyes began to be gladdened overmuch with her company; through which thing many times I had much unrest, and rebuked myself as a base person: also, many times I cursed the unsteadfastness of mine eyes, and said to them inwardly: 'Was not your grievous condition of weeping wont one while to make others weep? And will ye now forget this thing because a lady looketh upon you? who so looketh merely in compassion of the grief ye then showed for your own blessed lady. But whatso ye can, that do ye, accursed eyes! many a time will I make you remember it! for never, till death dry you up. should ye make an end of your weeping.' And when I had spoken thus unto mine eyes, I was taken again with extreme and grievous sighing. And to the end that this inward strife which I had undergone might not be hidden from all saving the miserable wretch who endured it, I proposed to write a sonnet, and to comprehend in it this horrible condition. And I wrote this which begins, 'The very bitter weeping.'

The sonnet has two parts. In the first, I speak to my eyes, as my heart spoke within myself. In the second, I remove a difficulty, showing who it is that speaks thus:

and this part begins here, ' So far.' It well might receive other divisions also; but this would be useless, since it is manifest by the preceding exposition.

> ' THE very bitter weeping that ye made
>   So long a time together, eyes of mine,
>   Was wont to make the tears of pity shine
> In other eyes full oft, as I have said.
> But now this thing were scarce rememberèd
>   If I, on my part, foully would combine
>   With you, and not recall each ancient sign
> Of grief, and her for whom your tears were shed.
> It is your fickleness that doth betray
>   My mind to fears, and makes me tremble thus
>   What while a lady greets me with her eyes.
> Except by death, we must not any way
>   Forget our lady who is gone from us.'
>   So far doth my heart utter, and then sighs.

The sight of this lady brought me into so unwonted a condition that I often thought of her as of one too dear unto me; and I began to consider her thus: ' This lady is young, beautiful, gentle, and wise: perchance it was Love himself who set her in my path, that so my life might find peace.' And there were times when I thought yet more fondly, until my heart consented unto its reasoning. But when it had so consented, my thought would often turn round upon me, as moved by reason, and cause me to say within myself: ' What hope is this which would console me after so base a fashion, and which hath taken the place of all other imagining?' Also there was another voice within me, that said: ' And wilt thou, having suffered so much tribulation through Love, not escape while yet thou mayst from so much bitterness? Thou must surely know that this thought carries with it the desire of Love, and drew its life from the gentle eyes of that lady who vouchsafed thee so much pity.' Wherefore I, having striven sorely and very often with myself, bethought me to say somewhat thereof in rhyme. And seeing that in the battle of

THE NEW LIFE

doubts, the victory most often remained with such as inclined towards the lady of whom I speak, it seemed to me that I should address this sonnet unto her : in the first line whereof, I call that thought which spake of her a gentle thought, only because it spoke of one who was gentle ; being of itself most vile.[1]

In this sonnet I make myself into two, according as my thoughts were divided one from the other. The one part I call Heart, that is, appetite ; the other, Soul, that is, reason ; and I tell what one saith to the other. And that it is fitting to call the appetite Heart, and the reason Soul, is manifest enough to them to whom I wish this to be open. True it is that, in the preceding sonnet, I take the part of the Heart against the Eyes ; and that appears contrary to what I say in the present ; and therefore I say that, there also, by the Heart I mean appetite, because yet greater was my desire to remember my most gentle lady than to see this other, although indeed I had some appetite towards her, but it appeared slight : wherefrom it appears that the one statement is not contrary to the other. This sonnet has three parts. In the first, I begin to say to this lady how my desires turn all towards her. In the second, I say how the soul, that is the reason, speaks to the Heart, that is, to the appetite. In the third, I say how the latter answers The second begins here, 'And what is this?' the third here, 'And the heart answers.'

A GENTLE thought there is will often start,
   Within my secret self, to speech of thee :
   Also of Love it speaks so tenderly
That much in me consents and takes its part.
' And what is this,' the soul saith to the heart,

---

[1] Boccaccio tells us that Dante was married to Gemma Donati about a year after the death of Beatrice. Can Gemma then be ' the lady of the window,' his love for whom Dante so contemns ? Such a passing conjecture (when considered together with the interpretation of this passage in Dante's later work, the *Convito*) would of course imply an admission of what I believe to lie at the heart of all true Dantesque commentary ; that is, the existence always of the actual events even where the allegorical superstructure has been raised by Dante himself.

'That cometh thus to comfort thee and me,
   And thence where it would dwell, thus potently
Can drive all other thoughts by its strange art?'
And the heart answers: 'Be no more at strife
   'Twixt doubt and doubt: this is Love's messenger
      And speaketh but his words, from him received;
And all the strength it owns and all the life
   It draweth from the gentle eyes of her
      Who, looking on our grief, hath often grieved.'

But against this adversary of reason, there rose up in me on a certain day, about the ninth hour, a strong visible phantasy, wherein I seemed to behold the most gracious Beatrice, habited in that crimson raiment which she had worn when I had first beheld her; also she appeared to me of the same tender age as then. Whereupon I fell into a deep thought of her: and my memory ran back, according to the order of time, unto all those matters in the which she had borne a part; and my heart began painfully to repent of the desire by which it had so basely let itself be possessed during so many days, contrary to the constancy of reason.

And then, this evil desire being quite gone from me, all my thoughts turned again unto their excellent Beatrice. And I say most truly that from that hour I thought constantly of her with the whole humbled and ashamed heart; the which became often manifest in sighs, that had among them the name of that most gracious creature, and how she departed from us. Also it would come to pass very often, through the bitter anguish of some one thought, that I forgot both it, and myself, and where I was. By this increase of sighs, my weeping, which before had been somewhat lessened, increased in like manner; so that mine eyes seemed to long only for tears and to cherish them, and came at last to be circled about with red as though they had suffered martyrdom: neither were they able to look again upon the beauty of any face that might again bring them to shame and evil: from which things it will appear that they were fitly guerdoned for their unsteadfastness. Wherefore I (wishing that mine abandonment of all such evil desires and vain temptations should be certified and made manifest, beyond all doubts which might have been suggested by the rhymes aforewritten) proposed to write a sonnet wherein I should express this purport. And I then wrote, 'Woe's me!'

I said, 'Woe's me!' because I was ashamed of the trifling of mine eyes. This sonnet I do not divide, since its purport is manifest enough.

WOE's me! by dint of all these sighs that come
  Forth of my heart, its endless grief to prove,
  Mine eyes are conquered, so that even to move
Their lids for greeting is grown troublesome.
They wept so long that now they are grief's home
  And count their tears all laughter far above;
  They wept till they are circled now by Love
With a red circle in sign of martyrdom.
These musings, and the sighs they bring from me,
  Are grown at last so constant and so sore
    That love swoons in my spirit with faint breath;
Hearing in those sad sounds continually
  The most sweet name that my dead lady bore,
    With many grievous words touching her death.

About this time, it happened that a great number of persons undertook a pilgrimage, to the end that they might behold that blessed portraiture bequeathed unto us by our Lord Jesus Christ as the image of His beautiful countenance [1] (upon which countenance my dear lady now looketh continually). And certain among these

---

[1] The Veronica (*Vera icon*, or true image); that is, the napkin with which a woman was said to have wiped our Saviour's face on His way to the cross, and which miraculously retained its likeness. Dante makes mention of it also in the *Commedia* (*Parad.* xxxi. 103), where he says:

> Quale è colui, che forse di Croazia
>   Viene a veder la Veronica nostra,
> Che per l'antica fama non si sazia,
>   Ma dice nel pensier, fin che si mostra:
> 'Signor mio Gesù Cristo, Dio verace,
>   Or fu sì fatta la sembianza vostra?' &c.

pilgrims, who seemed very thoughtful, passed by a path which is well-nigh in the midst of the city where my most gracious lady was born, and abode, and at last died.

Then I, beholding them, said within myself : 'These pilgrims seem to be come from very far ; and I think they cannot have heard speak of this lady, or know anything concerning her. Their thoughts are not of her, but of other things ; it may be, of their friends who are far distant, and whom we, in our turn, know not.' And I went on to say : 'I know that if they were of a country near unto us, they would in some wise seem disturbed, passing through this city which is so full of grief.' And I said also · 'If I could speak with them a space, I am certain that I should make them weep before they went forth of this city ; for those things that they would hear from me must needs beget weeping in any.'

And when the last of them had gone by me, I bethought me to write a sonnet, showing forth mine inward speech ; and that it might seem the more pitiful, I made as though I had spoken it indeed unto them. And I wrote this sonnet, which beginneth : ' Ye pilgrim-folk.' I made use of the word *pilgrim* for its general signification; for 'pilgrim' may be understood in two senses, one general, and one special. General, so far as any man may be called a pilgrim who leaveth the place of his birth ; whereas, more narrowly speaking, he only is a pilgrim who goeth towards or frowards the House of St. James. For there are three separate denominations proper unto those who undertake journeys to the glory of God. They are called Palmers who go beyond the seas eastward, whence often they bring palm-branches. And Pilgrims, as I have said, are they who journey unto the holy House of Gallicia ; seeing that no other apostle was buried so far from his birth-place as was the blessed Saint James. And there is a third sort who are called Romers ; in that they go whither these whom I have called pilgrims went : which is to say, unto Rome

This sonnet is not divided, because its own words sufficiently declare it.

Ye pilgrim-folk, advancing pensively
  As if in thought of distant things, I pray,
  Is your own land indeed so far away—
As by your aspect it would seem to be—
That this our heavy sorrow leaves you free
  Though passing through the mournful town midway;
  Like unto men that understand to-day
Nothing at all of her great misery?
Yet if ye will but stay, whom I accost,
  And listen to my words a little space,
    At going ye shall mourn with a loud voice.
It is her Beatrice that she hath lost;
  Of whom the least word spoken holds such grace
    That men weep hearing it, and have no choice.

A while after these things, two gentle ladies sent unto me, praying that I would bestow upon them certain of these my rhymes. And I (taking into account their worthiness and consideration,) resolved that I would write also a new thing, and send it them together with those others, to the end that their wishes might be more honourably fulfilled. Therefore I made a sonnet, which narrates my condition, and which I caused to be conveyed to them, accompanied by the one preceding, and with that other which begins, 'Stay now with me and listen to my sighs.' And the new sonnet is, 'Beyond the sphere.'

This sonnet comprises five parts. In the first, I tell whither my thought goeth, naming the place by the name of one of its effects. In the second, I say wherefore it goeth up, and who makes it go thus. In the third, I tell what it saw, namely, a lady honoured. And I then call it a 'Pilgrim Spirit,' because it goes up spiritually, and like a pilgrim who is out of his known country. In the fourth, I say how the spirit sees her such (that is, in such quality) that I cannot understand her; that is to say my thought rises into the quality of her in a degree that my intellect cannot comprehend, seeing that our intellect is, towards those blessed souls, like our eye weak against the sun; and this the Philosopher says in the Second of the Metaphysics.

In the fifth, I say that, although I cannot see there whither my thought carries me—that is, to her admirable essence—I at least understand this, namely, that it is a thought of my lady, because I often hear her name therein. And, at the end of this fifth part, I say, 'Ladies mine,' to show that they are ladies to whom I speak. The second part begins, 'A new perception'; the third, 'When it hath reached'; the fourth, 'It sees her such'; the fifth, 'And yet I know.' It might be divided yet more nicely, and made yet clearer; but this division may pass, and therefore I stay not to divide it further.

BEYOND the sphere which spreads to widest space
   Now soars the sigh that my heart sends above;
   A new perception born of grieving Love
Guideth it upward the untrodden ways.
When it hath reached unto the end, and stays,
   It sees a lady round whom splendours move
   In homage; till, by the great light thereof
Abashed, the pilgrim spirit stands at gaze.
It sees her such, that when it tells me this
   Which it hath seen, I understand it not,
     It hath a speech so subtile and so fine.
And yet I know its voice within my thought
Often remembereth me of Beatrice:
     So that I understand it, ladies mine.

After writing this sonnet, it was given unto me to behold a very wonderful vision:[1] wherein I saw things which determined me that I would say nothing further of this most blessed one, until such time as I could discourse more worthily concerning her. And to this end I labour all I can: as she well knoweth. Wherefore if it be His pleasure through whom is the life of all things,

---

[1] This we may believe to have been the Vision of Hell, Purgatory, and Paradise, which furnished the triple argument of the *Divina Commedia*. The Latin words ending the *Vita Nuova* are almost identical with those at the close of the letter in which Dante, on concluding the *Paradise*, and accomplishing the hope here expressed, dedicates his great work to Can Grande della Scala.

THE NEW LIFE

that my life continue with me a few years, it is my hope that I shall yet write concerning her what hath not before been written of any woman After the which, may it seem good unto Him who is the Master of Grace, that my spirit should go hence to behold the glory of its lady: to wit, of that blessed Beatrice who now gazeth continually on His countenance *qui est per omnia sæcula benedictus*.[1] *Laus Deo*.

---

[1] 'Who is blessed throughout all ages.'

THE END OF THE NEW LIFE.

I. Sonnet
TO BRUNETTO LATINI
Sent with the Vita Nuova

MASTER BRUNETTO, this my little maid
  Is come to spend her Easter-tide with you:
  Not that she reckons feasting as her due,—
Whose need is hardly to be fed, but read.
Not in a hurry can her sense be weigh'd,
  Nor mid the jests of any noisy crew:
  Ah! and she wants a little coaxing too
Before she'll get into another's head.
But if you do not find her meaning clear,
  You've many Brother Alberts [1] hard at hand,
    Whose wisdom will respond to any call.
Consult with them and do not laugh at her;
  And if she still is hard to understand,
    Apply to Master Janus last of all.

II. Sonnet [2]
Of Beatrice de' Portinari, on All Saints' Day

LAST All Saints' holy-day, even now gone by,
  I met a gathering of damozels:
  She that came first, as one doth who excels,
Had Love with her, bearing her company:
A flame burned forward through her steadfast eye,
  As when in living fire a spirit dwells:
  So, gazing with the boldness which prevails
O'er doubt, I knew an angel visibly.
As she passed on, she bowed her mild approof
  And salutation to all men of worth,
    Lifting the soul to solemn thoughts aloof.
In Heaven itself that lady had her birth,
I think, and is with us for our behoof:
  Blessed are they who meet her on the earth.

---

[1] Probably in allusion to Albert of Cologne. Giano (Janus), which follows, was in use as an Italian name, as for instance Giano della Bella; but it seems probable that Dante is merely playfully advising his preceptor to avail himself of the twofold insight of Janus the double-faced.

[2] This and the five following pieces seem so certainly to have

III. SONNET
To certain Ladies; when Beatrice was lamenting her Father's Death [1]

WHENCE come you, all of you so sorrowful ?
  An it may please you, speak for courtesy.
  I fear for my dear lady's sake, lest she
Have made you to return thus filled with dule.
O gentle ladies, be not hard to school
  In gentleness, but to some pause agree,
  And something of my lady say to me,
For with a little my desire is full.
Howbeit it be a heavy thing to hear :
  For Love now utterly has thrust me forth,
With hand for ever lifted, striking fear.
  See if I be not worn unto the earth ;
Yea, and my spirit must fail from me here,
  If, when you speak, your words are of no worth.

IV. SONNET
To the same Ladies; with their Answer

YE ladies, walking past me piteous-eyed,
  Who is the lady that lies prostrate here ?
  Can this be even she my heart holds dear ?
Nay, if it be so, speak, and nothing hide.
Her very aspect seems itself beside,
  And all her features of such altered cheer
  That to my thinking they do not appear
Hers who makes others seem beatified.

' If thou forget to know our lady thus,
  Whom grief o'ercomes, we wonder in no wise,
For also the same thing befalleth us.
  Yet if thou watch the movement of her eyes,
Of her thou shalt be straightway conscious.
  O weep no more ; thou art all wan with sighs.'

been written at the same time as the poetry of the *Vita Nuova*, that it becomes difficult to guess why they were omitted from that work. Other poems in Dante's *Canzoniere* refer in a more general manner to his love for Beatrice, but each among those I allude to bears the impress of some special occasion.

[1] See the *Vita Nuova*, at page 352.

V. Ballata

He will gaze upon Beatrice

Because mine eyes can never have their fill
Of looking at my lady's lovely face,
  I will so fix my gaze
That I may become blessed, beholding her.

Even as an angel, up at his great height
Standing amid the light,
  Becometh blessed by only seeing God:—
So, though I be a simple earthly wight,
Yet none the less I might,
  Beholding her who is my heart's dear load,
  Be blessed, and in the spirit soar abroad.
Such power abideth in that gracious one;
Albeit felt of none
  Save of him who, desiring, honours her.

VI. Canzone

He beseeches Death for the Life of Beatrice

Death, since I find not one with whom to grieve,
  Nor whom this grief of mine may move to tears,
    Whereso I be or whitherso I turn:
Since it is thou who in my soul wilt leave
  No single joy, but chill'st it with just fears
    And makest it in fruitless hopes to burn:
    Since thou, Death, and thou only, canst decern
Wealth to my life, or want, at thy free choice:—
It is to thee that I lift up my voice,
  Bowing my face that's like a face just dead. 10
I come to thee, as to one pitying,
In grief for that sweet rest which nought can bring
  Again, if thou but once be entered
Into her life whom my heart cherishes
Even as the only portal of its peace.

Death, how most sweet the peace is that thy grace
　Can grant to me, and that I pray thee for,
　　Thou easily mayst know by a sure sign,
If in mine eyes thou look a little space
　And read in them the hidden dread they store,—　20
　　If upon all thou look which proves me thine.
　　Since the fear only maketh me to pine
After this sort,—what will mine anguish be
When her eyes close, of dreadful verity,
　In whose light is the light of mine own eyes?
But now I know that thou wouldst have my life
As hers, and joy'st thee in my fruitless strife.
　　Yet I do think this which I feel implies
That soon, when I would die to flee from pain,
I shall find none by whom I may be slain.　30

Death, if indeed thou smite this gentle one
　Whose outward worth but tells the intellect
　　How wondrous is the miracle within,—
Thou biddest Virtue rise up and begone,
　Thou dost away with Mercy's best effect,
　　Thou spoil'st the mansion of God's sojourning.
　　Yea, unto nought her beauty thou dost bring
Which is above all other beauties, even
In so much as befitteth one whom Heaven
　Sent upon earth in token of its own.　40
Thou dost break through the perfect trust which hath
Been alway her companion in Love's path:
　The light once darkened which was hers alone,
Love needs must say to them he ruleth o'er,
'I have lost the noble banner that I bore.'

Death, have some pity then for all the ill
　Which cannot choose but happen if she die,
　　And which will be the sorest ever known.
Slacken the string, if so it be thy will,
　That the sharp arrow leave it not,—thereby　50
　　Sparing her life, which if it flies is flown.
　　O Death, for God's sake, be some pity shown!
Restrain within thyself, even at its height,
The cruel wrath which moveth thee to smite

Her in whom God hath set so much of grace.
Show now some ruth if 'tis a thing thou hast !
I seem to see Heaven's gate, that is shut fast,
   Open, and angels filling all the space
About me,— come to fetch her soul whose laud
Is sung by saints and angels before God.   60

Song, thou must surely see how fine a thread
   This is that my last hope is holden by,
      And what I should be brought to without her.
Therefore for thy plain speech and lowlihead
   Make thou no pause : but go immediately,
      Knowing thyself for my heart's minister,)
      And with that very meek and piteous air
Thou hast, stand up before the face of Death,
To wrench away the bar that prisoneth
   And win unto the place of the good fruit.   70
And if indeed thou shake by thy soft voice
Death's mortal purpose,—haste thee and rejoice
   Our lady with the issue of thy suit.
So yet awhile our earthly nights and days
Shall keep the blessed spirit that I praise.

VII. Sonnet

On the 9th of June 1290

Upon a day, came Sorrow in to me,
   Saying, ' I've come to stay with thee a while ; '
   And I perceived that she had ushered Bile
And Pain into my house for company.
Wherefore I said, ' Go forth—away with thee ! '
   But like a Greek she answered, full of guile,
   And went on arguing in an easy style.
Then, looking, I saw Love come silently,
Habited in black raiment, smooth and new,
   Having a black hat set upon his hair ;
And certainly the tears he shed were true.
   So that I asked, ' What ails thee, trifler ? '
Answering he said : ' A grief to be gone through ;
   For our own lady's dying, brother dear.'

VIII. TO CINO DA PISTOIA

Sonnet

He rebukes Cino for Fickleness

I THOUGHT to be for ever separate,
  Fair Master Cino, from these rhymes of yours;
  Since further from the coast, another course,
My vessel now must journey with her freight.[1]
Yet still, because I hear men name your state
  As his whom every lure doth straight beguile,
  I pray you lend a very little while
Unto my voice your ear grown obdurate.
The man after this measure amorous,
  Who still at his own will is bound and loosed,
    How slightly Love him wounds is lightly known.
If on this wise your heart in homage bows,
  I pray you for God's sake it be disused,
    So that the deed and the sweet words be one.

CINO DA PISTOIA TO DANTE ALIGHIERI

Sonnet

He answers Dante, confessing his unsteadfast Heart

DANTE, since I from my own native place
  In heavy exile have turned wanderer,
  Far distant from the purest joy which e'er
Had issued from the Fount of joy and grace,
I have gone weeping through the world's dull space,
  And me proud Death, as one too mean, doth spare;
  Yet meeting Love, Death's neighbour, I declare
That still his arrows hold my heart in chase.
Nor from his pitiless aim can I get free,
  Nor from the hope which comforts my weak will,
    Though no true aid exists which I could share.
One pleasure ever binds and looses me;
  That so, by one same Beauty lured, I still
    Delight in many women here and there.

---

[1] This might seem to suggest that the present sonnet was written about the same time as the close of the *Vita Nuova*, and that an allusion may also here be intended to the first conception of Dante's great work.

IX. TO CINO DA PISTOIA
Sonnet
Written in Exile

Because I find not whom to speak withal
  Anent that lord whose I am as thou art,
  Behoves that in thine ear I tell some part
Of this whereof I gladly would say all.
And deem thou nothing else occasional
  Of my long silence while I kept apart,
  Except this place, so guilty at the heart
That the right has not who will give it stall.
Love comes not here to any woman's face,
  Nor any man here for his sake will sigh,
    For unto such, 'Thou fool!' were straightway said.
Ah! Master Cino, how the time turns base,
  And mocks at us, and on our rhymes says 'Fie!'
    Since truth has been thus thinly harvested.

CINO DA PISTOIA TO DANTE ALIGHIERI
Sonnet
He answers the foregoing Sonnet, and prays Dante, in the name of Beatrice, to continue his great Poem

I know not, Dante, in what refuge dwells
  The truth, which with all men is out of mind;
  For long ago it left this place behind,
Till in ts stead at last God's thunder swells.
Yet if our shifting life most clearly tells
  That here the truth has no reward assign'd,—
  'Twas God, remember, taught it to mankind,
And even among the fiends preached nothing else.
Then, though the kingdoms of the earth be torn,
  Where'er thou set thy feet, from Truth's control,
    Yet unto me thy friend this prayer accord :—
Beloved, O my brother, sorrow-worn,
  Even in that lady's name who is thy goal,
    Sing on till thou redeem thy plighted word![1]

---

[1] That is, the pledge given at the end of the *Vita Nuova*. This may perhaps have been written in the early days of Dante's exile, before his resumption of the interrupted *Commedia*.

X. Sonnet

Of Beauty and Duty

Two ladies to the summit of my mind
  Have clomb, to hold an argument of love.
  The one has wisdom with her from above,
For every noblest virtue well designed :
The other, beauty's tempting power refined
  And the high charm of perfect grace approve :
  And I, as my sweet Master's will doth move,
At feet of both their favours am reclined.
Beauty and Duty in my soul keep strife,
  At question if the heart such course can take
    And 'twixt two ladies hold its love complete.
  The fount of gentle speech yields answer meet,
  That Beauty may be loved for gladness' sake,
    And Duty in the lofty ends of life.

XI. Sestina [1]

Of the Lady Pietra degli Scrovigni

To the dim light and the large circle of shade
I have clomb, and to the whitening of the hills,
There where we see no colour in the grass.
Natheless my longing loses not its green,
It has so taken root in the hard stone
Which talks and hears as though it were a lady.

---

[1] I have translated this piece both on account of its great and peculiar beauty, and also because it affords an example of a form of composition which I have met with in no Italian writer before Dante's time, though it is not uncommon among the Provençal poets (see Dante, *De Vulg. Eloq.*). I have headed it with the name of a Paduan lady, to whom it is surmised by some to have been addressed during Dante's exile ; but this must be looked upon as a rather doubtful conjecture. I have adopted the name chiefly to mark it at once as not referring to Beatrice ; and have ventured for the same reason to give a like heading to the sonnet which follows it.

Utterly frozen is this youthful lady,
Even as the snow that lies within the shade;
For she is no more moved than is the stone
By the sweet season which makes warm the hills   10
And alters them afresh from white to green,
Covering their sides again with flowers and grass.

When on her hair she sets a crown of grass
The thought has no more room for other lady,
Because she weaves the yellow with the green
So well that Love sits down there in the shade,—
Love who has shut me in among low hills
Faster than between walls of granite-stone.

She is more bright than is a precious stone;
The wound she gives may not be healed with grass: 20
I therefore have fled far o'er plains and hills
For refuge from so dangerous a lady;
But from her sunshine nothing can give shade,—
Not any hill, nor wall, nor summer-green.

A while ago, I saw her dressed in green,—
So fair, she might have wakened in a stone
This love which I do feel even for her shade;
And therefore, as one woos a graceful lady,
I wooed her in a field that was all grass
Girdled about with very lofty hills.   30

Yet shall the streams turn back and climb the hills
Before Love's flame in this damp wood and green
Burn, as it burns within a youthful lady,
For my sake, who would sleep away in stone
My life, or feed like beasts upon the grass,
Only to see her garments cast a shade.

How dark soe'er the hills throw out their shade,
Under her summer-green the beautiful lady
Covers it, like a stone cover'd in grass.

XII. Sonnet

To the Lady Pietra degli Scrovigni

My curse be on the day when first I saw
  The brightness in those treacherous eyes of thine,—
The hour when from my heart thou cam'st to draw
  My soul away, that both might fail and pine:
  My curse be on the skill that smooth'd each line
Of my vain songs,—the music and just law
  Of art, by which it was my dear design
That the whole world should yield thee love and awe.
Yea, let me curse mine own obduracy,
  Which firmly holds what doth itself confound—
    To wit, thy fair perverted face of scorn:
    For whose sake Love is oftentimes forsworn
So that men mock at him: but most at me
  Who would hold fortune's wheel and turn it round.

GUIDO CAVALCANTI

I. TO DANTE ALIGHIERI
Sonnet
He interprets Dante's Dream, related in the first Sonnet of the Vita Nuova[1]

Unto my thinking, thou beheld'st all worth,
  All joy, as much of good as man may know,
  If thou wert in his power who here below
Is honour's righteous lord throughout this earth.
Where evil dies, even there he has his birth,
  Whose justice out of pity's self doth grow.
  Softly to sleeping persons he will go,
And, with no pain to them, their hearts draw forth.
Thy heart he took, as knowing well, alas!
  That Death had claimed thy lady for a prey:
  In fear whereof, he fed her with thy heart.
But when he seemed in sorrow to depart,
  Sweet was thy dream; for by that sign, I say,
Surely the opposite shall come to pass.[2]

II. Sonnet
To his Lady Joan, of Florence

Flowers hast thou in thyself, and foliage,
  And what is good, and what is glad to see;
The sun is not so bright as thy visàge;
  All is stark naught when one hath looked on thee;
There is not such a beautiful personage
  Anywhere on the green earth verily;
If one fear love, thy bearing sweet and sage
  Comforteth him, and no more fear hath he.
Thy lady friends and maidens ministering
  Are all, for love of thee, much to my taste:
And much I pray them that in everything
  They honour thee even as thou meritest,
And have thee in their gentle harbouring:
  Because among them all thou art the best.

---

[1] See the *Vita Nuova*, at page 328.
[2] This may refer to the belief that, towards morning, dreams go by contraries.

III. Sonnet

He compares all Things with his Lady, and finds them wanting

Beauty in woman ; the high will's decree ;
  Fair knighthood armed for manly exercise ;
  The pleasant song of birds ; love's soft replies ;
The strength of rapid ships upon the sea ;
The serene air when light begins to be ;
  The white snow, without wind that falls and lies ;
  Fields of all flower ; the place where waters rise ;
Silver and gold ; azure in jewellery :—
Weighed against these the sweet and quiet worth
  Which my dear lady cherishes at heart
    Might seem a little matter to be shown ;
Being truly, over these, as much apart
As the whole heaven is greater than this earth.
  All good to kindred natures cleaveth soon.

IV. Sonnet

A Rapture concerning his Lady

Who is she coming, whom all gaze upon,
  Who makes the air all tremulous with light,
And at whose side is Love himself ? that none
  Dare speak, but each man's sighs are infinite.
  Ah me ! how she looks round from left to right,
Let Love discourse : I may not speak thereon.
Lady she seems of such high benison
  As makes all others graceless in men's sight.
The honour which is hers cannot be said ;
  To whom are subject all things virtuous,
    While all things beauteous own her deity.
Ne'er was the mind of man so nobly led,
  Nor yet was such redemption granted us
    That we should ever know her perfectly.

V. Ballata

Of his Lady among other Ladies

With other women I beheld my love;—
  Not that the rest were women to mine eyes,
Who only as her shadows seemed to move.

I do not praise her more than with the truth,
  Nor blame I these if it be rightly read.

But while I speak, a thought I may not soothe
  Says to my senses: 'Soon shall ye be dead,
  If for my sake your tears ye will not shed.'

And then the eyes yield passage, at that thought,
To the heart's weeping, which forgets her not.

VI.
TO GUIDO ORLANDI

Sonnet

Of a Consecrated Image resembling his Lady

Guido, an image of my lady dwells
  At San Michele in Orto, consecrate
  And duly worshipped. Fair in holy state
She listens to the tale each sinner tells:
And among them that come to her, who ails
  The most, on him the most doth blessing wait.
  She bids the fiend men's bodies abdicate;
Over the curse of blindness she prevails,
And heals sick languors in the public squares.
  A multitude adores her reverently:
    Before her face two burning tapers are;
    Her voice is uttered upon paths afar.
  Yet through the Lesser Brethren's [1] jealousy
She is named idol; not being one of theirs.

---

[1] The Franciscans, in profession of deeper poverty and humility than belonged to other Orders, called themselves *Fratres minores*.

GUIDO ORLANDI TO GUIDO CAVALCANTI

Madrigal

In answer to the foregoing Sonnet

If thou hadst offered, friend, to blessed Mary
    A pious voluntary,
  As thus : ' Fair rose, in holy garden set : '
Thou then hadst found a true similitude :
    Because all truth and good
  Are hers, who was the mansion and the gate
Wherein abode our High Salvation,
    Conceived in her, a Son,
  Even by the angel's greeting whom she met.
Be thou assured that if one cry to her,   10
    Confessing, ' I did err,'
  For death she gives him life ; for she is great.

Ah ! how may'st thou be counselled to implead
    With God thine own misdeed,
  And not another's ? Ponder what thou art ;
    And humbly lay to heart
That Publican who wept his proper need.
The Lesser Brethren cherish the divine
    Scripture and church-doctrine ;
Being appointed keepers of the faith   20
    Whose preaching succoureth :
For what they preach is our best medicine.

VII. Sonnet

Of the Eyes of a certain Mandetta, of Thoulouse, which resemble those of his Lady Joan, of Florence

A CERTAIN youthful lady in Thoulouse,
   Gentle and fair, of cheerful modesty,
   Is in her eyes, with such exact degree,
Of likeness unto mine own lady, whose
I am, that through the heart she doth abuse
   The soul to sweet desire. It goes from me
   To her; yet, fearing, saith not who is she
That of a truth its essence thus subdues.
This lady looks on it with the sweet eyes
   Whose glance did erst the wounds of Love anoint
   Through its true lady's eyes which are as they.
Then to the heart returns it, full of sighs,
   Wounded to death by a sharp arrow's point
   Wherewith this lady speeds it on its way.

VIII. Ballata

He reveals, in a Dialogue, his increasing Love for Mandetta

BEING in thought of love, I chanced to see
   Two youthful damozels.
  One sang: 'Our life inhales
   All love continually.'

Their aspect was so utterly serene,
   So courteous, of such quiet nobleness,
That I said to them: 'Yours, I may well ween,
   'Tis of all virtue to unlock the place.
   Ah! damozels, do not account him base
     Whom thus his wound subdues: 10
     Since I was at Thoulouse,
       My heart is dead in me.'

They turned their eyes upon me in so much
    As to perceive how wounded was my heart;
While, of the spirits born of tears, one such
    Had been begotten through the constant smart.
    Then seeing me, abashed, to turn apart,
        One of them said, and laugh'd:
            'Love, look you, by his craft
                Holds this man thoroughly.' 20

But with grave sweetness, after a brief while,
    She who at first had laughed on me replied,
Saying: 'This lady, who by Love's great guile
    Her countenance in thy heart has glorified,
    Look'd thee so deep within the eyes, Love sigh'd
        And was awakened there.
            If it seem ill to bear,
                In him thy hope must be.'

The second piteous maiden, of all ruth,
    Fashioned for sport in Love's own image, said: 30
'This stroke, whereof thy heart bears trace in sooth,
    From eyes of too much puïssance was shed,
    Whence in thy heart such brightness enterèd,
        Thou mayst not look thereon.
            Say, of those eyes that shone
                Canst thou remember thee?'

Then said I, yielding answer therewithal
    Unto this virgin's difficult behest:
'A lady of Thoulouse, whom Love doth call
    Mandetta, sweetly kirtled and enlaced, 40
    I do remember to my sore unrest.
        Yea, by her eyes indeed
            My life has been decreed
                To death inevitably.'

Go, Ballad, to the city, even Thoulouse,
    And softly entering the Dauràde,[1] look round
    And softly call, that so there may be found
Some lady who for compleasaunce may choose

[1] The ancient church of the Daurade still exists at Thoulouse. It was so called from the golden effect of the mosaics adorning it.

> To show thee her who can my life confuse.
>   And if she yield thee way, 50
>   Lift thou thy voice and say :
>   ' For grace I come to thee.'

DANTE ALIGHIERI TO GUIDO CAVALCANTI

Sonnet

He imagines a pleasant Voyage for Guido, Lapo Gianni, and himself, with their three Ladies.

Guido, I wish that Lapo, thou, and I,
  Could be by spells conveyed, as it were now,
  Upon a barque, with all the winds that blow
Across all seas at our good will to hie.
So no mischance nor temper of the sky
  Should mar our course with spite or cruel slip ;
  But we, observing old companionship,
To be companions still should long thereby.
And Lady Joan, and Lady Beatrice,
  And her the thirtieth on my roll,[1] with us
    Should our good wizard set, o'er seas to move
    And not to talk of anything but love :
And they three ever to be well at ease,
  As we should be, I think, if this were thus.

---

[1] That is, his list of the sixty most beautiful ladies of Florence, referred to in the *Vita Nuova* ; among whom Lapo Gianni's lady, Lagia, would seem to have stood thirtieth.

IX. TO DANTE ALIGHIERI

Sonnet

Guido answers the foregoing Sonnet, speaking with shame of his changed Love

If I were still that man, worthy to love,
  Of whom I have but the remembrance now,
  Or if the lady bore another brow,
To hear this thing might bring me joy thereof.
But thou, who in Love's proper court dost move,
  Even there where hope is born of grace,—see how
  My very soul within me is brought low:
For a swift archer, whom his feats approve,
Now bends the bow, which Love to him did yield,
  In such mere sport against me, it would seem
    As though he held his lordship for a jest.
  Then hear the marvel which is sorriest:—
  My sorely wounded soul forgiveth him,
Yet knows that in his act her strength is kill'd.

X. TO DANTE ALIGHIERI

Sonnet

He reports, in a feigned Vision, the successful Issue of Lapo Gianni's Love

Dante, a sigh that rose from the heart's core
  Assailed me, while I slumbered, suddenly:
So that I woke o' the instant, fearing sore
  Lest it came thither in Love's company:
Till, turning, I beheld the servitor
  Of Lady Lagia: 'Help me,' so said he,
'O help me, Pity.' Though he said no more,
So much of Pity's essence entered me,
That I was ware of Love, those shafts he wields
  A-whetting, and preferred the mourner's quest
    To him, who straightway answered on this wise:
'Go tell my servant that the lady yields,
  And that I hold her now at his behest:
    If he believe not, let him note her eyes.'

XI. TO DANTE ALIGHIERI

Sonnet

He mistrusts the Love of Lapo Gianni

I PRAY thee, Dante, shouldst thou meet with Love
  In any place where Lapo then may be,
  That there thou fail not to mark heedfully
If Love with lover's name that man approve;
If to our Master's will his lady move
  Aright, and if himself show fealty:
  For ofttimes, by ill custom, ye may see
This sort profess the semblance of true love.
Thou know'st that in the court where Love holds sway
  A law subsists, that no man who is vile
    Can service yield to a lost woman there.
    If suffering aught avail the sufferer,
  Thou straightway shalt discern our lofty style
Which needs the badge of honour must display.

XII. Sonnet

On the Detection of a false Friend [1]

LOVE and the Lady Lagia, Guido and I,
  Unto a certain lord are bounden all,
  Who has released us—know ye from whose thrall?
Yet I'll not speak, but let the matter die:
Since now these three no more are held thereby,
  Who in such homage at his feet did fall
  That I myself was not more whimsical,
In him conceiving godship from on high.
Let Love be thanked the first, who first discern'd
  The truth; and that wise lady afterward,
    Who in fit time took back her heart again;
And Guido next, from worship wholly turn'd;
  And I, as he. But if ye have not heard,
    I shall not tell how much I loved him then.

---

[1] I should think, from the mention of Lady Lagia, that this might refer again to Lapo Gianni, who seems (one knows not why) to have fallen into disgrace with his friends. The Guido mentioned is probably Guido Orlandi.

XIII. Sonnet

He speaks of a third Love of his

O THOU that often hast within thine eyes
  A Love who holds three shafts,—know thou from me
  That this my sonnet would commend to thee
(Come from afar) a soul in heavy sighs,
Which even by Love's sharp arrow wounded lies.
  Twice did the Syrian archer shoot, and he
  Now bends his bow the third time, cunningly,
That, thou being here, he wound me in no wise.
Because the soul would quicken at the core
  Thereby, which now is near to utter death,
    From those two shafts, a triple wound that yield.
  The first gives pleasure, yet disquieteth ;
And with the second is the longing for
    The mighty gladness by the third fulfill'd.

XIV. Ballata

Of a continual Death in Love

THOUGH thou, indeed, hast quite forgotten ruth,
Its steadfast truth my heart abandons not ;
But still its thought yields service in good part
    To that hard heart in thee.

Alas ! who hears believes not I am so.
Yet who can know ? of very surety, none.
From Love is won a spirit, in some wise,
    Which dies perpetually :

And, when at length in that strange ecstasy
    The heavy sigh will start,
    There rains upon my heart
    A love so pure and fine,
That I say : 'Lady, I am wholly thine.' [1]

---

[1] I may take this opportunity of mentioning that, in every case where an abrupt change of metre occurs in one of my translations it is so also in the original poem.

XV. Sonnet

To a Friend who does not pity his Love

If I entreat this lady that all grace
  Seem not unto her heart an enemy,
  Foolish and evil thou declarest me,
And desperate in idle stubbornness.
Whence is such cruel judgement thine, whose face,
  To him that looks thereon, professeth thee
  Faithful, and wise, and of all courtesy,
And made after the way of gentleness?
Alas! my soul within my heart doth find
  Sighs, and its grief by weeping doth enhance,
    That, drowned in bitter tears, those sighs depart:
And then there seems a presence in the mind,
  As of a lady's thoughtful countenance
    Come to behold the death of the poor heart.

XVI. Ballata

He perceives that his highest Love is gone from him

Through this my strong and new misaventure,
       All now is lost to me
Which most was sweet in Love's supremacy.

So much of life is dead in its control,
   That she, my pleasant lady of all grace,
Is gone out of the devastated soul:
   I see her not, nor do I know her place;
   Nor even enough of virtue with me stays
       To understand, ah me!
The flower of her exceeding purity.   10

Because there comes—to kill that gentle thought
   With saying that I shall not see her more—
This constant pain wherewith I am distraught,
   Which is a burning torment very sore,
   Wherein I know not whom I should implore.
       Thrice thanked the Master be
Who turns the grinding wheel of misery!

Full of great anguish in a place of fear
    The spirit of my heart lies sorrowing,
Through Fortune's bitter craft. She lured it here   20
    And gave it o'er to Death, and barbed the sting ;
    She wrought that hope which was a treacherous thing ;
        In Time, which dies from me,
She made me lose mine hour of ecstasy.

For you, perturbed and fearful words of mine,
    Whither yourselves may please, even thither go ;
But always burthened with shame's troublous sign,
    And on my lady's name still calling low.
    For me, I must abide in such deep woe
        That all who look shall see   30
Death's shadow on my face assuredly.

XVII. Sonnet

Of his Pain from a new Love

WHY from the danger did mine eyes not start,—
    Why not become even blind,—ere through my sight
    Within my soul thou ever couldst alight
To say : ' Dost thou not hear me in thy heart ? '
New torment then, the old torment's counterpart,
    Filled me at once with such a sore affright,
    That, Lady, lady, (I said,) destroy not quite
Mine eyes and me ! O help us where thou art !
Thou hast so left mine eyes, that Love is fain—
    Even Love himself—with pity uncontroll'd
        To bend above them, weeping for their loss :
Saying : ' If any man feel heavy pain,
    This man's more painful heart let him behold :
        Death has it in her hand, cut like a cross.' [1]

---

[1] Death (*la* Morte), being feminine in Italian, is naturally personified as a female. I have endeavoured to bear this in mind throughout my translations, but possibly some instances might be found in which habit has prevailed, and I have made Death masculine.

GUIDO ORLANDI TO GUIDO CAVALCANTI
Prolonged Sonnet
He finds fault with the Conceits of the foregoing Sonnet

FRIEND, well I know thou knowest well to bear
  Thy sword's-point, that it pierce the close-locked mail:
  And like a bird to flit from perch to pale:
And out of difficult ways to find the air:
Largely to take and generously to share:
  Thrice to secure advantage: to regale
  Greatly the great, and over lands prevail.
In all thou art, one only fault is there:
For still among the wise of wit thou say'st
  That Love himself doth weep for thine estate;
    And yet, no eyes no tears: lo now, thy whim!
Soft, rather say: This is not held in haste;
  But bitter are the hours and passionate,
    To him that loves, and love is not for him.

For me, (by usage strengthened to forbear
From carnal love,) I fall not in such snare.

GIANNI ALFANI TO GUIDO CAVALCANTI
Sonnet [1]
On the part of a Lady of Pisa

GUIDO, that Gianni who, a day agone,
  Sought thee, now greets thee (ay and thou mayst laugh!)
  On that same Pisan beauty's sweet behalf
Who can deal love-wounds even as thou hast done.
She asked me whether thy good will were prone
  For service unto Love who troubles her,
  If she to thee in suchwise should repair
That, save by him and Gualtier, 'twere not known:—
For thus her kindred of ill augury
  Should lack the means wherefrom there might be plann'd
    Worse harm than lying speech that smites afar.
I told her that thou hast continually
  A goodly sheaf of arrows to thy hand,
    Which well should stead her in such gentle war.

[1] From a passage in Ubaldini's Glossary (1640) to the *Documenti d'Amore* of Francesco Barberino (1300), I judge that Guido answered the above sonnet, and that Alfani made a rejoinder, from which a scrap

BERNARDO DA BOLOGNA TO GUIDO CAVALCANTI
Sonnet

He writes to Guido, telling him of the Love which a certain Pinella showed on seeing him

Unto that lowly lovely maid, I wis,
  So poignant in the heart was thy salute,
  That she changed countenance, remaining mute.
Wherefore I asked : ' Pinella, how is this ?
Hast heard of Guido ? know'st thou who he is ? '
  She answered, ' Yea ; ' then paused, irresolute ;
  But I saw well how the love-wounds acute
Were widened, and the star which Love calls his
Filled her with gentle brightness perfectly.
  ' But, friend, an't please thee, I would have it told,'
She said, ' how I am known to him through thee.
  Yet since, scarce seen, I knew his name of old,—
Even as the riddle is read, so must it be.
  Oh ! send him love of mine a thousand-fold ! '

XVIII. TO BERNARDO DA BOLOGNA
Sonnet

Guido answers, commending Pinella, and saying that the Love he can offer her is already shared by many noble Ladies

The fountain-head that is so bright to see
  Gains as it runs in virtue and in sheen,
Friend Bernard ; and for her who spoke with thee,
  Even such the flow of her young life has been :
So that when Love discourses secretly
  Of things the fairest he has ever seen,
He says there is no fairer thing than she,
  A lowly maid as lovely as a queen.
And for that I am troubled, thinking of
  That sigh wherein I burn upon the waves
    Which drift her heart,—poor barque, so ill bested !—
Unto Pinella a great river of love
  I send, that's full of sirens, and whose slaves
    Are beautiful and richly habited.

there printed appears to be taken. The whole piece existed, in Ubaldini's time, among the Strozzi MSS.

DINO COMPAGNI TO GUIDO CAVALCANTI
Sonnet
He reproves Guido for his Arrogance in Love

No man may mount upon a golden stair,
  Guido my master, to Love's palace-sill:
No key of gold will fit the lock that's there,
  Nor heart there enter without pure goodwill.
Not if he miss one courteous duty, dare
  A lover hope he should his love fulfil;
But to his lady must make meek repair,
  Reaping with husbandry her favours still.
And thou but know'st of Love (I think) his name:
  Youth holds thy reason in extremities:
  Only on thine own face thou turn'st thine eyes;
Fairer than Absalom's account'st the same;
And think'st, as rosy moths are drawn by flame,
  To draw the women from their balconies.[1]

XIX. TO GUIDO ORLANDI
Sonnet
In Praise of Guido Orlandi's Lady

A LADY in whom love is manifest—
  That love which perfect honour doth adorn—
Hath ta'en the living heart out of thy breast,
  Which in her keeping to new life is born:
For there by such sweet power it is possest
  As even is felt of Indian unicorn:[2]
And all its virtue now, with fierce unrest,
  Unto thy soul makes difficult return.
For this thy lady is virtue's minister
  In suchwise that no fault there is to show,
    Save that God made her mortal on this ground.
    And even herein His wisdom shall be found:
  For only thus our intellect could know
That heavenly beauty which resembles her.

---

[1] It is curious to find these poets perpetually rating one another for the want of constancy in love. Guido is rebuked, as above, by Dino Compagni; Cino da Pistoia by Dante (p. 391); and Dante by Guido (p. 411), who formerly, as we have seen (p. 404), had confided to him his doubts of Lapo Gianni.

[2] In old representations, the unicorn is seen often with his head in a virgin's lap.

GUIDO ORLANDI TO GUIDO CAVALCANTI

Sonnet

He answers the foregoing Sonnet, declaring himself his Lady's Champion

To sound of trumpet rather than of horn,
  I in Love's name would hold a battle-play
  Of gentlemen in arms on Easter Day;
And, sailing without oar or wind, be borne
Unto my joyful beauty; all that morn
  To ride round her, in her cause seeking fray
  Of arms with all but thee, friend, who dost say
The truth of her, and whom all truths adorn.
And still I pray Our Lady's grace above,
  Most reverently, that she whom my thoughts bear
    In sweet remembrance own her Lord supreme.
Holding her honour dear, as doth behove,—
  In God who therewithal sustaineth her
    Let her abide, and not depart from Him.

XX. TO DANTE ALIGHIERI

Sonnet

He rebukes Dante for his way of Life, after the Death of Beatrice [1]

I come to thee by daytime constantly,
  But in thy thoughts too much of baseness find:
  Greatly it grieves me for thy gentle mind,
And for thy many virtues gone from thee.
It was thy wont to shun much company,
  Unto all sorry concourse ill inclined:
  And still thy speech of me, heartfelt and kind,
Had made me treasure up thy poetry.
But now I dare not, for thine abject life,
  Make manifest that I approve thy rhymes;
    Nor come I in such sort that thou mayst know.
Ah! prythee read this sonnet many times:
So shall that evil one who bred this strife
    Be thrust from thy dishonour'd soul and go.

---

[1] This interesting sonnet must refer to the same period of Dante's life regarding which he has made Beatrice address him in words of noble reproach when he meets her in Eden (*Purg.* C. xxx).

XXI. Ballata

Concerning a Shepherd-maid

Within a copse I met a shepherd-maid,
More fair, I said, than any star to see.

She came with waving tresses pale and bright,
  With rosy cheer, and loving eyes of flame,
Guiding the lambs beneath her wand aright.
  Her naked feet still had the dews on them,
  As, singing like a lover, so she came;
Joyful, and fashioned for all ecstasy.

I greeted her at once, and question made
  What escort had she through the woods in spring?
But with soft accents she replied and said
  That she was all alone there, wandering;
  Moreover: 'Do you know, when the birds sing,
My heart's desire is for a mate,' said she.

While she was telling me this wish of hers,
  The birds were all in song throughout the wood.
' Even now then,' said my thought, ' the time recurs,
  With mine own longing to assuage her mood.'
  And so, in her sweet favour's name, I sued
That she would kiss there and embrace with me.

She took my hand to her with amorous will,
  And answered that she gave me all her heart,
And drew me where the leaf is fresh and still,
  Where spring the wood-flowers in the shade apart.
  And on that day, by Joy's enchanted art,
There Love in very presence seemed to be.[1]

---

[1] The glossary to Barberino, already mentioned, refers to the existence, among the Strozzi MSS., of a poem by Lapo di Farinata degli Uberti, written in answer to the above ballata of Cavalcanti. As this respondent was no other than Guido's brother-in-law, one feels curious to know what he said to the peccadilloes of his sister's husband. But I fear the poem cannot yet have been published, as I have sought for it in vain at all my printed sources of information.

XXII. Sonnet

Of an ill-favoured Lady

Just look, Manetto, at that wry-mouth'd minx;
  Merely take notice what a wretch it is;
  How well contrived in her deformities,
How beastly favoured when she scowls and blinks.
Why, with a hood on (if one only thinks)
  Or muffle of prim veils and scapularies,—
  And set together, on a day like this,
Some pretty lady with the odious sphinx;—
Why, then thy sins could hardly have such weight,
  Nor thou be so subdued from Love's attack,
    Nor so possessed in Melancholy's sway,
But that perforce thy peril must be great
  Of laughing till the very heart-strings crack:
    Either thou'dst die, or thou must run away.

XXIII. Sonnet

To a newly enriched Man; reminding him of the Wants of the Poor

As thou wert loth to see, before thy feet,
  The dear broad coin roll all thy hill-slope down,
  Till, 'twixt the cracks of the hard glebe, some clown
Should find, rub oft, and scarcely render it;—
Tell me, I charge thee, if by generous heat
  Or clutching frost the fruits of earth be grown,
  And by what wind the blight is o'er them strown,
And with what gloom the tempest is replete.
Moreover (an' it please thee), when at morn
  Thou hear'st the voice of the poor husbandman,
    And those loud herds, his other family,—
I feel quite sure that if Betthina's born
  With a kind heart, she does the best she can
    To wheedle some of thy new wealth from thee.[1]

---

[1] The original is very obscure. Bettina being the same name as Becchina, it suggests itself as possible that the person addressed may be Cecco Angiolieri after he inherited his father's property. (See his Poems further on, and the notice of him in the *Introduction to Part II.*)

XXIV. TO POPE BONIFACE VIII

Sonnet

After the Pope's Interdict, when the great Houses were leaving Florence

Nero, thus much for tidings in thine ear.
  They of the Buondelmonti quake with dread,
  Nor by all Florence may be comforted,
Noting in thee the lion's ravenous cheer;
Who more than any dragon giv'st them fear,
  In ancient evil stubbornly array'd;
  Neither by bridge nor bulwark to be stay'd,
But only by King Pharaoh's sepulchre.
Oh, in what monstrous sin dost thou engage,—
  All these which are of loftiest blood to drive
    Away, that none dare pause but all take wing!
Yet sooth it is, thou might'st redeem the pledge
  Even yet, and save thy naked soul alive,
    Wert thou but patient in the bargaining.

XXV. Ballata

In Exile at Sarzana

Because I think not ever to return,
    Ballad, to Tuscany,—
    Go therefore thou for me
      Straight to my lady's face,
      Who, of her noble grace,
    Shall show thee courtesy.

Thou seekest her in charge of many sighs,
  Full of much grief and of exceeding fear.
But have good heed thou come not to the eyes
  Of such as are sworn foes to gentle cheer:
  For, certes, if this thing should chance,—from her
    Thou then couldst only look
    For scorn, and such rebuke
    As needs must bring me pain;—
    Yea, after death again
    Tears and fresh agony.

Surely thou knowest, Ballad, how that Death
  Assails me, till my life is almost sped:
Thou knowest how my heart still travaileth
  Through the sore pangs which in my soul are bred:—
  My body being now so nearly dead, 21
      It cannot suffer more.
      Then, going, I implore
      That this my soul thou take
      (Nay, do so for my sake,)
      When my heart sets it free.

Ah! Ballad, unto thy dear offices
  I do commend my soul, thus trembling;
That thou mayst lead it, for pure piteousness,
  Even to that lady's presence whom I sing. 30
  Ah! Ballad, say thou to her, sorrowing,
      Whereso thou meet her then:—
      'This thy poor handmaiden
      Is come, nor will be gone,
      Being parted now from one
      Who served Love painfully.'

Thou also, thou bewildered voice and weak,
  That goest forth in tears from my grieved heart,
Shalt, with my soul and with this ballad, speak
  Of my dead mind, when thou dost hence depart. 40
  Unto that lady (piteous as thou art!)
      Who is so calm and bright,
      It shall be deep delight
      To feel her presence there.
      And thou, Soul, worship her
      Still in her purity.

XXVI. Canzone [1]

A Song of Fortune

Lo ! I am she who makes the wheel to turn ;
   Lo ! I am she who gives and takes away ;
      Blamed idly, day by day,
  In all mine acts by you, ye humankind.
For whoso smites his visage and doth mourn,
   What time he renders back my gifts to me,
      Learns then that I decree
No state which mine own arrows may not find.
Who clomb must fall ;—this bear ye well in mind,
Nor say, because he fell, I did him wrong.
      Yet mine is a vain song ;
For truly ye may find out wisdom when
King Arthur's resting-place is found of men.

Ye make great marvel and astonishment
   What time ye see the sluggard lifted up
      And the just man to drop,
  And ye complain on God and on my sway.
O humankind, ye sin in your complaint :
   For He, that Lord who made the world to live,
      Lets me not take or give
By mine own act, but as He wills I may.
Yet is the mind of man so castaway,
That it discerns not the supreme behest.
      Alas ! ye wretchedest,
And chide ye at God also ? Shall not He
Judge between good and evil righteously ?

Ah ! had ye knowledge how God evermore,
   With agonies of soul and grievous heats,
      As on an anvil beats
  On them that in this earth hold high estate,—

---

[1] This and the three following Canzoni are only to be found in the later collections of Guido Cavalcanti's poems. I have included them on account of their interest, if really his, and especially for the beauty of the last among them ; but must confess to some doubts of their authenticity.

Ye would choose little rather than much store,
　And solitude than spacious palaces;
　　　Such is the sore disease
　Of anguish that on all their days doth wait.
Behold if they be not unfortunate,
When oft the father dares not trust the son!
　　　O wealth, with thee is won
A worm to gnaw for ever on his soul
Whose abject life is laid in thy control!

If also ye take note what piteous death　　　　40
　They ofttimes make, whose hoards were manifold,
　　　Who cities had and gold
　And multitudes of men beneath their hand;
Then he among you that most angereth
　Shall bless me, saying, 'Lo! I worship thee
　　　That I was not as he
　Whose death is thus accurst throughout the land.'
But now your living souls are held in band
Of avarice, shutting you from the true light
　　　Which shows how sad and slight　　　　50
Are this world's treasured riches and array
That still change hands a hundred times a-day.

For me,—could envy enter in my sphere,
　Which of all human taint is clean and quit,—
　　　I well might harbour it
　When I behold the peasant at his toil.
Guiding his team, untroubled, free from fear,
　He leaves his perfect furrow as he goes,
　　　And gives his field repose
　From thorns and tares and weeds that vex the soil:
Thereto he labours, and without turmoil　　　　61
Entrusts his work to God, content if so
　　　Such guerdon from it grow
That in that year his family shall live:
Nor care nor thought to other things will give

But now ye may no more have speech of me,
　For this mine office craves continual use:
　　　Ye therefore deeply muse
　Upon those things which ye have heard the while:

Yea, and even yet remember heedfully 70
  How this my wheel a motion hath so fleet,
    That in an eyelid's beat
  Him whom it raised it maketh low and vile.
  None was, nor is, nor shall be of such guile
Who could, or can, or shall, I say, at length
    Prevail against my strength.
But still those men that are my questioners
In bitter torment own their hearts perverse.

Song, that wast made to carry high intent
  Dissembled in the garb of humbleness,— 80
    With fair and open face
To Master Thomas let thy course be bent.
Say that a great thing scarcely may be pent
  In little room : yet always pray that he
    Commend us, thee and me,
To them that are more apt in lofty speech :
For truly one must learn ere he can teach.

XXVII. Canzone

A Song against Poverty

O POVERTY, by thee the soul is wrapp'd
  With hate, with envy, dolefulness, and doubt.
    Even so be thou cast out,
  And even so he that speaks thee otherwise.
I name thee now, because my mood is apt
To curse thee, bride of every lost estate,
    Through whom are desolate
  On earth all honourable things and wise.
  Within thy power each blest condition dies :
By thee, men's minds with sore mistrust are made 10
    Fantastic and afraid :—
Thou, hated worse than Death, by just accord,
And with the loathing of all hearts abhorr'd.

Yea, rightly art thou hated worse than Death,
  For he at length is longed for in the breast.
    But not with thee, wild beast,
  Was ever aught found beautiful or good.

GUIDO CAVALCANTI

For life is all that man can lose by death,
Not fame and the fair summits of applause ;
       His glory shall not pause,
  But live in men's perpetual gratitude.
While he who on thy naked sill has stood,
Though of great heart and worthy everso,
       He shall be counted low.
Then let the man thou troublest never hope
To spread his wings in any lofty scope.

Hereby my mind is laden with a fear,
  And I will take some thought to shelter me.
       For this I plainly see :—
  Through thee, to fraud the honest man is led ;
To tyranny the just lord turneth here,
And the magnanimous soul to avarice.
       Of every bitter vice
  Thou, to my thinking, art the fount and head ;
From thee no light in any wise is shed,
Who bringest to the paths of dusky hell.
       I therefore see full well,
That death, the dungeon, sickness, and old age,
Weighed against thee, are blessed heritage.

And what though many a goodly hypocrite,
  Lifting to thee his veritable prayer,
       Call God to witness there
  How this thy burden moved not Him to wrath.
Why, who may call (of them that muse aright)
Him poor, who of the whole can say, 'Tis Mine ?
       Methinks I well divine
  That want, to such, should seem an easy path.
  God, who made all things, all things had and hath ;
Nor any tongue may say that He was poor,
       What while He did endure
For man's best succour among men to dwell :
Since to have all, with Him, was possible.

Song, thou shalt wend upon thy journey now :
  And, if thou meet with folk who rail at thee,
       Saying that poverty
Is not even sharper than thy words allow,—

Unto such brawlers briefly answer thou,
To tell them they are hypocrites; and then
    Say mildly, once again,
That I, who am nearly in a beggar's case,   60
Might not presume to sing my proper praise.

XXVIII. Canzone

He laments the Presumption and Incontinence of his Youth

The devastating flame of that fierce plague,
  The foe of virtue, fed with others' peace
    More than itself foresees,
  Being still shut in to gnaw its own desire;
Its strength not weakened, nor its hues more vague,
  For all the benison that virtue sheds,
    But which for ever spreads
  To be a living curse that shall not tire:
  Or yet again, that other idle fire
Which flickers with all change as winds may please:
    One whichsoe'er of these   11
At length has hidden the true path from me
    Which twice man may not see,
And quenched the intelligence of joy, till now
All solace but abides in perfect woe.

Alas! the more my painful spirit grieves,
  The more confused with miserable strife
    Is that delicious life
  Which sighing it recalls perpetually:
But its worst anguish, whence it still receives   20
  More pain than death, is sent, to yield the sting
    Of perfect suffering,
  By him who is my lord and governs me;
  Who holds all gracious truth in fealty,
Being nursed in those four sisters' fond caress
    Through whom comes happiness.
He now has left me; and I draw my breath
    Wound in the arms of Death,
Desirous of her: she is cried upon
In all the prayers my heart puts up alone.   30

How fierce aforetime and how absolute
  That wheel of flame which turned within my head,
    May never quite be said,
  Because there are not words to speak the whole.
It slew my hope whereof I lack the fruit,
  And stung the blood within my living flesh
    To be an intricate mesh
  Of pain beyond endurance or control;
Withdrawing me from God, who gave my soul
To know the sign where honour has its seat   40
    From honour's counterfeit.
So in its longing my heart finds not hope,
    Nor knows what door to ope;
Since, parting me from God, this foe took thought
To shut those paths wherein He may be sought.

My second enemy, thrice armed in guile,
  As wise and cunning to mine overthrow
    As her smooth face doth show,
  With yet more shameless strength holds mastery.
My spirit, naked of its light and vile,   50
  Is lit by her with her own deadly gleam,
    Which makes all anguish seem
  As nothing to her scourges that I see.
O thou the body of grace, abide with me
As thou wast once in the once joyful time;
    And though thou hate my crime,
Fill not my life with torture to the end;
    But in thy mercy, bend
My steps, and for thine honour, back again;
Till, finding joy through thee, I bless my pain.   60

Since that first frantic devil without faith
  Fell, in thy name, upon the stairs that mount
    Unto the limpid fount
  Of thine intelligence,—withhold not now
Thy grace, nor spare my second foe from death.
  For lo! on this my soul has set her trust;
    And failing this, thou must

Prove false to truth and honour, seest thou!
Then, saving light and throne of strength, allow
My prayer, and vanquish both my foes at last;   70
    That so I be not cast
Into that woe wherein I fear to end.
    Yet if it is ordain'd
That I must die ere this be perfected,—
Ah! yield me comfort after I am dead.

Ye unadornèd words obscure of sense,
  With weeping and with sighing go from me,
    And bear mine agony
(Not to be told by words, being too intense,)
    To His intelligence   80
Who moved by virtue shall fulfil my breath
In human life or compensating death.

XXIX. Canzone

A Dispute with Death

' O SLUGGISH, hard, ingrate, what doest thou?
  Poor sinner, folded round with heavy sin,
    Whose life to find out joy alone is bent.
I call thee, and thou fall'st to deafness now;
  And, deeming that my path whereby to win
    Thy seat is lost, there sitt'st thee down content,
    And hold'st me to thy will subservient.
But I into thy heart have crept disguised:
    Among thy senses and thy sins I went,
By roads thou didst not guess, unrecognised.   10
Tears will not now suffice to bid me go,
Nor countenance abased, nor words of woe.'

Now, when I heard the sudden dreadful voice
  Wake thus within to cruel utterance,
    Whereby the very heart of hearts did fail,
My spirit might not any more rejoice,
    But fell from its courageous pride at once,
    And turned to fly, where flight may not avail.
    Then slowly 'gan some strength to re-inhale

GUIDO CAVALCANTI

The trembling life which heard that whisper speak,
    And had conceived the sense with sore travail,   21
Till in the mouth it murmured, very weak,
Saying : ' Youth, wealth, and beauty, these have I :
O Death ! remit thy claim,—I would not die.'

Small sign of pity in that aspect dwells
    Which then had scattered all my life abroad
        Till there was comfort with no single sense :
And yet almost in piteous syllables,
    When I had ceased to speak, this answer flow'd :
    ' Behold what path is spread before thee hence.
    Thy life has all but a day's permanence.   31
And is it for the sake of youth there seems
    In loss of human years such sore offence ?
Nay, look unto the end of youthful dreams.
What present glory does thy hope possess,
That shall not yield ashes and bitterness ? '

But, when I looked on Death made visible,
    From my heart's sojourn brought before mine eyes,
        And holding in her hand my grievous sin,
I seemed to see my countenance, that fell,   40
    Shake like a shadow ; my heart uttered cries,
        And my soul wept the curse that lay therein.
    Then Death : ' Thus much thine urgent prayer shall win :—
I grant thee the brief interval of youth
    At natural pity's strong soliciting.'
And I (because I knew that moment's ruth
But left my life to groan for a frail space)
Fell in the dust upon my weeping face.

So when she saw me thus abashed and dumb,
    In loftier words she weighed her argument,   50
        That new and strange it was to hear her speak ;
Saying : ' The path thy fears withhold thee from
Is thy best path. To folly be not shent,
    Nor shrink from me because thy flesh is weak.
    Thou seest how man is sore confused, and eke

How ruinous Chance makes havoc of his life,
    And grief is in the joys that he doth seek ;
Nor ever pauses the perpetual strife
'Twixt fear and rage ; until beneath the sun
His perfect anguish be fulfilled and done.'   60

' O Death ! thou art so dark and difficult,
  That never human creature might attain
    By his own will to pierce thy secret sense,
Because, foreshadowing thy dread result,
He may not put his trust in heart or brain,
    Nor power avails him, nor intelligence.
    Behold how cruelly thou takest hence
These forms so beautiful and dignified,
    And chain'st them in thy shadow chill and dense,
And forcest them in narrow graves to hide ;   70
With pitiless hate subduing still to thee
The strength of man and woman's delicacy.'

' Not for thy fear the less I come at last,
  For this thy tremor, for thy painful sweat.
    Take therefore thought to leave (for lo ! I call)
Kinsfolk and comrades, all thou didst hold fast,—
  Thy father and thy mother,—to forget
    All these thy brethren, sisters, children, all.
    Cast sight and hearing from thee ; let hope fall ;
Leave every sense and thy whole intellect,   80
    These things wherein thy life made festival :
For I have wrought thee to such strange effect
That thou hast no more power to dwell with these
  As living man. Let pass thy soul in peace '

Yea, Lord. O thou, the Builder of the spheres,
  Who, making me, didst shape me, of thy grace,
    In thine own image and high counterpart ;
Do thou subdue my spirit, long perverse,
  To weep within thy will a certain space,
    Ere yet thy thunder come to rive my heart.   90
    Set in my hand some sign of what thou art,
Lord God, and suffer me to seek out Christ,—

>   Weeping, to seek Him in thy ways apart;
> Until my sorrow have at length suffic'd
> In some accepted instant to atone
> For sins of thought, for stubborn evil done.
>
> Dishevell'd and in tears, go, song of mine,
>   To break the hardness of the heart of man:
>   Say how his life began
> From dust, and in that dust doth sink supine:
>   Yet, say, the unerring spirit of grief shall guide
>   His soul, being purified,
> To seek its Maker at the heavenly shrine.

CINO DA PISTOIA

I. TO DANTE ALIGHIERI

Sonnet

He interprets Dante's Dream, related in the first Sonnet of the Vita Nuova [1]

> Each lover's longing leads him naturally
>   Unto his lady's heart his heart to show;
>   And this it is that Love would have thee know
> By the strange vision which he sent to thee.
> With thy heart therefore, flaming outwardly
>   In humble guise he fed thy lady so,
>   Who long had lain in slumber, from all woe
> Folded within a mantle silently.
> Also, in coming, Love might not repress
>   His joy, to yield thee thy desire achieved,
>   Whence heart should unto heart true service bring.
> But understanding the great love-sickness
>   Which in thy lady's bosom was conceived,
>   He pitied her, and wept in vanishing.

[1] See *ante*, p. 328

II. TO DANTE ALIGHIERI

Canzone

On the Death of Beatrice Portinari

Albeit my prayers have not so long delay'd,
  But craved for thee, ere this, that Pity and Love
  Which only bring our heavy life some rest ;
Yet is not now the time so much o'erstay'd
  But that these words of mine which tow'rds thee move
    Must find thee still with spirit dispossess'd,
    And say to thee : ' In Heaven she now is bless'd,
Even as the blessèd name men called her by ; '
    While thou dost ever cry,
' Alas ! the blessing of mine eyes is flown ! '   10
    Behold, these words set down
  Are needed still, for still thou sorrowest.
Then hearken ; I would yield advisedly
Some comfort : Stay these sighs ; give ear to me.

We know for certain that in this blind world
  Each man's subsistence is of grief and pain,
    Still trailed by fortune through all bitterness.
Blessèd the soul which, when its flesh is furl'd
  Within a shroud, rejoicing doth attain
    To Heaven itself, made free of earthly stress.   20
    Then wherefore sighs thy heart in abjectness,
Which for her triumph should exult aloud ?
    For He the Lord our God
Hath called her, hearkening what her Angel said,
    To have Heaven perfected.
  Each saint for a new thing beholds her face,
And she the face of our Redemption sees,
Conversing with immortal substances.

CINO DA PISTOIA

Why now do pangs of torment clutch thy heart
   Which with thy love should make thee overjoy'd,
     As him whose intellect hath passed the skies ?   31
Behold, the spirits of thy life depart
   Daily to Heaven with her, they so are buoy'd
     With their desire, and Love so bids them rise.
   O God ! and thou, a man whom God made wise,
To nurse a charge of care, and love the same !
      I bid thee in His Name
From sin of sighing grief to hold thy breath,
     Nor let thy heart to death,
     Nor harbour death's resemblance in thine eyes.
God hath her with Himself eternally,   41
Yet she inhabits every hour with thee.

Be comforted, Love cries, be comforted !
   Devotion pleads, Peace, for the love of God !
     O yield thyself to prayers so full of grace ;
And make thee naked now of this dull weed
   Which 'neath thy foot were better to be trod ;
     For man through grief despairs and ends his days.
   How ever shouldst thou see the lovely face
If any desperate death should once be thine ?   50
      From justice so condign
Withdraw thyself even now ; that in the end
     Thy heart may not offend
   Against thy soul, which in the holy place,
In Heaven, still hopes to see her and to be
Within her arms. Let this hope comfort thee.

Look thou into the pleasure wherein dwells
   Thy lovely lady who is in Heaven crown'd,
     Who is herself thy hope in Heaven, the while
To make thy memory hallowed she avails ;   60
   Being a soul within the deep Heaven bound,
     A face on thy heart painted, to beguile
     Thy heart of grief which else should turn it vile.
Even as she seemed a wonder here below,
      On high she seemeth so,—

428   CINO DA PISTOIA

Yea, better known, is there more wondrous yet.
    And even as she was met
First by the angels with sweet song and smile,
Thy spirit bears her back upon the wing,
Which often in those ways is journeying.   70

Of thee she entertains the blessed throngs,
    And says to them : ' While yet my body thrave
    On earth, I gat much honour which he gave,
Commending me in his commended songs.'
    Also she asks alway of God our Lord
    To give thee peace according to His word.

III. TO DANTE ALIGHIERI

SONNET

He conceives of some Compensation in Death [1]

DANTE, whenever this thing happeneth,—
    That Love's desire is quite bereft of Hope,
    (Seeking in vain at ladies' eyes some scope
Of joy, through what the heart for ever saith,)—
I ask thee, can amends be made by Death ?
    Is such sad pass the last extremity ?—
    Or may the Soul that never feared to die
Then in another body draw new breath ?
Lo ! thus it is through her who governs all
    Below,—that I, who entered at her door,
        Now at her dreadful window must fare forth.
Yea, and I think through her it doth befall
    That even ere yet the road is travelled o'er
        My bones are weary and life is nothing worth

---

[1] Among Dante's Epistles there is a Latin letter to Cino, which I should judge was written in reply to this Sonnet.

IV. Madrigal

*To his Lady Selvaggia Vergiolesi; likening his Love to
a search for Gold*

I AM all bent to glean the golden ore
  Little by little from the river-bed;
    Hoping the day to see
When Crœsus shall be conquered in my store.
  Therefore, still sifting where the sands are spread,
    I labour patiently:
Till, thus intent on this thing and no more,—
  If to a vein of silver I were led,
    It scarce could gladden me.
And, seeing that no joy's so warm i' the core
  As this whereby the heart is comforted
    And the desire set free,—
Therefore thy bitter love is still my scope,
  Lady, from whom it is my life's sore theme
More painfully to sift the grains of hope
  Than gold out of that stream.

V. Sonnet

To Love, in great Bitterness

O LOVE, O thou that, for my fealty,
  Only in torment dost thy power employ,
  Give me, for God's sake, something of thy joy,
That I may learn what good there is in thee.
Yea, for, if thou art glad with grieving me,
  Surely my very life thou shalt destroy
  When thou renew'st my pain, because the joy
Must then be wept for with the misery.
He that had never sense of good, nor sight,
  Esteems his ill estate but natural,
    Which so is lightlier borne: his case is mine.
    But, if thou wouldst uplift me for a sign,
  Bidding me drain the curse and know it all,
I must a little taste its opposite.

VI. Sonnet

Death is not without but within him

This fairest lady, who, as well I wot,
  Found entrance by her beauty to my soul,
    Pierced through mine eyes my heart, which erst was whole,
Sorely, yet makes as though she knew it not;
Nay, turns upon me now, to anger wrought;
  Dealing me harshness for my pain's best dole,
  And is so changed by her own wrath's control,
That I go thence, in my distracted thought
Content to die; and, mourning, cry abroad
  On Death, as upon one afar from me;
    But Death makes answer from within my heart.
  Then, hearing her so hard at hand to be,
I do commend my spirit unto God;
    Saying to her too, 'Ease and peace thou art.'

VII. Sonnet

A Trance of Love

Vanquished and weary was my soul in me,
  And my heart gasped after its much lament,
  When sleep at length the painful languor sent.
And, as I slept (and wept incessantly),—
Through the keen fixedness of memory
  Which I had cherished ere my tears were spent,
  I passed to a new trance of wonderment;
Wherein a visible spirit I could see,
Which caught me up, and bore me to a place
  Where my most gentle lady was alone;
    And still before us a fire seemed to move,
  Out of the which methought there came a moan
Uttering, 'Grace, a little season, grace!
    I am of one that hath the wings of Love.'

VIII. Sonnet

Of the Grave of Selvaggia, on the Monte della Sambuca

I was upon the high and blessed mound,
  And kissed, long worshipping, the stones and grass,
  There on the hard stones prostrate, where, alas !
That pure one laid her forehead in the ground.
Then were the springs of gladness sealed and bound,
  The day that unto Death's most bitter pass
  My sick heart's lady turned her feet, who was
Already in her gracious life renown'd.
So in that place I spake to Love, and cried :
  ' O sweet my god, I am one whom Death may claim
    Hence to be his ; for lo ! my heart lies here.'
    Anon, because my Master lent no ear,
  Departing, still I called Selvaggia's name.
So with my moan I left the mountain-side.

IX. Canzone

His Lament for Selvaggia

Ay me, alas ! the beautiful bright hair
  That shed reflected gold
    O'er the green growths on either side the way :
Ay me ! the lovely look, open and fair,
  Which my heart's core doth hold
    With all else of that best remembered day ;
    Ay me ! the face made gay
With joy that Love confers ;
Ay me ! that smile of hers
  Where whiteness as of snow was visible   10
Among the roses at all seasons red !
    Ay me ! and was this well,
O Death, to let me live when she is dead ?

Ay me ! the calm, erect, dignified walk ;
  Ay me ! the sweet salute,—
    The thoughtful mind,—the wit discreetly worn ;
Ay me ! the clearness of her noble talk,
  Which made the good take root
    In me, and for the evil woke my scorn ;
      Ay me ! the longing born   20
Of so much loveliness,—
The hope, whose eager stress
  Made other hopes fall back to let it pass,
Even till my load of love grew light thereby !
  These thou hast broken, as glass,
O Death, who makest me, alive, to die !

Ay me ! Lady, the lady of all worth ;—
  Saint, for whose single shrine
    All other shrines I left, even as Love will'd ;—
Ay me ! what precious stone in the whole earth,   30
  For that pure fame of thine
    Worthy the marble statue's base to yield ?
      Ay me ! fair vase fulfill'd
With more than this world's good,—
By cruel chance and rude
  Cast out upon the steep path of the mountains
Where Death has shut thee in between hard stones !
    Ay me ! two languid fountains
Of weeping are these eyes, which joy disowns.

Ay me, sharp Death ! till what I ask is done   40
  And my whole life is ended utterly,—
Answer—must I weep on
  Even thus, and never cease to moan Ay me ?

TO GUIDO CAVALCANTI

X. Sonnet

He owes nothing to Guido as a Poet

What rhymes are thine which I have ta'en from thee,
 Thou Guido, that thou ever say'st I thieve ? [1]
 'Tis true, fine fancies gladly I receive,
But when was aught found beautiful in thee ?
Nay, I have searched my pages diligently,
 And tell the truth, and lie not, by your leave.
 From whose rich store my web of songs I weave
Love knoweth well, well knowing them and me.
No artist I,—all men may gather it ;
 Nor do I work in ignorance of pride,
  (Though the world reach alone the coarser sense ;)
But am a certain man of humble wit
 Who journeys with his sorrow at his side,
  For a heart's sake, alas ! that is gone hence.

XI. Sonnet

He impugns the verdicts of Dante's Commedia

This book of Dante's, very sooth to say,
 Is just a poet's lovely heresy,
 Which by a lure as sweet as sweet can be
Draws other men's concerns beneath its sway ;
While, among stars' and comets' dazzling play,
 It beats the right down, lets the wrong go free,
 Shows some abased, and others in great glee,
Much as with lovers is Love's ancient way.
Therefore his vain decrees, wherein he lied,
 Fixing folks' nearness to the Fiend their foe,
  Must be like empty nutshells flung aside.
 Yet through the rash false witness set to grow,
French and Italian vengeance on such pride
  May fall, like Antony's on Cicero.

---

[1] I have not examined Cino's poetry with special reference to this accusation ; but there is a Canzone of his in which he speaks of having conceived an affection for another lady from her resemblance to Selvaggia. Perhaps Guido considered this as a sort of plagiarism *de facto* on his own change of love through Mandetta's likeness to Giovanna.

D. G. R.

XII. Sonnet

He condemns Dante for not naming, in the Commedia, *his friend Onesto di Boncima, and his Lady Selvaggia*

Among the faults we in that book descry
  Which has crowned Dante lord of rhyme and thought,
  Are two so grave that some attaint is brought
Unto the greatness of his soul thereby.
One is, that holding with Sordello high
  Discourse, and with the rest who sang and taught,
  He of Onesto di Boncima [1] nought
Has said, who was to Arnauld Daniel [2] nigh.
The other is, that when he says he came
  To see, at summit of the sacred stair,
    His Beatrice among the heavenly signs,—
He, looking in the bosom of Abraham,
  Saw not that highest of all women there
    Who joined Mount Zion to the Apennines.[3]

---

[1] Between this poet and Cino various friendly sonnets were interchanged, which may be found in the Italian collections. There is also one sonnet by Onesto to Cino, with his answer, both of which are far from being affectionate or respectful. They are very obscure, however, and not specially interesting.

[2] The Provençal poet, mentioned in C. xxvi of the *Purgatory*.

[3] That is, sanctified the Apennines by her burial on the Monte della Sambuca.

DANTE DA MAIANO

I. TO DANTE ALIGHIERI

Sonnet

He interprets Dante Alighieri's Dream, related in the First Sonnet of the Vita Nuova [1]

Of that wherein thou art a questioner
  Considering, I make answer briefly thus,
  Good friend, in wit but little prosperous:
And from my words the truth thou shalt infer,—
So hearken to thy dream's interpreter.
  If, sound of frame, thou soundly canst discuss
  In reason,—then, to expel this overplus
Of vapours which hath made thy speech to err,
See that thou lave and purge thy stomach soon.
  But if thou art afflicted with disease,
    Know that I count it mere delirium.
    Thus of my thought I write thee back the sum:
  Nor my conclusions can be changed from these
Till to the leech thy water I have shown.

II. Sonnet

He craves interpreting of a Dream of his

Thou that art wise, let wisdom minister
  Unto my dream, that it be understood.
To wit: A lady, of her body fair,
  And whom my heart approves in womanhood,
  Bestowed on me a wreath of flowers, fair-hued
And green in leaf, with gentle loving air;
  After the which, meseemed I was stark nude
Save for a smock of hers that I did wear.
Whereat, good friend, my courage gat such growth
  That to mine arms I took her tenderly:
With no rebuke the beauty laughed unloth,
  And as she laughed I kissed continually.
I say no more, for that I pledged mine oath,
  And that my mother, who is dead, was by.

[1] See *ante*, p. 328.

GUIDO ORLANDI TO DANTE DA MAIANO

Sonnet

He interprets the Dream [1] related in the foregoing Sonnet

On the last words of what you write to me
   I give you my opinion at the first,
   To see the dead must prove corruption nursed
Within you, by your heart's own vanity.
The soul should bend the flesh to its decree :
   Then rule it, friend, as fish by line amerced.
   As to the smock, your lady's gift, the worst
Of words were not too bad for speech so free.
It is a thing unseemly to declare
   The love of gracious dame or damozel,
     And therewith for excuse to say, I dream'd.
     Tell us no more of this, but think who seem'd
   To call you : mother came to whip you well.
Love close, and of Love's joy you'll have your share.

III. Sonnet

To his Lady Nina, of Sicily

So greatly thy great pleasaunce pleasured me,
   Gentle my lady, from the first of all,
   That counting every other blessing small
I gave myself up wholly to know thee :
And since I was made thine, thy courtesy
   And worth, more than of earth, celestial,
   I learned, and from its freedom did enthrall
My heart, the servant of thy grace to be.
Whereof I pray thee, joyful countenance,
   Humbly, that it incense or irk thee not,
If I, being thine, do wait upon thy glance
More to solicit, I am all afraid :
   Yet, lady, twofold is the gift, we wot,
Given to the needy unsolicited.

[1] There exist no fewer than six answers by different poets, interpreting Dante da Maiano's dream. I have chosen Guido Orlandi's,

IV. Sonnet

He thanks his Lady for the Joy he has had from her

Wonderful countenance and royal neck,
  I have not found your beauty's parallel!
  Nor at her birth might any yet prevail
The likeness of these features to partake.
Wisdom is theirs, and mildness: for whose sake
  All grace seems stol'n, such perfect grace to swell;
  Fashioned of God beyond delight to dwell
Exalted. And herein my pride I take
Who of this garden have possession,
  So that all worth subsists for my behoof
    And bears itself according to my will.
  Lady, in thee such pleasaunce hath its fill
That whoso is content to rest thereon
    Knows not of grief, and holds all pain aloof.

much the most matter-of-fact of the six, because it is diverting to find the writer again in his antagonistic mood. Among the five remaining answers, in all of which the vision is treated as a very mysterious matter, one is attributed to Dante Alighieri, but seems so doubtful that I have not translated it. Indeed, it would do the greater Dante, if he really wrote it, little credit as a lucid interpreter of dreams; though it might have some interest, as giving him (when compared with the sonnet at p. 435) a decided advantage over his lesser namesake in point of courtesy.

CECCO ANGIOLIERI, DA SIENA

I. TO DANTE ALIGHIERI

SONNET

On the last Sonnet of the Vita Nuova [1]

DANTE ALIGHIERI, Cecco, your good friend
  And servant, gives you greeting as his lord,
  And prays you for the sake of Love's accord,
(Love being the Master before whom you bend,)
That you will pardon him if he offend,
  Even as your gentle heart can well afford.
  All that he wants to say is just one word
Which partly chides your sonnet at the end.
For where the measure changes, first you say
  You do not understand the gentle speech
    A spirit made touching your Beatrice:
And next you tell your ladies how, straightway,
  You understand it. Wherefore (look you) each
    Of these your words the other's sense denies.

II. SONNET

He will not be too deeply in Love

I AM enamoured, and yet not so much
  But that I'd do without it easily;
  And my own mind thinks all the more of me
That Love has not quite penned me in his hutch.
Enough if for his sake I dance and touch
  The lute, and serve his servants cheerfully:
  An overdose is worse than none would be:
Love is no lord of mine, I'm proud to vouch.
So let no woman who is born conceive
  That I'll be her liege slave, as I see some,
    Be she as fair and dainty as she will.
Too much of love makes idiots, I believe:
  I like not any fashion that turns glum
    The heart, and makes the visage sick and ill.

[1] See *ante*, p. 384.

III. Sonnet

Of Love in Men and Devils

The man who feels not, more or less, somewhat
   Of love in all the years his life goes round
   Should be denied a grave in holy ground
Except with usurers who will bate no groat;
Nor he himself should count himself a jot
    Less wretched than the meanest beggar found.
   Also the man who in Love's robe is gown'd
May say that Fortune smiles upon his lot.
Seeing how love has such nobility
    That if it entered in the lord of Hell
     'Twould rule him more than his fire's ancient sting;
He should be glorified to eternity,
    And all his life be always glad and well
     As is a wanton woman in the spring.

IV. Sonnet

Of Love, in honour of his Mistress Becchina

Whatever good is naturally done
   Is born of Love as fruit is born of flower:
   By Love all good is brought to its full power:
Yea, Love does more than this; for he finds none
So coarse but from his touch some grace is won,
    And the poor wretch is altered in an hour.
   So let it be decreed that Death devour
The beast who says that Love's a thing to shun.
A man's just worth the good that he can hold,
    And where no love is found, no good is there;
     On that there's nothing that I would not stake.
So now, my Sonnet, go as you are told
    To lovers and their sweethearts everywhere,
     And say I made you for Becchina's sake.

V. Sonnet

Of Becchina, the Shoemaker's Daughter

WHY, if Becchina's heart were diamond,
   And all the other parts of her were steel,
   As cold to love as snows when they congeal
In lands to which the sun may not get round;
And if her father were a giant crown'd
   And not a donkey born to stitching shoes,
   Or I were but an ass myself;—to use
Such harshness, scarce could to her praise redound.
Yet if she'd only for a minute hear,
   And I could speak if only pretty well,
     I'd let her know that I'm her happiness;
That I'm her life should also be made clear,
   With other things that I've no need to tell;
     And then I feel quite sure she'd answer Yes.

VI. Sonnet

To Messer Angiolieri, his Father

IF I'd a sack of florins, and all new,
   (Packed tight together, freshly coined and fine,)
   And Arcidosso and Montegiovi mine,[1]
And quite a glut of eagle-pieces too,—
It were but as three farthings to my view
   Without Becchina. Why then all these plots
   To whip me, daddy? Nay, but tell me—what's
My sin, or all the sins of Turks, to you?
For I protest (or may I be struck dead!)
   My love's so firmly planted in its place,
     Whipping nor hanging now could change the grain.
And if you want my reason on this head,
   It is that whoso looks her in the face,
     Though he were old, gets back his youth again.

[1] Perhaps the names of his father's estates.

VII. Sonnet

Of the 20th June 1291

I'm full of everything I do not want,
   And have not that wherein I should find ease;
   For alway till Becchina brings me peace
The heavy heart I bear must toil and pant;
That so all written paper would prove scant
   (Though in its space the Bible you might squeeze,)
   To say how like the flames of furnaces
I burn, remembering what she used to grant.
Because the stars are fewer in heaven's span
   Than all those kisses wherewith I kept tune
     All in an instant (I who now have none!)
Upon her mouth (I and no other man!)
   So sweetly on the twentieth day of June
     In the new year [1] twelve hundred ninety-one.

VIII. Sonnet

In absence from Becchina

My heart's so heavy with a hundred things
   That I feel dead a hundred times a-day;
Yet death would be the least of sufferings,
   For life's all suffering save what's slept away;
Though even in sleep there is no dream but brings
   From dream-land such dull torture as it may.
And yet one moment would pluck out these stings,
   If for one moment she were mine to-day
Who gives my heart the anguish that it has.
   Each thought that seeks my heart for its abode
     Becomes a wan and sorrow-stricken guest:
Sorrow has brought me to so sad a pass
   That men look sad to meet me on the road;
     Nor any road is mine that leads to rest.

---

[1] The year, according to the calendar of those days, began on March 25. The alteration to January 1 was made in 1582 by the Pope, and immediately adopted by all Catholic countries, but by England not till 1752.

IX. Sonnet

Of Becchina in a Rage

When I behold Becchina in a rage,
  Just like a little lad I trembling stand
  Whose master tells him to hold out his hand.
Had I a lion's heart, the sight would wage
Such war against it, that in that sad stage
  I'd wish my birth might never have been plann'd,
  And curse the day and hour that I was bann'd
With such a plague for my life's heritage.
Yet even if I should sell me to the Fiend,
  I must so manage matters in some way
    That for her rage I may not care a fig;
Or else from death I cannot long be screen'd.
  So I'll not blink the fact, but plainly say
    It's time I got my valour to grow big.

X. Sonnet

He rails against Dante, who had censured his homage to Becchina

Dante Alighieri in Becchina's praise
  Won't have me sing, and bears him like my lord.
  He's but a pinchbeck florin, on my word;
Sugar he seems, but salt's in all his ways;
He looks like wheaten bread, who's bread of maize;
  He's but a sty, though like a tower in height;
  A falcon, till you find that he's a kite;
Call him a cock!—a hen's more like his case.
Go now to Florence, Sonnet of my own,
  And there with dames and maids hold pretty parles,
    And say that all he is doth only seem.
And I meanwhile will make him better known
  Unto the Count of Provence, good King Charles;[1]
    And in this way we'll singe his skin for him.

---

[1] This may be either Charles II, King of Naples and Count of Provence, or more probably his son Charles Martel, King of Hungary. We know from Dante that a friendship subsisted between himself and the latter prince, who visited Florence in 1295, and died in the same year, in his father's lifetime (*Paradise*, C. VIII).

XI. Sonnet

Of his four Tormentors

I'm caught, like any thrush the nets surprise,
   By Daddy and Becchina, Mammy and Love.
As to the first-named, let thus much suffice,—
   Each day he damns me, and each hour thereof;
Becchina wants so much of all that's nice,
   Not Mahomet himself could yield enough:
And Love still sets me doting in a trice
   On trulls who'd seem the Ghetto's proper stuff.
My mother don't do much because she can't,
   But I may count it just as good as done,
Knowing the way and not the will's her want.
   To-day I tried a kiss with her—just one—
To see if I could make her sulks avaunt:
   She said, 'The devil rip you up, my son!'

XII. Sonnet

Concerning his Father

The dreadful and the desperate hate I bear
   My father (to my praise, not to my shame,)
   Will make him live more than Methusalem;
Of this I've long ago been made aware.
Now tell me, Nature, if my hate's not fair.
   A glass of some thin wine not worth a name
   One day I begged (he has whole butts o' the same,)
And he had almost killed me, I declare.
'Good Lord, if I had asked for vernage-wine!'
   Said I; for if he'd spit into my face
   I wished to see for reasons of my own.
Now say that I mayn't hate this plague of mine!
   Why, if you knew what I know of his ways,
     You'd tell me that I ought to knock him down.[1]

---

[1] I have thought it necessary to soften one or two expressions in this sonnet.

XIII. Sonnet

Of all he would do

If I were fire, I'd burn the world away;
  If I were wind, I'd turn my storms thereon;
  If I were water, I'd soon let it drown;
If I were God, I'd sink it from the day;
If I were Pope, I'd never feel quite gay
  Until there was no peace beneath the sun;
    If I were Emperor, what would I have done?—
I'd lop men's heads all round in my own way.
If I were Death, I'd look my father up;
  If I were life, I'd run away from him;
    And treat my mother to like calls and runs.
If I were Cecco (and that's all my hope),
  I'd pick the nicest girls to suit my whim,
    And other folk should get the ugly ones.

XIV. Sonnet

He is past all Help

For a thing done, repentance is no good,
  Nor to say after, Thus would I have done:
In life, what's left behind is vainly rued;
  So let a man get used his heart to shun;
For on his legs he hardly may be stood
  Again, if once his fall be well begun.
But to show wisdom's what I never could;
  So where I itch I scratch now, and all's one.
I'm down, and cannot rise in any way;
  For not a creature of my nearest kin
    Would hold me out a hand that I could reach.
I pray you do not mock at what I say;
  For so my love's good grace may I not win
    If ever sonnet held so true a speech!

XV. Sonnet

Of why he is unhanged

Whoever without money is in love
  Had better build a gallows and go hang ;
  He dies not once, but oftener feels the pang
Than he who was cast down from Heaven above.
And certes, for my sins it's plain enough,
  If Love's alive on earth, that he's myself,
  Who would not be so cursed with want of pelf
If others paid my proper dues thereof.
Then why am I not hanged by my own hands ?
  I answer : for this empty narrow chink
    Of hope ;—that I've a father old and rich,
And that if once he dies I'll get his lands ;
  And die he must, when the sea's dry, I think.
    Meanwhile God keeps him whole and me i' the ditch.

XVI. Sonnet

Of why he would be a Scullion

I am so out of love through poverty
  That if I see my mistress in the street
  I hardly can be certain whom I meet,
And of her name do scarce remember me.
Also my courage it has made to be
  So cold, that if I suffered some foul cheat,
  Even from the meanest wretch that one could beat,
Save for the sin I think he should go free.
Ay, and it plays me a still nastier trick ;
  For, meeting some who erewhile with me took
    Delight, I seem to them a roaring fire.
So here's a truth whereat I need not stick ;—
  That if one could turn scullion to a cook,
    It were a thing to which one might aspire.

XVII. Sonnet

He argues his case with Death

Gramercy, Death, as you've my love to win,
  Just be impartial in your next assault ;
  And that you may not find yourself in fault,
Whate'er you do, be quick now and begin.
As oft may I be pounded flat and thin
  As in Grosseto there are grains of salt,
  If now to kill us both you be not call'd,—
Both me and him who sticks so in his skin.
Or better still, look here ; for if I'm slain
  Alone,—his wealth, it's true, I'll never have,
Yet death is life to one who lives in pain :
  But if you only kill Saldagno's knave,
I'm left in Siena (don't you see your gain ?)
  Like a rich man who's made a galley-slave.[1]

XVIII. Sonnet

Of Becchina, and of her Husband

I would like better in the grace to be
  Of the dear mistress whom I bear in mind
  (As once I was) than I should like to find
A stream that washed up gold continually :
Because no language could report of me
  The joys that round my heart would then be twin'd,
  Who now, without her love, do seem resign'd
To death that bends my life to its decree.
And one thing makes the matter still more sad :
  For all the while I know the fault's my own,
    That on her husband I take no revenge,
Who's worse to her than is to me my dad.
  God send grief has not pulled my courage down,
    That hearing this I laugh ; for it seems strange.

---

[1] He means, perhaps, that he should be more than ever tormented by his creditors.

XIX. Sonnet
On the Death of his Father

Let not the inhabitants of Hell despair,
  For one's got out who seemed to be locked in ;
  And Cecco's the poor devil that I mean,
Who thought for ever and ever to be there.
But the leaf's turned at last, and I declare
  That now my state of glory doth begin :
  For Messer Angiolieri's slipped his skin,
Who plagued me, summer and winter, many a year.
Make haste to Cecco, Sonnet, with a will,
  To him who no more at the Abbey dwells ;
    Tell him that Brother Henry's half dried up.[1]
He'll never more be down-at-mouth, but fill
  His beak at his own beck,[2] till his life swells
    To more than Enoch's or Elijah's scope.

XX. Sonnet
He would slay all who hate their Fathers

Who utters of his father aught but praise,
  'Twere well to cut his tongue out of his mouth ;
  Because the Deadly Sins are seven, yet doth
No one provoke such ire as this must raise.
Were I a priest, or monk in anyways,
  Unto the Pope my first respects were paid,
  Saying, 'Holy Father, let a just crusade
Scourge each man who his sire's good name gainsays.'
And if by chance a handful of such rogues
  At any time should come into our clutch,
    I'd have them cooked and eaten then and there,
If not by men, at least by wolves and dogs.
  The Lord forgive me ! for I fear me much
    Some words of mine were rather foul than fair.

---

[1] It would almost seem as if Cecco, in his poverty, had at last taken refuge in a religious house under the name of Brother Henry (*Frate Arrigo*), and as if he here meant that Brother Henry was now decayed, so to speak, through the resuscitation of Cecco. (See Introduction to Part II, p. 318.)

[2] In the original words, 'Ma di tal cibo imbecchi lo suo becco,' a play upon the name of Becchina seems intended, which I have conveyed as well as I could.

XXI.

TO DANTE ALIGHIERI

Sonnet

He writes to Dante, then in exile at Verona, defying him as no better than himself

Dante Alighieri, if I jest and lie,
  You in such lists might run a tilt with me:
  I get my dinner, you your supper, free;
And if I bite the fat, you suck the fry;
I shear the cloth and you the teazel ply;
  If I've a strut, who's prouder than you are?
  If I'm foul-mouthed, you're not particular;
And you're turned Lombard, even if Roman I.
So that, 'fore Heaven! if either of us flings
  Much dirt at the other, he must be a fool:
For lack of luck and wit we do these things.
  Yet if you want more lessons at my school,
Just say so, and you'll find the next touch stings—
  For, Dante, I'm the goad and you're the bull.

GUIDO ORLANDI [1]

Sonnet

Against the 'White' Ghibellines

Now of the hue of ashes are the Whites;
  And they go following now after the kind
  Of creatures we call crabs, which, as some find,
Will only seek their natural food o' nights.
All day they hide; their flesh has such sore frights
  Lest Death be come for them on every wind,
  Lest now the Lion's [2] wrath be so inclined
That they may never set their sin to rights.
Guelf were they once, and now are Ghibelline:
  Nothing but rebels henceforth be they named,—
    State-foes, as are the Uberti, every one.
Behold, against the Whites all men must sign
  Some judgement whence no pardon can be claim'd
    Excepting they were offered to Saint John.[3]

LAPO GIANNI

I. Madrigal

What Love shall provide for him

Love, I demand to have my lady in fee.

  Fine balm let Arno be;
The walls of Florence all of silver rear'd,
And crystal pavements in the public way.

  With castles make me fear'd,
Till every Latin soul have owned my sway.

---

[1] Several other pieces by this author, addressed to Guido Cavalcanti and Dante da Maiano, will be found among their poems.

[2] i.e. Florence.

[3] That is, presented at the high altar on the feast-day of St. John the Baptist; a ceremony attending the release of criminals, a certain number of whom were annually pardoned on that day in Florence. This was the disgraceful condition annexed to that recall to Florence which Dante received when in exile at the court of Verona; which others accepted, but which was refused by him in a memorable epistle still preserved.

Be the world peaceful ; safe throughout each path ;
        No neighbour to breed wrath ;
The air, summer and winter, temperate.

A thousand dames and damsels richly clad
        Upon my choice to wait,
Singing by day and night to make me glad.

Let me have fruitful gardens of great girth,
        Filled with the strife of birds,
With water-springs, and beasts that house i' the earth.

Let me seem Solomon for lore of words,
Samson for strength, for beauty Absalom.

        Knights as my serfs be given ;
And as I will, let music go and come ;
Till at the last thou bring me into Heaven.

II. Ballata

A Message in charge for his Lady Lagia

Ballad, since Love himself hath fashioned thee
  Within my mind where he doth make abode,
  Hie thee to her who through mine eyes bestow'd
Her blessing on my heart, which stays with me.

Since thou wast born a handmaiden of Love,
  With every grace thou shouldst be perfected,
    And everywhere seem gentle, wise, and sweet.
And for that thine aspect gives sign thereof,
  I do not tell thee, ' Thus much must be said : '—
    Hoping, if thou inheritest my wit,
    And com'st on her when speech may ill befit,
That thou wilt say no words of any kind :
But when her ear is graciously inclin'd,
    Address her without dread submissively.

Afterward, when thy courteous speech is done,
  (Ended with fair obeisance and salute
    To that chief forehead of serenest good)

LAPO GIANNI

Wait thou the answer which, in heavenly tone,
　Shall haply stir between her lips, nigh mute
　　For gentleness and virtuous womanhood.
　And mark that, if my homage please her mood,
No rose shall be incarnate in her cheek,
But her soft eyes shall seem subdued and meek,
　And almost pale her face for delicacy.

For, when at last thine amorous discourse
　Shall have possessed her spirit with that fear
　　Of thoughtful recollection which in love
Comes first—then say thou that my heart implores
　Only without an end to honour her,
　　Till by God's will my living soul remove:
　　That I take counsel oftentimes with Love;
For he first made my hope thus strong and rife,
Through whom my heart, my mind, and all my life,
　Are given in bondage to her seigniory.

Then shalt thou find the blessed refuge girt
　I' the circle of her arms, where pity and grace
　　Have sojourn, with all human excellence:
Then shalt thou feel her gentleness exert
　Its rule (unless, alack! she deem thee base):
　　Then shalt thou know her sweet intelligence:
　　Then shalt thou see—O marvel most intense!—
What thing the beauty of the angels is,
And what are the miraculous harmonies
　Whereon Love rears the heights of sovereignty.

Move, Ballad, so that none take note of thee,
　Until thou set thy footsteps in Love's road.
　Having arrived, speak with thy visage bow'd,
And bring no false doubt back, or jealousy.

DINO FRESCOBALDI

I. Sonnet

Of what his Lady is

This is the damsel by whom love is brought
  To enter at his eyes that looks on her ;
  This is the righteous maid, the comforter,
Whom every virtue honours unbesought.
Love, journeying with her, unto smiles is wrought,
  Showing the glory which surrounds her there ;
  Who, when a lowly heart prefers its prayer,
Can make that its trangression come to nought.
And, when she giveth greeting, by Love's rule,
  With sweet reserve she somewhat lifts her eyes,
    Bestowing that desire which speaks to us.
  Alone on what is noble looks she thus,
    Its opposite rejecting in like wise,
This pitiful young maiden beautiful.

II. Sonnet

Of the Star of his Love

That star the highest seen in heaven's expanse
  Not yet forsakes me with its lovely light :
  It gave me her who from her heaven's pure height
Gives all the grace mine intellect demands.
Thence a new arrow of strength is in my hands
  Which bears good will whereso it may alight ;
  So barbed, that no man's body or soul its flight
Has wounded yet, nor shall wound any man's.
Glad am I therefore that her grace should fall
  Not otherwise than thus ; whose rich increase
    Is such a power as evil cannot dim.
My sins within an instant perished all
  When I inhaled the light of so much peace.
    And this Love knows ; for I have told it him.

GIOTTO DI BONDONE

Canzone

Of the Doctrine of Voluntary Poverty

Many there are, praisers of Poverty;
The which as man's best state is register'd
    When by free choice preferr'd,
With strict observance having nothing here.
For this they find certain authority
Wrought of an over-nice interpreting.
    Now as concerns such thing,
A hard extreme it doth to me appear,
    Which to commend I fear,
For seldom are extremes without some vice.   10
    Let every edifice,
Of work or word, secure foundation find;
    Against the potent wind,
And all things perilous, so well prepar'd
That it need no correction afterward.

Of poverty which is against the will,
It never can be doubted that therein
    Lies broad the way to sin.
For oftentimes it makes the judge unjust;
In dames and damsels doth their honour kill;   20
And begets violence and villanies,
    And theft and wicked lies,
And casts a good man from his fellows' trust.
    And for a little dust
Of gold that lacks, wit seems a lacking too.
    If once the coat give view
Of the real back, farewell all dignity.
    Each therefore strives that he
Should by no means admit her to his sight,   29
Who, only thought on, makes his face turn white.

Of poverty which seems by choice elect,
I may pronounce from plain experience,—
 Not of mine own pretence,—
That 'tis observed or unobserved at will.
Nor its observance asks our full respect :
For no discernment, nor integrity,
 Nor lore of life, nor plea
Of virtue, can her cold regard instil.
 I call it shame and ill
To name as virtue that which stifles good.   40
 I call it grossly rude,
On a thing bestial to make consequent
 Virtue's inspired advent
To understanding hearts acceptable :
For the most wise most love with her to dwell.

Here may'st thou find some issue of demur :
For lo ! our Lord commendeth poverty.
 Nay, what His meaning be
Search well : His words are wonderfully deep,
Oft doubly sensed, asking interpreter.   50
The state for each most saving, is His will
 For each. Thine eyes unseal,
And look within, the inmost truth to reap
 Behold what concord keep
His holy words with His most holy life.
 In Him the power was rife
Which to all things apportions time and place.
 On earth He chose such case ;
And why ? 'Twas His to point a higher life.

But here, on earth, our senses show us still   60
How they who preach this thing are least at peace,
 And evermore increase
Much thought how from this thing they should escape.
For if one such a lofty station fill,
He shall assert his strength like a wild wolf,
 Or daily mask himself
Afresh, until his will be brought to shape ;
 Ay, and so wear the cape

That direst wolf shall seem like sweetest lamb
    Beneath the constant sham.   70
Hence, by their art, this doctrine plagues the world:
    And hence, till they be hurl'd
From where they sit in high hypocrisy,
No corner of the world seems safe to me.

Go, Song, to some sworn owls that we have known,
And on their folly bring them to reflect:
    But if they be stiff-neck'd,
Belabour them until their heads are down.

SIMONE DALL' ANTELLA

Prolonged Sonnet

In the last Days of the Emperor Henry VII

Along the road all shapes must travel by,
    How swiftly, to my thinking, now doth fare
    The wanderer who built his watchtower there
Where wind is torn with wind continually!
Lo! from the world and its dull pain to fly,
    Unto such pinnacle did he repair,
    And of her presence was not made aware,
Whose face, that looks like Peace, is Death's own lie.
Alas, Ambition, thou his enemy,
    Who lurest the poor wanderer on his way,
But never bring'st him where his rest may be,—
    O leave him now, for he is gone astray
Himself out of his very self through thee,
    Till now the broken stems his feet betray,
And, caught with boughs before and boughs behind,
Deep in thy tangled wood he sinks entwin'd.

GIOVANNI QUIRINO
TO DANTE ALIGHIERI
Sonnet

*He commends the work of Dante's Life, then drawing to
its close; and deplores his own deficiencies*

GLORY to God and to God's Mother chaste,
  Dear friend, is all the labour of thy days :
  Thou art as he who evermore uplays
That heavenly wealth which the worm cannot waste :
So shalt thou render back with interest
  The precious talent given thee by God's grace :
  While I, for my part, follow in their ways
Who by the cares of this world are possess'd.
For, as the shadow of the earth doth make
  The moon's globe dark, when so she is debarr'd
    From the bright rays which lit her in the sky,—
So now, since thou my sun didst me forsake,
  (Being distant from me), I grow dull and hard,
    Even as a beast of Epicurus' sty.

DANTE ALIGHIERI TO GIOVANNI QUIRINO
Sonnet

*He answers the foregoing Sonnet; saying what he feels
at the approach of Death*

THE King by whose rich grace His servants be
  With plenty beyond measure set to dwell
  Ordains that I my bitter wrath dispel
And lift mine eyes to the great consistory ;
Till, noting how in glorious quires agree
  The citizens of that fair citadel,
  To the Creator I His creature swell
Their song, and all their love possesses me.
So, when I contemplate the great reward
  To which our God has called the Christian seed,
    I long for nothing else but only this.
And then my soul is grieved in thy regard,
  Dear friend, who reck'st not of thy nearest need.
    Renouncing for slight joys the perfect bliss.

APPENDIX TO PART II

I. FORESE DONATI. CECCO D'ASCOLI

WHAT follows relates to the very filmiest of all the will-o'-the wisps which have beset me in making this book. I should be glad to let it lose itself in its own quagmire, but am perhaps bound to follow it as far as may be.

Ubaldini, in his Glossary to Barberino (published in 1640, and already several times referred to here), has a rather startling entry under the word *Vendetta*.

After describing this 'custom of the country', he says :—

'To leave a vengeance unaccomplished was considered very shameful; and on this account Forese de' Donati sneers at Dante, who did not avenge his father Alighieri: saying to him ironically :—

"Ben sò che fosti figliuoli d'Alighieri ;
Ed accorgomen pure alla vendetta
Che facesti di lui sı bella e netta ;"

and hence perhaps Dante is menaced in Hell by the Spirit of one of his race.'

Now there is no hint to be found anywhere that Dante's father, who died about 1270, in the poet's childhood, came by his death in any violent way. The spirit met in Hell (C. XXIX) is Geri, son of Bello Alighieri, and Dante's great-uncle; and he is there represented as passing his kinsman in contemptuous silence on account of *his own* death by the hand of one of the Sacchetti, which remained till then unavenged, and so continued till after Dante's death, when Cione Alighieri fulfilled the *vendetta* by slaying a Sacchetti at the door of his house. If Dante is really the person addressed in the sonnet quoted by Ubaldini, I think it probable (as I shall show presently when I give the whole sonnet) that the ironical allusion is to the death of Geri Alighieri. But indeed the real writer, the real subject, and the real object of this clumsy piece of satire, seem about equally puzzling.

Forese Donati, to whom this Sonnet and another I shall quote are attributed, was the brother of Gemma Donati, Dante's wife, and of Corso and Piccarda Donati. Dante introduces him in the *Purgatory* (C. XXIII) as expiating the sin of gluttony. From what is there said, he seems to have been well known in youth to Dante, who speaks also of having wept his death; but at the same time he hints that the life they led together was disorderly and a subject for regret. This can hardly account for such violence as is shown in these sonnets, said to have been written from one to the other; but it is not impossible, of course, that a rancour, perhaps temporary, may have existed at some time between them, especially as Forese probably adhered with the rest of his family to the party hostile to Dante. At any rate, Ubaldini, Crescimbeni, Quadrio, and other writers on Italian Poetry, seem to have derived this impression from the poems which they had seen in MS. attributed to Forese. They all combine in stigmatizing Forese's supposed productions as very bad poetry, and in fact this seems the only point concerning them which is beyond a doubt. The four sonnets of which I now proceed to give such translations as I have found possible were first published together in 1812 by Fiacchi, who states that he had seen two separate ancient MSS. in both of which they were attributed to Dante and Forese. In rendering them, I have no choice but to adopt in a positive form my conjectures as to their meaning; but that I view these only as conjectures will appear afterwards.

I

DANTE ALIGHIERI TO FORESE DONATI

He taunts Forese, by the Nickname of Bicci

O BICCI, pretty son of who knows whom
  Unless thy mother Lady Tessa tell,—
  Thy gullet is already crammed too well,
Yet others' food thou needs must now consume.
Lo! he that wears a purse makes ample room
  When thou goest by in any public place,
  Saying, 'This fellow with the branded face
Is thief apparent from his mother's womb.'
And I know one who's fain to keep his bed
  Lest thou shouldst filch it, at whose birth he stood
  Like Joseph when the world its Christmas saw.
Of Bicci and his brothers it is said
  That with the heat of misbegotten blood
  Among their wives they are nice brothers-in-law.

II

FORESE DONATI TO DANTE ALIGHIERI

He taunts Dante ironically for not avenging Geri Alighieri

RIGHT well I know thou'rt Alighieri's son;
  Nay, that revenge alone might warrant it,
  Which thou didst take, so clever and complete,
For thy great-uncle who awhile agone
Paid scores in full. Why, if thou hadst hewn one
  In bits for it, 'twere early still for peace!
  But then thy head's so heaped with things like these
That they would weigh two sumpter-horses down.
Thou hast taught us a fair fashion, sooth to say,—
  That whoso lays a stick well to thy back,
    Thy comrade and thy brother he shall be.
As for their names who've shown thee this good play,
  I'll tell them thee, so thou wilt tell me back
    All of thy fears, that I may stand by thee.

III

DANTE ALIGHIERI TO FORESE DONATI

He taunts him concerning his Wife

To hear the unlucky wife of Bicci cough,
  (Bicci,—Forese as he's called, you know,—)
You'd fancy she had wintered, sure enough,
  Where icebergs rear themselves in constant snow:
  And Lord! if in mid-August it is so,
How in the frozen months must she come off?
  To wear her socks abed avails not,—no,
Nor quilting from Cortona, warm and tough.
Her cough, her cold, and all her other ills,
  Do not afflict her through the rheum of age,
    But through some want within her nest, poor spouse!
This grief, with other griefs, her mother feels,
  Who says, 'Without much trouble, I'll engage,
    She might have married in Count Guido's house!'

IV

FORESE DONATI TO DANTE ALIGHIERI

He taunts him concerning the unavenged Spirit of Geri Alighieri

THE other night I had a dreadful cough
  Because I'd got no bed-clothes over me;
And so, when the day broke, I hurried off
  To seek some gain whatever it might be.
And such luck as I had I tell you of.
  For lo! no jewels hidden in a tree
I find, nor buried gold, nor suchlike stuff,
  But Alighieri among the graves I see,
Bound by some spell, I know not at whose 'hest,—
  At Solomon's, or what sage's who shall say?
Therefore I crossed myself towards the east;
  And he cried out: 'For Dante's love I pray
Thou loose me!' But I knew not in the least
  How this were done, so turned and went my way.

Now all this may be pronounced little better than scurrilous doggrel, and I would not have introduced any of it, had I not wished to include everything which could possibly belong to my subject.

Even supposing that the authorship is correctly attributed in each case, the insults heaped on Dante have of course no weight, as coming from one who shows every sign of being both foul-mouthed and a fool. That then even the observance of the *vendetta* had its opponents among the laity, is evident from a passage in Barberino's *Documenti d'Amore*. The two sonnets bearing Dante's name, if not less offensive than the others, are rather more pointed; but seem still very unworthy even of his least exalted mood.

Accordingly Fraticelli (in his *Minor Works of Dante*) settles to his own satisfaction that these four sonnets are not by Dante and Forese; but I do not think his arguments conclusive enough to set the matter quite at rest. He first states positively that Sonnet I (as above) is by Burchiello, the Florentine barber-poet of the fifteenth century. However, it is only to be found in one edition of Burchiello, and that a late one, of 1757, where it is placed among the pieces which are very doubtfully his. It becomes all the more doubtful when we find it there followed by Sonnet II (as above), which would seem by all evidence to

APPENDIX TO PART II

be at any rate written by a different person from the first, whoever the writers of both may be. Of this sonnet Fraticelli seems to state that he has seen it attributed in one MS. to a certain Bicci Novello; and adds (but without giving any authority) that it was addressed to some descendant of the great poet, also bearing the name of Dante. Sonnet III is pronounced by Fraticelli to be of uncertain authorship, though if the first is by Burchiello, so must this be. He also decides that the designation, 'Bicci, vocato Forese', shows that Forese was the nickname and Bicci the real name; but this is surely quite futile, as the way in which the name is put is to the full as likely to be meant in ridicule as in earnest. Lastly, of Sonnet IV Fraticelli says nothing.

It is now necessary to explain that Sonnet II, as I translate it, is made up from two versions, the one printed by Fiacchi and the one given among Burchiello's poems; while in one respect I have adopted a reading of my own. I would make the first four lines say—

> Ben sò che fosti figliuol d'Alighieri:
> Ed accorgomen pure alla vendetta
> Che facesti di lui, sì bella e netta,
> Dell' *avolin* che diè cambio l'altrieri.

Of the two printed texts one says, in the fourth line—

> Dell' aguglin ched ei cambiò l'altrieri;

and the other,

> Degli auguglin che diè cambio l'altrieri.

'Aguglino' would be 'eaglet', and with this, the whole sense of the line seems quite unfathomable: whereas at the same time 'aguglino' would not be an unlikely corrupt transcription, or even corrupt version, of 'avolino, which again (according to the often confused distinctions of Italian relationships) might well be a modification of 'avolo' (grandfather), meaning greatuncle. The reading would thus be, 'La vendetta che facesti *di lui* (i.e.) *dell' avolino* che diè cambio l'altrieri;' translated literally, 'The vengeance which you took for him,—for your great-uncle who gave change the other day.' Geri Alighieri might indeed have been said to 'give change' or 'pay scores in full' by his death, as he himself had been the aggressor in the first instance, having slain one of the Sacchetti, and been afterwards slain himself by another.

I should add that I do not think the possibility, however questionable, of these sonnets being authentically by Dante and Forese, depends solely on the admission of this word 'avolino'.

The rapacity attributed to the 'Bicci' of Sonnet I seems a tendency somewhat akin to the insatiable gluttony which Forese is represented as expiating in Dante's *Purgatory*. Mention is also there made of Forese's wife, though certainly in a very different strain from that of Sonnet III ; but it is not impossible that the poet might have intended to make amends to her as well as in some degree to her husband's memory. I am really more than half ashamed of so many 'possibles' and 'not impossibles' ; but perhaps, having been led into the subject, am a little inclined that the reader should be worried with it like myself.

At any rate, considering that these Sonnets are attributed by various old manuscripts to Dante and Forese Donati ;—that various writers (beginning with Ubaldini, who seems to have ransacked libraries more than almost any one) have spoken of these and other sonnets by Forese against Dante,—that the feud between the Alighieri and Sacchetti, and the death of Geri, were certainly matters of unabated bitterness in Dante's lifetime, as we find the *vendetta* accomplished even after his death,—and lastly, that the sonnets attributed to Forese seem to be plausibly referable to this subject,—I have thought it pardonable towards myself and my readers to devote to these ill-natured and not very refined productions this very long and tiresome note.

Crescimbeni (*Storia della Volgar Poesia*) gives another sonnet against Dante as being written by Forese Donati, and it certainly resembles these in style. I should add that their obscurity of mere language is excessive, and that my translations therefore are necessarily guesswork here and there ; though as to this I may spare particulars except in what affects the question at issue. In conclusion, I hope I need hardly protest against the inference that my translations and statements might be shown to abound in dubious makeshifts and whimsical conjectures ; though it would be admitted, on going over the ground I have traversed, that it presents a difficulty of some kind at almost every step.

There is one more versifier, contemporary with Dante, to whom I might be expected to refer. This is the ill-fated Francesco Stabili, better known as Cecco d'Ascoli, who was burnt by the Inquisition at Florence in 1327, as a heretic, though the exact nature of his offence is involved in some mystery. He was a narrow, discontented, and self-sufficient writer ; and his incongruous poem in *sesta rima*, called *L'Acerba*, contains various references to the poetry of Dante (whom he knew personally) as well as to that of Guido Cavalcanti, made chiefly in a supercilious spirit. These allusions have no poetical or biographical value whatever, so I need say no more of them or their author. And indeed perhaps the 'Bicci' sonnets are quite enough of themselves in the way of absolute trash.

II. GIOVANNI BOCCACCIO

SEVERAL of the little-known sonnets of Boccaccio have reference to Dante, but, being written in the generation which followed his, do not belong to the body of my first division. I therefore place three of them here, together with a few more specimens from the same poet.

There is nothing which gives Boccaccio a greater claim to our regard than the enthusiastic reverence with which he loved to dwell on the *Commedia* and on the memory of Dante, who died when he was seven years old. This is amply proved by his Life of the Poet and Commentary on the Poem, as well as by other passages in his writings both in prose and poetry. The first of the three following sonnets relates to his public reading and elucidation of Dante, which took place at Florence, by a decree of the State, in 1373. The second sonnet shows how the greatest minds of the generation which immediately succeeded Dante already paid unhesitating tribute to his political as well as poetical greatness. In the third sonnet, it is interesting to note the personal love and confidence with which Boccaccio could address the spirit of his mighty master, unknown to him in the flesh.

I

To one who had censured his public Exposition of Dante

IF Dante mourns, there wheresoe'er he be,
    That such high fancies of a soul so proud
    Should be laid open to the vulgar crowd,
(As, touching my Discourse, I'm told by thee,)
This were my grievous pain; and certainly
    My proper blame should not be disavow'd;
    Though hereof somewhat, I declare aloud
Were due to others, not alone to me.
False hopes, true poverty, and therewithal
    The blinded judgement of a host of friends,
    And their entreaties, made that I did thus.
But of all this there is no gain at all
    Unto the thankless souls with whose base ends
    Nothing agrees that's great or generous.

II

Inscription for a Portrait of Dante

DANTE ALIGHIERI, a dark oracle,
  Of wisdom and of art, I am ; whose mind
  Has to my country such great gifts assign'd
That men account my powers a miracle.
My lofty fancy passed as low as Hell,
  As high as Heaven, secure and unconfin'd ;
  And in my noble book doth every kind
Of earthly lore and heavenly doctrine dwell.
Renownéd Florence was my mother,—nay,
  Stepmother unto me her piteous son,
Through sin of cursed slander's tongue and tooth.
Ravenna sheltered me so cast away ;
  My body is with her,—my soul with One
For whom no envy can make dim the truth.

III

To Dante in Paradise, after Fiammetta's death

DANTE, if thou within the sphere of Love,
  As I believe, remain'st contemplating
  Beautiful Beatrice, whom thou didst sing
Erewhile, and so wast drawn to her above ;—
Unless from false life true life thee remove
  So far that Love's forgotten, let me bring
  One prayer before thee : for an easy thing
This were, to thee whom I do ask it of.
I know that where all joy doth most abound
  In the third Heaven, my own Fiammetta sees
The grief which I have borne since she is dead.
O pray her (if mine image be not drown'd
  In Lethe) that her prayers may never cease
Until I reach her and am comforted.

I add three further examples of Boccaccio's poetry, chosen for their beauty alone. Two of these relate to Maria d'Aquino, the lady whom, in his writings, he calls Fiammetta. The last has a playful charm very characteristic of the author of the *Decameron* ; while its beauty of colour (to our modern minds, privileged to review the whole pageant of Italian Art,) might recall the painted pastorals of Giorgione.

IV

Of Fiammetta singing

LOVE steered my course, while yet the sun rode high,
   On Scylla's waters to a myrtle-grove:
    The heaven was still and the sea did not move;
Yet now and then a little breeze went by
Stirring the tops of trees against the sky:
   And then I heard a song as glad as love,
   So sweet that never yet the like thereof
Was heard in any mortal company.
' A nymph, a goddess, or an angel sings
   Unto herself, within this chosen place,
    Of ancient loves;' so said I at that sound.
And there my lady, mid the shadowings
   Of myrtle-trees, 'mid flowers and grassy space,
    Singing I saw, with others who sat round.

V

Of his last sight of Fiammetta

ROUND her red garland and her golden hair
   I saw a fire about Fiammetta's head;
    Thence to a little cloud I watched it fade,
Than silver or than gold more brightly fair;
And like a pearl that a gold ring doth bear,
   Even so an angel sat therein, who sped
   Alone and glorious throughout heaven, array'd
In sapphires and in gold that lit the air.
Then I rejoiced as hoping happy things,
   Who rather should have then discerned how God
    Had haste to make my lady all His own,
Even as it came to pass. And with these stings
   Of sorrow, and with life's most weary load
    I dwell, who fain would be where she is gone.

VI

Of three Girls and of their Talk

By a clear well, within a little field
   Full of green grass and flowers of every hue,
   Sat three young girls, relating (as I knew)
Their loves. And each had twined a bough to shield
Her lovely face ; and the green leaves did yield
   The golden hair their shadow ; while the two
   Sweet colours mingled, both blown lightly through
With a soft wind for ever stirred and still'd.
After a little while one of them said,
   (I heard her,) 'Think ! If, ere the next hour struck,
   Each of our lovers should come here to-day,
Think you that we should fly or feel afraid ? '
   To whom the others answered, ' From such luck
   A girl would be a fool to run away.'

I have now, as far as I know, exhausted all the materials most available for my selections, among those which exist in print. I have never visited Italy and enjoyed the opportunity of making my own researches in the libraries for everything which might belong to my subject. Some day I still hope to do so, and then to enrich this series, especially as regards its second division, with an appendix of valuable matter which is as yet beyond my reach.

THE END.

INDEX OF FIRST LINES OF POEMS

	PAGE
A little while a little love	135
A remote sky, prolonged to the sea's brim	143
Along the grass sweet airs are blown	99
And did'st thou know indeed, when at the font	150
And now Love sang: but his was such a song	119
And thou, O Life, the lady of all bliss	131
Andromeda, by Perseus saved and wed	101
Around the vase of Life at your slow pace	129
As he that loves oft looks on the dear form	150
As two whose love, first foolish, widening scope	122
As when desire, long darkling, dawns, and first	107
As when two men have loved a woman well	128
At Antwerp, there is a low wall	155
At length their long kiss severed, with sweet smart	109
Because our talk was of the cloud-control	117
Beholding youth and hope in mockery caught	129
Between the hands, between the brows	132
Clench thine eyes now,—'tis the last instant, girl	143
Consider the sea's listless chime	139
Could you not drink her gaze like wine?	95
Death, of thee do I make my moan	102
Dusk-haired and gold-robed o'er the golden wine	144
Each hour until we meet is as a bird	114
Eat thou and drink; to-morrow thou shalt die	124
Get thee behind me. Even as, heavy-curled	128
Girt in dark growths, yet glimmering with one star	116
Give honour unto Luke Evangelist	146
Have you not noted, in some family	112
Heavenborn Helen, Sparta's queen	9
Here meet together the prefiguring day	145
'How should I your true love know'	100
I did not look upon her eyes	137
I have been here before	134
I plucked a honeysuckie where	138

INDEX OF FIRST LINES OF POEMS

	PAGE
I said: 'Nay, pluck not—let the first fruit be'	126
I sat with Love upon a woodside well	119
I stood where Love in brimming armfuls bore	114
In a soft-complexioned sky	133
In our Museum galleries	12
Inside my father's close	105
Is it the moved air or the moving sound	153
It was Lilith the wife of Adam	18
John of Tours is back with peace	104
Lady of Heaven and earth, and therewithal	102
Lazy laughing languid Jenny	62
Like the sweet apple which reddens upon the topmost bough	106
Look in my face; my name is Might-have-been	130
Master of the murmuring courts	5
Mother, is this the darkness of the end	141
Mother of the Fair Delight	23
Mystery: God, Man's Life, born into man	154
Mystery: Katharine, the bride of Christ	154
Not in thy body is thy life at all	115
Not that the earth is changing, O my God!	149
'O have you seen the Stratton flood'	83
'O Hector, gone, gone, gone! O Hector, thee'	148
O Lord of all compassionate control	111
O thou who at Love's hour ecstatically	108
O ye, all ye that walk in Willowwood	120
Of Adam's first wife, Lilith, it is told	146
Of Florence and of Beatrice	48
Once more the changed year's turning wheel returns	124
One flame-winged brought a white-winged harp-player	111
Our Lombard country-girls along the coast	32
Peace in her chamber, wheresoe'er	133
Rend, rend thine hair, Cassandra: he will go	148
Say, is it day, is it dusk in thy bower	135
Scarcely, I think; yet it indeed *may* be	142
She fell asleep on Christmas Eve	97
She fluted with her mouth as when one sips	151
She hath the apple in her hand for thee	147
She wept, sweet lady	40
So it is, my dear	99
So sang he, and as meeting rose and rose	120
Some ladies love the jewels in Love's zone	110
Sweet dimness of her loosened hair's downfall	113
Sweet stream-fed glen, why say 'farewell' to thee	152

INDEX OF FIRST LINES OF POEMS

	PAGE
Tell me now in what hidden way is	101
The blessed damozel leaned out	1
The changing guests, each in a different mood	121
The gloom that breathes upon me with these airs	123
The hour which might have been yet might not be	121
The lost days of my life until to-day	127
The mother will not turn, who thinks she hears	118
The wind flapped loose, the wind was still	138
There came an image in Life's retinue	118
These little firs to-day are things	139
Think thou and act; to-morrow thou shalt die	125
This feast-day of the sun, his altar there	123
This is that blessed Mary, pre-elect	144
This is her picture as she was	73
This sunlight shames November where he grieves	152
Those envied places which do know her well	113
'Thou Ghost,' I said, 'and is thy name To-day?'	116
'Tis of the Father Hilary	156
To all the spirits of love that wander by	110
To-day Death seems to me an infant child	131
Under the arch of Life, where love and death	147
Warmed by her hand and shadowed by her hair	112
Was *that* the landmark? What,—the foolish well	122
Watch thou and fear; to-morrow thou shalt die	125
Water, for anguish of the solstice:—nay	142
Weary already, weary miles to-night	151
What is the sorriest thing that enters Hell?	126
What of the end, Pandora? Was it thine	149
What shall be said of this embattled day	117
What smouldering senses in death's sick delay	109
What thing unto mine ear	88
When do I see thee most, beloved one?	108
When first that horse, within whose populous womb	127
'When that dead face, bowered in the furthest years'	115
When vain desire at last and vain regret	132
Whence came his feet into my field, and why?	130
'Who owns these lands?' the Pilgrim said	26
'Why did you melt your waxen man?'	76
'Why wilt thou cast the roses from thine hair?'	145

INDEX OF FIRST LINES OF TRANSLATIONS

(*ENGLISH AND ITALIAN*)

	PAGE
A CERTAIN youthful lady in Thoulouse *Una giovine donna di Tolosa*	400
A day agone, as I rode sullenly *Cavalcando l'altrier per un cammino*	334
A fresh content of fresh enamouring *Novella gioia e nova innamoranza*	273
A gentle thought there is will often start *Gentil pensiero che parla di vui*	379
A lady in whom love is manifest *La bella donna dove Amor si mostra*	410
Alas for me, who loved a falcon well! *Tapina me che amava uno sparviero*	291
Albeit my prayers have not so long delay'd *Avvegna ched io m'aggio più per tempo*	426
A little wild bird sometimes at my ear *Augelletto selvaggio per stagione*	293
All my thoughts always speak to me of Love *Tutti li miei pensier parlan d'Amore*	340
All the whole world is living without war *Tutto lo mondo vive senza guerra*	196
All ye that pass along Love's trodden way *O voi che per la via d'amor passate*	330
Along the road all shapes must travel by *Per quella via che l'altre forme vanno*	455
A man should hold in very dear esteem *Ogni uomo deve assai caro tenere*	242
Among my thoughts I count it wonderful *Pure a pensar mi par gran meraviglia*	206
Among the dancers I beheld her dance *Alla danza la vidi danzare*	270
Among the faults we in that book descry *Infra gli altri difetti del libello*	434
And every Wednesday, as the swift days move *Ogni Mercoledì corredo grande*	256

472 INDEX OF FIRST LINES

	PAGE
And in September, O what keen delight *Di Settembre vi do diletti tanti*	252
And now take thought, my sonnet, who is he *Sonetto mio, anda o' lo divisi*	254
And on the morrow, at first peep o' the day *Alla domane al parere del giorno*	258
As I walk'd thinking through a little grove *Passando con pensier per un boschetto*	290
A spirit of Love, with Love's intelligence *Ispirito d'Amor con intelletto*	272
As thou wert loth to see, before thy feet *Se non ti caggia la tua Santalena*	413
A thing is in my mind *Venuto m'è in talento*	209
At whiles (yea oftentimes) I muse over *Spesse fiate venemi alla mente*	344
A very pitiful lady, very young *Donna pietosa e di novella etate*	357
Ay me, alas! the beautiful bright hair *Ohimè lasso quelle treccie bionde*	431
Ballad, since Love himself hath fashioned thee *Ballata poi che ti compose Amore*	450
Beauty in woman; the high will's decree *Beltà di donna e di saccente core*	397
Because I find not whom to speak withal *Poich' io non trovo chi meco ragioni*	392
Because I think not ever to return *Perch' io non spero di tornar giammai*	414
Because mine eyes can never have their fill *Poichè saziar non posso gli occhi miei*	388
Because ye made your backs your shields, it came *Guelfi per fare scudo delle reni*	246
Being in thought of love, I chanced to see *Era in pensier d' amor quand' io trovai*	400
Be stirring, girls! we ought to have a run' *State su donne che debbiam noi fare*	289
Beyond the sphere which spreads to widest space *Oltre la spera che più larga gira*	384
By a clear well, within a little field *Intorno ad una fonte in un pratello*	466
By the long sojourning *Per lunga dimoranza*	239
Canst thou indeed be he that still would sing *Sei tu colui ch' hai trattato sovente*	354

OF TRANSLATIONS 473

	PAGE
Dante Alighieri, a dark oracle *Dante Alighieri son Minerva oscura*	464
Dante Alighieri, Cecco, your good friend *Dante Alighier Cecco tuo servo ed amico*	438
Dante Alighieri, if I jest and lie *Dante Alighier s' io son buon begolardo*	448
Dante Alighieri in Becchina's praise *Lassar vuol lo trovare di Becchina*	442
Dante, a sigh that rose from the heart's core *Dante un sospiro messagger del core*	403
Dante, if thou within the sphere of Love *Dante se tu nell' amorosa spera*	464
Dante, since I from my own native place *Poich' io fui Dante dal mio natal sito*	391
Dante, whenever this thing happeneth *Dante quando per caso s' abbandona*	428
Death, alway cruel, Pity's foe in chief *Morte villana di Pietà nemica*	332
Death, since I find not one with whom to grieve *Morte poich' io non trovo a cui mi doglia*	388
Death, why hast thou made life so hard to bear *Morte perchè m' hai fatta sì gran guerra*	228
Do not conceive that I shall here recount *Non intendiate ch' io qui le vi dica*	274
Each lover's longing leads him naturally *Naturalmente chere ogni amadore*	425
Even as the day when it is yet at dawning *Come lo giorno quando è al mattino*	267
Even as the moon amid the stars doth shed *Come le stelle sopra la Diana*	271
Even as the others mock, thou mockést me *Con l' altre donne mia vista gabbate*	342
Fair sir, this love of ours *Messer lo nostro amore*	231
Flowers hast thou in thyself, and foliage *Avete in voi li fiori e la verdura*	396
For a thing done repentance is no good *A cosa fatta già non val pentire*	444
For August, be your dwelling thirty towers *D' Agosto sì vi do trenta castella*	252
For certain he hath seen all perfectness *Vede perfettamente ogni salute*	365
For grief I am about to sing *Di dolor mi conviene cantare*	199

INDEX OF FIRST LINES

	PAGE
For January I give you vests of skins *Io dono vai nel mese di Gennaio*	248
For July, in Siena, by the willow-tree *Di Luglio in Siena sulla saliciata*	251
For no love borne by me *Non per ben ch' io ti voglia*	292
For Thursday be the tournament prepar'd *Ed ogni Giovedì torniamento*	257
Friend, well I know thou knowest well to bear *Amico saccio ben che sai limare*	408
Glory to God and to God's Mother chaste *Lode di Dio e della Madre pura*	456
Gramercy, Death, as you've my love to win *Morte mercè sì ti priego e m' è in grato*	446
Guido, an image of my lady dwells *Una figura della donna mia*	398
Guido, I wish that Lapo, thou, and I *Guido vorrei che tu e Lapo ed io*	402
Guido, that Gianni who, a day agone *Guido quel Gianni che a te fu l'altrieri*	408
Hard is it for a man to please all men *Greve puot' uom piacere a tutta gente*	207
He that has grown to wisdom hurries not *Uomo ch' è saggio non corre leggiero*	206
Her face has made my life most proud and glad *Lo viso mi fa andare allegramente*	218
I am afar, but near thee is my heart *Lontan vi son ma presso v' è lo core*	265
I am all bent to glean the golden ore *Io mi son dato tutto a tragger oro*	429
I am enamoured, and yet not so much *Io sono innamorato ma non tanto*	438
I am so out of love through poverty *La povertà m' ha sì disamorato*	445
I am so passing rich in poverty *Eo son sì ricco della povertate*	231
I come to thee by daytime constantly *Io vegno il giorno a te infinite volte*	411
If any his own foolishness might see *Chi conoscesse sì la sua fallanza*	224
If any man would know the very cause *Se alcuu volesse la cagion savere*	207
If any one had anything to say *Chi Messer Ugolin biasma o riprende*	269

OF TRANSLATIONS

                PAGE

If, as thou say'st, thy love tormenteth thee
Se vi stringesse quanto dite amore 244

If Dante mourns, there wheresoe'er he be
Se Dante piange dove ch' el si sia 463

I felt a spirit of love begin to stir
Io mi sentii svegliar dentro dal core 361

If I'd a sack of florins, and all new
S' io avessi un sacco di fiorini 440

If I entreat this lady that all grace
S' io prego questa donna che pietate 406

If I were fire, I'd burn the world away
S' io fossi foco arderei lo mondo 444

If I were still that man, worthy to love
S' io fossi quello che d'amor fù degno 403

If thou hadst offered, friend, to blessed Mary
Se avessi detto amico di Maria 399

If you could see, fair brother, how dead beat
Fratel se tu vedessi questa gente 273

I give you horses for your games in May
Di Maggio sì vi do molti cavagli 250

I give you meadow-lands in April, fair
D' Aprile vi do la gentil campagna 250

I have it in my heart to serve God so
Io m' aggio posto in core a Dio servire . . . 213

I hold him, verily, of mean emprise
Tegno di folle impresa allo ver dire 204

I know not, Dante, in what refuge dwells
Dante io non odo in qual albergo suoni . . . 392

I laboured these six years
Sei anni ho travagliato 222

I look at the crisp golden-threaded hair
Io miro i crespi e gli biondi capegli 279

I'm caught, like any thrush the nets surprise
Babbo Becchina Amore e mia madre 443

I'm full of everything I do not want
Io ho tutte le cose ch' io non voglio 441

In February I give you gallant sport
Di Febbraio vi dono bella caccia 249

In March I give you plenteous fisheries
Di Marzo sì vi do una peschiera 249

In June I give you a close-wooded fell
Di Giugno dovvi una montagnetta 251

I play this sweet prelude
Dolce cominciamento 264

INDEX OF FIRST LINES

	PAGE
I pray thee, Dante, shouldst thou meet with Love *Se vedi Amore assai ti prego Dante*	404
I thought to be for ever separate *Io mi credea del tutto esser partito*	391
I've jolliest merriment for Saturday *E il Sabato diletto ed allegranza*	258
I was upon the high and blessed mound *Io fui in sull' alto e in sul beato monte*	431
I would like better in the grace to be *Io vorrei innanzi in grazia ritornare*	446
Just look, Manetto, at that wry-mouth'd minx *Guarda Manetto quella sgrignutuzza*	413
Ladies that have intelligence in love *Donne che avete intelletto d' Amore*	347
Lady, my wedded thought *La mia amorosa mente*	234
Lady of Heaven, the mother glorified *Donna del cielo gloriosa madre*	230
Lady, with all the pains that I can take *Donna io forzeraggio lo podere*	263
Last All-Saints' holy-day, even now gone by *Di donne io vidi una gentile schiera*	386
Last, for December, houses on the plain *E di Dicembre una città in piano*	254
Let baths and wine-butts be November's due *E di Novembre petriuolo e il bagno*	253
Let Friday be your highest hunting-tide *Ed ogni Venerdì gran caccia e forte*	257
Let not the inhabitants of Hell despair *Non si disperin quelli dello Inferno*	447
Lo! I am she who makes the wheel to turn *Io son la donna che volgo la rota*	416
Love and the gentle heart are one same thing *Amore e cor gentil son una cosa*	350
Love and the Lady Lagia, Guido and I *Amore e Monna Lagia e Guido ed io*	404
Love hath so long possessed me for his own *Sì lungamente m' ha tenuto Amore*	366
Love, I demand to have my lady in fee *Amore io chero mia donna in domino*	449
Love's pallor and the semblance of deep ruth *Color d' amore e di pietà sembianti*	377
Love steered my course, while yet the sun rode high *Guidommi Amor ardendo ancora il Sole*	465

OF TRANSLATIONS

	PAGE
Love taking leave, my heart then leaveth me *Amor s' eo parto il cor si parte e dole*	244
Love will not have me cry *Amor non vuol ch' io clami*	215
Many there are, praisers of Poverty *Molti son quei che lodan povertade*	453
Marvellously elate *Maravigliosamente*	213
Master Bertuccio, you are called to account *Messer Bertuccio a dritto uom vi cagiona*	269
Master Brunetto, this my little maid *Messer Brunetto questa pulzelletta*	386
Mine eyes beheld the blessed pity spring *Videro gli occhi miei quanta pietate*	376
My body resting in a haunt of mine *Poso il corpo in un loco mio pigliando*	240
My curse be on the day when first I saw *Io maladico il dì ch' io vidi imprima*	395
My heart's so heavy with a hundred things *Io ho sì tristo il cor di cose cento*	441
My lady carries love within her eyes *Negli occhi porta la mia donna amore*	351
My lady looks so gentle and so pure *Tanto gentile e tanto onesta pare*	365
My Lady mine, I send *Madonna mia a voi mando*	217
My lady, thy delightful high command *Madonna vostro altero piacimento*	224
Nero, thus much for tidings in thine ear *Novella ti so dire odi Nerone*	414
Never was joy or good that did not soothe *Gioia nè ben non è senza conforto*	233
Next, for October, to some sheltered coign *Di Ottobre nel contà ch' ha buono stallo*	253
No man may mount upon a golden stair *Non vi si monta per iscala d' oro*	410
Now of the hue of ashes are the Whites *Color di cener fatti son li Bianchi*	449
Now these four things, if thou *Quattro cose chi vuole*	275
Now to Great Britain we must make our way *Ora si passa nella Gran Bretagna*	282
Now, when it flowereth *Oramai quando flore*	211

478 INDEX OF FIRST LINES

	PAGE
Now with the moon the day-star Lucifer *Quando la luna e la stella diana*	255
O Bicci, pretty son of who knows whom *Bicci novel figliuol di non so cui*	458
Often the day had a most joyful morn *Spesso di gioia nasce ed incomenza*	240
Of that wherein thou art a questioner *Di ciò che stato sei dimandatore*	435
O lady amorous *Donna amorosa*	261
O Love, O thou that, for my fealty *O tu Amore che m' hai fatto martire*	429
O Love, who all this while hast urged me on *Amor che lungiamente m' hai menato*	259
On the last words of what you write to me *Al motto diredan prima ragione*	436
O Poverty, by thee the soul is wrapped *O Povertà come tu sei un manto*	418
'O sluggish, hard, ingrate, what doest thou' *O lento pigro ingrato ignar che fai*	422
O thou that often hast within thine eyes *O tu che porti negli occhi sovente*	405
Pass and let pass,—this counsel I would give *Per consiglio ti do dè passa passa*	270
Prohibiting all hope *Levandomi speranza*	245
Remembering this—how Love *Membrando ciò che Amore*	219
Right well I know thou'rt Alighieri's son *Ben so che fosti figliuol d'Alighieri*	459
Round her red garland and her golden hair *Sovra li fior vermigli e i capei d' oro*	465
Sapphire, nor diamond, nor emerald *Diamante nè smeraldo nè zaffino*	215
Say, wouldst thou guard thy son *Vuoi guardar tuo figliuolo*	279
Set Love in order, thou that lovest Me *Ordina quest' Amore o tu che m' ami*	198
So greatly thy great pleasaunce pleasured me *Sì m' abbellìo la vostra gran piacenza*	436
Song, 'tis my will that thou do seek out Love *Ballata io vo che tu ritruovi Amore*	337
Stay now with me, and listen to my sighs *Venite a intender li sospiri miei*	372

OF TRANSLATIONS

	PAGE
Such wisdom as a little child displays *Saver che sente un picciolo fantino*	236
That lady of all gentle memories *Era venuta nella mente mia*	375
That star the highest seen in heaven's expanse *Quest' altissima stella che si vede*	452
The devastating flame of that fierce plague *L' ardente fiamma della fiera peste*	420
The dreadful and the desperate hate I bear *Il pessimo e il crudel odio ch' io porto*	443
The eyes that weep for pity of the heart *Gli occhi dolenti per pietà del core*	370
The flower of Virtue is the heart's content *Fior di virtù si è gentil coraggio*	247
The fountain-head that is so bright to see *Ciascuna fresca e dolce fontanella*	409
The King by whose rich grace His servants be *Lo Re che merta i suoi servi a ristoro*	456
The lofty worth and lovely excellence *Lo gran valore e lo pregio amoroso*	221
The man who feels not, more or less, somewhat *Chi non sente d' Amore o tanto o quanto*	439
The other night I had a dreadful cough *L'altra notte mi venne una gran tosse*	460
There is among my thoughts the joyous plan *Io ho pensato di fare un gioiello*	255
There is a time to mount; to humble thee *Tempo vien di salire e di scendere*	201
There is a vice prevails *Par che un vizio pur regni*	276
There is a vice which oft *Un vizio è che laudato*	275
The sweetly-favoured face *La dolce ciera piacente*	226
The thoughts are broken in my memory *Ciò che m' incontra nella mente more*	343
The very bitter weeping that ye made *L' amaro lagrimar che voi faceste*	378
Think a brief while on the most marvellous arts *Sè 'l subietto preclaro O Cittadini*	197
This book of Dante's, very sooth to say *In verità questo libel di Dante*	433
This fairest lady, who, as well I wot *Questa leggiadra donna ched io sento*	430

INDEX OF FIRST LINES

	PAGE
This fairest one of all the stars, whose flame *La bella stella che sua fiamma tiene* .	292
This is the damsel by whom love is brought *Questa è la giovinetta ch' amor guida*	452
Though thou, indeed, hast quite forgotten ruth *Se m' hai del tutto obliato mercede* .	405
Thou sweetly-smelling fresh red rose *Rosa fresca aulentissima*	189
Thou that art wise, let wisdom minister *Provvedi saggio ad esta visione*	435
Thou well hast heard that Rollo had two sons *Come udit' hai due figliuoli ebbe Rollo*	285
Through this my strong and new misaventure *La forte e nova mia disavventura*	406
To a new world on Tuesday shifts my song *E il Martedì li do un nuovo mondo* .	256
To every heart which the sweet pain doth move *A ciascun' alma presa e gentil core* .	328
To hear the unlucky wife of Bicci cough *Chi udisse tossir la mal fatata*	459
To see the green returning *Quando veggio rinverdire*	227
To sound of trumpet rather than of horn *A suon di tromba innanzi che di corno*	411
To the dim light and the large circle of shade *Al poco giorno ed al gran cerchio d' ombra* .	393
Two ladies to the summit of my mind *Due donne in cima della mente mia* .	393
Unto my thinking, thou beheld'st all worth *Vedesti al mio parere ogni valore* .	396
Unto that lowly lovely maid, I wis *A quella amorosetta forosella* .	409
Unto the blithe and lordly fellowship *Alla brigata nobile e cortese* .	247
Upon a day came Sorrow in to me *Un dì si venne a me Melancolìa* .	390
Upon that cruel season when our Lord *Quella crudel stagion che a giudicare* .	243
Vanquished and weary was my soul in me *Vinta e lassa era già l' anima mia* .	430
Weep, Lovers, sith Love's very self doth weep *Piangete amanti poi che piange Amore* .	332
Were ye but constant, Guelfs, in war or peace *Così faceste voi o guerra o pace* .	246

	PAGE
Wert thou as prone to yield unto my prayer *Così fossi tu acconcia di donarmi*	272
Whatever good is naturally done *Qualunque ben si fa naturalmente*	439
Whatever while the thought comes over me *Quantunque volte lasso mi rimembra*	373
What rhymes are thine which I have ta'en from thee *Quai son le cose vostre ch' io vi tolgo*	433
Whence come you, all of you so sorrowful *Onde venite voi così pensose*	387
When God had finished Master Messerin *Quando Iddio Messer Messerin fece*	268
When I behold Becchina in a rage *Quando veggio Becchina corrucciata*	442
When Lucy draws her mantle round her face *Chi vedesse a Lucia un var cappuzzo*	201
When the last greyness dwells throughout the air *Quando l' aria comincia a farsi bruna*	292
Whether all grace have fail'd I scarce may scan *Non so s' è mercè che mo vene a meno*	243
Whoever without money is in love *Chi è senza denari innamorato*	445
Who is she coming, whom all gaze upon *Chi è questa che vien ch' ogn' uom la mira*	397
Whoso abandons peace for war-seeking *Chi va cherendo guerre e lassa pace*	236
Who utters of his father aught but praise *Chi dice di suo padre altro che onore*	447
Why from the danger did mine eyes not start *Perchè non furo a me gli occhi dispenti*	407
Why, if Becchina's heart were diamond *Se di Becchina il cor fosse diamante*	440
Within a copse I met a shepherd-maid *In un boschetto trovai pastorella*	412
Within the gentle heart Love shelters him *Al cor gentil ripara sempre Amore*	202
With other women I beheld my love *Io vidi donne con la donna mia*	398
Woe's me! by dint of all these sighs that come *Lasso per forza de' molti sospiri*	381
Wonderful countenance and royal neck *Viso mirabil gola morganata*	437
Yea, let me praise my lady whom I love *Io vo del ver la mia donna lodare*	204

482 INDEX OF FIRST LINES OF TRANSLATIONS

	PAGE
Ye graceful peasant-girls and mountain-maids *Vaghe le montanine e pastorelle*	288
Ye ladies, walking past me piteous-eyed *Voi donne che pietoso atto mostrate*	387
Ye pilgrim-folk, advancing pensively *Deh peregrini che pensosi andate*	383
Your joyful understanding, lady mine *Madonna vostra altera canoscenza*	237
You that thus wear a modest countenance *Voi che portate la sembianza umile*	353